healthy foods from healthy soils

a hands-on resource for educators

ELIZABETH PATTEN and KATHY LYONS

ILLUSTRATED BY HELEN STEVENS

TILBURY HOUSE  PUBLISHERS

GARDINER, MAINE

Tilbury House, Publishers
2 Mechanic Street
Gardiner, Maine 04345
800–582–1899
www.tilburyhouse.com

First Edition: March 2003
Revised Edition: January 2007

10 9 8 7 6 5 4 3 2

This book is printed on Williamsburg Recycled paper, which contains 30% post-consumer waste.

Cover design by Geraldine Millham, Westport, Massachusetts
Editing and production by Audrey Maynard, Jennifer Bunting, Barbara Diamond, and Karen Fisk
Printing and binding by Versa Press, East Peoria, IL
Cover photographs: Kathy Lyons, Elizabeth Patten, Jodie DeBois, Wendy Wenerstrom, and Lynn Walters

For Michael, Tyler, and Miles, with love and gratitude —E. P.

For David, my love, and Rebekah Rose, my joy —K. L.

For Anne S. Johnson (1928–2004), who planted the seed

No ray of sunshine is ever lost. But the green which it awakens into existence needs time to sprout. And it is not always granted for the sower to see the harvest. All work that is worth anything is done in faith. —*Albert Schweitzer*

Acknowledgments

To all of the following people—for your generous sharing of time and experience, we thank you sincerely, and hope that if we've inadvertently omitted your name, you'll call us on it!

The late Anne S. Johnson, our matchmaker and indefatigable supporter, whom we miss dearly; Mary Casciotti and Annie Brown who started us rolling; the Food and Consumer Service of the USDA for our original grant "seed money"; and the teachers, administrators, and community members who trusted us in the beginning and nudged us toward compiling the lessons: Victoria Baker, Gene Berg, Kristen Billington, Bonnie Blair, Connie Carter, David Dowe, Nancy Fitch, Mame Gardner, Gail Garthwaite, Sue Gauthier, Catherine Atkinson Greenwood, JoAnn Hall, Karla Harkin, Judy Higbea, Sarah Holman, Dian Jordan, Cynthia Kimball-Strout, Phil LaPierre, Terry Lincoln, the inimitable Walter Lunt, Sally Martin, Monsieur T. McKibben, Lynn McPherson, Janet Metcalf, Allyson Miller, Mike Morcom, Joyce Murdock, Susan Neel, Anne O'Brien, Amy Parker, Holly Ranks, Kyle Rhoads, Bob Robinson, Janice Smith, Linda Smith, Lois Soucy, Carol Taylor, Jim Verrill, Jane Weinstein, Cheryl White, Debbie White, Steve Whitney, and Cecilia Ziko.

Larry and Jane Levine, for your early strong support and constructive criticism (and some terrific oatmeal hospitality).

We could write another whole book of equal volume in appreciation for the many contributions of the students and families in Freeport and Orono and beyond who learned along with us, donated materials and time, tended the gardens, prepared fresh local foods, provided child and red wiggler care, offered enthusiastic support, agricultural expertise, field trip and summer gardening help, and use of land and tools: Kathy Bither, Kristen Britain for our original "worm-toon" illustrations, Kate Butler, Joe Cannon, Chris and Dave Colson of New Leaf Farm, Richard Connelly, Gloria DeGrandpré, Glenn Dickey, Ken Dupuis, Sarah Firth, Freeport Public Library staff, Bill Getty, Judy Goodenow and school nutrition staff, Laura Girr, Gleason Gray of the Penobscot County Cooperative Extension, Carey Hotaling, Colleen Kelley for the loan of her massive worm file early on, Kevin McElroy, Eric Meyer of Good Earth Farm, Peter Milholland, Steve Niles, Tom Preble and the wonderful Penobscot County Master Gardeners, Joan and Scott Samuelson, Horticultural Specialist Lois Stack with the University of Maine Cooperative Extension, former Curator Bill Reed of the Page Farm and Home Museum, Alice and Charlie Smith, David Suchoff, Mark Taggart, Mary Wade, Emily Wesson, University of Maine Roger's Farm, Wolfe's Neck Farm Teach Maine Americorps members, and the custodial staff at all the schools.

For manuscript review and timely, valuable suggestions: Michael Alpert, the late Mary Appelhof (the original wormwoman), Debra Ballou, Scott Belanger, Dede Bennell, Joyce Benson, Martha Carton, Chris Colson, Jim Cook, George Criner, Judy Donnelly, Mahmoud El-Begearmi, Jean English, Sue Erich, Tim Forsman, José Garcia, Steven Garrett, Carol Giesecke, Sue Gorman, Katie Greenman, Tracey Grimsley, Zoie Guernsey, Alison Harmon, MaryAnn Healey, Dorothy Hebert, Deanne Herman, Carey Hotaling, Marjorie Hundhammer, Irene Jackson, Allison Keef, Stephanie Kempf, Russell Libby, Deb Lippoldt, Judy Kellogg Markowsky, MaryAnn McGarry, Stu Nunnery, Beedy Parker, Barbara Patten, Bryant Patten, Miriam Patten, Ellen Port, Rebecca Reilly, Nancy Ross, Kris Sader, Kathy Savoie, Marina Schauffler, Judy Sims, Nancy Sleeth, Stewart Smith, Rice Spann, Lois Stack, Paul Super,

Randall Wade Thomas, Lisa Turner, Mary Turner, Lynn Walters, and Adrienne White (with special thanks for her specific and comprehensive suggestions).

For consistent professional support and friendships (including some marathon teacher-training road trips): Judy Gatchell (who astutely directed the original grant proposal our way), Linda Kennedy, Tamra Montgomery, Barbara Raymond, Sheila Reed, Chris Sady, and the Maine Nutrition Network teachers.

To MaryAnn McGarry, whose dedication to detail ensured that our book was aligned with the Benchmarks for Science Literacy.

To our talented illustrator, Helen Stevens, our ever-encouraging editor Audrey Maynard, and our unflappable publisher Jennifer Bunting, without whom this manuscript would not have become A Book.

For wonderful, supportive friends: Nancy Adams, the late Diana Becker, Steve Doughty, Sarah Firth, Hilary Forrest, John Gleason, Carey Hotaling, Deb Lippoldt, Robin Lurie, Tracy McCallum, Jeannie McMorrow, Coleen O'Connell, Karen O'Rourke, Cathy Robie, Denise Sullivan, Katrina Van Dusen, and Linda Wheatley.

To Annelida, our spokesworm, who opened doors to many young people's hearts and made our jobs as educators that much more fun.

And finally,

(K. L.) To my folks, Rita and J. Robert Savage (who always told me I should write a book), my brother John and his family— Rachelle, Ben, and Sam—thanks for your belief in me, and to my husband, David, and dog, Zoe, who with love and humor helped me survive the ups and downs of writing this book. And finally, to Rebekah Rose (and her birth parents) for the gift and joy of the most amazing job of all—motherhood.

(E. P.) To my late grandfather, Bryant McLellan Patten, whose ripe garden tomatoes, cucumbers, rhubarb, and corn I can still savor in my taste buds' memories; my parents Mimi and Amory Patten, who've nourished me with their generosity from start to "finish"; my siblings Barbara and Bryant and their families, for your continual love and support; and my extraordinary family—Michael, Tyler, and Miles—who help me keep Life in perspective.

—Elizabeth Patten

—Kathy Lyons

Introduction

Thank you for picking up this book! From glancing at the cover and table of contents you've likely recognized our belief that food is a catalyst for all kinds of topics: what we choose to eat blends personal health, local economics, and global environmental concerns. We want children to have the opportunity to examine their foods in relation to these topics, and to consider ways that they might help create a healthier and more sustainable future.

Healthy Foods from Healthy Soils weaves down-to-earth activities from a variety of disciplines into one interconnected cycle, illustrating where food comes from, how our bodies use food, and what happens to food waste. Take this manual into the garden or kitchen with your students, get it soiled, dripped on, and maybe eventually even compost it (plenty of fiber)! We have confidence you'll find this guide an ally in both your indoor and outdoor classrooms.

Not so long ago, a curriculum guide designed to help children learn about food's origins and the connection between healthy soils and nourishing foods would have seemed unnecessary. Just two to three generations ago many people lived those connections, and no formal education was needed. Now that so many of us are living with the health consequences of being a "fast-food nation," a program that addresses these issues in a lively and enjoyable manner is vital.

To that end, we provide you with the direction, knowledge, and self-assurance to use this practical hands-on project that kids have benefitted from since 1995. At that time, Kathy Lyons and I started a pilot venture called "Healthy Foods from Healthy Soils," thanks to funding from the Food and Consumer Service of the U. S. Department of Agriculture. This manual grew out of that original program. In this book, you'll find a cyclic guided tour: growing foods in soil amended with organic matter (compost), eating whole foods from the farm or garden, and turning food wastes back into compost to improve the soil for the next planting, continuing the cycle into the following growing season and another crop of students. Experiential activities such as gardening, preparing and eating food together, composting, observing and documenting help children think critically. The lessons involve cooperative learning, invite lots of discussion, and generate plenty of quality ideas, allowing students to examine those opinions and ideas without needing to find a singular "right" answer. Children are encouraged to take responsibility for their personal choices and decisions, and to become involved citizens.

In this way, young people everywhere can connect with their own communities—with rural neighbors and urban gardeners, senior citizens and local businesses—learning that we are all part of an interrelated food system that involves agriculture, waste management, human and environmental health, education and compassion. We believe, along with an increasing number of colleagues, that a more equitable food system is not only possible, but *necessary*—everyone should have ample nutritious food available no matter where s/he lives. To reach the attainable goal of food security for all, the first steps are being aware of the food system, and recognizing what our local communities provide.

We encourage you and your students to consider the impact our food choices have—on natural resources, on fellow citizens, and on the economy—while using this book for guidance. ¡Vamos!

—E. P.

How to Use This Guide

We think you'll have lots of fun with **HEALTHY FOODS FROM HEALTHY SOILS**. It's a great resource for engaging children in a diverse and lively set of activities to learn about the food cycle from "farm to plate" (and back!). This guide is adaptable and can be used in many different settings besides the classroom. Parents, environmental educators, home-schoolers, volunteer coordinators, clubs, and service groups will also find a wealth of interesting activities and useful information in this guide.

The lessons we've included move across traditional disciplines. As educators, we are passionate about building a curriculum that is not only science focused. We have found that approaching subjects in a multi-disciplinary way is uniquely effective in reaching all the children in a classroom. Our **HEALTHY FOODS FROM HEALTHY SOILS** activities give children opportunities to sing, act, make models, grow food, create collages, taste new food, keep journals, chart food waste, and learn to love worms.

A number of lessons in the guide ask the children to reflect on their own choices, and to look at how those choices may affect their personal health or the health of their communities. We think that one of the best ways to make the study of any subject meaningful to children is to connect the materials, the ideas, and the concepts to their own personal lives. We have taken that challenge to heart.

Organization:

There are four main sections in **HEALTHY FOODS FROM HEALTHY SOILS:**

- **Where Does Food Come From?** explores the origins of our food;
- **Choosing Food for Body and Soul** examines food systems and nutrition issues in detail;
- **Putting "Garbage" to Work** delves into ways to better manage our waste stream; and
- **Let's Grow Our Own!** demonstrates the planting cycle and identifies methods for introducing children to simple gardening—indoors or outdoors.

Each lesson is keyed to the ***Benchmarks for Science Literacy.*** Each provides simple **Goals**; **Key Points**, which are generally written in "kid" language to help easily convey main concepts; ample **Background** information to complement the activity; clear **How to** instructions; followed by **Classroom Conversations** which are integral to each lesson; suggestions for further discussion (**Want to Do More?**); **Lesson Links** to connect you to related activities; wonderful suggestions for children's **Literature Links**; and relevant annotated **Resources**. Many activities include **Action Steps** to encourage tangible outcomes, and tips to make teacher planning easier (**Getting Ready**).

Create Your Own Lesson Sequence and Go at Your Own Pace!

Nutrition, agriculture, and recycling provide exceptional opportunities for exploring science, math, the arts, and language, not to mention feeding the body and soul. **HEALTHY FOODS FROM HEALTHY SOILS** can be used as either a supplement to traditional coursework—by providing a guide to resources and complementary activities—or as a comprehensive program. Teachers can start anywhere in this guide and develop a sequence that fits their needs. Because the lessons all have links to each other, it's possible to weave through the book in a variety of ways. For example, some teachers explore just the food and health dimension and leave out the farming and gardening components. There are teachers who dive right into the world of worms and composting and then later work into gardening; the following year they enjoy their own classroom garden produce. And then, there are teachers who've been using these lessons for years who have yet to touch a worm! The activities in this guide were developed with grades K-6 in mind, but have been taught successfully with pre-schoolers through adults.

Making Connections: Taking **Healthy Foods from Healthy Soils** Home

It is crucial to be respectful in the area of food and family. How we choose to nourish ourselves is often bound by personal preferences and/or cultural and economic realities. Most families have strong feelings about the food they provide for their children. We encourage you to have ongoing communication with families about this program so they are aware of the goals of the lessons and support their children in the activities. Note that each lesson has "goals" and these can be copied and included in your class newsletter or put up on the parent bulletin board.

The Urban–Rural Divide

This guide is designed to be valuable to educators everywhere—whether you work with children in Phoenix, Arizona; Boone, North Carolina; downtown Manhattan; Thetford Center, Vermont; or Kansas City, Missouri. We've taken the differences between urban and rural classrooms into consideration, and you'll find helpful suggestions for making our activities work in your own particular setting. If your school doesn't have a garden plot, you can still raise sprouts or grow plants (lettuce, for instance) under lights. And composting with worms can be done in any indoor setting! No matter where they live, children will benefit from increased awareness about food and health and nature's cycles.

Using the Benchmarks

The *Benchmarks for Science Literacy* is a nationally recognized tool prepared by the American Association for the Advancement of Science. It was selected after examining various national curriculum standards that could be aligned with **Healthy Foods from Healthy Soils** lessons. The *Benchmarks* book was created by a large cross-section of K–12 teachers and administrators, as well as education, math, science, engineering, and history professionals, and was based on published research. It promotes science literacy through recommending what students should know and be able to do at certain grade levels. Grouped in three clusters—K–2, 3–5, and 6–8—the standards are to be used as a strategy, not a set curriculum or framework, in order to encourage educators to shape their own curricula.

Using this *Benchmarks* tool can help with implementing or adhering to state and district requirements, and is adaptable to varied student backgrounds, interests, teacher preferences, and local environments. It can be used by cross-subject and cross-grade teacher groups, for helping prepare assessments, tests, or research.

The *Benchmarks* are listed by grades and subject matter, and have specific citations that allow you to readily see how each activity meets one or more national standard. They are comprehensive and in straightforward easy-to-understand language, laying out criteria for school and classroom accountability.

For the *Benchmarks* listed, it is important to note that not all parts of the *Benchmark*, in some cases, are addressed in the activity; the reader can determine the parts of it that most carefully align. The alignment can be found in any number of sections of the activity description: the goals, background, procedure, or follow-up discussion questions.

By reading the aligned *Benchmarks* first, an educator can make sure to address different components of it as he or she facilitates the activity. In some cases, relevant *Benchmarks* for grades targeted below the grade level listed for the activity are included to provide the teacher with information on the progressive development of the knowledge and skills through the grade spans.

The aligned *Benchmarks* in this guide are listed in the order in which they are organized in the *Benchmarks for Science Literacy* book. They are not listed in this guide in order of priority or strongest alignment with the activity. Naturally, certain *Benchmarks* are much more tightly aligned than others. Educators should make professional decisions about which ones should receive more attention and then emphasize these and teach them in multiple ways to ensure that all students meet these *Benchmarks*.

The numbers and letters with each *Benchmark* refer to the chapter and section in the *Benchmarks for Science Literacy* and are helpful, quick references for looking up the full context of the particular one cited.

The *Benchmarks* was prepared as a tool to be used by everyone engaged in efforts to transform learning in science, mathematics, and technology.

You can find further background on *The Benchmarks* and its complete text at http://www.project2061.org/publications/bsl/default.htm

Growing Our Future

When we received the funding from USDA to pilot our original program, we dreamed that the project would one day lead to the growth of healthier communities by involving children in actions that would promote a more sustainable future. We still hold on to that dream, and we want to share it with other educators.

What we have learned over the years of teaching others about **HEALTHY FOODS FROM HEALTHY SOILS** is that, just as with gardening and cooking, your creativity is the key. If you use quality ingredients that you find locally (your students) combined with your skill and experience, the wonderful result will be informed, critical thinkers. Of course, we hope they will become the leaders in our communities in the future.

Finally, remember that nutrition and food systems education are best taught through the taste buds, so *bon appétit!*

Suggestions for Success

- **Start locally!** The more connections you have and create within your community, the easier it will be.
- **Find one or two (or more) committed individuals or groups.** A parent, another teacher, principal, parent-teacher organization or community member, or local farmer/gardener who's willing to coordinate details and troubleshoot is very helpful. For most teachers, such assistance is crucial. Your school food service or physical education staff is often a valuable ally here.
- **This guide is intended to assist you.** Do not consider this an additional burden—use this to enhance and energize the considerable work you're already doing!
- **Build school interest and administrative support.** Students, once involved, are your best ambassadors. Also, don't forget to enlist your custodial staff—they're the ones who'll likely help with cleaning up the classroom pasta-making or the compost creations!
- **Tap existing resources—use your assets!** Start "where you are," and where your strengths are. You are likely teaching some of these topics already. For example, if you're teaching about the human body or planning a unit on animal habitats or soils, use the **HEALTHY FOODS FROM HEALTHY SOILS** cycle as a basis for those established units. Later, work in additional year-round **HEALTHY FOODS FROM HEALTHY SOILS** concepts which build on areas where you're already familiar.
- **Start small.** Build on success! Start in just one or a few classrooms in the beginning. By the way, this project doesn't require large amounts of money to get started. Necessities for a year-round program include: outdoor area or indoor/outdoor container space for gardening, room for preparing and eating food in class, a worm composting container—which can be purchased or constructed—and red wiggler worms. Most other materials, such as tools, food, and seeds/seedlings can often be donated. Ask your school nutrition manager about the possibility of using "commodity foods."
- **Use good resources.** As you're aware, there is excellent material currently available—no need to "reinvent the wheel." Take advantage of the materials we offer and please contribute suggestions to us that have worked well for you.
- **Remain flexible.** (You know that already!) Even if you've never gardened, taught outdoors, used puppets, or considered the thought of composting, much less vermi-composting, this is a chance to learn along with your students.

If we all waited for experience, we might never start! In fact, learning together may cause a camaraderie and group spirit that a leader might not instill. —Barbara Britz, Urban Agriculture Program, Eugene, Oregon, in *Youth Gardening*

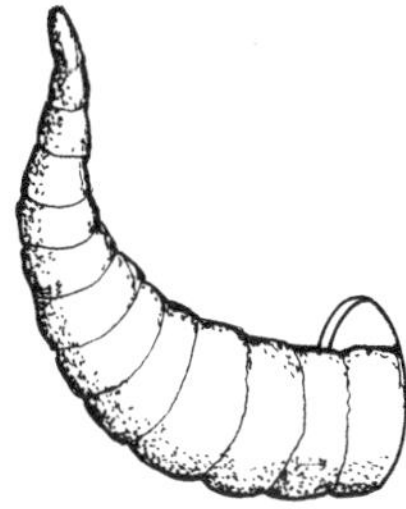

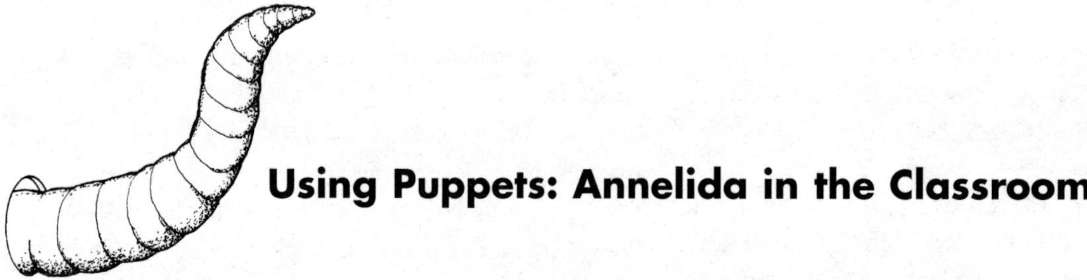

Using Puppets: Annelida in the Classroom

Our earthworm puppet, Annelida, transformed the work we did with children. In her presence children were willing to try new foods, pay attention, and ask questions they never would have thought of had she not been there wiggling with the best of them. Since many teachers we encountered over the years have asked us for tips on using a puppet in the classroom, we decided to include a chapter on the subject. Our hope is that you'll feel inspired to begin using puppets and discover the wonder they bring. Some helpful hints on using puppets in the classroom follow, and you'll find instructions for making your own puppets in several lessons and in the Appendix.

You will get a flavor of the fun of having a puppet assistant by meeting Annelida in this guide. She is the **Healthy Foods from Healthy Soils** mascot. She squirms her way through the guide and provides you with lots of tips, quips, information, facts, and jokes for you to enjoy and share!

A Little Background, So to Speak . . .

Annelida's career break came in the summer of 1991 when she was conceived and constructed to entertain and educate Acadia National Park visitors about the new recycling program. She worked with "Pete," the soda bottle puppet, every Saturday night at Seawall Campground. Pete encouraged the recycling of glass, aluminum, and plastics. Annelida, the worm puppet, reminded visitors that nature recycled long before it became popular in the waste management world. In fact, she would say, "nature reuses and recycles every minute of every day."

For two summers she often asked people to imagine if everything that landed on the forest floor in one year (i.e., leaves, pine needles, dead plants, bugs and animals, animal poop, acorns, bark, trees, etc.) just accumulated! And, what would happen if it just piled up, year after year? Wiggling with delight, she would launch into her favorite topic—nature's decomposers/recyclers—the uncelebrated bacteria, fungi, animals, insects, and worms—who make sure that there are no waste disposal problems where they live.

So it was a natural move for Annelida to join **Healthy Foods from Healthy Soils** in 1995 when we started! She was only too delighted to help with the worm composting—a place where she realized right from the start that worms were appreciated. None of us could have predicted that she would embrace every aspect of the **Healthy Foods from Healthy Soils** cycle! She set us straight about her involvement in the whole show, "I love kids, I love worm hugs, I think composting is tops, and you can't have a proper garden without worms!" We also knew that she loved to eat and was choosy about her diet. That's when she became an official part of the project.

Since that day, she's been "worming" her way into the hearts of children, teachers, and parents as she spreads cheer and handy information about the food cycle on which we all depend. Right, Annelida?

Why Annelida Is in the Book

Although you might assume that a worm puppet should be relegated to the worm composting section, Annelida runs through the entire book. Why? Well, as in nature, everything is connected—composting is just one part of the nutrient cycle. Without sun, soil, water, or air there would be no plants; without plants—no food; without food—no leftovers; without leftovers—no compost/no dinner for Annelida!; without compost—no food for the soil; without food for the soil . . . and so on. That's just the way it is! Annelida is fond of cycles. In fact when Annelida squirms around to touch her mouth and tail, she creates a circle. It is the position she uses to give her famous worm hugs. She is very fond of children (very willing to give them worm hugs) and very eager to help teachers educate! We hope you will allow her to worm her way into your heart and your classroom the way she has in so many classrooms, libraries, workshops, scout meetings, and gardens.

Annelida's Tips for Using Puppets in the Classroom

Not familiar with using puppets? Not sure how to start? Worried about what Annelida should sound like or act like? Allow Annelida to help set those worries aside. Our friendly spokesworm likes to say, "Anyone can make a puppet come to life, especially when you like the puppet you are using."

Basically, a puppet is any inanimate object brought to life by a puppeteer and the imagination of a viewer. By that definition, a puppet can be anything and can appear anywhere. Contrary to what most people think about puppets, you don't need a stage, nor a cast of characters, script, sound effects, or props. And if you speak for the puppet, you don't even have to hide your mouth or be a ventriloquist. (Remember Jim Henson? When he took Kermit to TV interviews, the two of them would sit on the set. Jim would talk for himself and then look at Kermit while he voiced Kermit's words—with no attempt to hide the fact that he was talking for Kermit. He was asked about that and replied that people were watching Kermit! They didn't care what he was doing!) Puppets come to life because of imagination and belief—on the part of the viewer and puppeteer. When you know the personality of your puppet, when you are enjoying what you are doing—something magical flows from your hand to the puppet and we all believe.

Why use a puppet with your students?

- **To give you flexibility; to allow children to discuss things they might not otherwise; to inject playfulness, joy, and laughter into a lesson.** Annelida likes to dress up for Halloween as something she might eat in a worm bin. Each year one class got to choose. I made her "costume" big enough for her to fit into, i.e., an apple, orange—so that she could hide inside it. When children would say the magic words in unison as instructed (sometimes in a whisper, sometimes in a yell), she would pop out of the costume and usually have something to say about her favorite holiday. Sometimes the

magic words were "Happy Halloween" and sometimes they were "Trick or Treat." This game was enjoyed so much by both the children and Annelida that she kept her costume around all year!

- **To encourage children to become less tentative and more engaged.** Annelida is approachable—most puppets are. When she expresses emotions or thoughts that children are familiar with, they identify with her. If she asks them a question, they will answer her, not you. Annelida may even be allowed to say, ask, or do things a particular child wouldn't allow you as the teacher to do.
- **To provide opportunities for children to excel and show off what they know.** Children loved the Annelida quizzes we conducted from time to time. Questions relating to recent concepts involving the HEALTHY FOODS FROM HEALTHY SOILS are written on slips of paper and put into a basket. Children draw a question and read it to Annelida. Sometimes she gets the answer perfectly right, sometimes she needs hints from the kids, and sometimes she gives wrong or silly answers on which the children can correct her.
- **To help focus attention, quiet a group, draw interest.** A tradition soon developed where Annelida would hug every child in the group before she had to leave or go back to sleep (in her Halloween costume or a cozy container). Annelida absolutely refused to be hugged by an unruly group. At the end of a lesson, once the children were seated quietly, she would go around the room and hug each child (wrapping her head and tail around their necks

and saying something nice). Or if the children were leaving, she would hug them one by one as they filed past her saying so long.

Also, Annelida likes everyone to hear her, so if there is too much noise, she will be quiet and whisper things to the puppeteer. The puppeteer responds so the children close by can hear. Soon the whole group is listening intently to the private conversation which is probably about . . . why the children aren't listening to her.

I've made every mistake you can make with a speaking mouth puppet and both my audience and I still enjoyed ourselves. I used Annelida's voice for mine and vice versa. When I realized this, Annelida and I looked at each other in shock and then laughed! I forgot to move her mouth when she was talking, or moved her mouth when I was talking. Our voices started out sounding different, but became the same voice within minutes. But with all of that, Annelida was still adored, partly because of the personality that emerged from her, partly because I really liked Annelida, and largely because the children wanted to believe!

Some important things to keep in mind when using Annelida or any puppet:

- **A puppet should always be treated with respect whether in use or not.** This means the children should be told that Annelida is very sensitive and doesn't appreciate being handled roughly. She should leave (be put in her box, etc.) if the children break a rule you've communicated to them. This also means that when the puppet is not in use, it should be placed in a safe place—a place for comfort and resting.
- **People generally like to be looked in the eye when being spoken to—even by a puppet**. This relies on your hand position. With a mouth puppet, bend your hand at the wrist and point your fingers (which are in the mouth) at the eyes of the listener. For Annelida, you may want to slope her mouth down a bit more as her eyes are on top of her head.
- **Some very young children may be afraid of a new puppet.** When approaching pre-schoolers for the first time, be gentle with their first interaction. No surprise pop-ups or loud yells. Allow them to touch the puppet, keeping her very still and telling the children how much the puppet likes them.
- **It may be easier for you to use puppets with children in grades 3 and younger.** If you are very comfortable with using a puppet and know your children well, you can introduce Annelida to older children. It all depends on your comfort level and the coolness factor of the group of kids with whom you are working. If they are "too old" for puppets, these children work best when they can make and manipulate their own puppets.
- **When you are talking, the puppet is still and listening to you. When the puppet is speaking, you are listening to her.**
- **As you get comfortable with Annelida, you will find ways for her to express surprise, sadness, shyness, frustration, excitement, and laughter.** She can say a lot with body language—experiment with this. Her tail can be used as a hand in pointing to things, raising her hand, scratching her head while thinking. . . .
- **Talk to Annelida as you take her out of her container and as you put her away.** She can speak to you as well.
- **Every puppet has a personality.** Annelida is sweet, kind, rambunctious, curious, silly, sometimes shy, sometimes very bold, but always considerate of others' feelings. She is passionate about **Healthy Foods from Healthy Soils** and loves children. She loves to congratulate children for trying and for doing things well. However, Annelida's voice, personality, age, habits, and specific interests will vary from puppeteer to puppeteer. It is the character you feel from her and that you give to her that will make her an easy co-teacher and a believable, lovable puppet. For instance, a teacher who feels uncomfortable speaking for Annelida may have an Annelida puppet who only whispers things in the teacher's ear to tell the children. What's important is that you have a feeling for what she would want to say.

You'll find instructions for puppets from recycled materials on page 143, vegetable pop-up puppets on page 179, and instructions for making sock puppets and a nylon wiggler in the Appendix, page 225. We hope you'll bring your own Annelida to life!

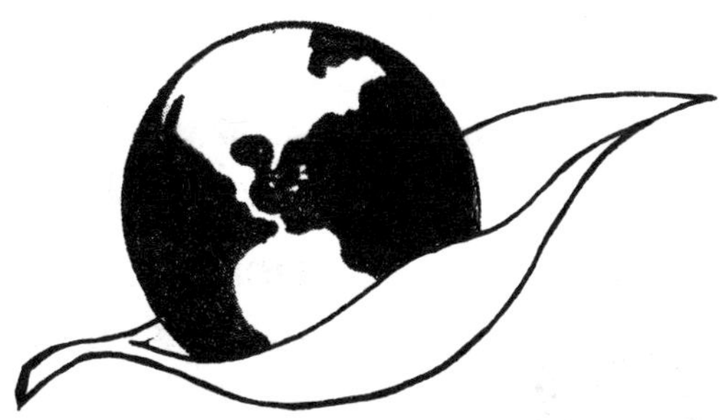

WHERE DOES FOOD COME FROM?

"Eating is an agricultural act." —*Wendell Berry*

Most children today (and many adults) give very little thought to the source of their food. We have become accustomed to the idea that food "comes from" the grocery store, the kitchen, or often a fast-food restaurant. Although children are aware of the way food looks, how it is packaged, and—of course—how it tastes, they often don't know how it's grown, prepared, or whose job it is to do that work. In this section we aim to take children "back to the basics" and introduce them to the fundamentals of food production and agriculture.

Let's Get Grounded The six engaging activities included here will help children appreciate why healthy soil is so critical to the production of the food they eat. Children will learn how food is grown from the soil up and how plants' habitat needs parallel their own.

Who Grows Our Food? Like teaching, small-scale farming is multifaceted and labor-intensive. Two generations ago, there wasn't much mystery about where food came from or who grew it. Today, very few children know anything about the people who make a living growing food. The activities in this section will change that and help to put faces on the people who work on farms.

It's important to *reconnect* children to their environment, so they can understand that—at least to start—it is nature, not a supermarket, that is the source of their food. As their information about food builds, children have an increasing chance to understand how it might be true that "eating is an agricultural act."

Let's Get Grounded

Sun, soil, water, space, shelter, and air are essential for the survival of both plants and animals. We are much more aware of the dangers of air and water pollution today than we were decades ago, partly because it is more noticeable when water is dirty or air is polluted, but we are less likely to be protective of the quality of our soil. This section reviews the role of these natural resources, particularly the neglected element: soil. Later lessons delve into the life of a seed, which supplies both plants and humans with nutrient-filled food. Most of the world's population depends on seeds for sustenance and protein.

It's a Small World[1]

Demonstrate the finite nature of earth's resources

Recommended Grades 3–6
- **Math**
- **Geography**

"They're making people every day, but they ain't makin' any more dirt." —*Will Rogers*

"People must fully understand the irreplaceable value of prime farmlands, and the ominous meaning of the war between the bulldozer and the plow. When farmland goes, food goes. Asphalt is the land's last crop." —*M. Rupert Cutler, former Assistant Secretary of Agriculture for Natural Resources*

Goals

Learn that soil is an important and finite natural resource and see how little arable land is available for food production. "As topsoil goes, so goes the food."

Key Points

- We have less and less farmable land left for growing food.
- Knowing this makes us realize how precious soil is.

Background

Most plants can't grow without soil. In the U.S. today, only about one-half acre (0.2 ha) of arable land per person is available for food production.[2] The earth's soil surface can be likened to the skin of fruits and vegetables—often the most nutritious layer of the food. This "skin" is made up of minerals, rocks, organic matter, microorganisms, air, and water in varying proportions from one part of the globe to another. It is this thin and fragile layer of topsoil on the earth's surface that supports our entire agricultural ecosystem, permitting us to grow vast quantities of food. However, the volume of productive healthy topsoil is diminishing at the same time as the human population escalates.[3] Productive topsoil can be degraded or lost to erosion by moving wind and water, development, pollution, pesticide use, intensive single-crop agriculture, and by poor soil management or grazing practices.

Once lost or degraded, topsoil takes a long time to regenerate. It can take up to 1,000 years for a single inch of topsoil (25 mm) to accumulate.[4] But through proper land-use planning and soil conservation techniques, soil can be saved and improved. For instance, farmers can use cover crops, field rotation, windbreaks, and contour planting (tilling and planting parallel to slopes and drainage) to reduce soil loss. They can replace nutrients and improve soil quality by adding organic matter to the soil. Towns can plan carefully where new houses and businesses will be built and preserve farmland for open space. Urban areas can control run-off water from paved surfaces, protect exposed soil by planting grasses or native plants, and construct new streets mindful of environmental impacts. All of these things can help the long-term economic, ecological, and social condition of a community.

1 Adapted from: The Natural Resources Conservation Service, Conservation Communications Staff, PO Box 2890, Washington, DC 20013.

2 "Ecological Resources and Agricultural Sustainability" by David Pimentel in *Proceedings of A Life Cycle Approach to Sustainable Agriculture Indicators,* Feb 26-27, 1999. Dr. Pimentel states, "Per capita world cropland is .27 ha."

3 Ibid; http://css.snre.umich.edu/ To sustain adequate crop production, a soil depth of 6 inches (150 mm) is needed. Center for Sustainable Systems, University of Michigan.

4 USDA Natural Resources Conservation Serivce: www.nrcs.usda.gov/feature/education/squirm/skQ11.html

What You'll Need

Large apple(s); cutting board; knife; compost bucket (optional); OR paper; crayons/pencils; and scissors.

Getting Ready

Decide whether you want to prepare one "apple" diagram for each student or just demonstrate the activity.

How to Do It

Begin by using a large apple (with washed skin) to represent earth. Ask the class: How much of the earth-apple represents the soil in which food can grow (also known as arable land)?

Demonstrate in front of the class—"Julia Child" style—while your students follow along with their own apples or paper apples. Younger children or those with special needs can draw a picture of an apple with the skin on it (a generous circle, with a stem and leaf). The "skin" should be drawn/colored only on the circumference. If using paper apples, label each piece that is cut.

Cut the apple into four equal sections. Ask students what these represent. (Three parts represent the earth's water: oceans, lakes, rivers, and streams, one part represents the land.) Put aside the three water parts.

Cut the land portion in half lengthwise. One part represents deserts, swamps, Arctic/Antarctic terrain, and mountains. The other part symbolizes where people live and grow food. Set aside the non-usable land part.

Slice into four equal parts the remaining piece (which represents land where food may be grown). Put aside three of them for the places that are too rocky, wet, hot, developed, or degraded to grow food. (The piece left is 1/32 of the apple.)

Peel the last piece. This small bit of peel represents the earth's soil on which the whole earth's population depends for food.[1]

Next, ask students for their reactions to the exercise. With so little of the earth available for growing food, what can be done to save soil or create new soil? (Soil conservation techniques help retain topsoil and compost application helps return nutrients and structure.) Describe how composting can help build up topsoil from food waste. (See composting information in A Worm's-Eye View of Compost beginning on page 147.)

Where does your lunch come from? Most of what you and the rest of the world eats is grown on just 1/32 of our planet's "skin."

Then, have them taste some of the apple—as a metaphor for all the different foods we eat from the earth. Hold up the remaining apple parts and discuss the options for "disposing" of them. If your class is already composting, or you have a compost system at home, collect the apple parts to compost. (This may be a good place to get your students interested in composting as the creation of soil amendments helps save soils.)

Classroom Conversations

- What would happen if we lost most of our topsoil?
- Why are some areas losing farmland?
- Of all the apple parts discarded as undesirable for growing food (i.e., oceans, deserts, developed or degraded land, land that's too wet or too dry), could any of them be altered in some way to turn into arable land?
- Invite your students to discuss what will happen if we have smaller and smaller amounts of soil yet more and more people who need food. Is that why some people are hungry? (Some of the reasons people are hungry include poverty, too few jobs with adequate pay, inequitable global income distribution, lack of education—especially for women, natural disasters, social injustice, political causes, and lack of access to nutritious food. See the Resources in Grow a Row, pages 187–89.)

[1] Please note that this exercise is representational only and not an exact numerical calculation.

Action

Start a school bulletin board, mural, or poster about the earth's soils. Title it "Save Our Soils" and list the things the class knows about soil, what they want to learn, and what they can do to save it. Have students collect magazine photos of all different types of everyday objects and figure out which ones come from the land, especially which ones come from farmland.

Want to Do More?

- Ask older students to think about their own community. Do they have farmland? If not, did their community once have farmland, and what happened to it? How could we protect the farmland we have left? Invite them to research and calculate and/or map the diminished land available for farming due to development and sprawl. (Check with your municipal office, library, historical society, state agriculture department.)

Q: What's the difference between soil and dirt?
A: Dirt is what's under your fingernails.

- Use the apple exercise to practice applying fractions or percentages. At the end of each cut, ask what fraction remains?
- Create a compost pile or vermicomposting system (see related lessons in A Worm's-Eye View of Composting, page 147).
- Make a bulletin board illustrating the soil layer, using information and diagrams available from your regional Cooperative Extension office or Natural Resources Conservation Service.
- Current events assignment: Watch the news for items related to soil loss, areas of famine or drought, or other farm-related news.
- Connect history to this activity by discussing the Dust Bowl era. (Listen to or teach Woody Guthrie's *Dust Bowl Ballads* (includes the original liner notes). www.woodyguthrie.org for online catalog and song lyrics. See the *Smithsonian* article, "The Dust Bowl" by Michael Parfit, Volume 20, Issue 3, June 1989. *The Grapes of Wrath* by John Steinbeck also describes the Dust Bowl.

Lunchbox Locator

Here is a sample lunch. Ask students to figure out the ingredients in and origins of the six food items in this lunchbox. (Examples of possible answers appear in parenthesis.)

Salad (carrots, lettuce, celery, tomatoes, soil)
Juice (fruit, tree, soil)
Bread (grains [wheat, corn, rye?], water, yeast, salt, soil)
Cheese (cow [grass and grains], soil)
Fruit salad (oranges, apples, bananas, watermelon, mint leaves, water, soil)
Cookies (eggs [chickens and grain], flour [wheat], oats, sugar [cane], nuts, spices, water, soil)

Then have them trace their last meal to its source.

Sing and act the "Dirt Made My Lunch" song.

Dirt Made My Lunch

Chorus
Dirt made my lunch, dirt made my lunch.
Thank you dirt, thanks a bunch!
For my salad, my sandwich, my milk, my lunch.
Dirt made my lunch!

Dirt is a word we often use
When we talk about the earth beneath our shoes.
It's a place where plants can sink their toes,
And in a little while a garden grows.

Chorus

A farmer's plow will tickle the ground.
You know the earth has laughed when wheat is found.
The grain is taken and flour is ground,
For making a sandwich to munch on down.

Chorus

A stubby green beard grows upon the land.
Out of the soil the grass will stand.
But under hoof it must bow,
For making milk by way of cow.

Chorus

Used with permission. Written by the Banana Slug String Band, 888-327-5847 www.bananaslugstringband.com

Lesson Links

Are All Soils Created Equal?
Food Security (Appendix)
Grow a Row (pages 187–89)
What Is Locally Grown?

Literature Links

Pumpkins: A Story for a Field by Mary Lyn Ray
One Good Apple by Catherine Paladino
Our Endangered Planet: SOIL by Suzanne Winckler and Mary M. Rodgers
Farming (Ecology Alert) by Jane Featherstone
The Wump World by Bill Peet
City Green by Dyanne DiSalvo-Ryan
Why the Sky is Far Away: A Nigerian Folktale by Mary Joan Gerson

Resources

- See American Farmland Trust web site, www.farmlandinfo.org for the yearly *Census on Agriculture.* Click on the statistics or state tabs for information on changes in agriculture (economics, numbers of farms, and the amount of land currently being farmed in the U.S. or in your state). Or go to National Agricultural Statistics Service's site, www.nass.usda.gov and click on "Census of Agriculture" or "Statistics by State." To see this lesson graphically, go to www.farmland.org, click on "news" and then "audio/video clips" for *Apple as Planet Earth*. American Farmland Trust, 202-331-7300.
- The Cooperative Extension (USDA) publishes a host of information on farming, soils, and other topics. Contact your state Cooperative Extension or check the National web site: www.csrees.usda.gov/Extention/index/html
- The Banana Slug String Band has audiotapes and CDs of "Dirt Made My Lunch" and other songs, along with many other science-related topics. See www.bananaslugstringband.com.
- Contact the Natural Resources Conservation Service for information on soils written for teachers and students: http://www.nrcs.usda.gov
- www.nacdnet.org. Click on Education and Outreach and choose Soil and Water Stewardship 2006—*Water Wise*; *2005—Celebrate Conservation*; or 2004—*The Living Soil*. From *The Living Soil* page, click on Educators' Guide for *Soil Is Not Trivial,* for lesson plans for grades 5-12 and a list of additional web sites on soil. 509 Capital Court NE, Washington, DC 20002; 202-547-6223.
- *Reclaiming the Commons* by Brian Donahue and Wes Jackson, Yale University Press, 2001. Reviewer writes, "combines social and natural history to examine how our culture and economy favor development and consumerism at the expense of the environment."
- *Empty Breadbasket? The Coming Challenge to America's Food Supply and What We Can Do about It.* The Cornucopia Project. Rodale Press, 1984. Analyzes how America's abuse of natural resources endangers the future food supply and recommends ways to improve the food system.
- Sustainable Agriculture Resources: USDA National Agricultural Library (NAL) or Alternative Farming Systems Information Center (AFSIC) www.nal.usda.gov/afsic/AFSIC_pubs/k-12.htm or www.ams.usda.gov/; Center for Sustainable Agriculture www.uvm.edu/~susagctr/; Nat'l Campaign for Sustainable Agriculture. www.sustainableagriculture.net; Cloud Institute for Sustainability Education: www.sustainabilityed.org
- USDA/ARS Wind Erosion Research Unit at www.weru.ksu for information, resources, and photos concerning the Dust Bowl era and recent dust storms (and soil erosion) in the U.S. and all over the world!

Benchmarks

The Physical Setting: 4C—Processes That Shape the Earth, p. 73
Grades 6-8
"Human activities, such as . . . intensive farming, have changed the earth's land. . . . Some of these changes have decreased the capacity of the environment to support some life forms."

The Living Environment: 5E—Flow of Matter and Energy, p. 119
Grades 3-5
"Over the whole earth, organisms are growing, dying, decaying, and new organisms are being produced by the old ones."

The Designed World: 8A—Agriculture, p. 184
Grades 3-5
"The kinds of crops that can grow in an area depend on the climate and soil."

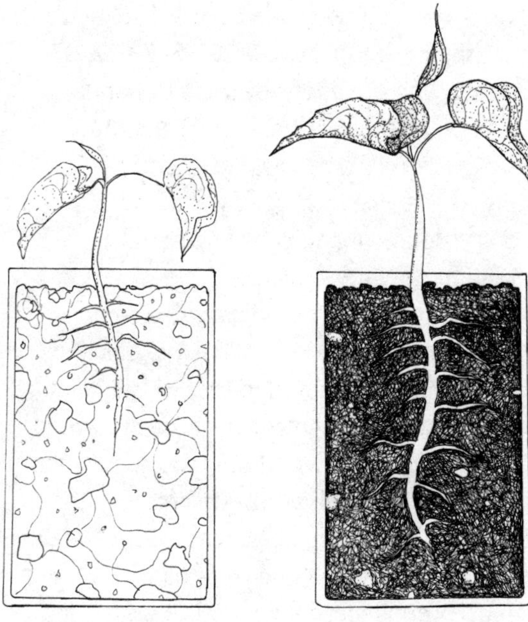

Are ALL Soils Created Equal?

Make soil quality comparisons

Recommended Grades: 2-6
- **Scientific Method**
- **Math**
- **Language Arts**

Goals

Using the scientific method, observe the effects of different soils on plants and see that some soils are better than others for growing plants.

Key Points

- Since good food depends on healthy soils, the quality of soil is important to farmers and gardeners.
- Soils missing certain ingredients (nutrients) will not support healthy plant growth.
- Organic matter such as compost is needed for good soil.

Background

Many factors affect a soil's health—particle size, minerals, organic matter, and soil organisms. To nourish plant growth, soil requires both water and oxygen. Soils with too much clay have poor drainage, holding water that deprives plant roots of oxygen. Sandy soils dry out quickly, dehydrating the plant. A proper mix of particle sizes creates soil with the capacity to hold some water but still maintain good drainage and pockets for air. Healthy soil is generally dark brown, earthy-smelling, and granular. It is neither hard and clumpy (like clay), nor all consisting of individual particles (like sand).[1]

Plants rely on soil nutrients to stimulate healthy root development, increase resistance to disease, and generate high-quality fruits and grains. These nutrients nationally come from decomposing organic matter and dissolved minerals in the soil. Farmers and gardeners pay close attention to three nutrients in particular—nitrogen, phosphorus, and potassium—because they are most often the ones found to be deficient in soils. Yet, just as with people, plants also depend on the dozen or so lesser-known nutrients found in the soil. (See Appendix, pages 219–20.)

Organic matter makes up just 1–5 percent by weight of most healthy soils, yet it is a vital component. Whether soil is clay, sand, or loam, the presence of organic matter improves the way that soil particles cluster together (thereby improving moisture retention, soil structure, water drainage, and soil aeration). Plants grown in soils with high organic matter are less vulnerable to drought or flooding. Organic matter also supports worms and beneficial bacteria, another important component of healthy soil. In fact, healthy soil, with microorganisms intact is a living ecosystem of its own.

I have to brag just a little about how important worms and my other friends are to soils, plants, and people!!!

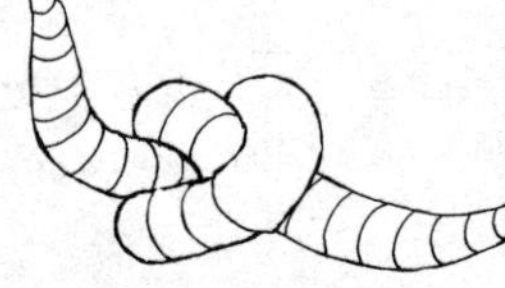

[1] Personal communication with M. Susan Erich, Professor of Plant and Soil Chemistry, University of Maine, January 2002.

What You'll Need

An uprooted plant (with roots intact), preferably a weed; seeds (radish, lettuce or another rapidly germinating type); permanent markers; enough pots with drainage holes to allow one per student or pair of students (single-serving yogurt containers with holes in the bottom work well); a ground cloth or tarp; several trays to hold pots; three large bowls or buckets (labeled A, B, and C) each filled with a different soil mix; a selection of ingredients for soil mix: garden or playground soil, purchased potting mix (perhaps a local nursery or agricultural supply company will donate this), sand, clay, peat moss, compost, or vermicompost, etc. *Caution:* Avoid vermiculite as a potting medium since the airborne particles pose a health risk if inhaled.

Note: This activity takes several weeks to complete.

Getting Ready

Prepare three soil mixes from your choice of the ingredients listed above. Include one sample of obviously poor growing soil and one sample of good growing soil.

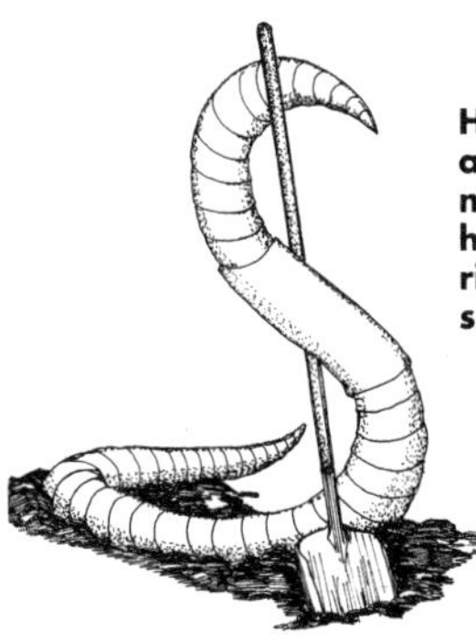

Heavy garden soil should be amended with sand and peat moss, or coir (ground-up coconut husks) for indoor growing. Nutrient-rich worm compost can be used sparingly. A little goes a long way!

How to Do It

Begin by showing your class an uprooted plant and discuss how soil helps a plant (anchors it in the ground, supplies important minerals, holds water for it to absorb, etc.). Draw student attention to the roots as this experiment will be testing the availability of nutrients to the roots and the root growth can indicate the health of the plant. Ask what types of soils might be best for growing plants and record students' ideas. Indicate that the class will do an experiment to observe the effects different soils have on plant growth. (Show them soil mix A, B, and C.) Since the variable in the experiment is the soil sample, all other conditions affecting the seed and plant need to be kept constant. Ask students what these conditions would be. Make a plan for how they will regulate these variables, ie., have a consistent watering schedule, allocate the same volume of soil and number of seeds to each pot, and place pots in the same location.

Next, decide how they will chart their observations. What will they look for (plant height, numbers of leaves, color)? How will they record and organize their data (graph, chart, journal, class poster)? Ask the class for predictions. What do they think will happen to the seeds? Which soil sample (A, B, or C) will grow the strongest plants and which the weakest? Why? What variables will indicate strong plants or weak plants? Will the seeds all come up at once? Record their predictions.

Then, divide the class into three working groups. Using a ground cloth to protect the floor, set up a potting area with three soil samples in labeled buckets or bowls (A, B, C—each one associated with one group of students). Have the groups of students clearly label the small cups or pots (A, B, or C) and fill them with the corresponding soil mix. Take time to study and describe the visible attributes of each soil sample, and plant the same number of seeds in each pot.

Place cups or pots on trays labeled as A, B, or C. (It may help to use different colored pots for each group.) Place pots on a lighted grow stand or windowsill, with all plants getting equal amounts of light.

Finally, over the next few weeks, have student groups water pots evenly (in measured amounts) as needed, take data, and make observations. Record these in a journal or class chart or graph. Initially, all seedlings will be using nutrients from the seed to sprout. Once the energy from the seed is used up, the plants will be dependent on soil nutrients and may begin to exhibit differences in growth and health from sample to sample. Have students record their conclusions. If possible, present a report of the findings to another class, local garden group, or science fair. Be sure to report results with thank-yous to any companies that donated materials for your project.

Classroom Conversations

- How would you compare the growth of plants in soil mix A, B, and C? Which ones grew faster, taller, etc? Which have the best color? Which appear strongest?
- How do the results compare with their predictions (hypotheses)?
- How healthy are the roots in the different soil mixes? Dig out one plant per sample group (A, B, C) and carefully remove soil from the roots. Compare the plants' root growth.
- Decide as a class what to do with the plants once the experiment is done (compost, continue to grow, take home, give as gifts, use for fundraiser).

Want to Do More?

- Document the class data on a poster, with photographs if possible. Have students report on what they observed and how their experiment confirmed or disproved their hypotheses.
- Using your classroom samples, explore more into the world of soils through other available experiments in publications and web sites. (See Resources, below, or Bibliography.)
- Have students write in journals about how the plants can be likened to people. If healthy plants are those that receive all they need from the sun, soil, water, and air, what conditions make for healthy humans (those who consume nutritious food, exercise, and have clean water and air)? Invite students to compare themselves to the plants that didn't grow well, imagining that they live in a setting without adequate food or clean water. What happens when a body doesn't get enough nutrients? What does that feel like? What effect would it have on their bodies? Where do people live in these conditions (near or far from home)?
- Provide students with different soil ingredients and ask them to make their own "soil recipe" and repeat the experiment. Ask them what they'd recommend for a planting mixture, based on what they learned from this soil experiment. Have them record the proportions of each soil type in their mix.
- Ask students how plants get water during dry weather. Record their comments and find a few ideas the class agrees on. Have them moisten a cup of clayey soil until it makes a mud cake, then place the "cake" on a tray or piece of cardboard labeled "just soil." In another container, they can moisten and mix one-half cup of soil with one-quarter cup of wet sawdust or peat moss to make a mud cake. Place this cake on a tray or cardboard labeled "soil with organic matter." Have them put both cakes in the sun, checking them every hour or two. Record observations until each mud cake is completely dry. Have students try breaking the mud cakes with their hands: what happens? Discuss why the different cakes react differently. See the discussion of organic matter in Background—the sawdust acts the same way—making plants less subject to drought or excess water.
- Explore how soils vary naturally from region to region and how each soil type has a name. Some soils are named for the towns or areas where they are located.

Action

Plant a surprise! Find a place somewhere in your area that needs a little boost. Using good topsoil or potting mix and some vermicompost, plant something beautiful—à la *Miss Rumphius* (story by Barbara Cooney)—where others wouldn't expect to see it. It's probably best to use bulbs or non-edible plants, since you won't be able to control the surrounding growth conditions.

Lesson Links

It's a Small World
Alive and Thriving!
Go to Seed!
Vermi-Condos

Literature Links

A Handful of Dirt by Raymond Bial
Living Earth: Soil by Eleonore Schmid
Earthworms, Dirt, and Rotten Leaves by Molly McGlaughlin
The World Beneath Our Feet: The Story of Soil by Martin Keen
Annelida the Wonder Worm by Katie B. Diepenbrock
Science Fun with Mud and Dirt by Rose Wyler

Mrs. Rose's Garden by Elaine Greenstein

Resources

- *Dig In! Hands-On Soil Investigations* by Tom Levermann. National Science Teachers Association and Natural Resources Conservation Service, 2001, for soil activities for grades K-4; www.nsta.org/scistore
- Ask a local garden group to donate materials in return for having students present their findings to the group.
- See related activities in: *Wonderful World of Wigglers* by Julia Hand, Food Works, 1995; and *Worms Eat Our Garbage* by Mary Appelhof, Mary Frances Fenton, and Barbara Loss Harris, Flower Press, 1993.
- Visit Cedar Meadow Farm at www.cedarmeadowfarm.com to learn about their no-till vegetable production and other sustainable cropping systems.
- The Community Alliance with Family Farmers (CAFF) is a California-based organization promoting family-scale farming that is environmentally sound and sustains local economies. www.caff.org
- For more soil-exploring ideas see *Soils Alive! From Tiny Rocks to Compost (4H Cycling Back to Nature Series, 1995).*
- Soil questions? Ask S. K. Worm, the official annelid of the USDA's National Resources Conservation Service: www.nrcs.usda.gov/Feature/education/squirm/skworm.html
- Natural Resources Conservation Service (NRCS) Soil Education site http://soils.usda.gov/education for soil facts, science, experiments, songs, quotations, soil science glossary, state soils, Smithsonian Soils Exhibit, Tools for Educators, and more.
- See the USDA/ARS Wind Erosion Research unit's website www.weru.ksu for sobering information on the damaging effects wind errosion continues to have on agriculture today.

Benchmarks

The Physical Setting: 4C—Processes That Shape the Earth, pp. 72-73

Grades 3-5

"Soil is made partly from weathered rock, partly from plant remains—and also contains many living organisms."

Grades 6-8

"The composition and texture of soil and its fertility and resistance to erosion are greatly influenced by plant roots and debris, bacteria, fungi, worms, insects, rodents, and other organisms."

Alive and Thriving!

Play a micro-farm game to learn what plants need

Recommended Grades 2–6
- **Science**
- **Dramatic Play**

Goals

To grow and thrive, plants and animals need a healthy habitat. Explore what plants need for healthy growth and discover that the basic habitat needs of plants and children are similar.

Key Points

- All living things need food, water, air, shelter, and space (a habitat) in order to survive.
- Plants specifically need sun, air, water, soil, space, and shelter.
- The quality of a habitat is important for a plant or animal's health.

Background

When a gardener or farmer grows food, he or she becomes the provider of that plant's habitat needs. On a basic level (to survive), a plant needs sun, soil, air, water, space, and shelter. Like people, when plants' habitat needs are met, they survive; when they are provided with top-quality habitat components like nutrient-rich soil, full sunlight, TLC, clean air, and the right amount of clean water, they *thrive*. In most habitat lessons, the concentration is on the basics—only what an organism needs to survive, but in this lesson, we are interested in what is needed to grow healthy, thriving plants!

Plants manufacture their own "food" through the wonderful and mysterious process of photosynthesis—a plant uses *air* (carbon dioxide) and *water* to store the *sun*'s energy into "food energy" (carbohydrates and starch). But a plant still needs *soil* for the nutrients necessary for growth, repair, and overall health, *water* to carry these dissolved nutrients into the plant from the soil, *space* for growth—spreading leaves out to the sun and sending roots out for water and nutrients—and *shelter* for protection from high winds, flooding, drought, insects, or animals.

A farmer may use many things to help enhance a plant's habitat—tractors and tools to ease the work; compost, cow manure, worms and other soil microorganisms to enhance the soil; bats and beneficial insects to prey on insect pests; honey bees, hummingbirds, and wild pollinators to increase fruit production; fences; trees as windbreaks; irrigation; and a greenhouse or row covers to protect and shelter. In this activity encourage students to look at the options available for providing the optimum habitat for their crops.

What You'll Need

Note: Although we believe space and shelter are essential for healthy plant growth, these concepts are difficult to represent on a concrete level in this activity. Please discuss these with your "farmers" and suggest they keep these important points in mind as they build their farms.

Representative ingredients for "Healthy Farm Habitat" (4–6 of each, depending on the number of groups you have):

- Enough for one per group: jars of soil; air (can substitute with inflated balloon representing carbon dioxide); water; sunlight (flashlight, light bulb, or cut-out of sun).
- Pictures or toys representing toy tractors; garden tools; plastic worms and/or soil microorganisms; honey bees and/or native pollinating insects; bats; hummingbirds; cow manure; compost; fences; irrigation; mini greenhouse; etc. (Get ideas from a seed catalog.)
- Words to the songs "Have to Have a Habitat" by Bill Oliver and "Sun, Soil, Water, and Air" by the Banana Slug String Band. (See next page.)

Getting Ready

Gather materials and set them out on a table. Review the concept of habitat with your students if it's unfamiliar to them.

Note: This activity can be done without all the props. Just provide each group with a list of the items suggested above.

How to Do It

Begin by asking students to identify things they use from plants (food, furniture, medicine, oxygen, clothing). Make a list on the board. (Older students could identify which plants these products come from.) Do we absolutely need the things we listed in order to survive? Since plants are important to our survival, shouldn't we know what *plants* need to survive? Are their needs similar to ours? Challenge your students to start thinking about what plants need. Remind them of the habitat concept.

Next, break students into small groups and explain this scenario. Each group owns a "Healthy Farm Habitat"—in its first year of operation. They plan to grow vegetables to sell at a farm stand. As farmers, they must provide the vegetables' habitat needs. Because they are first-year farmers, they have a limited budget and workforce so can provide just a little bit more than the basics. Point out the table with the "Healthy Farm Habitat" pieces where each group can choose five pieces, each (no doubling up on one ingredient) to help them grow their vegetables. Their goal is to grow the healthiest and best-tasting vegetables they can.

Then, send each group up one at a time to gather five different pieces. (You may need to limit their time.) Once they agree on their five, they need to develop good reasons why they made each choice. When all groups have had a chance up at the table, allow a second trip to make any trades. Ask them to record their reasons for the five things they chose.

Finally, have each group report to the class what five items it felt it needed for its first year of farming (for its plant habitat). Write these on the board. See which items are common from group to group. Try to determine what the habitat basics were. Find out how each farm hoped to enhance its plants' habitat. Discuss how the various pieces on the table could affect a plant's life. Ask each group what additional items it would like and why. Allow it to add one or two.

Classroom Conversations

- Allow children to "micro-farm" with their "Healthy Farm Habitat" ingredients—set up a farm on their desks. Start posing "what if" questions to the farmers to see how the vegetables on their farms would fare in different scenarios: Your soil lost nutrients. You didn't get enough rain. A huge flock of birds landed in the fields and started eating your plants. You had an infestation of pest insects. There was a drought. The stream got polluted. A herd of deer appeared near your farm. The wind threatens to blow away your soil and damage your crops. The farmer was sick and unable to farm. Is it possible to create the perfect farm? Why or why not?
- Learn words to one or both songs: "Have to Have a Habitat" and "Sun, Soil, Water, and Air." Invite students to add a verse on soil or farms to "Have to Have a Habitat."

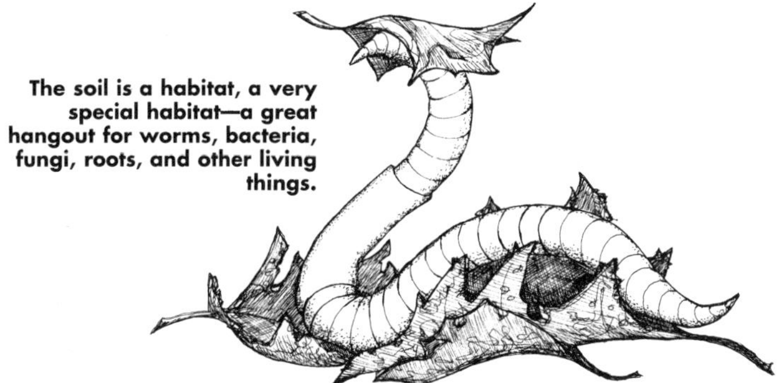

The soil is a habitat, a very special habitat—a great hangout for worms, bacteria, fungi, roots, and other living things.

Have to Have a Habitat

Lyrics by Bill Oliver

Chorus

Habitat, habitat, have to have a habitat,
Habitat, habitat, have to have a habitat,
Habitat, habitat, have to have a habitat,
You have to have a habitat to carry on.

The ocean is a habitat, a very special habitat.
It's where the deepest water's at, it's where the biggest mammal's at.
It's where our future food is at, it keeps the atmosphere intact.
The ocean is a habitat that we depend on.

Chorus

The forest is a habitat, a very special habitat.
It's where the tallest trees are at, it's where a bear can scratch a back.
It keeps the ground from rolling back, renews the oxygen, in fact.
The forest is a habitat that we depend on.

Chorus

The river is a habitat, a very special habitat.
It's where the freshest water's at, for people, fish, and muskrats.
But when the people dump their trash the river takes the biggest rap.
The river is a habitat that we depend on.

Chorus

People are different than foxes and rabbits.
Affect the whole world with their bad habits.
Better to love it while we still have it.
Or rat-ta-tat-tat, our habitat's gone.

Chorus

Used with permission from Bill Oliver, Mr. Habitat, Mrhabitat@aol.com; www.mrhabitat.net

And two more verses from Kathy Lyons:

The prairie is a habitat, a very special habitat.
It's where the bison herds are at, where antelope can get a snack.
The prairie dogs make it their home, the coyote he can roam alone.
The prairie is a habitat that we depend on.

Chorus

Communities are habitats, they're very special habitats.
Where folks like you and I are at, with homes and food and dogs and cats,
And schools and friends and neighborhoods all working for the common good.
Communities are habitats that we depend on.

Chorus

Sun, Soil, Water, and Air

By Steve Van Zandt, 1987

(To be chanted in a round)

Sun, soil, water, air.
Sun, soil, water, air.
Everything you eat
And everything you wear
Comes from
Sun, soil, water, air.

Used with permission. Written by the Banana Slug String Band, 888-327-5847; www.bananaslugstringband.com

Action

Choose to improve a plant habitat in your area: clean up trash, weed, water, plant, add compost, etc. Work with another group in your community to help you accomplish the goal.

Want to Do More?

- Test plants' needs for sun, soil, water, air, space, and shelter by setting up a few experiments. Predict results ahead of time and track in a journal what happens.

  Sun: Put one plant in the sun and one in darkness. Compare plant growth over time.

  Soil: Plant seeds in potting soil, sawdust, wet paper towels and note what happens to the plant over time.

  Water: Water one plant regularly, over-water one, and water another very little. Note what happens to the plants over time.

  Air: Cover some plant leaves with oil or petroleum jelly so these leaves cannot "breathe." Note what happens to the air-deprived leaves compared with the others.[1]

  Space: In two equal size pots with potting soil, plant a handful of seeds in one and two seeds in the other. Observe their growth and vigor over time.

  Shelter: Place a plant very near a hot air vent, air conditioner, or fan and another under similar light conditions, but protected from the harsher conditions. Watch the plants for changes over time.
- Have students create slogans reminding us all of basic needs and that these needs should be clean, unpolluted, etc. Example: "Everyone needs to eat well—even the soil"; "Feed the soil, feed yourself"; "What if there were no clean water?; What if ______?"
- Have students role-play some of the physical work that is required to maintain a farm: shoveling, hauling, planting, harvesting, working on machinery, etc. Consider how much labor is needed compared to most (sedentary) jobs today.
- Ask students what it would be like if we humans could manufacture our own food *directly* from the sun, soil, water, and air as plants do. Write about the experience. Compare the basic habitat needs of plants and children.
- Explore ways a garden or farm can become a healthy habitat for other living thing. (See Literature Links and Resources.)

Lesson Link

Are All Soils Created Equal?

Literature Links

Mrs. Rose's Garden by Elaine Greenstein
More Than Just a Vegetable Garden by Dwight Kuhn
The Lady and the Spider by Faith McNulty
Looking at Plants by David Suzuki
Straight from the Bear's Mouth: The Story of Photosynthesis by Bill Ross
Seeds, Stems, and Stamens: The Ways Plants Fit into Their World by Susan Goodman

Resources:

- Visit Cedar Meadow Farm at www.cedarmeadowfarm.com to learn about their no-till vegetable production and other sustainable cropping systems.
- The Community Alliance with Family Farmers (CAFF) is a California-based organization promoting family-scale farming that is environmentally sound and sustains local economies. www.caff.org
- FoodRoutes Network is a national nonprofit organization dedicated to rebuilding local, community-based food systems. Their goal is "reintroducing Americans to their food—the seeds it grows from, the farmers who produce it, and the routes that carry it from the fields to their tables." www.foodroutes.org
- Banana Slug String Band for tapes and CDs: www.bananaslugstringband.com "Sun, Soil, Water and Air" (words on page 12).
- Bill Oliver, "Mr. Habitat," writer of "Have to Have a Habitat" (words on page 12), has six albums of eco-music. www.mrhabitat.net/
- *The Farm As Natural Habitat: Reconnecting Food Systems with Ecosystems* by Dana and Laura Jackson, Island Press, 2002. Essays discussing how agriculture can protect and co-exist with native species while growing healthy food.
- See Bullfrog Films (under Organizations in Bibliography) for films related to timely agriculture and recycling issues.

[1] Idea adapted with permission from *Project Seasons* by Deb Parrella, Shelburne Farms, 1995, p. 224.

Benchmarks

The Living Environment: 5C—Cells, p. 111

Grades K-2

"Most living things need water, food, and air."

The Living Environment: 5D—Interdependence of Life, pp. 116-17

Grades 3-5

"Many plants depend on animals for carrying their pollen to other plants or for dispersing their seeds."

"Changes in an organism's habitat are sometimes beneficial to it and sometimes harmful."

Grades 6-8

"In all environments . . . organisms with similar needs may compete with one another for resources, including food, space, water, air, and shelter. In any particular environment, the growth and survival of organisms depend on the physical conditions."

"Relationships may be competitive or mutually beneficial. Some species have become so adapted to each other that neither could survive without the other."

The Living Environment: 5E—Flow of Matter and Energy, p. 119

Grades K-2

"Plants . . . need to take in water. . . . In addition, plants need light."

Grades 3-5

"Some source of 'energy' is needed for all organisms to stay alive and grow."

The Designed World: 8A—Agriculture, p. 184

Grades K-2

"Most food comes from farms. . . . To grow well, plants need enough warmth, light, and waste. Crops also must be protected from weeds and pests that can harm them."

Go to Seed![1]

Welcome a classroom visitor to illustrate seed germination

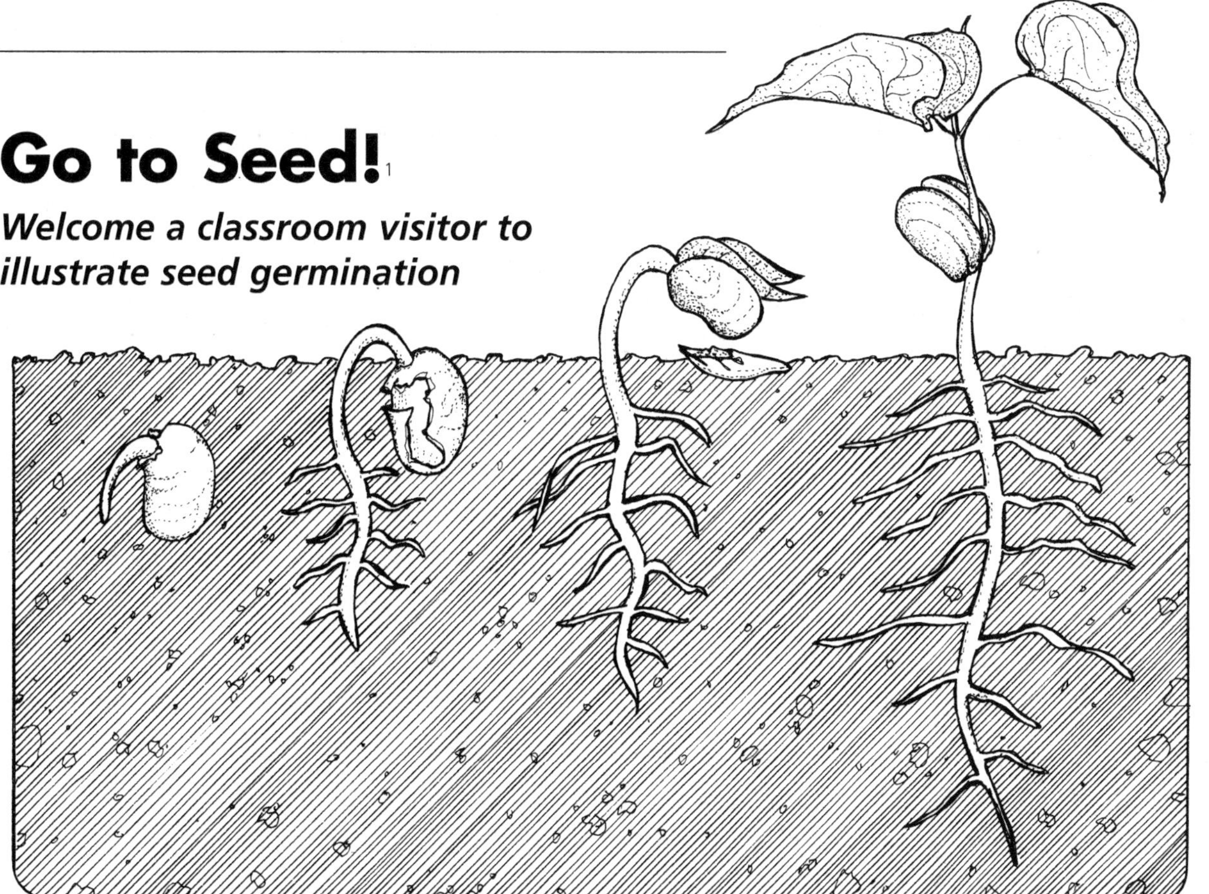

Recommended Grades: K–4

- **Science**
- **Performing Arts**

Goal

Learn about the germination process and, using scientific names, identify the parts of seeds.

Key Points

- To sprout, seeds need air, water, and the right temperature.
- The food supply that gives a seed its healthy start is the same food supply that helps humans grow.

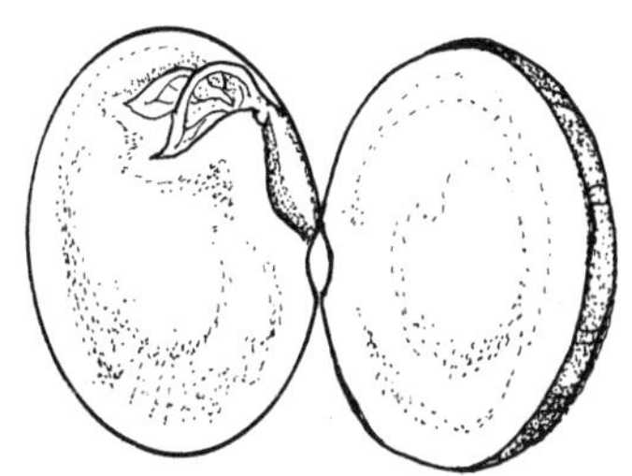

Background

A cycle—by nature—has no beginning or end, but seeds are a terrific starting place for examining a plant's life cycle. Students will get a close-up look at the components of a seed when they meet a life-sized seed.

Seeds are amazing packages of potential protected by a hard shell called a seed coat. These embryos contain a plant's first leaves, embryonic roots, and a supply of food energy—stored either in special leaves called cotyledons (rhymes with "mottle edens") or in an endosperm—a sac around the embryonic plant. The nutrient-packed food supply that enables a seed to get its healthy start is the same food supply that provides human beings with important proteins, fats, and carbohydrates when they eat seeds.

What You'll Need

For the skit: large raincoat with hood, preferably; day pack containing: a bag of edible seeds and nuts; water bottle or plant mister; green hat, scarf, and gloves; white rope or string; five signs, one for each plant part (cotyledon, leaves, roots, food, seed coat); and clothespins. For seed observation: various sizes and types of seeds (from small radish seeds to a coconut, for example) to show students; hand lenses; soaked seeds (large beans such as lima or

[1] Adapted with permission from "Little Sprout" from *Project Seasons*, by Deb Parrella, Shelburne Farms, 1995.

scarlet runner beans); drawing of seed for overhead projector (optional).

Caution: We recommend not including peanuts for this seed snack because so many children are allergic to them.

Getting Ready

Locate a parent or fellow teacher who likes to ham it up to be "Seedy" and go over the skit with him or her.

Sprout some seeds ahead of time. (Wrap seeds in wet paper towel, place in plastic bag, and set in a dark place, or see The Classroom is Sprouting, page 190.) Bean seeds are a good choice for this.

How to Do It

Begin by asking students: What is in a seed? What causes a seed to grow? (Guide them to recall what plants need for growth: sun, soil, water, air, space, shelter (and TLC!).

Show them a variety of seeds. What seeds do they eat? While students observe these seeds, a special guest enters the classroom.

Next, this guest is dressed with a raincoat worn over a backpack. The backpack represents the cotyledons and contains food (a bag of seeds and nuts to eat), tiny new leaves (a green hat, scarf, and gloves), and a new root (length of white rope). The guest could also carry moisture (a water bottle or mister). When Seedy walks in, the teacher could plant him or her and ask the kids what would happen next. The guest hunches over into a ball and makes noises (as if trying to break free of something).

The guest looks up to the class and says, "Hi, my name is Seedy," and explains that s/he is a seed and feels the days getting longer and the soil getting warmer, but the seed coat is just not soft enough to break out of. Ask if a student will help by raining on the soil/seed. The volunteer is given a mister and mists the seed. (The kids love this part so the teacher may need to remind "the rain" that flooding a seed is not such a good thing.)

The seed unzips the seed coat with a sigh of relief. A volunteer is asked to hang it in the classroom and attach the seed coat label to the coat with a clothespin. (This will be done with each of the seed components.) The backpack contains all the seed parts: cotyledons (bag of food—which feeds the plant until its leaves are grown), roots (rope—which brings in water and nutrients from the soil), and leaves (the hat, scarf, and gloves—which will manufacture the plants energy from the sun).

At this point, Seedy begins to grow. S/he can ask students for assistance, i.e., to first locate and label the cotyledons' food, the root, then the green parts inside the backpack that can be worn to get energy from the sun. Seedy dons each part and acts out the seed's growth—reaching up to the sun with a flourish, discarding the backpack (cotyledons) that is no longer needed. The seed takes a bow. (S/he's going to seed!)

Then, pass out the "plant food" (the nuts and seeds) to the class for a snack break, and review what just happened. Ask them if they can see the seed parts in the nuts and seeds they are eating.

Hand out sprouted beans or other seeds and hand lenses to explore the inside of the seed. Locate the seed coat, leaves, roots, and cotyledon.

Classroom Conversations

- What kind of seed was Seedy? Are all seeds like Seedy? (All seeds contain those basic parts. They might look different and sprout different plants.)
- Where did Seedy come from?
- What would have happened to Seedy if the backpack had no food left, the rain didn't stop, it never rained, etc.? Discuss why seeds are important.

Want to Do More?

- Dress Seedy back up, having students explain what all the parts are as a way to apply what they learned.
- Invite students to create their own seed story, starting with, "One day, a bird dropped a seed. . . ."
- Go WILD with seeds: grow them, cook them, sort or categorize, save seeds from the garden or a field, look at seed catalogs, make art with seeds, eat seeds, explore the history of seeds.
- Have children create their own Seedy character skit and share with another classroom.

Lesson Links

Sprout Yourself!

The Global Staff of Life
The Classroom Is Sprouting!

Literature Links

Carlos and the Cornfield/Carlos y la milpa de maiz by Jan Romero Stevens
The Carrot Seed by Ruth Krauss
The Magic School Bus Activity Guide: Plants and Seeds: A Book About How Living Things Grow by Joanna Cole and Bruce Degen
Pumpkin Circle: The Story of a Garden by George Levenson
How a Seed Grows by Helene Jordan

Resources

- For many wonderful activities and ideas about seeds, gardens, and soil: *Project Seasons,* by Deb Parrella, Shelburne Farms, 1995. www.shelburnefarms.org

For information on saving seeds:

- Seed Savers Exchange, 3076 N. Winn Road, Decorah, IA 52101; 563-382-5990; www.seedsavers.org. Oldest and most active nonprofit group in preserving heirloom seeds worldwide.
- Native Seeds/SEARCH, 526 N. Fourth Ave., Tucson, AZ 85705; www.nativeseeds.org.
- Eastern Native Seed Conservancy www.enscseeds.org. no longer an active organization but stays online to provide information. The links page, "Seedsaving and Seedsavers' Resources," provides a global list of web sites, organizations, books, and more.
- Kids in Bloom Seed Co., PO Box 344, Zionsville, IN 46077; 317-636-3977. Your class can become "Seed Guardians" who help grow, save, and learn about heirloom seeds.
- Heirloom Seed Project, Medomak Valley High School, www.msad40.org/schools.mvhs. Click on Heirloom Seed Project for a catalog and more information on saving seeds.
- *Beyond the Bean Seed* by Nancy Jurenka and Rosanne Blass, Libraries Unlimited, 1996, to connect gardening to children's books.

Benchmarks

The Physical Setting: 4D—Structure of Matter, p. 77

Grades 3-5

"Many kinds of changes occur faster under hotter conditions."

The Physical Setting: 4E—Energy Transformations, pp. 83-84

Grades K-2

"The sun warms the land, air, and water."

Grades 3-5

"Things that give off light also give off heat."

The Living Environment: 5C—Cells, p. 111

Grades K-2

"Most living things need water, food, and air."

The Designed World: 8A—Agriculture, p. 184

Grades K-2

"To grow well, plants need enough warmth, light, and water. . . ."

Common Themes: 11B—Models, p. 268

Grades K-2

"A model of something is different from the real thing but can be used to learn something about the real thing."

Common Themes: 11C—Constancy & Change, p. 272

Grades K-2

"Things can change in different ways, such as in size, weight, color, and movement. . . ."

Sprout Yourself![1] *Take a storytelling break*

Recommended Grades: K–2

- **Science**
- **Performing Arts**

Goal

This is a fun activity for classrooms that don't get a visit from Seedy.

Key Point

- Seeds are an essential part of the growing cycle of plants.

Background

Once the parts and needs of a seed are understood, a guided imagery activity can bring seeds to life in the imaginations of children. By enacting a story, students trace the life of a seed from storage before planting to seed-saving in the fall. Such an exercise can reinforce themes discussed throughout this section: soil, seed and plant needs, and cycles.

What You'll Need

Imagination and a sense of play; story text; large feather to simulate insects; spray bottle.

Getting Ready

Read through the story yourself, and note any words that might need an explanation for your students. Use the Glossary at the back of the book for helpful explanations.

How to Do It

Begin by asking your students to think of a type of vegetable or fruit seed. Tell them that they will pretend to be these seeds in their seed coats, curled up with their seed buddies, silent inside paper seed packets (children could wear jackets or sweaters to simulate their own seed coats). Ask them to crouch on the floor as seeds—closing their eyes, listening carefully, and acting out what happens. Be sure they are spread out, leaving room for their own growth!

Next, lower the lights in the room and read:

The Earth is not ready for growing seeds. [Use reasons appropriate to your region: the ground is frozen, it is too hot and dry, this is the hurricane season, etc.] Above the ground [for northern climates] winds are cold blowing snow all around and piling it in drifts. [For southern climates—winds are strong, the sun bakes the earth dry.] You don't sense these things because you are asleep. Time passes, days, weeks, maybe months, but you don't notice because you are safe in your seed coat.

[1] Adapted with permission from "To Be a Seed" in *EarthChild 2000: Earth Science for Young Children* by Kathryn Sheehan and Mary Waidner, Council Oak Books, 1998.

There are important changes. The winds blow more gently, now. [Fill in with climate changes typical for your area at the start of a growing season.] Everything is just right—the sunshine, the rain, the warmth of the soil. One morning, just at sunrise a person picks up you and your seed buddies. Somehow you know it's planting day! The ground was prepared for you yesterday and the person places you and your other seed buddies into the warm, moist earth along with some dark, healthy compost and then covers you up. With a pat, pat, pat on top of the soil, the person is gone and you are alone in the quiet comfort of some beautiful, dark soil.

As seeds in the ground, you begin to wake up *very* slowly. Moisture from rain reaches down into the ground near you. [With a spray bottle, spray the air above the children to simulate rain. Continue reading.] You begin to drink it in. You are so thirsty that you drink until you are puffed with water! Your coat softens and splits as you swell. The soil around you is warmed by the sun and is just the right temperature—it feels great. You begin to tremble and tingle as the warmth and moisture awaken you from your slumber.

But you aren't the only one down here in this healthy soil! Earthworms are squirming around on their way to find food. They are making little tunnels that will eventually help bring air and water to your roots. They are eating rotting leaves and plant parts from last year, turning them into nutrients that you can use to grow strong.

Very slowly, you stretch a tiny root into the soil to absorb more water. It digs straight down, growing longer and longer each day. You drink the water and eat the food from your seed lobes (cotyledons). Soon you are strong enough to push your tiny stem and leaves through the ground and into the bright sunshine. Ahhhh! Open your eyes as you come up out of the ground.

Next, [brighten the lights in the room and continue]. Your little leaves spread open and catch the sun's warmth. You no longer need the food from your seed because you can now make your own! Your green leaves combine air, water from the earth, and energy from the sun to make delicious sugar and starch for your growing body. With each day, you grow bigger and stronger!

In the hot summer sunshine, you grow into a beautiful plant. On some days, a warm gentle rain falls on your new leaves and soaks down to your thirsty roots. [Use "rain" from the spray bottle sparingly. Continue reading.] You drink up not only the water but also dissolved nutrients from tiny rock particles and broken down plant and animal matter.

Some of you have a beautiful flower. The honeybees come to visit, tickling your petals with their furry bodies. [Use feather lightly.] As they turn to leave, they brush off some of the pollen they have collected from other flowers. In a while your flower (or perhaps your root) turns into a fruit or a vegetable.

People come to pick you and take you home for their dinner. Imagine what they'll make with you. Applesauce? Pumpkin pie? Whatever it is, it will be just scrumptious! And many of the vitamins and minerals you contain can nourish the boy or girl who eats you with their dinner!

Meanwhile, as the growing season comes to an end, the plant that grew you begins to weaken or get ready for a rest. [For northern climates, it can be shortening days, cooler temperatures, less daylight, etc.] Become that plant and let your leaves droop and fall to the ground. Your dead leaves and stems will feed the earthworms. They will get the soil ready for another season. Some of you left seeds behind for next time. Gardeners visit you to gather those seeds and put them in packets for the next growing season.

It's been a good growing cycle. As seeds once again, you are ready for a well-deserved rest. Ahhhhhhh.

Then, when finished reading, pause, and tell your students at the count of three to open their eyes and turn back into humans again. Take some time for them to tell everyone what they decided to be and what it was like to experience life as a seed. Review the cycle they experienced going from seed to plant to new seed. Ask them to explain how they got their food and water.

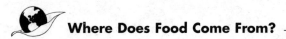

Classroom Conversations

- Identify the different parts of the cycle in the story.
- Ask "What if?" questions. Would changes in the cycle affect their growth as plants? What changes and why?

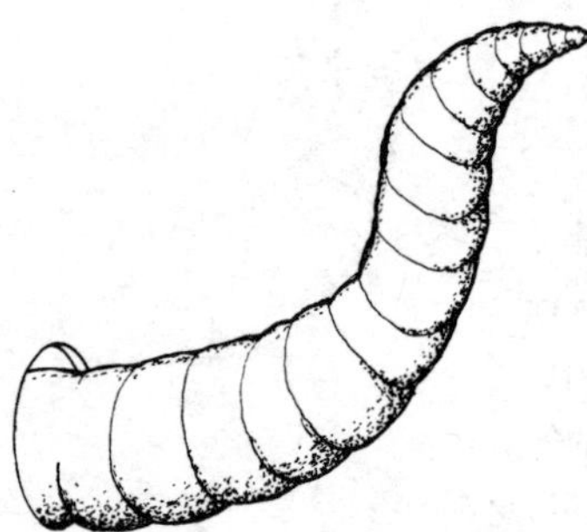

Did you know that seeds are packed with power? If you fill a small film canister with seeds almost to the very top and add water, they will swell so much that they'll POP the top right off the container!

Want to Do More?

- Have students do painted illustrations of some of the images they thought of during the story. When you hang them on the wall, arrange them in a cyclical growing sequence.
- Invite Annelida the spokesworm into the classroom after the experience. Have her ask the children what they saw underground and if they noticed any of her worm friends. She can ask them what the worms were doing. Start a list of what the class knows about earthworms and what they would like to know. Use this list as you go out to garden or start your own worm compost bin.

Lesson Links

What Does Your Garden Grow?
The Classroom Is Sprouting!
Go to Seed!
Alive and Thriving!
Vegetable Pop-Up Puppets

Literature Links

The Tiny Seed by Eric Carle
Pumpkin, Pumpkin by Jean Titherington
From Seed to Pear by Ali Mitgutsch
From Seed to Plant by Gail Gibbons
Grandpa's Garden Lunch by Judith Casely
The Pumpkin Book by Gail Gibbons
Seeds-Pop, Stick, Glide by Patricia Lauber

Resources

- *Growing with Plants: 4H—Youth Development Washington* by Linda Watts and Steven Garrett, State University Cooperative Extension, 1995. www.nal.usda.gov/Kids/4hplants.htm
- See seed-saving resources in the Go to Seed! lesson on page 17.
- Free seeds are available a few times a year through America the Beautiful; 800-522-3557; www.america-the-beautiful.org
- National Gardening Association has great Teacher's Guides for growing indoors. See *Growlab: A Complete Guide to Gardening in the Classroom,. NGA, 1988,* and *Growlab: Activities for Growing Minds, NGA,* 1994; 800-538-7476; www.kidsgardening.com

Benchmarks

The Physical Setting: 4B—The Earth, p. 67
Grades K-2
"Some events in nature have a repeating pattern. The weather changes some from day to day, but things such as temperature and rain (or snow) tend to be high, low, or medium in the same months every year."

The Designed World: 8A—Agriculture, p. 184
Grades K-2,
"To grow well, plants need enough warmth, light, and water. . . ."

Bark and Seeds for Breakfast[1]

Play a guessing game and snack on plant parts

Recommended Grades: 1–6
- **Science**
- **Language Arts**
- **Music**

Goals

Identify and classify various foods as parts of plants, and taste some unfamiliar foods.

Key Points

- Common foods we eat can be grouped by where they come from on a plant: seeds, roots, stems, leaves, flowers, and fruits.
- Exploring foods as plants helps us better understand where foods come from.
- Knowing which parts of the plant were edible was a matter of life or death to people foraging for their food before the dawn of agriculture. Some plant parts are poisonous!

I sometimes tell students that I had one of my favorite breakfasts that morning: I had some ground-up, cooked seeds sprinkled with bits of powdered bark, covered with thick sap, and topped with tiny blue fruit that comes from a low-growing bush—and it was DELICIOUS! Then I ask, "Can you tell what I ate?"
Answer: Oatmeal with cinnamon, maple syrup, and blueberries!

Background

Fruit or vegetable? In common language, we refer to many foods as vegetables when they are actually fruits, botanically speaking. For example, a zucchini is the fruit of the plant because it holds the seeds. One dictionary definition of fruit is: "The ripened, seed-bearing part of a plant, especially when fleshy and edible." It derives from the Latin *fructus,* to enjoy! Have older students look up and compare the meanings of the following words: fruit, fruitful, fruition, fruitcake, fruit fly, fruitless, fruity.

Caution: It's rare that we eat ANY whole plant in its entirety, even though plants make up the bulk of what we eat. Emphasize that not all parts of plants are edible, and in fact some are poisonous. One example is rhubarb, whose cooked stems are prized for their unique flavor and color, but whose leaves contain a substance that can make you sick. Another is potatoes. The potato itself is edible, but the rest of the plant could kill you. The potato is in the deadly nightshade family. Did you know that tomatoes were once thought to be poisonous?

How to Do It

Begin by asking, "Did you eat any plant parts today?" Write the six plant part classifications across the top of the board in a row. Ask students to think of any that they might have eaten. List their ideas under the appropriate column heading. Mention some of the features of various plant parts—protein found in seeds helps us grow, fiber in stems gets rid

[1] Adapted with permission from *The Growing Classroom: Garden-Based Science,* by Roberta Jaffe and Gary Appel, Addison-Wesley, 1990.

Plant Part	Plant Benefit	Human Benefit	Examples
SEEDS	Store energy needed to begin initial growth	Provide high levels of protein, supplying more than 50 percent of the protein that humans consume	Rice, wheat, corn kernels and popcorn, millet, nuts, peas, lentils, soybeans, dry/shell beans, sunflower or pumpkin seeds, coffee beans
ROOTS	Take up water and nutrients for the plant	Contain a lot of complex carbohydrates, providing the best energy source for the body	Carrots, turnips, radishes, parsnips, beets, potatoes (actually tubers, a type of underground stem), sweet potatoes, onions (bulbs are another kind of underground stem), and parsnips
STEMS	Act as spines that support a plant's leaves and fruits; carry food in "tubes" from the leaves to the entire plant as well as delivering water and nutrients from the roots	Provide a good source of fiber, which helps the body remove waste efficiently and prevent disease	Celery, rhubarb, asparagus, sugar cane, bamboo shoots, fennel, broccoli (stems), bok choy
FLOWERS	Form seeds which produce the new plant	Strengthen vision and keep mucus membranes functioning normally	Broccoli (heads), cauliflower, artichokes (when humans consume flowers, such as broccoli, it is before the plant has converted the flower into a seed)
FRUITS	Form once the flower is pollinated; the "seed suitcase" holds, nurtures, and protects the seeds	Contain vitamins A and C (which help heal cuts, scrapes, and can reduce the severity of some cold viruses)	String beans, snow peas, peppers, tomatoes, cucumbers, berries, apples, eggplant, corn on the cob, kiwis, strawberries, citrus, cantaloupe
LEAVES	Convert the sun's energy into food through the process of photosynthesis, the plant's "food factory"	Are a significant nutrition source containing iron, calcium, vitamin C, and fiber (especially the darker leaves)	Lettuce, spinach, cabbage, Chinese greens, herbs (basil, parsley)

We earthworms often pull leaves into our burrows for snacks, believe it or not. (My parents don't mind food in the bedroom!)

of wastes in our bodies, etc. (Refer to chart.)

Next, ask if the plant really needs all these parts. "Think of yourself as a plant. What if your stem were missing?" That would be like a human missing its spine! (Not just because of the structure it provides, but also because of the nutrients carried up the stem.) "Just as you need good food, the plant needs its food to grow and develop also."

Then, hold up different foods, and ask the students to identify them. What is it? How does it grow? Ask if anyone has ever eaten it? What was it like? What plant part is it? Add to the plant parts list if it isn't already there. Allow students to come up with more, now that they've had a chance to think about it. Use the list to help plan a "Plants Part-y." Make plans for who will bring the plant part snacks and schedule the tasting party.

Classroom Conversations

- Ask students to look at the plant parts list and ask if they realized that all the foods listed were actual plant parts?
- Why might it be important to know what plant parts you eat?
- Challenge students to come up with an answer to these questions: What's important about each plant part? What does each plant part do for the plant and in turn do for us when we eat it? (Discuss or assign them to research specific plant parts and prepare a report, poster, or skit.)

Want to Do More?

- Make a chart using a week's worth of school lunches or breakfasts to see how many foods come from different plants—categorize them according to the six plant parts.
- Learn the song "Roots, Stems, Leaves," by Steve Van Zandt of the Banana Slug String Band and

Roots, Stems, Leaves Song

By Steve Van Zandt

Chorus

Roots, stems, leaves, flowers, fruits and seeds,
Roots, stems, leaves, flowers, fruits and seeds,
Roots, stems, leaves, flowers, fruits and seeds,
Roots, stems, leaves, flowers, fruits and seeds,
That's six parts, six parts, six plant parts,
That plants and people need.

The roots hold the plant in the ground,
They gather up the water that falls around,
And there's a root inside of me,
Because a carrot is a root that I eat.

Chorus

A stem is an elevator growing up from the ground,
The water goes up and the sugar back down,
And there's a stem inside of me,
Because celery is a stem that I eat.

Chorus

The leaves are the kitchens where the food is done,
They breathe the air and catch rays from the sun,
And there's a leaf inside of me,
Because lettuce is a leaf that I eat.

Chorus

The flowers are dressed so colorfully,
They hold the pollen and attract the bees,
And there's a flower inside of me,
Because cauliflower is a flower that I eat.

Chorus

The fruit gets ripe, then it falls on down,
It holds the seeds and feeds the ground,
And there's a fruit inside of me,
Because an apple is a fruit that I eat.

Chorus

The seeds get buried in the earth,
And the cycle starts again with a new plant's birth,
And there are seeds inside of me,
Because sunflower is a seed that I eat.

Chorus

Now you know what this whole world needs,
It's roots, stems, leaves, flowers, fruits and seeds,
There's six plant parts inside of me,
Because a garden salad is what I eat.

Handout from *Healthy Foods from Healthy Soils*

create a Plant Parts Parade using student illustrations. Sing the song to accompany the procession. Perform for younger grade students if possible.

- Do art prints from various discarded plant parts such as carrot tops (preferably not wasting plants that could be used for food). Create a collage from a variety of food prints.
- Cook up a soup recipe using as many plant parts as you can.
- Create a plant parts poster or "table talker" for the school cafeteria or bulletin board.
- Have students bring in menus from restaurants (or make a teacher-created one) that they then rewrite as a Plant Parts Menu.

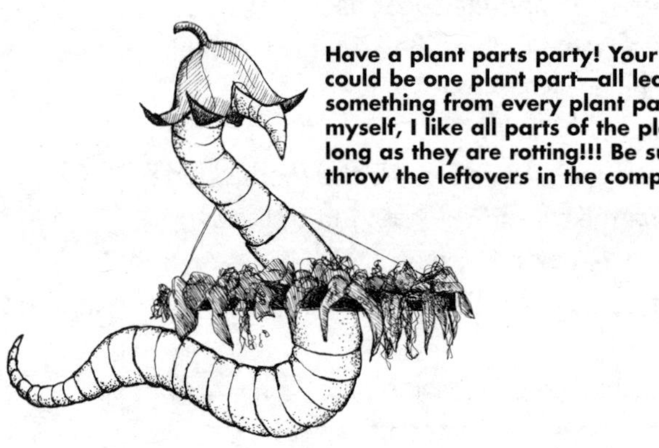

Have a plant parts party! Your menu could be one plant part—all leaves! Or something from every plant part! For myself, I like all parts of the plant, as long as they are rotting!!! Be sure to throw the leftovers in the compost!

Lesson Links

The Classroom Is Sprouting
What Is Locally Grown?
Vegetable Pop-Up Puppets

Literature Links

Gardening Wizardry for Kids by Patricia Kite
Tops and Bottoms by Janet Stevens
The Reason for a Flower by Ruth Heller
A Kids Guide to: How Flowers Grow; How Fruits Grow; How Herbs Grow; How Plants Grow; How Trees Grow; and *How Vegetables Grow,* all by Patricia Ayers
Green Power: Leaf and Flower Vegetables by Meredith Sayles Hughes
Healthy Body Cookbook: Over 50 Fun Activities and Delicious Recipes for Kids by Joan D'Amico and Karen E. Drummond
Fruits, Roots, and Fungi: Plants We Eat by Isamu Sekido

Resources

- To order the 200 "paper food models" (item #0012N, includes a leader guide), go through your state or regional affiliate of the Dairy Council. Call the national office at 847-803-2000 to find the Dairy Council nearest you; www.nationaldairycouncil.org
- Your local school nutrition or food services program may be willing to help provide some supplies or assist with snack preparation or space.
- These books all provide many lessons and activities on plants: *How to Teach Nutrition to Kids* by Connie Liakos Evers, 24 Carrot Press, 2006; *Project Seasons* by Deb Parrella, Shelburne Farms, 1995; *Growing with Plants* by Linda Watts and Steven Garrett, WSU Cooperative Extension, 1995; and *GrowLab: Activities for Growing Minds,* National Gardening Association, 1990.
- See the Top Ten Vegetables and Fruits (in Appendix, page 224) for some nutrition facts that may apply to the fruits, stems, flowers, leaves, seeds, or roots.
- The Food Timeline at www.foodtimeline.org was created by the Morris County, New Jersey, librarians to help students, parents, and teachers locate food history and period recipes. It is not a single website, but a collection of related web pages.
- *Roots, Stems, Leaves* by The Banana Slug String Band can be found (along with other songs relating to science) on their audiotapes and CDs;. www.bananaslugstringband.com

Benchmarks

The Living Environment: 5A—Diversity of Life, pp. 102-04

Grades K -2

" Plants . . . have features that help them live in different environments."

Grades 3-5

" A great variety of kinds of living things can be sorted into groups in many ways using various features to decide which things belong to which group."

Grades 6-8

"Similarities among organisms are found in internal anatomical features, which can be used to infer the degree of relatedness among organisms. . . ."

Who Grows Our Food?

"Food should have a place, a face, and a taste," asserts farmer and activist Russell Libby. Putting taste aside for a moment, we can look at some of the countless people (faces) and farms (places) that provide us with nourishment: our local and distant neighbors who sustain the food system.

Food production today is a complicated process that is difficult for young children to understand. In a nutshell, the food system is powered by natural and human resources, and involves food production, transformation, distribution, access, and consumption. It helps to start with the basics—how food is grown, where it comes from, and where it goes—before touching on some of the relevant social and economic issues.

Spending just $10 a week on local food can have far-reaching effects. "If each household in a town of 2,000 households spends $10 a week for 20 weeks on local food, for instance, that would gross $400,000 for local growers—and some of that money would be passed on to local farm supply stores, hardware stores, and the other services that growers use, thus strengthening communities."[1]

This section offers opportunities for you and your students to look at long-term changes in the nature of farming; to observe seasonal changes through the eyes of the farmer; and to meet some local growers.

[1] Personal communication, Russell Libby, MOFGA—Maine Organic Farmers and Gardeners Association, Fall, 2001.

What Is Locally Grown?

Map the sources of the food you eat

Recommended Grades: 3–6
- **Language Arts**
- **Geography**
- **Social Studies**

Goals

Discover where the produce we eat comes from by surveying the readily available goods in our own homes and communities. Surveying where produce comes from helps children become more thoughtful consumers.

Key Points

- Most of our food travels a long way to reach us.
- Food from many places is available in supermarkets almost any time of the year. If we had to eat only what was grown locally and seasonally, what would our meals be like?
- We can make a difference in a local farmer's life by purchasing the food grown on his or her farm.

Background

Many of us are aware of global environmental issues such as climate warming or rainforest destruction, but generally know less about what affects our own local food supply. Choosing to support and eat food produced in one's area means food is fresher and

likely more nutritious, has fewer "travel miles" on it, has less handling and processing, and there's less time between harvest and consumption. Buying locally decreases transportation costs and keeps dollars in the local economy. It may help encourage local agricultural economies to produce food crops rather than non-edible crops that deplete soils or create a dependency on foreign trade.[1] As reported by Brian Halweil of the Worldwatch Institute, "One Iowa study found that the ingredients for a meal made from local sources traveled an average of 45 miles (74 kilometers) to reach their destination, compared with 1,550 miles (2,577 kilometers) if the same ingredients had been bought from the usual distant sources nationwide."[2]

Teacher Tips

If you have an urban classroom, the borders for "local" may be farther afield than for rural classrooms. But the farmers on the outskirts of your city are probably providing produce for local wholesalers who stock supermarkets or small stores, or for a farmers' market in the city. It will still be an adventure for your students to find out where the produce they eat comes from.

Availability of locally grown produce will vary depending on the growing season in your area. You could conduct the survey at different times of the year to make this point with your students.

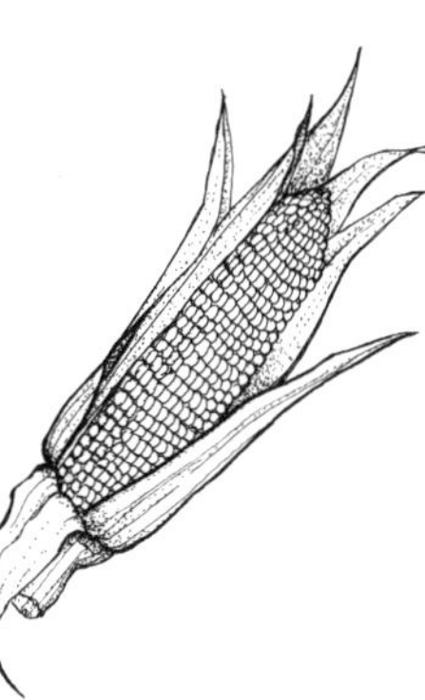

What You'll Need

Fruit or vegetables whose place of origin can be identified (some local, some out- of-state and some foreign—your local supermarket should be able to provide you with "country of origin" lists for its produce); maps or globes; U.S. agriculture map (see www.usda.gov).

[1] Personal communication with José Garcia, Community Food Systems and Sustainable Agriculture Program Coordinator, University of Missouri.

[2] Brian Halweil, *Home Grown: The Case for Local Food in a Global Market*. Worldwatch Institute, Paper 163, November 2002. ISBN *1-878071-66-1*.

How to Do It

Begin by asking, "What does local mean?" (The root of the word comes from Latin, meaning "place." Thinking about local food would mean place-based food, then.) Have the class define "local" or "regional." Ask students to think about what food is produced in their local area, region, or state—in particular think about any fresh produce—vegetables, fruits, etc. Pass around the samples you brought in and determine where these foods are from. Note that stores don't always display a food's source, but will provide it if asked. (Some produce boxes or stickers identify the place it was grown.) Use a map or globe to locate the food origins. Which would be considered local, according to their definitions; which would not?

Next, have students generate a collective list of the fruits and vegetables they commonly consume. Ask the class where these food items are grown. Do their homes contain any local produce? Does the nearest food store sell locally grown food? How might they find out?

Then, have students conduct a survey of their home kitchens to see if they can identify where the produce items come from. Are there any from local sources? (Older students can work in small teams to do this survey in a nearby grocery store as part of a field trip.)

Classroom Conversations

- Discuss the results of their home surveys. Are there local growers in your area? If so, who buys the food produced by those growers? (Local restaurants, health food stores, farmers' markets?) If not, if all of your food comes from outside the local area or region, what does this mean?
- What might be some reasons to eat locally grown food? (See Sidebar on page 29.)
- Are there any benefits to eating

food from far away? (Diversity of diet, supports growers in other communities—do the farmers in distant countries benefit from the food we buy here?)

Action

Check out your local market. If they sell produce, ask them to display place-of-origin information for consumers, if they don't already do this. Make up a regional food guide for your area, as Cornell has done for the Northeast. (See Resources.) Find out from your Cooperative Extension office if there are any CSA (community supported agriculture/subscription farms, see page 40) projects in your vicinity.

Want to Do More?

- Organize a "Local Foods" party in your classroom. Research what foods are grown or processed locally or regionally.
- Create regional/local maps representing foods grown in your region. See www.greenmap.com and click on the "Youth" icon.
- Invite a local farmer, rancher, or farmers' market grower into the classroom to speak to your students about their livelihood and where and how they sell their products.
- Find out if the cafeteria serves local food. Work with the school nutrition or food service employees and local farmers to plan a "Local Foods Day."
- Encourage students to compare labels of clothing as well as food labels. Fiber is an important agricultural commodity, and origins of clothing can be another way to determine "point of origin" information.

Lesson Links

Pyramids Near You
Farm to Table
Figuring Out Our Food System
Read the Small Print

Literature Links

Harvest Year by Cris Peterson
Leah's Pony by Elizabeth Friedrich
Supermarket by Kathleen Krull
The American Family Farm: A Photo Essay by George Ancona, text by Joan Anderson
Farmers' Market by Paul B. Johnson
Market! by Ted Lewin
Portrait of a Farm Family by Raymond Bial

Resources

- Most agricultural commodities, ranked by state, can be found at www.nass.usda.gov. From the site, find your state's department of agriculture for local growers, farmers' markets, growing season charts, agricultural fairs, etc. For local Community Supported Agriculture (CSA) farms, go to www.nal.usda.gov/afsic/csa or www.localharvest.org/csa or www.foodroutes.org
- Northeast Regional Food Guide Pyramid Poster and Fact Sheets—a color poster and educational handouts that promote regional, seasonal eating in one area. By Jennifer Wilkins and Jennifer Bokaer-Smith, Cornell Cooperative Extension, Cornell University Resource Center, 7 Business and Technical Park, Ithaca, NY 14850; www.nutrition.cornell.edu/foodguide/archive/index.html
- Your state Agriculture in the Classroom organization may have agricultural materials and contacts with local or regional farmers; www.agclassroom.org Click on "State Programs."
- See the dietary guidelines for sustainability in the Appendix for the context in which student's food choices can be examined.
- The Wisconsin Foodshed Research Project provides tools and resources for activists and eaters who are changing the way we grow, process, market, and eat food; www.cias.wisc.edu/foodshed/index/html
- Local Harvest connects consumers to local producers as well as small farms and products;. www.localharvest.org
- The Leopold Center for Sustainable Agriculture in Ames, Iowa, offers information and graphics that illustrate food issues, including the distance produce often must travel to reach the market. www.leopold.iastate.edu/pubs/other/files/food_chart.pdf
- *Coming Home to Eat: The Pleasures and Politics of Local Foods* by Gary Nabhan, Norton, 2001, makes a case for eating locally.

Supporting a Locally Grown Food System[1]

- Local agriculture can help make food affordable and accessible by providing a wide variety of fresh, high-quality produce and agricultural products sold at their peak of flavor and nutritional value.
- Buying locally grown food supports local jobs. Agriculture (along the coasts, that includes aquaculture) is a vital part of a state's economy. Thousands of people are employed by agriculture and farms and, in turn, economically support state and local businesses—keeping rural communities alive.
- Support for local agriculture keeps regional farms viable. By selling directly to consumers at the farm, farmers earn a greater share of the consumer dollar[2]—better sustaining farm operations in the face of rising property values and encroaching development. The high cost of trucking and the wholesaler or "middleman" is largely eliminated from the picture.
- Farm fields and pastures enhance a region's quality of life, providing scenic vistas, and open space and wildlife habitat. These attract tourism, recreation, and outdoor sports, which contribute significantly to the economy of any region.
- Food that is shipped long distances is often coated with wax or sprayed with agents to prevent spoiling or discoloration during storage and transport; buying locally avoids this treatment.
- Locally grown foods require less energy to transport, thus reducing their cost to consumers and their environmental impact. Additionally, farming helps reduce potentially damaging greenhouse gases because crops act as a "sink," consuming carbon dioxide and giving off oxygen.
- Taxation studies have shown repeatedly that agricultural land can provide more than residential land does in terms of revenue. Residential development often costs more in services than it yields in taxes. In fact, one study concluded that farms might be *subsidizing* sprawl because farms' excess contribution reduces the true cost of the services demanded by sprawl.
- As the number of local farms decrease, concerns grow about the ability of future generations to feed themselves in a healthy sustainable way. Stronger regional food systems create greater food security.

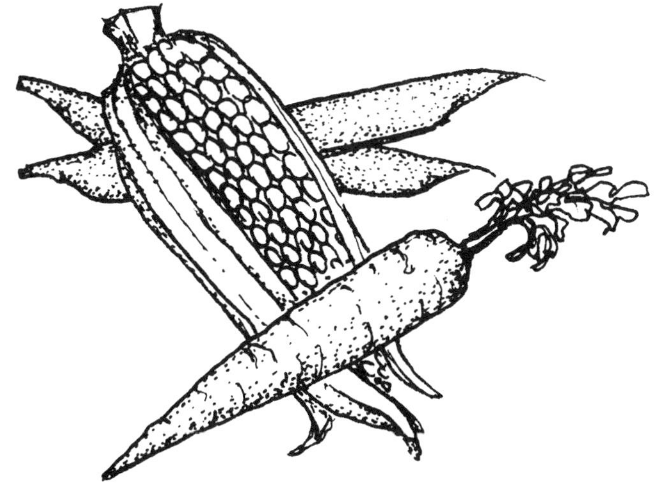

[1] Adapted with permission from *Massachusetts Agriculture in the Classroom Newsletter,* Spring 1999; www.aginclassroom.org. Information compiled from Kathy Ruhf of New England Small Farms Institute, Irene Winkler of the Pilgrim RC&D, Hilare Downey of the Heritage Farm Coast Trust, Barbara Ruhs of the Massachusetts Department of Education, and Joyce Benson of the Maine State Planning Office.

[2] According to the Community Alliance with Family Farms, "the farmer today gets less than 10 cents of the retail food dollar." From a "Five Reasons to Buy Local Food" flyer.

Benchmarks

Human Society: 7C—Global Interdependence, p. 176

Grades 3-5

"Many of the things people eat . . . come from other countries. . . . Decisions made in one country about what is produced there may have an effect on other countries."

The Designed World: 8A—Agriculture, p. 184

Grades 3-5

"Places too cold or dry to grow certain crops can obtain food from places with more suitable climates. Much of the food eaten by Americans comes from other parts of the country and other places in the world."

"Heating, salting, smoking, drying, cooling, and airtight packaging are ways to slow down the spoiling of food by microscopic organisms. These methods make it possible for food to be stored for long intervals before being used."

Grades 6-8

"In agriculture, as in all technologies, there are always trade-offs to be made. Getting food from many different places makes people less dependent on weather in any one place, yet more dependent on transportation and communication among far-flung markets. Specializing in one crop may risk disaster if changes in weather or increases in pest populations wipe out that crop. Also, the soil may be exhausted of some nutrients, which can be replenished by rotating the right crops."

"Many people work to bring food . . . to U.S. markets. With improved technology, only a small fraction of workers in the United States actually plant and harvest the products that people use. Most workers are engaged in processing, packaging, transporting, and selling what is produced."

The Designed World: 8C—Energy Sources and Use, p. 193

Grades 3-5

"People try to conserve energy in order to slow down the depletion of energy resources and/or to save money."

Old-Fashioned Food[1]

Conduct a mini oral history project

Recommended Grades: 3–6
- **History**
- **Language and Visual Arts**
- **Life Skills**

Goals

Gain a historic perspective on food, diet, and agriculture through interviews with community elders. Compile memories, facts, and stories from the past while conecting with people in your community.

Key Points

- "History is not simply what you read in a book or study in a classroom—every person and every community has a history worth preserving."[2]
- You can learn about the past by talking to older people in the community.
- The food we eat today is not necessarily the same as what people ate in the past.

Background

How food gets from farm to table has changed tremendously. For thousands of years, agriculture relied on farmers' knowledge and the power of human and animal labor. Farms operated on a small, family scale—the way they're depicted in "Old McDonald Had a Farm" and *Charlotte's Web.* In 1800, 97 percent of the U.S. population lived on farms. Strenuous physical activity was a part of everyday life. Farm products were usually sold directly to the consumer and people knew where their food came from.

[1] Adapted with permission from *The Three Sisters: Exploring an Iroquois Garden* by Marcia Eames-Sheavly, Cornell Cooperative Extension Publication 142LM15, p. 6.

[2] Ibid.

As farming has changed, so has the food we eat: the food in our refrigerators and cupboards is vastly different from the whole food harvested from the land. It is cooked and processed before it reaches our kitchen—a big difference from a few generations ago when most meals were cooked "from scratch." TV dinners, "instant" packaged microwaveable products, and fast food are all relatively recent developments.

Children are often fascinated by how things used to be different from what they take for granted as "the norm" today. Interviewing older people about their memories concerning food opens the door to many classroom conversations about food, history, culture, choices, and the future.

Getting Ready

An oral history is different from a regular interview. Oral historians, when successful, encourage elaboration and capture the voice and story-telling style of the person interviewed. To help students collect an oral history, train them to ask follow-up questions and elicit stories and memories beyond the list of questions on their list. This will require some practice or role playing before the interview, as well as some comfort using the tape recorder.[1]

What You'll Need

Tape recorder; microphone; and camera (optional).

How to Do It

Begin by asking how traditions, knowledge, and history were passed along in cultures before tape recorders, television, and especially before written language was used extensively—for instance, how did people know which foods were poisonous to eat (through spoken stories and oral legends)? How do we learn about the past, now? Explore the idea that all individuals have memories of the past and that many experiences and memories of regular people and places are not necessarily collected in our modern-day history books.

Explain that they will have a chance to collect some local history through interviews with older people in their community. They will collect "oral histories" with a focus on food and agriculture.

[1] Irene Jackson, author of *Hot Biscuits and Shanty Boys: The Maine Folklife Curriculum Guide,* 2001.

Have students brainstorm possible local residents they could interview—guide students to people who may have had experience with a part of the food system (agriculture, grocery store, food processing, trucking—or just cooking and eating). Young people may ask grandparents or other older relatives, a neighbor, a resident of an adult home, or a community historian or librarian. Record student choices.

Next, develop a list of questions related to food—avoid too many yes/no questions. (Use the list below to get started.) Think up some follow-up questions. Sample questions:

- What is one of your earliest memories of food?
- When you were a little child, what did you usually have for breakfast, lunch, dinner? How was it different from what we can have today?
- What were your favorite foods when you were little?
- What did you eat for snacks? Did you eat "junk food"?
- How did your parents shop for food? Did you ever help make the food?
- How did you store your food?
- Did you grow any food at home or raise any farm animals? Did you know anyone who did?
- Did you ever work on a farm? Did you have a garden? What did you grow?
- What are some of the biggest changes that you have seen in the food you eat and the way it's grown, processed, packaged, sold, or cooked?
- What kinds of cooking tools and appliances did you have? Were they the same ones that we have today? What was different?
- What foods do you miss from your childhood?
- How has your life changed as more machines and conveniences have come along? How has it not changed? What do and don't you like about it?

Then, set up some practice sessions or role-playing opportunities. Both the role playing and interviewing may be easier to do in pairs where one student is primarily the interviewer and the other is the recorder. Coach and encourage. When they are prepared, have students schedule an interview time with their community members.

Following the interview, have students transcribe the recorded interviews soon after their meeting, if possible. Send thank-you notes to the

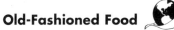

elders for having participated in the class project and offer to share your final "history" if s/he would like. Have students write up highlights of their interviews for the school paper or a display. Include photographs of senior community members and younger students, if possible.

Classroom Conversations

- Discuss what the interview process was like. How did they feel about spending time with a senior citizen? How willing was the person to share his or her experiences? What did you learn from your experience? What was fun about the experience? What were some of the observations that surprised you?
- Did you learn things from the interview that you have not read in a book?
- Choose some questions from the list to concentrate on and ask students what they found out.
- Looking at the broader picture, how has life and food changed? How have farming and gardening practices changed?
- What would they do differently if they did another oral history?

. . . and we didn't have all that fast food in my childhood!

Want to Do More?

- Awareness of one's history can help with shaping the future. Bind the students' "Oral Food Histories" into a book, and make copies for school, public libraries, and a local elders association or local historical society.
- Have students interpret and discuss their own meaning for the following Chinese proverb:

> *If we do not change the direction we are going, we are likely to end up where we are headed.*

Lesson Links

Once Upon a Farm
Visiting a Grower
Traditions at the Table

Literature Links

My Backyard History Book by David Weitzman
Early Stores and Markets by Bobbie Kalman
Sugaring Time by Kathryn Lasky
Once Upon a Farm by Bob Artley
Keep the Buttered Side Up: Food Superstitions from Around the World by Kathlyn Gay
Cooking the Mexican Way by Rosa C. Coronado (One of 40 *Easy Menu Ethnic Cookbooks)*
The Farms (Settling America Series) by Raymond Bial

Resources

- Local historical society for accurate historical details, photographs, or documents related to your community's past.
- Local library or elders' organization resources on local history or research on your locality's and community members' history.
- *Foxfire* books for interviews of elders and *Sometimes a Shining Moment: The Foxfire Experience* by Eliot Wigginton, Anchor Books, 1985, for commentary on his experiences conducting oral histories with students.
- *Hot Biscuits and Shanty Boys: The Maine Folklife Center Curriculum Guide* by Irene Jackson, 1998; www.umaine.edu/folklife/curriculum.htm Includes one section on preparing students for conducting oral histories in their communities.
- *Cooking Up U.S. History: Recipes and Research to Share with Children* by Suzanne I. Barchers and Patricia C. Marden, Teacher Ideas Press, 1991, and *Hasty Pudding, Johnny Cakes, and Other Good Stuff: Cooking in Colonial America* by Loretta F. Ichord, Millbrook Press, 1998, for some old-time food and a bit of tasty history.
- Community Alliance for Family Farmers provides many helpful resources for people interested in supporting family-size farms; www.caff.org
- Food Routes Network is a national nonprofit organization dedicated to rebuilding local, community-based food systems. Their goal is "reintroducing Americans to their food—the seeds it grows from,

the farmers who produce it, and the routes that carry it from the fields to their tables." www.foodroutes.org

- *Pickled, Potted, and Canned: How the Art of Food Preserving Changed the World* by Sue Shephard, Simon & Schuster, 2001. A history of food preservation.

Benchmarks

The Designed World: 8A—Agriculture, p. 184

Grades 3-5

"Heating, salting, smoking, drying, cooling, and air-tight packaging are ways to slow down the spoiling of food by microscopic organisms. These methods make it possible for food to be stored for long intervals before being used."

"Modern technology has increased the efficiency of agriculture so that fewer people are needed to work on farms than ever before."

Even though science is not listed as a discipline for this activity, the background section on how farming has changed could focus on the above concepts. Elements of the above *Benchmarks* could also be incorporated into the interview questions.

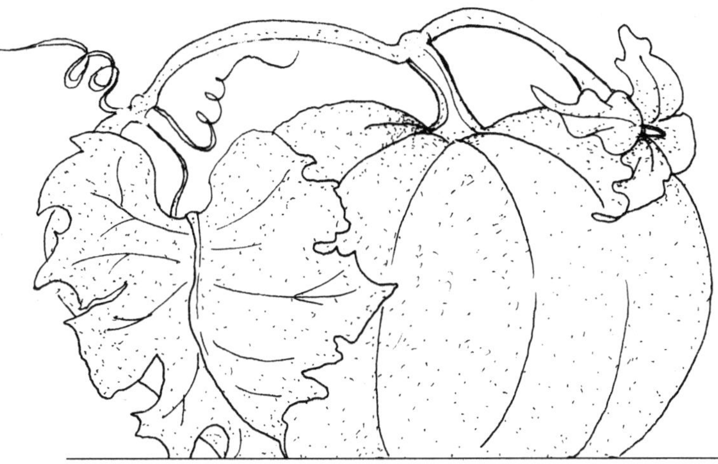

Once Upon a Farm

Take a storytelling break: visit the agricultural life gone by

Recommended Grades: 1–3
- **History**
- **Language**
- **Performing Arts**

Goals

Dramatize the story of old-fashioned farm life to learn how farming is affected by the cycles of nature and how the "face and place" of agriculture have been transformed.

Key Points

- Younger students can imagine life on a northern farm before modern times and inventions and understand how farming life has changed.
- The seasons play an important role in farming life.

Background

So few children today have direct contact with a farm or farmer that it's helpful to read about the history of our nation through the lens of a farm family. Literature on agricultural history is one place to start.

What You'll Need

The story below. You could also bring in books describing mid-nineteenth-century farm life, such as those by Laura Ingalls Wilder.

How to Do It

Begin by finding out what your students know about farming: ask them what farmers grow, when they plant, when they harvest, and how they sell goods. Ask them to describe a farmer's life: what time they rise in the morning, what they do during the day, and when they finish work, what they do in different seasons, and what farmers need to know about nature. Write their answers down for later reference.

Next, ask them the same questions about farms before gasoline-powered tractors and electricity. What do they perceive as the differences? Ask them what—at their age—they would do for work on the farm if they lived in those earlier times. Write these responses down as well.

Finally, ask the children to imagine themselves within this story. Suggest that they note what jobs boys and girls had and how life may be different today. "We'll take a time machine back a hundred and fifty years or more, to around the time when your great-great-grandparents were born. Imagine you are either Emma or John."

Farm Story from the Past

The days are getting shorter as the winter solstice draws close, the longest night of the whole year. And during this long night, twin brother and sister John and Emma lie snuggled in their beds under wool blankets and homemade quilts—sound asleep and dreaming. In her dream, Emma prances around a colorful maypole with her friends and some frisky new spring lambs. John has a dream about the last day of school on a warm day in spring when he goes to play in the nearly empty hayloft with his friends after class.

Emma and John wake up early the next morning and roll out of bed. Their dreams of spring vanish as their bare feet hit the cold wooden floor.

It's still dark out, and there's frost on the windows. Quickly they put on hand-knitted wool socks Grandma made for them. John slips on a thick sweater and warm pants, and Emma wears her hand-me-down winter dress. After rinsing the sleep from their eyes using cold water from the water bucket, they race each other to the warmth of the kitchen. Their parents have already started a warm fire in the cookstove with the wood that John carried in yesterday. Even though their stomachs growl, they start their morning chores before breakfast.

John must check on the animals: feed and water the pigs, sheep, and chickens, clean out the stalls, and help milk the cows—chores he does twice every day. Emma gathers the eggs, fetches butter from the icehouse, helps with breakfast, and sets the table. When chores are done, the whole family sits down to a filling breakfast next to the warm cookstove—eggs, potatoes, ham, and some apple cider. Emma remembers picking the apples in the fall with John and their mother. The best part was when the whole family helped press the apples into sweet cider with the big cider press.

John and Emma walk to school, past the pond where their father cuts ice every winter for the icehouse. Their school is a one-room building where they learn alongside students in grades 1–8. School started late this year because the haying season went later than usual and most of the older students were needed to help out at home. All the children at the school live on farms. John thinks back to haying time, the dust and smells of the grass, and remembers the warmer weather and the flavor of switchel, his favorite drink on those hot work days. Emma daydreams about the smells in the kitchen at summer's end—boiling fruit for jam, drying apples, and bunches of herbs hung up to dry.

After school, John likes to split "biscuit wood"—that's what his mother calls firewood for the big kitchen cookstove. He helped stack this wood last year and will help his father chop down trees for next winter's wood. When John stops in the kitchen after school before starting his barn chores, Emma is kneading bread and getting ready to help her mother make a pie. John can't wait—will it be raspberry, apple, or blueberry?—this time, Emma gets to choose.

Emma loves to be sent down to the cool root cellar where they keep potatoes and squash in bins, carrots in sand, and the summers' fruit and vegetables in glass canning jars! She's always tempted to bring up jars of canned peaches and plums for dessert! You can tell what season it is by what's left in the root cellar. By the time spring rolls around, only the smallest potatoes are left, the squash is long gone, and they are enjoying the last of the jams and jellies.

The sun sets long before supper. A few more chores to be done, even in the dark. Goodnight to the cows, sheep, pigs, and chickens. By the time John and Pa have finished the chores in the barn, and Emma's pie is ready, you need a lantern to see. And, everyone is REALLY hungry!

Next, the time machine brings you back to the present day.

Vocabulary

Biscuit wood: Dry pieces often cut from last year's woody plants, such as alder. It burns quickly and hot, and is perfect for browning biscuits or other baked goods in a wooden cookstove.

Cider press: Machine used to crush and release juice from fresh apples.

Hayloft: The upper part of the barn, where the hay is stored.

Haying: To cut and store (and in more modern times, bale) dried grass to be used later for animal feed.

Icehouse: A building where large blocks of ice are stored, usually packed in sawdust to keep them from melting.

Kneading: To mix dough by folding, pressing, and squeezing it with the hands.

Maypole: Tall decorated pole that is put up for traditional May Day celebrations.

Root cellar: Basement or underground storage space for root vegetables and long-keeping crops.

Classroom Conversations

- Ask the students if the story was what they imagined farm life to be like back then. What were some of the things you knew already? Were there any surprises? Why?
- How did Emma and John's lives differ from your own? How was physical activity different then than now?

Seasonal Farm Wheel: Emma and John's Chores[1]

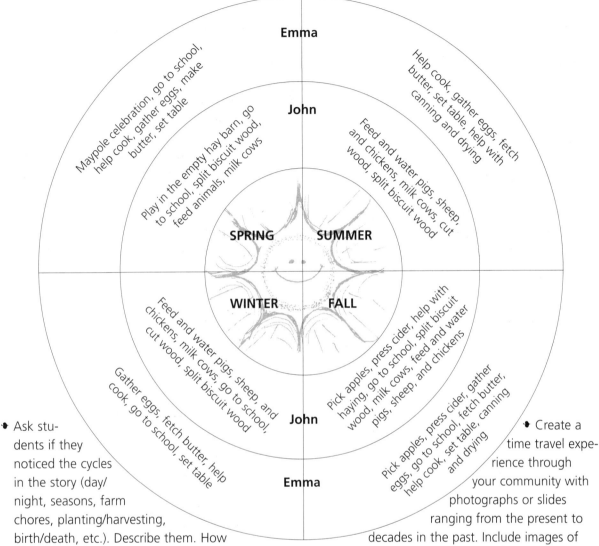

- Ask students if they noticed the cycles in the story (day/night, seasons, farm chores, planting/harvesting, birth/death, etc.). Describe them. How is farm life affected by these cycles? What cycles are in your lives? Are they different?
- Have students compare the food system (for example, food from field to table) from 150 years ago to now. What are some of the major changes/differences?

Want to Do More?

- Create a seasonal farm wheel based on the story.
- Invite a former or current farmer to class to answer questions from the class.
- Visit your state agricultural or history museum. See Resources below.
- Interview relatives and neighbors to discover their role in agriculture in the past. If they farmed, find out what their daily or yearly schedule entailed.
- Create a time travel experience through your community with photographs or slides ranging from the present to decades in the past. Include images of familiar landmarks. Show the photographs or slides in reverse chronological order. In most communities, you will see the buildings disappear and farms and open land appear. Discuss the change in their community from urban (present) to small town and rural communities. Discuss the role agriculture played in their community in the past and present.[2]
- Have a classroom snack based on food from "the olden days": biscuits with jam or jelly, dried fruit, and switchel to drink, etc.

[1] Adapted with permission from "Seasonal Round of Activities," Tobias Walker Farm, Kennebunk, Maine. Freeport Historical Society, www.freeporthistoricalsociety.org.

[2] From Lois Berg Stack, University of Maine Cooperative Extension.

Lesson Links

Visiting a Grower
What Is Locally Grown?
Figuring Out the Food System
How to Keep a Good Thing Going
The Global Staff of Life
Old-Fashioned Food

Literature Links

Farmer Boy by Laura Ingalls Wilder (and other books in the *Little House* series)
Portrait of a Farm Family by Raymond Bial
Farming by Jane Featherstone
Farmers' Market by Paul Brett Johnson
Century Farm: One Hundred Years on a Family Farm by Cris Peterson
If You Were a Farmer by Virginia Schomp
Tortilla Factory by Gary Paulsen
Corn is Maize: The Gift of the Indians by Aliki
A Farmer's Alphabet by Mary Azarian
The Story of George Washington Carver by Eva Moore
Clouds of Terror by Catherine A. Welch
A Farm through Time: The History of a Farm from Medieval Times to the Present Day by Angela Wilkes
The Farm Book by Rien Poortlvliet

Resources

- *Earth Child:2000: Earth Science for Young Children* by Kathryn Sheehan and Mary Waidner, Council Oak Books, 1998. Contains stories, games, crafts and book ideas for children and families.
- *Native American Gardening: Stories, Projects, and Recipes for Families* by Michael Caduto and Joseph Bruchac, Fulcrum, 1996. Includes Native gardening ideas and stories, crafts, and foods.
- Local historical societies, a state museum, or agricultural museums for the agricultural history of your area. To locate agricultural museums in your area try searching www.musee-online.org or www.museumstuff.com
- *Cooking up U.S. History: Recipes and Research to Share with Children* by Suzanne I. Barchers and Patricia C. Marden, Teacher Ideas Press, 1991.
- The Food Timeline is a collection of related web sites for parents and teachers on food history and traditions across cultures. This site links to multiple lesson plans. www.foodtimeline.org
- Harvest of History is an interactive web site featuring video clips of farming (past and present) a database of museum objects and documents, and a fourth-grade curriculum. www.harvestof history.org.

Benchmarks

The Designed World: 8A—Agriculture, p. 184

Grades K-2

"Machines improve what people get from crops by helping in planting and harvesting, in keeping food fresh by packaging and cooling. . . ."

Grades 3-5

"Irrigation and fertilizers can help crops grow in places where there is too little water or the soil is poor." The explanation for the *Benchmarks* for grades 3-5 states, "To appreciate the rigors of agriculture, students should learn about life in earlier times and the great effort that went into planting, nurturing, harvesting, and using crops. . . ."

Switchel Recipe

1 gallon water
1 1/2 cups brown sugar (24 tablespoons)
1/2 cup apple cider vinegar (8 tablespoons)
1 teaspoon dried ginger or 1 tablespoon fresh ginger juice (or more to taste)

Add brown sugar, apple cider vinegar, and ginger to the water. Stir until mixed. Add ice (chipped off an ice block for historic accuracy) and serve. Don't let the ingredients fool you. This drink is actually very refreshing on a hot day and kids loved it on planting day!

Did you ever wonder what people drank in the days before soda pop? They made their own Switchel—a strange but tangy mix of water, apple cider vinegar, molasses or brown sugar, and ginger! On those hot summer days it whets—WETS?—your whistle better than any modern-day bottled drink!

Visiting a Grower

Organize a field trip to an "outdoor classroom"

Recommended Grades: K–5
- **Language Arts**
- **Physical Education**

Goal

Field trips provide us with opportunities to synthesize what we've learned about farming, food, and food production.

Key Points

- Visiting a grower can be done in any setting: urban, rural, or suburban.
- Farmers' daily chores depend on seasonal cycles.
- Farmers and gardeners live by nature's rhythms and their lives are tied closely to the earth and its weather.

Background

Agriculture is an ever-evolving art and science. New tools, machinery, and techniques have helped farmers for generations improve their crops and ease their workload. However, not all changes in agriculture have been advantageous. Statistics from the USDA Census may lead one to believe that family farms are alive and well in the United States, but examining the numbers reveals a trend that has been and will continue to reduce the number of families making their living off their own land.

Although family farmers are the large majority of farmers in the United States, they are struggling to make a decent living on the farm. In 2003 family farmers barely covered costs from their farming operations. Even with off-farm jobs, their net income was 86% of the U.S. average. They live with the constant threat of losing their farm. In contrast, very large commercial farms, just 10% of all full-time farms, averaged a net cash farm income of $172,147.00—371% of the U.S. average.[1] With modern day advances, farming has become less of a shared livelihood and more of a large, efficient business—far removed from the lives of the majority of people.

If you are visiting a farm with your students, you may want to discuss and/or research the different kinds of farms that exist—family farm, partnership, corporate, organic, subsistence, diversified, sustainable, industrial—and compare them to the farm described in the lesson "Once Upon a Farm."

Getting Ready

Research field trip possibilities: a local farm that gives tours; a farming or botanical museum that offers school programs; an area greenhouse or nursery; a farmers' or green market; or an urban or rural community garden where growers would be willing to host a tour (contact your local Cooperative Extension for assistance). Many cities have active community garden programs: www.communitygarden.org

"At Thanksgiving time, why are students cutting out paper turkeys in their classrooms? They should be out seeing real turkeys." *On the necessity of visiting a farm, Joseph Kiefer of Vermont Food Works*[2]

[1] Global Development and Environment Institute Working Paper No. 05-02: "Understanding the Farm Problem; Six Common Errors in Presenting Farm Statistics," by Timothy A. Wise. tim.wise@tufts.edu.
[2] Joshua Brown in "Planning Your Farm Visit," *School to Farm Directory Supplement* (NOFA-VT), 1999.

Teacher Tip

Try to arrange a time during your area's growing season to visit a farm or garden; this can be tricky in some parts of the country! You might instead choose a dairy or other year-round operation. If a farm visit is not feasible, try asking a farmer or grower to come to the school. If possible, arrange some hands-on activity during the trip such as grinding grains, gathering vegetables, or making cider. Example: Have students try identifying root crops—leeks, onions, turnips, winter squash, beets, etc. (Optional: Create a scavenger hunt check-off sheet for students to use during the field trip, based on their interests and your knowledge of the site.)

How to Do It

Begin by reviewing the field trip tips in the sidebar, "Field Trip Planning," noting the items that you'll want to consider for your trip. Start to guide students in formulating questions for the grower. Ask them to list things they want to learn on the trip. Has anyone ever visited a farm/garden/greenhouse? Why are farms located outside cities? Why are these growing places important? What does a farmer/gardener do? What are some challenges that growers face, especially weather-related? What might one expect to see on a farm/garden/greenhouse this time of year? What changes has the farmer or grower seen in farming since he or she started? Does the grower use organic methods or pesticides or something in between—why? (For older students.) Do they hire help—local labor, migrant workers, or apprentices? How long is an average growing season workday for them?

On the day of the field trip, review the schedule and safety rules.

Next, enjoy field trip! During a tour break, provide students with paper and art materials to create drawings of what they see. Discuss as a group.

Finally, send thank-you letters or illustrations to the farmer/greenhouse/garden tour guide expressing what students learned during their visit.

Classrooom Conversations

- Following the visit, ask the students what they remember most from the experience.
- They saw a snapshot of farm/garden/greenhouse life—what must it be like during other times or seasons? Describe how weather or seasons changes a farmer's jobs.
- How was the field trip site different from what they expected?
- Have them list foods grown at the site and discuss how those compare to what is found in local supermarkets.

What's a CSA?

A CSA (Community Supported Agriculture) is a partnership between farmers and their communities. Before crops are even put in the ground, local community members purchase "shares" from the farm (the cost and agreements vary from one CSA to another). Some farms even "sell" shares for labor during the growing season. In either case, an agreement is made in good faith that shareholders will receive a portion of the farm's crops—usually over the course of several months. If the farmer has a bad year, the shares purchase less—in a banner year, shareholders get more food than they can eat! And the farmer is paid for the food at the beginning of the growing season when cash is needed. In this way, "CSA members are supporting a regional food system, securing the agricultural integrity of their area, and participating in a community-building act that even helps bridge socio-economic gaps. . . . Knowing you like good, fresh food has nothing to do with money, status, or where you live. Members range from people who use food stamps to those who pay extra to have their vegetables delivered. Together they guarantee that local farmers survive." —Robyn Van En, quoted in *Coming Home to Eat: The Pleasures and Politics of Local Foods* by Gary Nabhan, Norton, 2002; ISBN 0-393-32374-9, p. 127.

Want to Do More?

- Stress personal hygiene and the need to wash all fruits and vegetables before eating them. (See "Germs and the Cinnamon Trick" in "Making Food with Children" in the Appendix.) Create a snack or meal from food picked or purchased on the field trip—make soup!
- Have students write and illustrate a story about their visit to the farm or garden or how they imagine the farm as described by a grower visiting

the classroom. Create a four-season mural of the farm as they imagine it.

- Involve your students in the study of their seasonal changes (phenology). As they become weather-aware, they may begin to understand climate and weather's effect on more than their own lives from day to day. Invite them to make more of a connection between the availability of food and the climate and weather events occurring around the world. Like most phenologists, start in your own backyard. (A search for "phenology" will turn up many interesting web sites.)
- Choose one topic, such as the seasonal availability of food, and create a calendar of foods in season in your state/region.

Lesson Links

Figuring Out Our Food System
What Is Locally Grown?
Once Upon a Farm
Old-Fashioned Food
Pyramids Near You
Figuring Out Our Food System

Literature Links

I'll Meet You at the Cucumbers by Lillian Moore and Sharon Wooding
Seasons of Arnold's Apple Tree by Gail Gibbons
First Day in Grapes by L. King Perez
Market! by Ted Lewin
Harvest Year by Cris Peterson
If You Were a Farmer by Virginia Schomp
City Green by DyAnne Disalvo-Ryan
Seedfolks by Paul Fleischman
Tractor by Craig Brown
Portrait of a Farm Family by Raymond Bial

Resources

- If you don't have a farmer in mind, try contacting farmers participating in regional farmers' markets at www.ams.usda.gov/farmersmarkets/
- Check with the American Community Gardening Association for community gardens in your area. They are also a source of information on gardening; www.communitygarden.org
- City Farmer's "Children and Urban Agriculture" web pages include brief descriptions of projects and links to these sites; www.cityfarmer.org
- The web site for the Leopold Center for Sustainable Agriculture offers information and graphics that illustrate food issues, including "How Far Has Your Produce Traveled?"; www.leopold.iastate.edu/pubs/staff/ppp/index.html
- Sustainable agriculture and "no till" farming are practiced at Cedar Meadow Farm in Pennsylvania. This farm was one of five in the world that were featured on a PBS documentary about sustainable agriculture; www.cedarmeadowfarm.com

Benchmarks

The Designed World: 8A—Agriculture, p. 184
Grades K-2
"Most food comes from farms either directly as crops or as the animals that eat the crops. . . ."
"Machines improve what people get from crops by helping in planting and harvesting, in keeping food fresh by packaging and cooling. . . ."
Grades 3-5
"Modern technology has increased the efficiency of agriculture so that fewer people are needed to work on farms than ever before."

The explanatory text for the Grades 3-5 *Benchmarks* states, "Where possible, students should visit markets, farms, grain elevators, and processing plants, and as many other parts of the 'technological food chain' as possible."

Habits of Mind: 12D—Manipulations and Observations, p. 293
Grades 3-5
"Keep a notebook that describes observations made, carefully distinguishes actual observations from ideas and speculations about what was observed. . . ."

FIELD TRIP PLANNING[1]

Goals and Objectives

- Be sure you and your students know the purpose of the trip.
- Develop pre- and post-trip activities to enhance these goals.

Choosing a Farm/Garden/Greenhouse/Nursery

- Ask colleagues for recommendations of sites visited in the past.
- Check with your state's Farm Bureau for suggestions.
- Your state Cooperative Extension or Agriculture in the Classroom organization may know possible sites.
- Find a farm that matches your field trip needs (goals, subject area, time, etc.).
- In urban areas, look for farmers' markets or community gardens to visit.

Planning

- Explain the reason for the trip to the farmer/grower—what your class is studying.
- Prepare the farmer for the age and background knowledge of your group.
- Share ideas for organizing and focusing students as well as ways to actively involve them. Discuss possible learning stations or stops to make with groups. (Can some stops be facilitated by a volunteer?)
- Determine the basics: washroom facilities for emergencies? Area for a picnic? A place to get out of the rain? Or alternatives: a picnic area or local school your group could use before or after the trip.
- Acquaint yourself with the route to travel and any noteworthy sights along the way.
- Determine where the bus can park and turn around.
- Negotiate any special requests or conditions you or the farmer may have.
- Establish safety rules with the farmer.
- Insurance: Be sure the school board covers field trips and suggest the farmer notify his/her insurance. (If an additional premium is required of the farmer, the school should offer to cover costs.)
- Arrange for adult volunteers and communicate in advance the role they will play on the farm.
- Ask students and volunteers to wear appropriate clothing and foot gear.

Pre-Trip Activities

- Have students brainstorm what they think they will see, hear, and smell on the farm.
- Ask them to develop a list of acceptable behaviors on the trip.
- Share what you know about the site and have them research similar operations—collect magazine and newspaper articles related to the visit site.
- Develop a list of questions to answer before the trip and ask at the site. (You might want to send the list of questions to the site owner before your field trip.)
- Practice interview skills before the visit. Practice use of tape recorder, camera, and/or camcorder if they will be used by students as part of the experience.
- Create a scavenger hunt for the visit. Have students be on the lookout for items such as: pest damage (insect, animal, etc.), soil creatures, signs of non-farm visitors (people, animals), plants that animals eat, something green and smooth, evidence of water or lack of water, etc.

Getting There

- Enhance your trip with activities along the way.
- Have students predict things they might see as they travel. Develop a bingo game from this list to check off during the trip.
- Create a crossword puzzle dependent upon observations made during the ride to the farm.
- Sing related songs.
- Have groups or individuals tally observations along the way: types of farms, silos, animals, tractors, mailboxes, etc.

1 Adapted with permission from Minnesota Agriculture in the Classroom, St. Paul, MN; 651-201-6688; www.mda.state.mn.us/maitc

At the Site

Safety Considerations and Guidelines of Conduct

- The visit site is a business (and maybe a home) for the owner. The property should be respected as such.
- Know what areas are out-of-bounds and respect these boundaries.
- Communicate rules about touching, handling, or moving around animals. Being too noisy or moving suddenly can frighten farm animals.
- Be aware of dangers: slippery surfaces, tools, machinery, chemicals, electric fences, hoses, etc.
- Keep off fences, gates, machines, etc.
- Groups should stay together at all times.
- Students should not pick or eat anything unless invited to do so.

Have a Plan

- Small groups (determined beforehand) should be formed following a general farm introduction. (Each group should be with a responsible adult prepared to monitor student behavior.)
- If possible, rotate groups of students through "learning stations" as small groups can get closer, ask more questions, and be less daunting to an adult facilitator.
- At the end of the visit, wash hands thoroughly—especially before eating.

After the Visit

- Create a display, bulletin board, or model based on the visit.
- Write an article for the school or community newspaper.
- Compare the brainstorm list of what they thought they would see, hear, smell, and what they actually did.
- Follow up the trip with visits to related sites: supermarket, farmers' market, restaurant, stockyard, food processing plant, etc.
- Invite people with other links in the food system cycle to the class: farm equipment dealer, seed salesperson, butcher, farmer, trucker, composter, etc.
- Send a written thank-you to the field trip site owner and include some of the students' work and impressions. They appreciate knowing their effort was worthwhile for your students.

Figuring Out Our Food System[1]

Create a food system collage

Recommended Grades: 3–6
- **Visual and Language Arts**

"A sustainable agriculture does not deplete soils or people."
—*Wendell Berry*

Goal

Learn what's involved in food production and delivery to understand the connection between healthy soils and healthful foods.

Key Points

- Our food system is powered by the sun and works because of natural cycles and countless human workers, including farmers and farm workers, food processors, shippers, grocers, consumers, and waste handlers.
- The HEALTHY FOODS FROM HEALTHY SOILS [nutrient] cycle is an example of a very basic food system—a sustainable system where nutrients are returned to the soil.
- Ecology is the study of relationships within a natural community or system—what happens to one member will have some impact on another.
- We can look at our food system ecologically speaking—what happens to one part of the system will have an impact on another part.
- Our food choices really can make a difference—what we buy and eat is like a "vote" for the product, the farmers, companies, or systems that produced it.

Background

In the late 1800s, a farmer WAS the agricultural or food system—or at least was the largest part—doing nearly everything on the farm.[2] Saved seeds were planted for cash crops, food, and animal feed; crops were harvested and stored at or near the farm; and the farmer sold products from the farm—milk, vegetables, hay, etc. The "middle man" played a very small role. Now the farmer makes up the smallest portion of the agricultural system.

Picture the agricultural system in three parts: (1) "Inputs"—the people and businesses who manufacture and sell goods and services to farmers (farming machinery, animals, pesticides, fertilizers, seeds, loans, etc.); (2) the farmers who grow the food; and (3) the "marketing" people and businesses who

[1] Adapted with permission from *Project Seasons* by Deb Parrella, 1995.

[2] "Sustainable Agriculture and Public Policy" by Stewart Smith, *Maine Policy Review,* April 1993.

process, transport, store, advertise, and deliver food from the farm to the consumer.[1] Each sector costs money and makes profits. There are benefits and costs to these changes.

Following World War II, agriculture became increasingly industrialized (more an agri-business than agri-culture). Economics forced small farms to sell out. The large farms that resulted from the consolidation of these small farms now use more and bigger equipment, greater amounts of gasoline, chemical fertilizers, and pesticides, increased livestock management, and new high-yield hybrid or patented seed varieties. Fewer farmers can produce more food using less land. From an economical perspective, agri-business is a success—but this success comes at a price: diminished farm communities, contaminated wells from pesticides and fertilizers, depleted soils, and the loss of autonomy for the farmer. At 9 percent or less of the agri-business or industrial-agriculture system, farmers have the least power and are dependent upon the input and marketing sectors for their livelihood. As consumers, we support the current agricultural system and reap the benefits of abundant, inexpensive food. We also bear the costs—but not at the grocery store, since these social and environmental costs are not reflected in the prices we pay at the checkout counter. Our food system and its alternatives contain thought-provoking fodder for teachers and students to chew on. Don't try to digest it all at once!

What You'll Need

Magazines and newspapers with pictures of food system components: trucks, farms, people, stores, etc.; glue, markers, large sheets of paper cut into pieces manageable for groups of three or four; food item (choose an item that you know most of your students will recognize, such as popcorn, breakfast cereal, or bread).

How to Do It

Begin by asking your students how food gets to their school cafeteria or dinner table and write their answers on the board.

Next, hold up a food item and ask the class to brainstorm all the steps it took to get this specific food item to them. Record their answers and make some connections with arrows. Solicit details not mentioned (specific natural resources used, labor, animals, machines, gasoline, factories, pollution, paper, packaging, waste products).

Then, divide the students into small working groups, hand out materials, and ask each group to choose one product as a "starting point" to create its own food system collage.

Give them a reasonable time limit. Walk around the room helping the groups make decisions, draw connecting arrows, and identifying additional steps in their food systems. Suggest labeling or drawing where needed.

Finally ask each group to present its collage to its classmates, explaining the steps, the needed ingredients, natural resources, etc., (called inputs), and the wastes produced (called outputs).

Classroom Conversations

- Ask the students for their reactions to the activity. Did they realize so much went into food's production? Who might they know who does any of the jobs they placed on their charts? What were the common inputs, outputs? Were any of the collages very simple or very complicated? Why?
- Discuss the collages from an ecological/relationships point of view. Bring up the concept of interdependence and what might happen to their system when one or more of its parts are changed or removed. (Examples: the price of gas just went up, the last farm in their area sold for housing, or the local grocery store closed.) Who decides on what happens along the food system continuum? What are the consequences of those decisions?

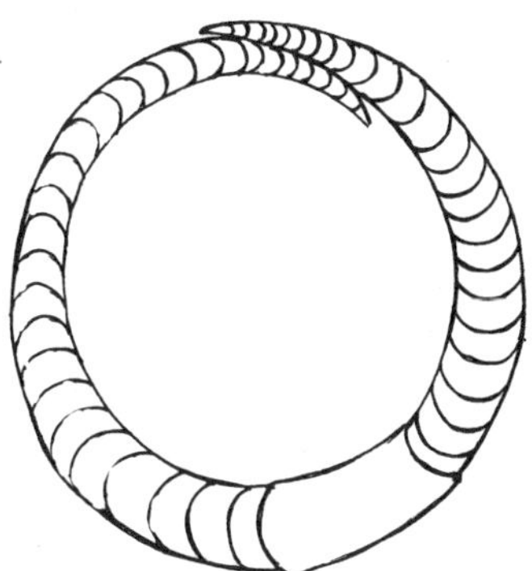

Everything is connected to everything else, and do you know what? There is no such thing as a free lunch!

[1] The three sectors in 1910 were Inputs 15%, Farming 41%, and Marketing 44%. In 1990 they were Inputs 24%, Farming 9%, and Marketing 67%.

- Write Barry Commoner's "Laws of Ecology" on the board (see Appendix): Everything is connected to everything else; Everything must go somewhere; Nature knows best; There is no such thing as a free lunch. Ask: How does eating something connect you to some of these laws? (Buying the food may/may not support the workers or farmers, the use of certain resources, the production of the pollution, etc.)
- Notice that the system literally starts in the soil and usually stops with people, the consumers. Is anything wrong with this picture? Who puts the nutrients back into the soils that grew the food we eat? How can this be done? Nature works in cycles.

Want to Do More?

- Look at ways to reduce the waste outputs (recycling, purchasing less packaging, buying locally).
- Research and discuss sustainable agriculture, "a kind of farming that encourages the farmer to earn a decent living growing good food on healthy land"[1]—and, as often stated, is economically viable, environmentally sound, and socially acceptable.

Action

Have students discuss how they and their school/class/families are contributing to a particular problem, and how they could change their behavior to have a more positive impact on our planet. Then, students choose an immediate problem such as litter in their neighborhood and brainstorm what changes they might make. (See Ten Steps to Action on page 214 in the Appendix for suggestions on tackling a task together.)

Lesson Links

What Is Locally Grown?
French Fries and Couch Potatoes
Dollars and $ense
Farm to Table
It All Adds Up
Recycled Art

1 "A Farming Revolution: Sustainable Agriculture" by Verlyn Klinkenborg. *National Geographic,* December 1995, page 68.

Bubble Mapping

Bubble-mapping is one way to think about consequences: What would happen if . . . I only ate a certain set of foods? If I took action— or didn't? If I chose to live my life in a particular way?

By connecting the dots, you can link one action with its implications or results, both positive and negative. This can be a helpful tool in brainstorming or planning goals, allowing you to envision some of the outcomes of your choices.

How to Do It

Begin with a blank sheet of paper. Think of a food-related topic (such as having a farmers' market, buying microwaveable lunches every day, or composting with worms). It can be a problem, an issue, or a question.

Next, write it in the center of the page, and draw a circle around it.

Then, think: What is related or connected to this? What leads to this or from it? What else does it have to do with? Write your answers in bubbles surrounding the original one, and connect them with lines. Add as many as you can which you think relate to the original topic. The circles may even connect to each other, not just to the center one, and a web of connections may become apparent.

Finally, Make more connections and then consider if any of your actions might have an impact that you could influence. Use the bubble map to reflect on better choices that you might make.

For younger students, doing just the bubbles as a brainstorming exercise (examining the connections between creatures in a worm bin, for example) will be fun.

Literature Links

How to Make an Apple Pie and See the World by Marjorie Priceman
Food Watch—Protecting Our Planet by Martyn Bramwell and Catriona Lennox
In the Supermarket (Machines at Work) by Henry Pluckrose
Market! by Ted Lewin
What is a Farmer's Market? by Deborah Patraker
Early Stores and Markets by Bobbie Kalman
Supermarket by Kathleen Krull
Amelia's Road by Linda Jacobs Altman
La Mariposa by Francisco Jimenez

Resources

For background on the concept of the food system, further activities, and related resources:

- *The Food System: Building Youth Awareness through Involvement* by Alison Harmon, Rance Harmon, and Audrey Maretzki, Penn State College of Agricultural Sciences, 1999. Guidebook introduces the concept of the food system, emphasizes interactive learning, skill building, and using the community as a classroom. For parents and educators of youth in grades 4-12.
- Food Routes Network is a national nonprofit organization dedicated to rebuilding local, community-based food systems. Their goal is "reintroducing Americans to their food—the seeds it grows from, the farmers who produce it, and the routes that carry it from the fields to their tables." www.foodroutes.org
- Local Food Solutions is a well-designed site by the Wisconsin Foodshed Project that provides tools and resources for eaters and educators who want to change the way we grow, process, market, and eat food; www.cias.wisc.edu/foodshed/index.html Click on "Articles."

Benchmarks

Human Society: 7C—Global Interdependence, p. 176

Grades 3-5

"Many of the things people eat . . . come from other countries. . . . Decisions made in one country about what is produced there may have an effect on other countries."

Grades 6 -8

"Trade between nations occurs when natural resources are unevenly distributed and the costs of production are very different in different countries. A nation has a trade opportunity whenever it can create more of a product or service at lower cost than another."

"The global environment is affected by national policies and practices relating to energy use, waste disposal, ecological management, manufacturing, and population."

The Designed World: 8A—Agriculture, p. 184

Grades 3-5

"Places too cold or dry to grow certain cops can obtain food from places with more suitable climates. Much of the food eaten by Americans comes from other parts of the country and other places in the world."

"Heating, salting, smoking, drying, cooling, and airtight packaging are ways to slow down the spoiling of food by microscopic organisms. These methods make it possible for food to be stored for long intervals before being used."

Grades 6-8

"In agriculture, as in all technologies, there are always trade-offs to be made. Getting food from many different places makes people less dependent on weather in any one place, yet more dependent on transportation and communication among far-flung markets. Specializing in one crop may risk disaster if changes in weather or increases in pest populations wipe out that crop. Also, the soil may be exhausted of some nutrients, which can be replenished by rotating the right crops."

"Many people work to bring food . . . to U.S. markets. With improved technology, only a small fraction of workers in the United States actually plant and harvest the products that people use. Most workers are engaged in processing, packaging, transporting, and selling what is produced."

The Designed World: 8C—Energy Sources and Use, p. 193

Grades 3-5

"People try to conserve energy in order to slow down the depletion of energy resources and/or to save money."

The ART in AgRiculTure

Harvest a crop of poems

Recommended Grades: K–6

- **Language Arts**

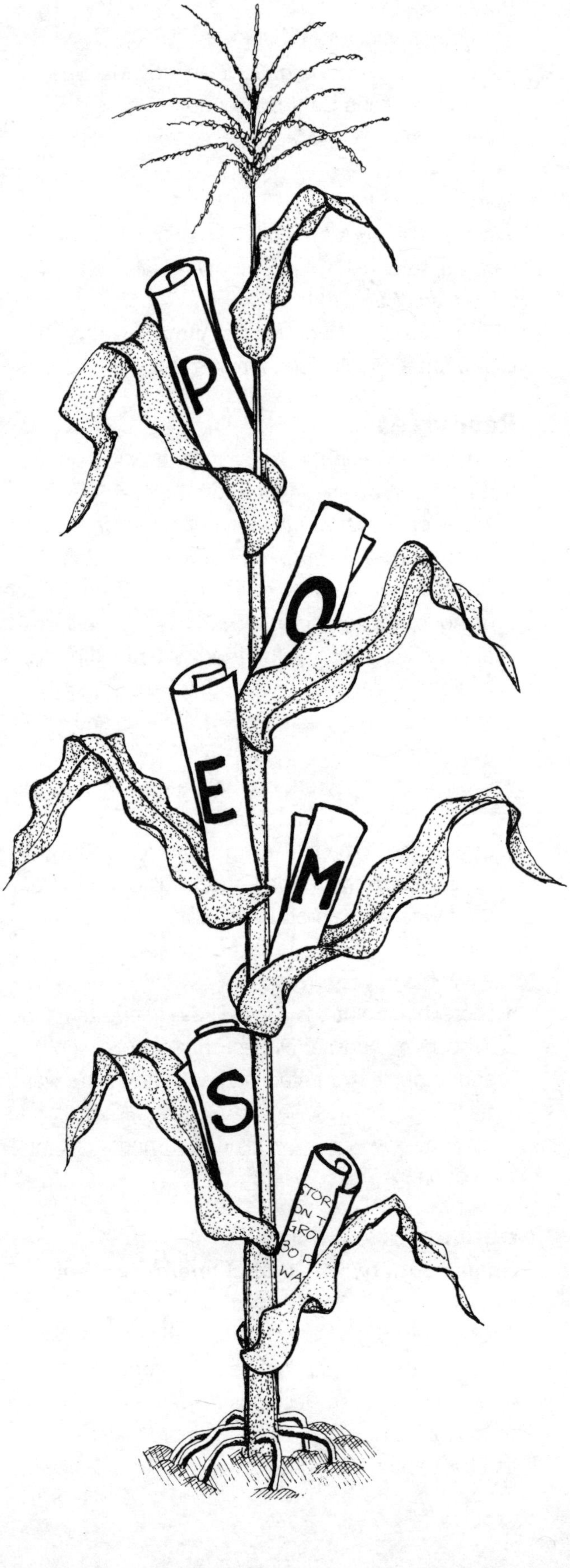

Goals

Move across the curriculum and have the opportunity to express what we've learned in a different discipline. Identify what "makes" a poem, practice poem-writing skills, and create our own poems based on recent class field trip experiences.

Key Points

- Poetry writing, like creating art or music, is another way to express ourselves.
- For thousands of years, farming and agricultural land has inspired many writers and artists.

"I think it's more through the arts that one keeps that [sense of] wonder alive. One of the sad things that has happened is the arts have been separated out from science, social science, and other disciplines. The arts have been isolated to a half-hour with crayons. And yet art, myth, they're the kind of thing that needs to pervade everything, that needs to come before, I think, a rigorous approach to things. It instills in kids a sense of wonder and beauty. Plus, I think that emotion is at the root of all teaching and art tends to be more inclusive of emotion." —Malcolm Margolin[1]

Background

Introducing children to poetry is not a one-time class event. Plan to have the creative processes flow over several classes—you know how long your students will need for re-working their pieces. You may want to enlist the help a local art teacher if you would like the children to be inspired by artwork depicting nature, instead of relying on memories of their field trips. If so, look for artwork by Monet, O'Keefe, van

[1] Sara Marcellino, "Educating with a Sense of Wonder: An Interview with Malcolm Margolin."

Gogh, Breughel, Millet, and Grandma Moses as examples.

This poetry exposure and subsequent writing could be used as good indoor activities during an inclement gardening season, especially if you were planning to work outdoors—or could take place in a quiet "outdoor classroom" if space is available to you.

Getting Ready

Precede lesson with a field trip or outdoor experience in a garden, etc.

What You'll Need

Garden-related poetry. See Literature Links and Resources. (See "Pumpkin Head" poem below.)

How to Do It

Begin by asking: What do you know about poetry and what makes a poem different from a story? Read a rhyming book or a food- or garden-related poem, depending on the age of the children (*Chicken Soup with Rice* by Maurice Sendak; the poem "Last Night I Dreamed of Chickens" in *Something Big Has Been Here* by Jack Prelutsky; *Jamberry* by Bruce Degen; any of the *I Spy Picture Riddle Books* by Jean Marzollo). Guide them to understand the rhythm or "beat" of the poems. Explain and read examples of various kinds of poetry such as non-rhyming poems, cinquain, or haiku.

For younger children, you may teach them to recite the poem by having them repeat each line after you. Practice it several times throughout the day and during your unit on growing food.

Next, have children close their eyes. Ask them to remember their recent class visit to a grower, elder community member, greenhouse, or farmer's market—encourage them to consider smells, sounds, colors, textures, tastes, etc. After a few minutes, have them open their eyes and tell you some of what they "saw" in their mind's eye. Note on the board some words and phrases that the children recall from their field trips.

If you want their poems to rhyme, brainstorm some words that rhyme with the terms they've remembered.

Then, have students start to write their own poems, cinquain, or haiku about food, nature, or gardening. Start small! Assist with vocabulary and rhythm and make suggestions for edits. Younger students may choose to illustrate a poem the class chooses, or dictate one to you for recording.

Classroom Conversations

Once poems have been worked on and re-written, have students share their poems with the rest of the class. Discuss. They could then compile them into a classroom poetry anthology, with illustrations, if desired.

The word poem comes originally from the Greek word *poi'ma*, meaning "to make." Did you know that March is designated both National Poetry Month and National Nutrition Month?

Want to Do More?

- Have students try to recite their poems to their families; you might include them in a parent or school newsletter. For younger children, they might remember the poem better if it's taught with motion—showing the size of the small seed or the tall plant for corresponding lines in a poem, for instance. Or, try music: they might use a familiar tune to sing their "lyrics." (See *The Soup Garden Song* on page 177.)
- Students choose a garden book or poem to share with the class.
- Use the Dr. Seuss book *If I Ran the Circus* and convert the theme from a circus to a garden. (The rhyming story starts out with the boy clearing a vacant lot and creating an imaginary circus.)
- Discuss native planting rituals, moon cycles, etc.
- Students can illustrate the "Pumpkin Head" poem or another garden/food-related poem they like.

Lesson Links

Visiting a Grower
Old-Fashioned Food
Lunch at the Dump
Once Upon a Farm

Literature Links

Read-Aloud Rhymes for the Very Young selected by Jack Prelutsky

Sing a Song of Popcorn: Every Child's Book of Poems edited by Beatrice de Regniers
Honey, I Love and Other Love Poems by Eloise Greenfield
Children of Long Ago Poems by Lessie Jones Little
Chicken Soup with Rice by Maurice Sendak
Oddhopper Opera: A Bug's Garden of Verses by Kurt Cyrus
Kinder Spirits: Children Helping Children in the Fight Against Hunger by Vicki Hubbard and Nancy Killion
Something Big Has Been Here by Jack Prelutsky
Food Fight: Poets Join the Fight against Hunger with Poems to Favorite Foods edited by Michael J. Rosen
Doodle Dandies: Poems That Take Shape by Patrick J. Lewis
Poem-Making: Ways to Begin Writing Poetry by Myra Cohn Livingston

Resources

- For some ideas and guidance on teaching poetry, see these books: *Teaching Poetry Yes You Can!* by Jacqueline Sweeney, Gr. 4-8, Scholastic, 1992; *Reading and Writing Poetry: A Guide for Teachers* by Judith W. Steinbergh, Gr. K-4, Scholastic, 1993; *The Poetry Break: An Annotated Anthology with Ideas for Introducing Children to Poetry* by Caroline Feller Bauer, H.W. Wilson, 1995; *Beyond Words: Writing Poems with Children: A Guide for Parents and Teachers* by Judith W. Steinbergh, Talking Stone Press, 1999.
- *Nature Journaling: Learning to Observe and Connect with the World Around You* by Clare W. Leslie and Charles E. Roth, Storey Books, 1998. Use these simple techniques in a farm, garden, or park and create a work of art by learning to see your surroundings in a new way.
- *Cultivating a Child's Imagination through Gardening* by Nancy Jurenka, Libraries Unlimited, 1996, for lots of ways to connect art and agriculture!

Benchmarks

The Human Organism: 6D—Learning, p. 140

K-2

Background: "Children are most interested in learning about their surroundings and all the ways they can interact with these surroundings. They should be encouraged to notice how they learn. . . ."

"People use their senses to find out about their surroundings and themselves. Different senses give different information."

Grades 3-5

Background: "They should be given many opportunities to explore areas of personal interest and to develop new skills. . . . Their concern with learning is how it can help them achieve in their areas of interest."

"Human beings have different interests, motivations, skills, and talents."

"Human beings can use the memory of their past experiences to make judgments about new situations."

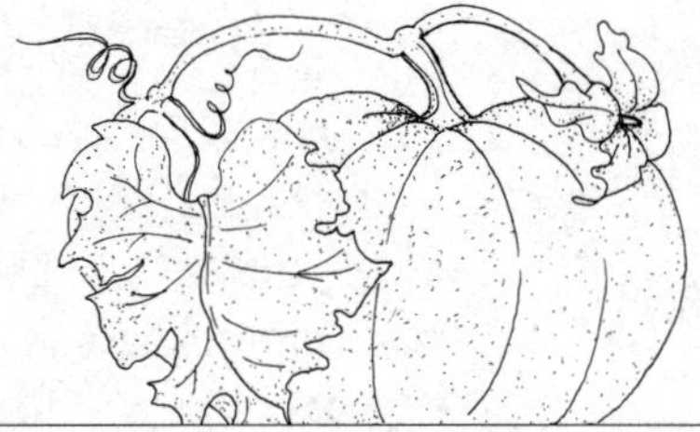

Pumpkin Head

Spring's Sprung, Singity-Sung,
Scoop a cup of mud,
Plop it on your brother's head,
Give it a good rub.

Spring's Sprang, Singity-Sang,
Pick a pumpkin pit,
Plant it on your brother's head,
Then you water it.

Spring's Sprong, Singity-Song
Watch the pumpkin grow,
Brother's head is stuck inside,
He makes a great scarecrow.

—Victoria Baker

CHOOSING FOOD FOR BODY & SOUL

"Healthy citizens are the greatest asset any country can have." —*Winston Churchill*

"The first wealth is health." —*Ralph Waldo Emerson*

If we teach children basic nutrition, if we encourage them to spend time *reflecting* on their food choices, and if we give them fundamental consumer skills, they will have a real opportunity to make a lifetime of better food choices for themselves.

Among U.S. adults, four of the seven leading causes of death are diet-related! Poor health in adults often stems from habits or circumstances that began in youth; unsound eating behaviors from childhood may be linked to heart disease, some forms of cancer, stroke, and diabetes. Infrequent exercise in youth often leads to poor physical activity habits in adults.

Surveys document consistently growing numbers of young people at risk both for being overweight as well as for being undernourished. Over 66 percent of U.S. adults and 16 percent of children ages 6-11 (up from 4 percent only two decades before) are overweight.[1]

The premise of this section—and this book—is not to dwell on alarming statistics but to provide a smorgasbord of nutrition activity ideas for students (and families) which encourage healthier food choices.

Choosing for Health The ten activities featured in this section will inspire children to think about their personal food world by keeping a health diary, learning to read labels, and analyzing television's influence on food choices. Identifying and understanding some of the outside pressures that influence their food world will help them as they grow into adults and learn to manage their own health.

Choosing for Taste Taste is personal! Taste is cultural! Ultimately it is taste (and the related sense of smell) that most strongly affects our choice of food. The activities in this section allow children to sample cuisine from different parts of the world while identifying the common ingredients they share. Eating different foods may be the most vital way to help children appreciate global diversity.

Choosing for Costs If your students calculate the costs of bringing food to their table and learn to compare the nutrutional value of different foods, they'll gain some real dollars and "sense" savvy.

We become creatures of habit. Children are at the stage of development where their food choices will have a significant impact on their health over their lifetimes. By encouraging them to assess these habits early on, we can build a healthier nation and reverse current trends.

[1] Results from the 1999-2002 National Health and Nutrition Examination Survey (NHANES) indicate that an estimated 16 percent of children and adolescents ages 6-19 years are overweight. This represents a 45 percent increase from the overweight estimates of 11 percent obtained from NHANES III (1988-94). http://www.cdc.gov/nchs/fastats/overwt.htm

Choosing for Health

Why is it important to start health education early? If young people learn how to treat their bodies well, they can develop food habits that will help them grow well, respect their bodies, and make sound nutrition, physical activity, and lifestyle choices throughout their lives. Optimal health clearly depends on many factors (food, exercise, attitude, family history, economic environment, and social support, among others); food is one of the primary aspects we can control. This section helps students determine which foods are best for their health and helps them cultivate a taste for healthful foods.

Reflect on the "What if . . .?" question. What if children don't learn to respect their bodies, and don't receive education about ways they can keep themselves healthy?

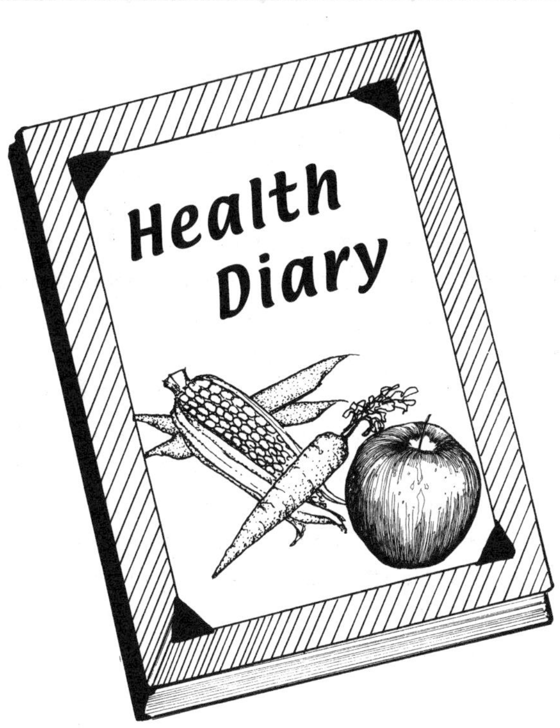

Dear Diary. . . .

Keep a food and health diary

Recommended Grades: 3–6

- **Health**
- **Math**
- **Language Arts**
- **Physical Education**

Goals

Record in a diary what we eat and drink, and do for activity in order to better assess health habits.

Key Point

- Children can become more aware of how and what they're eating, and how much they're moving their bodies.

Background

Do this lesson after students are already familiar with the food pyramid and dietary guidelines (see the back of the Health Diary handout and the Appendix). This Dear Diary activity can be done early in the unit or year and again at the end—it's fun for students to compare the changes they make. By revisiting this journaling activity, you'll observe even more the second time.

Generating health diaries from your class will not supply you with scientific study data, but will stimulate thinking and talking about daily health routines. We encourage you as the teacher or parent to keep your own health diary along with students, since adults are the primary role models for young people. You may determine the length of time to record data—one day provides a snapshot, while several consecutive days yields a more typical consumption pattern.

Save the results of this class activity to see if any changes are made over time. (Refer to companion lesson, Dear Diary . . . Again.) For simplicity's sake, we'll emphasize and evaluate (through graphing) fruit and vegetable consumption, as well as amount of activity. Keeping track of one's food and exercise habits is the first step in becoming aware of those habits—with the goal of improving them in small ways. Make up a student-created chart on the wall—so they can log in their entries from the previous day.

What You'll Need

Reproduce the two-sided Health Diary handout for each student for the number of days you'll be recording foods; examples of typical produce serving portions (see the back of the handout); fruit juice(s) and examples of a fruit (flavored) drink, cocktail, punch, -ade, or beverage (none of which is actual juice); measuring cups; and paper food models (optional).

You may enlist a local registered dietitian or licensed nutritionist (or a health professional such as the school nurse who's familiar with children) to do the presentation on keeping a health diary—someone who can describe serving sizes and help with evaluation. You'll also find helpful food and nutrition information in the Appendix.

How to Do It

Begin by discussing the purpose for keeping a journal or diary. For example, have they used a journal for science, or for writing skills? Discuss the reason for having a health diary: for observation and to collect data. *This is not a judgment on what individuals are eating;* it's to help us all be aware and evaluate the choices we make *as a group.* We shouldn't modify our regular eating habits for this exercise—we want a *typical* daily pattern for each person, if possible.

Next, ask students to name some of their favorite fruits and vegetables. Show serving sizes of common produce items—using real food examples, paper food models, or measuring cups. To help prepare the kids for keeping their health journals at home, school, or elsewhere, have them practice estimating portion sizes for *only* fruits and vegetables using paper food models or typical measuring utensils—they do not need to write down other foods eaten. One hundred percent fruit juice can be recorded as a fruit serving. *Note that with beverages, the first ingredient should be 100 percent juice, otherwise it cannot be considered juice.* Show examples of juice drinks, which may have a small percentage of real fruit juice, if any. Review the serving size table on the back of the reproducible diary page.

Then, explain to children that they will record all foods and beverages containing fruits and vegetables for a specific amount of time—typically one to three days, and create their own diary or use the form provided. Make sure to include any produce snacks on the record as well as meals. (Many children's snacks contain more calories than any single one of their meals.) For combination foods such as pizza or soup, use the best estimate of the amount of vegetables included. Foods eaten away from home provide a large part of daily calories for most of us—ask students to try to keep track of the fruit and vegetable foods they eat even when they're away from home. Additionally, list exercise in terms of number of minutes at recess, playing sports, walking to and from school, etc.

On the board, demonstrate how to fill out the diary by tallying the following:

- date or day;
- name of foods that contain fruit or vegetables, as well as juices consumed—using one line for each item;
- the quantity of each food (best "guesstimate");
- serving sizes in fruit or vegetable category (check marks under appropriate column);
- exercise—what kind and for how long?

Next, go through the current day and have students write down any fruit and vegetable foods or juices they've had, recording them to see that they understand how to keep the diary correctly.

Then, as their homework project, have them record in the health diary for a specified number of days and return them to class. You may choose to send a letter home to parents (see sample) explaining the observational nature of this assignment and that the journal will be used to make a total *class* tally, with the ultimate goal of trying to improve habits as a group. Review daily diary progress if possible.

Finally, remind students that this journal is for observation, not criticism. With students, create a large bar graph showing the collective amounts of fruits, vegetables, and amount of activity done by class for the journal time period. Focus on the class total, not any individual student's amounts of activity or foods eaten. Make observations about results. Save the tallied chart for the Dear Diary . . . Again activity on page 128.

Classroom Conversations

- We are advised to eat one and a half cups of fruit and two and a half cups of vegetables a day. Did the classroom meet that challenge? This will require some numerical calculations.
- Refer to USDA Dietary Guidelines and the Dietary Guidelines for Sustainability in the Appendix. Compare recorded foods to these guidelines. How do the food items listed in your diaries match up? Why or why not?
- What did you notice about doing your health diary? How hard was it to keep track of what you ate and drank?
- Did it change what you typically ate?
- Did charting your physical activity

Health Diary

Name______________________________**Class**____________

Dates: from__________________**to**______________________

Day	Food Name	Amount (measure)	Fruit	Vegetable	Exercise	Amount (time)

- **Fruits and vegetables really are nutrition superstars. They give you a host of vitamins and minerals you won't find easily elsewhere, as well as fiber and usually plenty of water.**
- **If you eat a larger portion, count it as more than one serving. For example, a cup of fruit salad would count as two servings of fruit.**

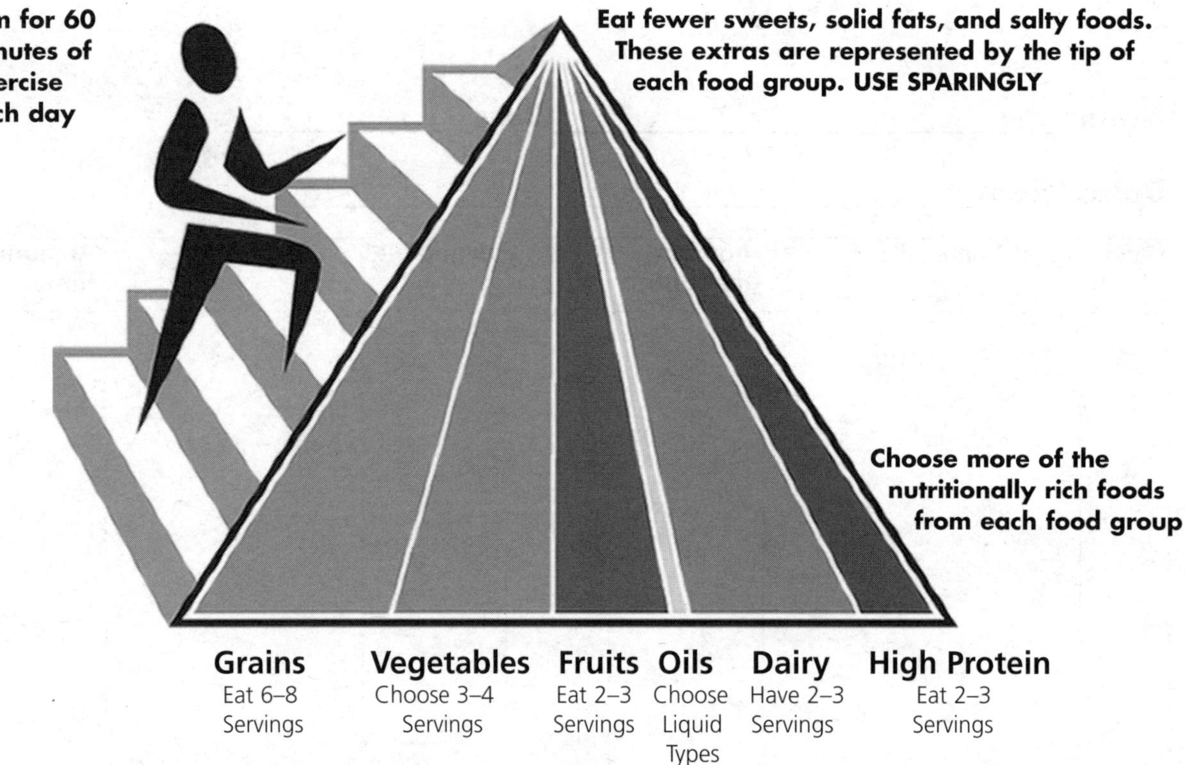

Use the Food Pyramid to help you eat better. The **wwwMyPyramid.gov** web site will help you set personalized goals for a healthy diet and enough exercise. Start with plenty of whole grains, vegetables, and fruit. Add a few dairy and other protein foods, and go easy on the extras. Get your oils from fish, nuts, seeds, and liquid oils such as olive, corn, canola or soybean oils. Find a balance between food and fun. Move more. Aim for at least 60 minutes on most days.

TYPICAL SERVING SIZES:

Vegetable Group—Choose for color!

- 1 cup of raw leafy vegetables
- 1/2 cup of other vegetables—cooked or raw
- 3/4 cup of vegetable juice

Fruit Group—Try to get fresh types.

- 1 medium apple, banana, orange, pear
- 1/2 cup of chopped, cooked, or canned fruit
- 3/4 cup of 100% fruit juice

Grain Group—Look for whole grain products.

- 1 slice of bread
- 1 ounce ready-to-eat cereal
- 1/2 cup cooked cereal, rice, or pasta

Dairy Group—Choose non-fat or 1% varieties for children over two

- 1 cup of milk or yogurt
- 1 1/2 ounces of natural cheese

High Protein Group

- 1/2 cup of cooked dry beans
- 1 egg
- 1/4 cup nuts or seeds
- 1-2 ounces fish, poultry, or lean meat

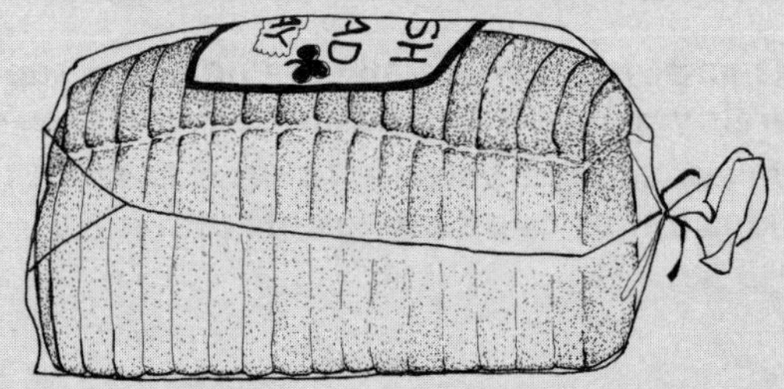

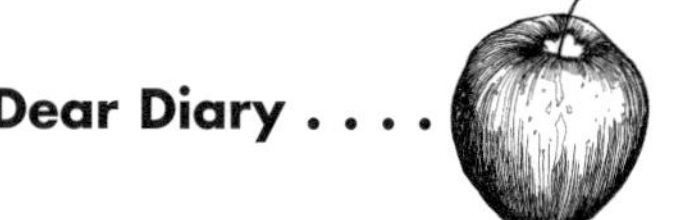

make any difference in the amount of exercise you got?

Want to Do More?

- Do the same exercise along with another class in your school. Contrast the results of both groups.
- Compare what you eat with dietary recommendations using a dietary analysis tool: www.mypyramidtracker.gov/
- Older students might want to record some additional data as well, to use for later comparison: All foods and beverages consumed over a certain time span; how hungry they felt at the time of eating (on a scale of 1 to 5); how to recognize their body's *signals* regarding how much to eat; and how they felt at the time (for example: rushed, relaxed, stressed, lonely, or bored).

Action

- Enlist the help of your school's food service staff to promote a classroom goal of everyone eating at least five servings from the vegetable and fruit groups. Brainstorm easy ways to reach the goal—enjoying favorite colorful crunchy raw vegetables, whole fruits, frozen 100 percent fruit juice bars, dried fruit, etc. Encourage schoolwide participation.
- How would you like to have gym every day? Rates of childhood obesity are increasing in this country. One way to counter that would be to have more regular activity for all students. If you agree, lobby your local school board to encourage more recess or gym time for your system—five days a week. (Some school systems combine lunch and recess into one hour-long mid-day break.) In the meantime, institute a ten- or fifteen-minute walking period at a specified time each day.

Lesson Links

Pyramids Near You
What is Locally Grown?
Dear Diary . . . Again
Read the Small Print
Farm to Table

Literature Links

Elliot's Extraordinary Cookbook by Christina Bjork
Gregory, the Terrible Eater by Mitchell Sharmat
Food Rules! What You Munch, Its Punch, Its Crunch, and Why Sometimes You Lose Your Lunch by Bill Haduch

Resources

- A school food service director might contribute food measurement tools and techniques.
- A local health professional can assist with instructions for keeping a food and activity diary. To find a professional in your area who works with common ethnic and cultural groups, see www.eatright.org (choose "Find a Nutrition Professional" or do a search for "Networking Groups") or www.dietitians.ca (Canada).
- Use The Top Ten Vegetables and Fruits list (Appendix) for helpful nutrition information.
- For a colorful reproducible snack handout: www.fns.usda.gov/tn/Educators/yrslf07.pdf
- Paper food models—#0012N with leader guide (created by the National Dairy Council) will help with portion size estimation. Go through the national office to locate an affiliate near you at 847-803-2000.
- Sites for dietary guidelines and pyramid information: www.mypyramid.gov and www.sne.org/mypyramid
- For more information on health and fitness, see the following groups/programs in the Organizations section of the bibliography: American Alliance of Health, Physical Education, Recreation, and Dance; Division of Nutrition and Physical Activity at CDC; President's Council on Physical Fitness and Sports.
- The Children's Health and Nutrition site is designed for kids: bright graphics and good information on many subjects relating to their own health: www.kidshealth.org/kid/stay_healthy
- *Surgeon General's Call to Action to Prevent and Decrease Overweight and Obesity* www.surgeongeneral.gov/topics/obesity/calltoaction/toc.htm for more information on the issue.

Benchmarks

The Human Organism: 6E—Physical Health, pp. 144–45

Grades 3-5

"Food provides energy and materials for growth and repair of body parts. . . ."

Grades 6-8

"The amount of food energy (calories) a person requires varies with body weight, age, sex, activity level, and natural body efficiency."

Habits of Mind: 12A—Values and Attitudes, p. 286

Grades 3-5

Background: ". . . students should be required to keep written records in bound notebooks of what they did, what data they collected, and what they think the data mean."

"Keep records of . . . observations and not change the records later."

Grades 6-8

Background: "Time needs to be found to enable students to pursue scientific questions that truly interest them. . . . Such projects also establish realistic contexts in which to emphasize the importance of scientific honesty in . . . recording data, . . . and reporting conclusions."

"Know why it is important in science to keep honest, clear, and accurate records."

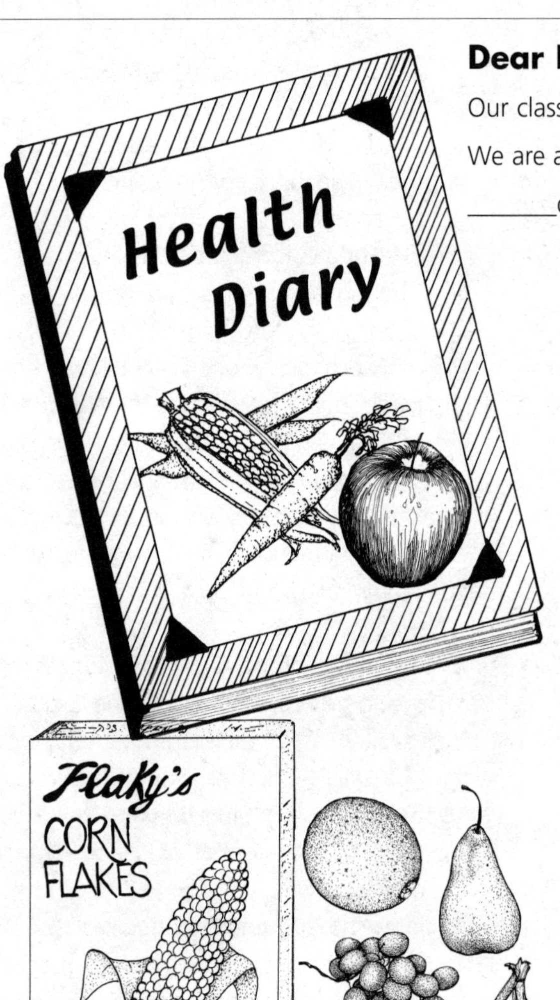

Dear Parent,

Our class is studying ways to build healthy, fit bodies. We are asking students to fill out a health diary for ______day(s).

The goal behind keeping this log is to observe usual eating and activity patterns. Students are not to change their regular routine just because they are writing it down. We will look at overall class totals for the three items that students are asked to record: foods containing fruits and vegetables as well as 100 percent fruit and vegetable juices, and activity amounts. (A personal diary becomes a class act!)

Please note that this is NOT a judgment on what individual children are eating or getting for exercise; it's to help the whole class be aware of the choices we make as a group—with the ultimate goal of trying to improve habits.

Thank you for helping your child with keeping the diary. Please contact me if you have any questions.

Handout from *Healthy Foods from Healthy Soils* by Elizabeth Patten and Kathy Lyons, Tilbury House, Publishers.

Pyramids Near You

Plan a regional menu using the food pyramid

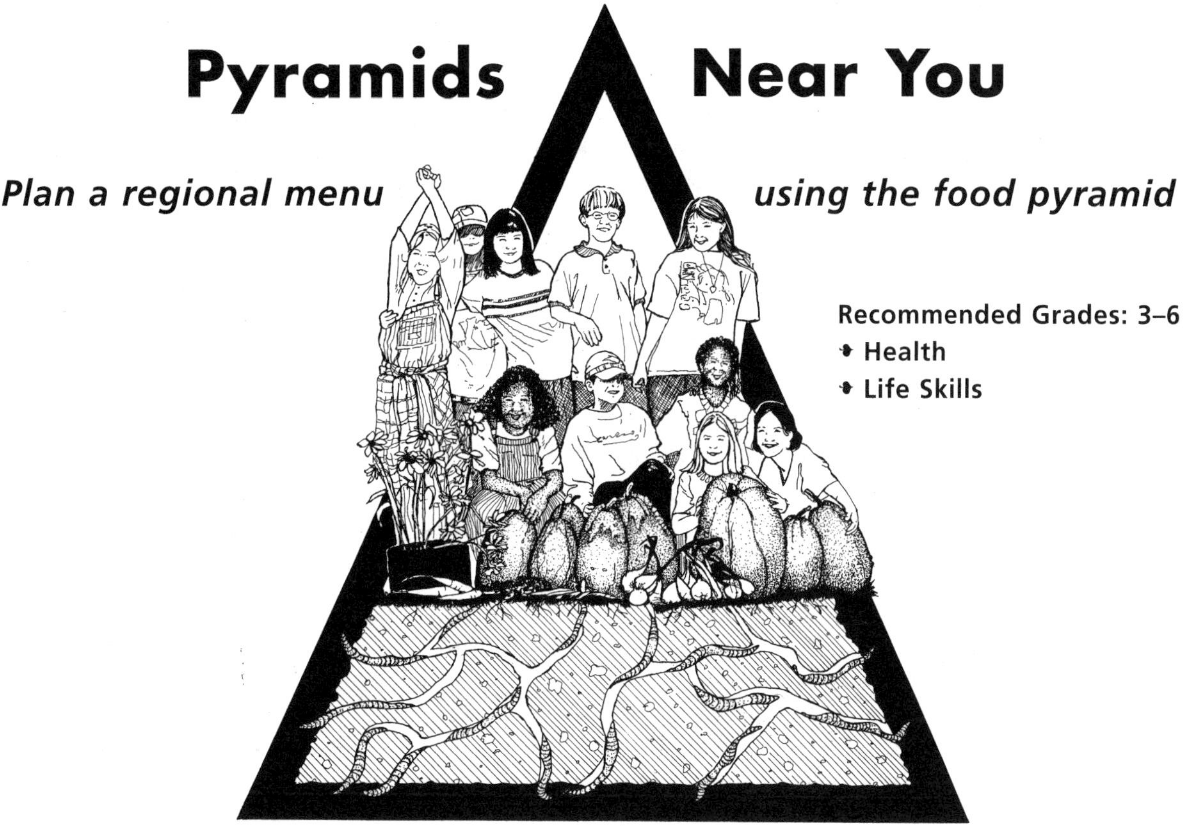

Recommended Grades: 3–6
- **Health**
- **Life Skills**

Goals

Design and prepare a meal using local, seasonal, or regional foods from the five (healthy) food groups. This will help us become more aware of locally available foods.

The experience of meal planning while using the nutrition pyramid is an important life skill. This activity also challenges students to think about eating "locally" and to discuss the advantages that doing so would mean to local growers.

Key Points

- Using the food pyramid to plan what you eat each day will help you choose a better diet.
- Eating foods from "closer to home" can help you, local farmers, and the environment.

Background

Note: Use this activity after students are already familiar with the food pyramid concepts (see page 56 and the Appendix).

Eating food grown locally has at least three major points in its favor: it is healthier, increases economic stability of the area, and reduces pollution. Purchasing from a local grower or growing your own food is not only satisfying but also ecologically beneficial. When grown locally, your food may be more nutritious, because fewer nutrients are lost due to travel time, handling, transport, packaging, time on the shelf, or refrigeration. (For more background, see Supporting a Locally Grown Food System on page 29.)

The Northeast Regional Food Guide Pyramid, developed by Jennifer Wilkins and Jennifer Bokaer-Smith from Cornell Cooperative Extension, emphasizes regional eating—and can be used as a model or adapted to your own home region. Learning more about the bountiful harvest of our own locality and sampling those foods can help us choose a healthier diet.[1]

This lesson provides a good opportunity to emphasize the dietary guidelines, especially eating five a day—eat at least two servings of fruit and at least three servings of vegetables each day. For optimum nutrition, choose dark-green leafy vegetables,

[1] *The Northeast Regional Food Guide Pyramid* by Jennifer Wilkins and Jennifer Bokaer-Smith, Cornell University Resource Center, Ithaca, NY.

orange fruits and vegetables, and cooked dry peas and beans often.

What You'll Need

Blank food pyramid; paste or glue sticks; pictures of local foods in season at the time of the class (optional); list of regional foods from your state agriculture office or Cooperative Extension; assortment of local foods to show and/or sample. (*Note:* In some locales and seasons, the amount of local fresh foods that are in season may not be as abundant—in that case, use canned, dried, etc. as long as they're originally from the area. Students will still be able to discover what's available at the time of the lesson.)

How to Do It

Begin by reviewing the idea of locally grown foods. (See "What is Locally Grown? page 26.) Have students brainstorm a list of local foods and write their ideas on the board. Use local foods you've brought in to help with the brainstorming (or taste testing!).

Next, provide each student or pair of students with a large blank food pyramid form and have them label each section alongside the triangular image (as grains, vegetables, fruits, protein, dairy, extras). If anyone remembers the number of servings recommended in each group (see Dear Diary lesson), label those as well. Paste in photos of local foods provided (optional), or write in food names based on lists or charts from local agencies.

Ask students to make up a lunch or snack menu using as many regional foods as possible. The class convenes and votes on a single healthy luncheon or snack they'd like to make. Guide them in outlining the steps they'll follow in order to prepare the meal, using the directive: What do we want to do? How do we get there? Then, what's next? (Example: How do we make a meal for our class? Ask someone who's done it before: school nutrition staff!) Pairs or small groups of students will each take a step in the process: gathering recipes, obtaining ingredients, collecting utensils, preparing in advance, following proper hygiene, preparing on the day of meal, etc; clean up, etc.

Then, with cooperation from the school lunch director, help the class prepare the selected snack or meal centered on regional foods. Invite others and enjoy!

What Do Girls (and Boys), Gorillas, and Guinea Pigs Have In Common?

Why do we need to eat fresh fruits and vegetables? Getting enough vitamin C is one big reason. A curious fact about vitamin C is that almost all mammals make it in their own livers, and so, logically, would never be deficient.

However, humans (along with apes and guinea pigs) cannot! We must get it from our food. Without vitamin C, a disease called scurvy develops.

Long before man knew about vitamins, it had been observed that when people couldn't get certain types of foods, diseases would develop. Sailors, for instance, who went on long trips and couldn't get fresh vegetables would get a disease called scurvy. In the seventeenth century British sailors were given lemons and limes to prevent this disease. And this, by the way, is why British sailors got the nickname "limeys."

Classroom Conversations

- Following the meal, ask if students would make any changes if preparing locally grown foods another time.
- What difference does it make if we eat foods from near where we live? Discuss the advantages and disadvantages of eating locally and eating globally. (Why would we choose to eat local foods rather than those from farther away? What foods would be unavailable to the students if they ate only foods from within their region?)
- What nutrients might they lack by not eating a variety of foods? (See What If All I Ate Were Potato Chips? on page 87.) What if we didn't eat citrus, for example. Explain how sailors on long trips in the old days came down with scurvy due to a lack of fresh fruit, particularly vitamin C. What foods in your region provide vitamin C? (Citrus, potatoes, cherries, green peppers, broccoli, tomatoes, melon, berries.)
- How does your growing season affect food production, quantity, and variety?
- What if you compared the ingredients in a fast food meal and a locally produced meal, with respect to the pyramid? Are there any locally grown foods in the fast food meals? Are locally grown foods available at your nearest market? What if every family in their class or school spent $5-10 of its weekly food budget on local foods?

Actions

- Come up with menu suggestions with help from the school food service to offer a locally grown lunch/snack.
- Have students assist with family food shopping to demonstrate their knowledge of the food pyramid in selecting local and regional foods. (Use list of foods selected from regional/local food pyramids in class.)

Want to Do More?

- Have small groups choose different regions and create regional food pyramids. (See Oldways in Resources.)
- A "foodshed" is similar to a watershed, and has surfaced as one conceptual way to think about the origins and destinations of foods in a particular region. Older students can learn about watersheds, and then help identify their geographic "foodshed" by looking at a map and seeing what farms lie within their own idea of where that area lies.
- Provide small taste-test examples of local food that may not be familiar to students, for instance: rhubarb, spring garlic greens, fennel, parsnips, or an unusual variety of winter squash.
- Take a field trip to a farmers' market, sometimes called a "green market."

Lesson Links

What is Locally Grown?
Visiting a Grower
Farm to Table
What If All I Ate Were Potato Chips?

Literature Links

Good Enough to Eat: A Kid's Guide to Food & Nutrition by Lizzy Rockwell
The Edible Pyramid: Good Eating Every Day by Loreen Leedy
Vegetables by Susan Wake
Sugar by Elaine Landau
Food Pyramid by Joan Kalbacken
Oliver's Vegetables by Vivian French

Resources

- Northeast Regional Food Guide Pyramid Poster and Fact Sheets. Color poster and educational handouts promoting regional seasonal eating in one area by Jennifer Wilkins & Jennifer Bokaer-Smith, Cornell Cooperative Extension. Cornell University Resource Center, 7 Business & Technical Park, Ithaca, NY 14850; www.nutrition.cornell.edu/foodguide/
- *The Victory Garden Cookbook* by Marian Morash, Alfred Knopf, 1982, is filled with vegetables—planting and harvesting tips, recipes (some high fat), and wonderful photographs.

- *How to Teach Nutrition to Kids,* Connie Liakos Evers, 24 Carrot Press, 2006. Includes cooking ideas.
- Contact the Cooperative Extension in your area or state Department of Agriculture for regional/ seasonal food suggestions.
- Ask your school food service program director or area supermarket manager to help with food samples.
- Oldways Food Preservation and Trust has published the "healthy eating pyramids," a set of dietary guides based on worldwide dietary traditions closely associated with good health: Asian, Latin American, Mediterranean, and Vegetarian diets. Oldways Preservation & Exchange Trust, 266 Beacon St., Boston, MA 02116; 617-421-5500; www.oldwayspt.org
- The Chefs Collaborative; www.chefscollaborative.org and the Slow Food Movement; www.slowfoodusa.org both, in different ways, strive to promote enjoyment of locally grown food.
- To locate a farmer's market or green market in your area: www.ams.usda.gov/farmersmarkets
- Center for Science in the Public Interest *Healthy Eating Pyramid* or any pyramid model that differentiates between processed/less processed foods, i.e., Oregon Dairy Council materials.
- *Ethnic and Regional Food Practices: A Series,* American Dietetic Association and American Diabetes Association, Inc. (1995-98). ADA, 216 West Jackson Boulevard, Chicago, IL, 60606-6995; ADA Customer Service 800-877-1600, ext. 5000. The ADA also has a set of 11" x 14" color Pyramid Posters including: vegetarian, children's, older Americans, Mexican, Chinese, Indian, traditional Southern/Soul, Italian, and Native American.

Benchmarks

The Human Organism: 6E—Physical Health, p. 144

Grades 3-5

"Eating a variety of healthful foods . . . helps people to stay healthy." (The *Benchmark* addresses the concept in the activity of recognizing and applying the five healthy pyramid food groups.)

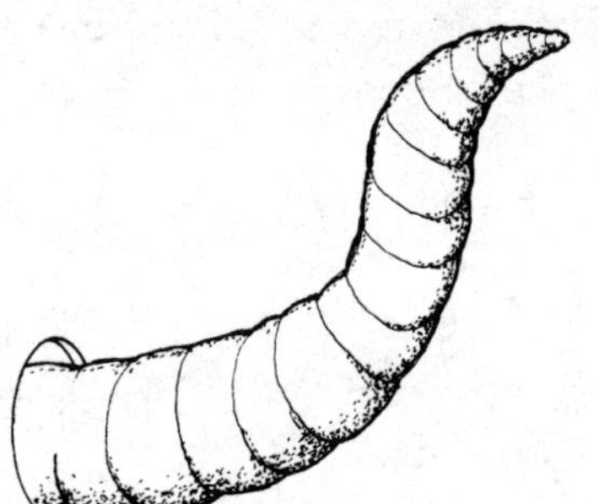

What WOULD it feel like to go on a journey through the body?! See Anatomy in Action, next. Using a magnifying glass, you can actually watch food traveling on its journey if you look carefully at a young red wiggler!

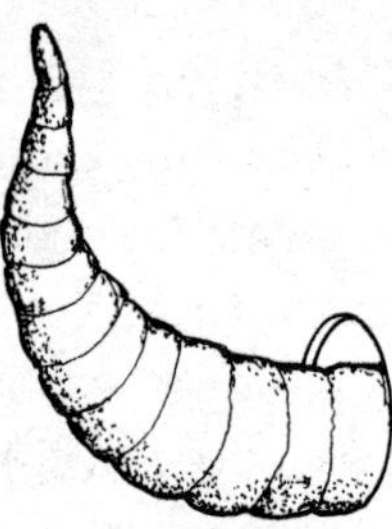

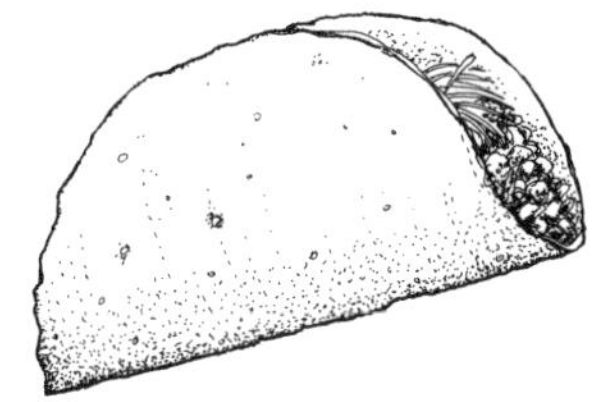

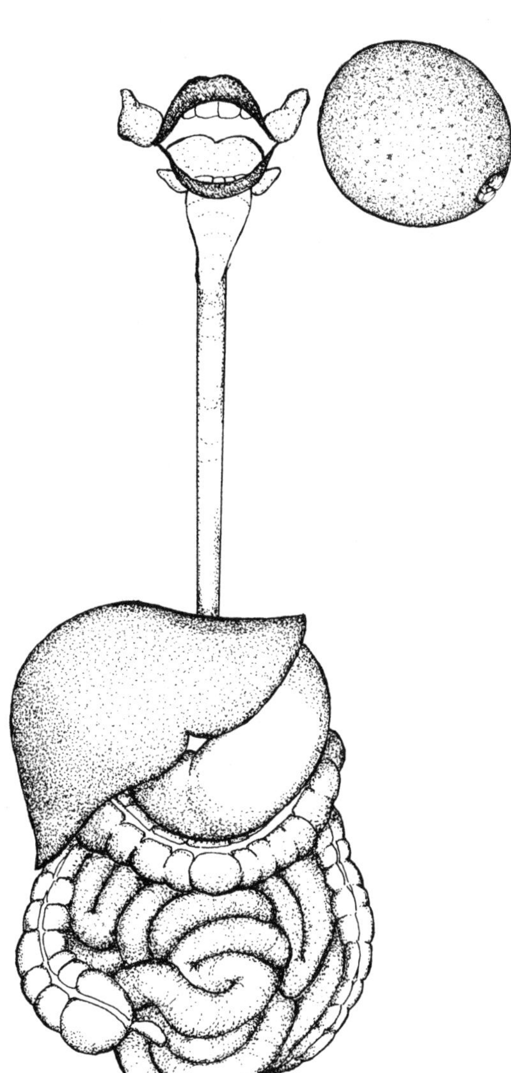

Anatomy in Action

Build a model digestive tract

Recommended Grades: 4–6

- **Science**
- **Health**
- **Language Arts**
- **Visual Arts**

Goals

Research parts of the digestive system to discover what happens to food in the body. Then, build a life-size model of the digestive system!

Key Points

- Food travels a long way during its journey through our bodies; the distance is dependent on our age and height.
- There are five key steps in a nutrient's path through the digestive system: First it's broken up into pieces, then it's mixed and blended, then the blood picks up the nutrients and circulates them throughout the body. Once we use the energy from the nutrients our body gets rid of what it doesn't need.
- These steps are called digestion, absorption, circulation, metabolism, and excretion.

Background

Digestion means breaking food down into millions of tiny pieces so it can be used by the body. This amazing process starts in the mouth. Food travels down the esophagus to the stomach, which acts as a human blender, mixing all the pieces together. The soup mixture that leaves the stomach heads to the small intestine, a 20-foot-long (6 meters) organ where most digestion takes place as nutrients are **absorbed** through its walls into the blood. Arteries then carry nutrients and oxygen to cells throughout the body thanks to the network of blood vessels (similar to our roadways) that are called the

circulatory system. The nutrients carried in blood give us the building blocks for energy, healing, maintenance, and growth. Each cell of the body is like a tiny factory, taking nutrients and producing energy, growth, and replacement parts (**metabolism**). Not all parts of food can be used by the body: material that cannot be absorbed moves into the 7-foot-long (2 meters) large intestine where it combines with water and eventually leaves the body (**excretion**).[1]

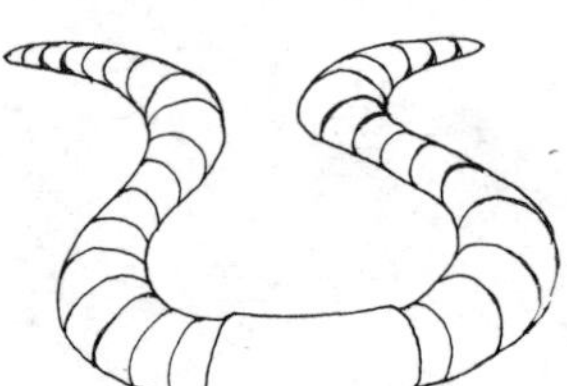

What about cows—how many stomachs do they have?—Can you find out why?

What You'll Need

Access to a library for information; props to make digestive tract model (Students can choose necessary "ingredients," for example, a set of false teeth for mouth, snorkel or other tube representing the esophagus, a hot water bottle or plastic milk jug for stomach, a 20-foot rope for the lengthy small intestine, a 7-foot larger-diameter rope or tube for the large intestine, and a toilet paper tube or tube-shaped balloon with end cut for the rectum); duct tape (how appropriate to connect all these body ducts!).

Getting Ready

This lesson would benefit from some prior study of the human body, including having students make full-sized paper tracings of their bodies (optional).

How to Do It

Begin, as a class, by talking about what students think happens to food in the body. For example, the teeth grind it up into small pieces (that's why Annelida always says to chew your food carefully!); and the salivary glands make chemicals that allow food to start digesting the moment it enters the body. Later, the stomach blends the particles up, like a cement mixer. The small and large intestine are primarily responsible for sending the nutrients into the bloodstream and then removing water from what remains before it leaves the body. Define and briefly research digestion, absorption, circulation, metabolism, and excretion to confirm or change their opinions of what happens.

Next, break into five groups (1. mouth; 2. esophagus; 3. stomach; 4. small intestine; 5. large intestine) and challenge each small group to investigate one tract section. They should be able to describe where each part is located, what precedes and follows their section, and what happens to food there. Last but not least, we suggest the teacher (for obvious reasons) completes the gastro-intestional tract by researching and explaining the function of the rectum and anus.

Later, ask students to name the parts of the digestive system in sequence. Brainstorm what materials they might need to construct a life-size human digestive tract.

During the next few class periods, gather materials and have the class construct and connect the model pieces in sequence. In other words, build your body! The final "trick" is to try and fit it all into an appropriately sized human body "containment vessel"! (Suggestion: an illustrated paper grocery bag, cloth sack, or backpack could be used to hold the digestive sections.)

Why is it called the LARGE intestine if it's shorter than the SMALL intestine? (It's a wider diameter tube.)

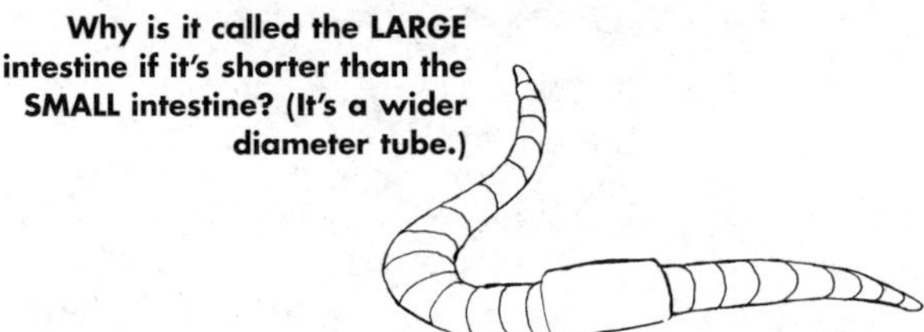

Classroom Conversations

- Have each group present its findings to the class using the 3-D model (they may want to name the figure they've created! GI Jane? GI Joe?).
- Take your body "on the road" to show it to other classes. Starting from the mouth, each group does its presentation by gradually pulling sections out of the "body." At the end of the individual group's presentations, the whole system is OUT OF THE BAG. You can demonstrate and measure its length by spreading all the connected pieces out on the classroom floor or school hallway.
- Food is needed as fuel to power the action of the digestive tract (and everything else we do!). What

[1] Definitions adapted with permission from *How to Teach Nutrition to Kids* by Connie Liakos Evers, 24 Carrot Press, 2006.

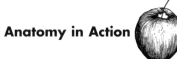

would happen if you didn't get enough food or enough water? (See the box below.)
- How does the food get out of the tube and go into the body's cells? (See Background.)
- Does all the food we eat end up being excreted?

Want to Do More?

- Decorate t-shirts with fabric paint or markers to depict the digestive tract, and wear them to celebrate "I'm a Healthy Body" day.
- Investigate the actual length of the digestive tract for each student. For approximate total measure, use a string to estimate the distance:
  1. Mouth to stomach (via esophagus) = distance from lip corner around your ear to the center spot on your chest (sternum);
  2. Stomach = distance from outstretched thumb to tip of pinky finger;
  3. Small intestine = body height, times three; and
  4. Large intestine = from middle fingertip to middle fingertip with outstretched arms

Literature Links

What Happens to Your Food? by Alastair Smith
Food Rules! What You Munch, Its Punch, Its Crunch, and Why Sometimes You Lose Your Lunch by Bill Haduch
Inside the Human Body (*Magic School Bus* series) by Joanna Cole
Food and Digestion by Steve Parker
The Digestive System by Helen Frost
Eating a Meal: How You Eat, Drink, and Digest by Steve Parker
What Happens to a Hamburger by Paul Showers
Elliot's Extraordinary Cookbook by Christina Bjork

Resources

- *How to Teach Nutrution to Kids* by Connnie Liakos Evers. 24 Carrot Press, 2006. For additional related activities.
- School or local librarian (give advance notice to gather books on human anatomy and nutrition for children).
- Stanford University's online healthy library, The Anatomy of Nutrition, is an excellent resource for older students who want to learn more about the digestive process: http://healthlibrary.stanford.edu/resources/internet/bodysystems/gi_intro.html#anatomy

Does your school have convenient, working water fountains so that you can get a free refreshing drink whenever you need one? If not, find out why, and lobby your school administration to fix the problems.

The BEST Thirst-Quencher!

Water is the most essential nutrient—for humans, plants, and other living things, but the vital role that water plays in humans is often overlooked. Water helps regulate body temperature, maintains mineral balance, eliminates wastes, carries nutrients and oxygen to the cells, and assists in many chemical reactions. The average person's body is 55 to 75 percent water by weight, about the same proportion that makes up all animals and plants. Also, 75 percent is the same proportion found on earth as water or ice. (However, only 1 percent of the earth's total water is available for human use; 97 percent is salty and 2 percent is frozen.)

Water is *always* moving. Our bodies lose water through sweating, breathing, urine, and feces. In fact, the average person loses about 10 cups (2.4 liters) of water daily, so it's important to replace fluids by drinking plenty of water and eating foods with a high water content (such as fruit). Lack of water can contribute to daytime fatigue.

Sodas, juices, and other beverages are not as good a choice as water because they are high in simple sugars and may not quench thirst as well as water. Although they are made of water, they are low in nutrient density. That is, the amount of other nutrients they provide is quite low compared to the amount of calories they add. Choose water because it is portable, inexpensive (except in bottled form), readily available, not loaded with calories, and quickly absorbed. It's just what your body needs!

- Digestive Tract features a good, reproducible illustration and article suitable for middle-school children: http://digestive.niddk.nih.gov/ddiseases/pubs/yrdd/index.htm

Benchmarks

The Human Organism: 6C—Basic Functions, pp. 136–37

Grades 3-5

"From food, people obtain energy and materials for body repair and growth. The undigestible parts of food are eliminated."

Grades 6-8

"For the body to use food for energy and building materials, the food must first be digested into molecules that are absorbed and transported to cells."

"The urinary system disposes of dissolved waste molecules, the intestinal tract removes solid wastes. . . ."

Common Themes: 11B—Models, pp. 268–69

Grades 3-5

Background: "Students can begin to formulate their own models to explain things they cannot observe directly."

Grades 6-8

"Models are often used to think about processes. . . ."

"Different models can be used to represent the same thing. Choosing a useful model is one of the instances in which intuition and creativity come into play in science. . . ."

Nutrition Facts	
Serving Size 1/2 cup (126g)	
Servings Per Container about 6	
Amount Per Serving	
Calories 50	Calories from Fat 10
	% Daily Value*
Total Fat 1g	**2%** [2]
Saturated Fat 0g	**0%**
Trans Fat 0g	
Cholesterol 0mg	**0%**
Sodium 540mg	**23%**
Total Carbohydrate 10g	**3%**
Dietary Fiber 3g	**12%**
Sugars 7g	
Protein 2g	
Vitamin A 8% • Vitamin C 15%	
Calcium 2% • Iron 8%	

*Percent Daily Values are based on a 2,000 calorie diet. Your daily values may be higher or lower depending on your calorie needs:

	Calories:	2,000	2,500
Total Fat	Less than	65g	80g
Sat Fat	Less than	20g	25g
Cholesterol	Less than	300mg	300mg
Sodium	Less than	2,400mg	2,400mg
Total Carbohydrate		300g	375g
Dietary Fiber		25g	30g

Calories per gram:
Fat 9 • Carbohydrate 4 • Protein 4

Read the Small Print[1]

Practice consumer skills

Recommended Grades: 3–6

- **Language Arts**
- **Math**
- **Health**
- **Life Skills**

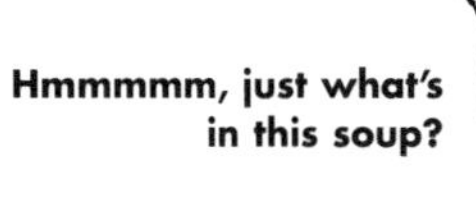
Hmmmmm, just what's
in this soup?

Goals

By learning to read the fine print on labels, see that advertisers sometimes make foods sound more nutritious than they really are.

Key Points

- On packaged foods, nutrition fact labels and ingredient listings are usually the best place to find out nutrient information.
- Serving sizes are one of the most important parts of the nutrition facts label.
- Humans need fat, but too much fat, especially saturated fat or trans fat, can cause health problems.

Background

Nutrition information on labels is a relatively new feature of food packaging. It's very helpful if you want to know more about what you're eating. A logical place to start is with the serving size, which tells you how much of the food you're supposed to eat in order to get the nutrients listed. It's measured in various ways—metric or standard—and even in terms that we are more likely to understand, such as the quantity or volume (the number of crackers, for example, or a one-cup serving). *Note:* The term "serving size" refers to the amount the food producer or the USDA deems you should eat. The term "portion" is used to describe the amount of food YOU eat normally of that particular food.

Manufacturers decide how much a serving size will be, and it varies considerably from brand to brand. For example, a serving size for some cereals is one cup, but a serving size for other cereals is 3/4 cup or even 1 1/4 cups. One product might state that three or four of their mini-cookies make up a single serving, but another company might list only one of their big cookies as a serving—even if they're the same type of cookie! Consider that many items sold as single portions actually provide two servings or more: a 20-ounce soft drink, a 12-ounce steak, a 3-ounce bag of chips, or a large bagel or muffin. The bottom line is that you can't determine how many nutrients or calories are in your foods without checking to see how your portion compares to what they claim is a serving. If you're concerned about nutrition, check out your portion before enjoying the food. You can get many more calories than you expect if you eat more than the product tells you that you should eat!

For children, whose calorie needs are extremely varied, there is no hard-and-fast rule about exactly

[1] Lesson adapted with permission from Earthsave Foundation's *Healthy Schools Lunch Action Guide* and Connie Liakos Evers's *How to Teach Nutrition to Kids*., 24 Carrot Press, 2006.

[2] Fat quantities may be .5g or less, and were rounded up to 1 g. total on this label.

how much fat they should eat. Note that current recommendations call for us to eat fewer than 30 percent of our calories from fat (averaged over all of a day's food). This exact information is not found on the label, but can be easily calculated by dividing the total "Calories" by the "Calories from Fat," both of which are listed on the nutrition label. Check the line just below "Amount Per Serving." This gives you the percentage of fat in this one food.

Fat generally gets a bad rap, but the problem really is *too much* fat or the *wrong types* of fat (avoid saturated, trans, and partially hydrogenated types). We wouldn't be able to live without some! Fat is a good source of energy (in the fuel sense), especially for children, because it contains more than twice as many calories by weight as protein or carbohydrate. (Annelida says, "See if you can find where that information is listed on the label.") Fat helps us absorb the fat-soluble vitamins A, D, E, and K, and it provides essential fatty acids that we need for healthy hearts, cells all over the body, skin, and hormones. Fats in the body act as shock absorbers to cushion body organs, and the fat layer under the skin helps insulate us. For most people in developed countries, total fat in the diet can stand to be lowered or types of fat changed, but it shouldn't be eliminated entirely.

What You'll Need

Overhead transparency of food label. **For Part 1:** bags or containers of popcorn, pretzels, corn chips, corn tortillas, or other snack food with many small morsels (not for consumption); package from plain popcorn kernels and air popped corn; trays or small containers; measuring cups. **For Part 2:** packaging with nutrition labels from rolled oats and several brands of granola bars; clean discarded labels or packages (with nutritional information) from some favorite processed snack foods (or use labels from Part I); math manipulatives, checkers, dominoes, or other stackable items (each one representing 4.3 grams or 1 teaspoon of fat).

How to Do It

Begin by explaining that packaged foods have labels with (1) ingredients, listed in order of highest to lowest quantity, and (2) Nutrition Facts, listing nutrient and guideline percentages and amounts. Many

What's a gram? If you're talking nutrition, it's probably not what I call my grandmother, "Gram"! It's a measure of weight and it equals about the weight of a shoelace.

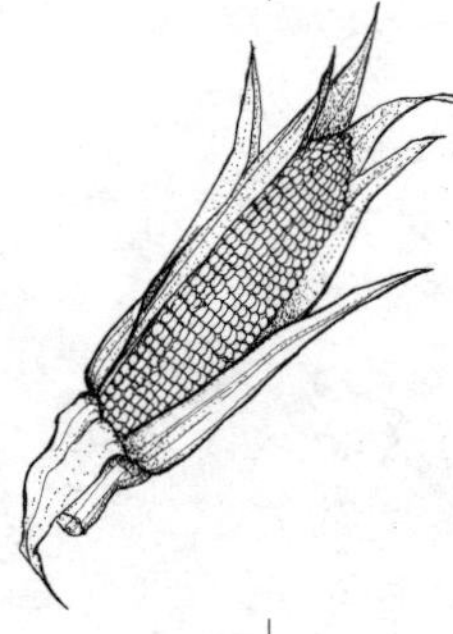

How FAT?

Food Item	Serving Size	Fat (in grams)	Trans Fat (in grams)
Part 1—Snack Food/Corn			
Air popped popcorn, popped	4 cups	<2.0	0
Microwave popcorn, popped	4 cups	12	2.2
Corn, cooked	1/2 cup	<.5	0
Corn chips	1-oz bag	10	0
Corn tortilla	1	<1	0
FILL IN YOUR FAVORITE SNACK	____	____	____
Part 2—Granola Bars/Oats			
Rolled oats, cooked	1/2 c	3	0
Low fat (oat) granola bars	2 bars	6	0.5
FILL IN YOUR OWN GRANOLA BAR	____	____	____

How does your portion size compare to the recommended serving size?

Handout from *Healthy Foods from Healthy Soils* by Elizabeth Patten and Kathy Lyons, Tilbury House, Publishers.

foods, such as fresh fruits and vegetables don't have labels. (Why?)

Next, (Part I: Snack food and serving size) break the class into small groups and have them look at the labels. For the purposes of this lesson, discuss two main features: serving size and amount of fat. For serving size: help students locate it and discuss its purpose. Explain that on a product label, the "Serving Size" tells you how much food you need to eat to get the amounts of nutrients listed. The "Servings Per Container" tells you how many servings are in the whole package. (Figure out how many servings would be in a product if there were 48 count and a serving represented 3 pieces.) Have several students at a time pour out the amount of pretzels, corn chips, popcorn, etc., they would *normally* eat for a snack and record the amount, using measuring tools and bowls. (Remind them that this is a demonstration and the food is not to be eaten as it's being handled by too many people.) After everyone has had a turn, ask one student to read aloud the serving amount listed on the label. Discuss any differences between the standard label serving size and the amount students might usually consume (portion). Remind students that the nutrition information listed refers to the standard label serving size and review the implications of any differences between what you and the manufacturer think is "normal."

Then, (Part 2: Granola bar, oats, and fat) have students look for "Total Fat" on the label. Compare the two products you have—rolled oats and granola bars—for differences in "Total Fat" and "Trans Fat." Distribute other snack food packages with nutrition labels to graphically demonstrate the amount of actual "Total Fat" in various products by stacking objects such as checkers, dominoes, math manipulative pieces, etc., to represent every 4 grams (or approx. 1 teaspoon) of fat. To be accurate, 4.3 grams = 1 teaspoon. Compare the piles.

Finally, encourage them to do comparisons with other foods such as crackers or other snack "munchies," chicken products, and fast-food choices.

Also look for products that have little saturated, trans, or partially hydrogenated fats—what type of foods do they tend to be? (They're fruits and vegetables, and grains.)

Classroom Conversations

- Name some of the ways that fat is beneficial (see Background). Like anything, "too much of a good thing" isn't necessarily good. But, what happens if you don't get enough fat?
- What are some of the ways you can reduce the most damaging types of fat but maintain enough fat to help you grow? (Use liquid oils rather than butter or margarine, eat fish and lean meats, limit most fats that are solid at room temperature, etc.)
- Discuss if this statement is true or false: Low fat means low calorie. (Sometimes extra sugars are added to low-fat foods, and they may be just as high, if not higher, in calories.)

Want to Do More?

- Make the comparison only of different serving sizes within a particular class of foods—such as crackers, snack chips, cookies, or cereals, and create a large graph with your findings. Post in the class or cafeteria, with permission and help from the food service staff.
- Research what happens if you don't get enough calories. (Children in developing countries typically eat a fraction of the average 2,300 calories a day that a 10-year-old child from the United States eats.) Explore hunger issues in your state, country or another country. (See World Hunger Year, Kids Can Make a Difference, and Food First/The Institute for Food and Development Policy listed in Bibliography under Organizations.)
- Do the same kinds of comparisons with "Lunchables" or prepared luncheon snack meals.

Lesson Links

What If All I Ate Were Potato Chips?
Sugar Detectives
The Global Staff of Life
Dear Diary Lessons
What Are Whole Foods
Dollars and $ense

Literature Links

Sugaring Time by Kathryn Lasky
Sugar by Elaine Landau
Mr. Sugar Came to Town/La visita del Sr. Azucar by Harriet Rohmer and Gomez Cruz
Gregory, the Terrible Eater by Mitchell Sharmat

Fats (Food Power! series) by Alvin Silverstein, Virginia Silverstein, and Robert Silverstein

Resources

- For label reading information, and to try a fun label-reading quiz, see the FDA's Center for Food Safety and Applied Nutrition site: www.cfsan.fda.gov/~dms/lab-gen.html
- For a list of nutrients humans need, see Selected Nutrition Information in the Appendix.
- For nutrient composition data, see USDA's Nutrient Data Laboratory: www.nal.usda.gov/fnic/foodcomp/search/
- Ask a local life skills or family and consumer science teacher, or USDA Cooperative Extension Educator for nutrient information or to be a classroom speaker on topics of food labeling.
- See *Bowes & Church's Food Values of Portions Commonly Used*, 18th ed. by Jean A. T. Pennington and Judith S. Douglass. Lippincott, Williams & Wilkins, 2004, a nutrient reference guide for commonly eaten foods.
- School Food Services director for pyramid posters/materials.
- *Consuming Passions: The Anthropology of Eating* by Peter Farb and George Armelagos, Houghton Mifflin 1983.
- *How to Teach Nutrition to Kids* by Connie Liakos Evers, 24 Carrot Press, 2006; www.nutritionforkids.com
- Center for Science in the Public Interest (very helpful with food additive information); www.cspinet.org.

Benchmarks

The Nature of Mathematics: 2C—Mathematical Inquiry

Grades 3-5

The background section states, "Students should be encouraged to describe all sorts of things mathematically. . . ."

"Numbers . . . —and operations on them—help to describe and predict things about the world. . . ."

The Mathematical World: 9A—Numbers, p. 212

Grades 3-5

"When people care about what is being counted or measured, it is important for them to say what the units are. . . ."

The Mathematical World: 9C—Shapes, p. 223

If information on the chart created in the activity is graphed, then the *Benchmarks* below apply.

Grades 3-5

"Graphical display of numbers may make it possible to spot patterns that are not otherwise obvious, such as comparative size and trends."

Grades 6-8

"The graphical display of numbers may help to show patterns such as trends. . . ."

The Human Organism: 6E—Physical Health, p. 144

Grades 3-5

"Food provides energy and materials for growth and repair of body parts. Vitamins and minerals, present in small amounts in foods, are essential to keep everything working well."

Grades 6-8

"The amount of food energy (calories) a person requires varies with body weight, age, sex, activity, level, and natural body efficiency."

"Changing dietary habits to reduce the in take of such things as animal fat increases the chances of living longer."

Habits of Mind: 12D—Communication Skills, p. 296

Grades 3-5

"Use numerical data in describing and comparing objects and events."

Grades 6-8

"Organize information in simple tables and graphs and identify relationships they reveal."

Habits of Mind: 12—Critical-Response Skills, p. 298

The background states the following, "In everyday life, people are bombarded with claims—claims about products . . . about their health. . . . In trying to separate sense from nonsense, knowledge helps."

Grades 3-5

"Buttress their statements with facts . . . and identify the sources used. . . ."

Grades 6-8

"Compare consumer products and consider reasonable personal trade-offs. . . ."

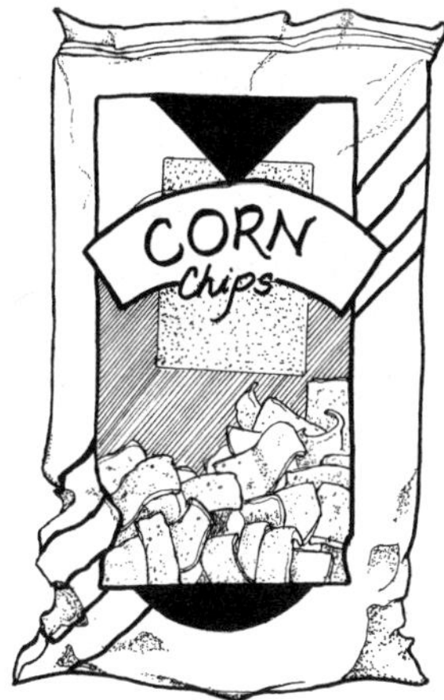

What are "Whole Foods"?

Differentiate between processed and unprocessed foods

Recommended Grades: 3–6

- **Language Arts**
- **Health**
- **Math**
- **Life Skills**

Goals

Discover that processed foods generally have more sugar, salt, and fat than their unprocessed cousins.

Key Points

- There is a difference between foods in their fresh (unprocessed, whole) state and once they've been changed somehow (processed).
- Differences can include nutrition, amount of additives and preservatives, and quantities of sugar, salt, and fat.
- The Nutrition Facts label and ingredients list on a food package can help you learn how processed or how healthful it is.

Background

". . . it is a fair generality that the more a food is processed, the fewer nutrients it contains. Processing has this overall degrading effect because it eliminates vitamins and minerals—by removal as in refining, or by destruction as in high-heat processing—and because it dilutes the remaining nutrients by adding cheap fillers: water, fats, starches, sugars."[1]
—Joan Gussow, Professor Emeritus, Columbia Teacher's College, New York, NY

For centuries humans have processed food through methods such as cooking, milling, pounding, salting, smoking, canning, drying and freezing. There are pros and cons to any method. Modern methods of producing food often rely on processing techniques such as oil refining, high heat treatment, and high-volume grain refining that reduce important minerals, fiber, vitamins, and flavor in our food supply. Some foods are enriched or fortified to replace or add nutrients. Many modern processed foods have altered nutritional value compared to their "whole" counterparts. Processed foods require increased packaging, and the food processing industry is among the nation's renowned polluters.[2] Yet consumers routinely choose processed foods because they find them easier to prepare, readily available, they can be eaten in any season, they do not necessarily need refrigeration, and they can be transported around the globe. (That's why they are called convenience foods!) Such products are usually heavily advertised.

Sound nutrition depends on a foundation of whole foods—ones that come directly from nature

1 "Agriculture, Food and Nutrition" by Joan Dye Gussow, in *Progress as If Survival Mattered* (as excerpted in *Earthfriends* manual).
2 P2Rx The Pollution Prevention Resource Exchange is a national network of regional information centers dedicated to improving the dissemination of pollution prevention information www.p2rx.org/

without undue processing (such as grains, beans, nuts, seeds, fruits, vegetables, meats, poultry, fish, some dairy products, and herbs). These foods contain no *added* preservatives, artificial colors or flavors, refined sweeteners, oils, or synthetic substances. Yet even whole foods may be affected by the widespread use of pesticides, fertilizers, or antibiotics. For these concerns and more, some people choose foods that are grown organically or sustainably. Eating whole foods can improve our nutrition, since they are naturally free of additives. Eating whole foods can also minimize the negative environmental impact we have, since whole foods tend to have less packaging, less processing, and fewer travel miles.

Note: Students should already be familiar with the food pyramid. Also, in reviewing labels with students, note that the serving size on the package may vary considerably from what you'd consider a normal portion size. (See Read the Small Print, page 67.) The Percent Daily Values listed on the label do not always relate to children's calorie needs (about 1,800 calories for a typical 4-6-year-old, and approximately 2,000 for an average 7-10-year-old).

What You'll Need

Overhead transparency of Nutrition Facts/ingredient label; have students bring in clean discarded labels or packages (with nutritional information) from food items containing oranges or tomatoes (concentrated orange juice, orange soda, and ketchup if you want to use the chart). For additional study use labels from cereal, crackers, snack foods (including "fruit" snacks), bread, luncheon meats, margarine, juice, whole grain cereals, fruits, vegetables, meats, and milk; food guide pyramids with foods listed; Center for Science in the Public Interest's food additive information or other food additive source (see Bibliography).

The number of individuals and families eating meals away from the home grows annually. Families now spend fifty cents of every dollar on foods eaten out, up from twenty-nine cents in 1970. Unfortunately, that translates into poor nutrition and correlates with rising rates of overweight Americans. Are convenient foods the culprit?*

Teacher Tip:

Bring in an orange and tomato as well as nutrition labels (or containers) from various orange and tomato products to help present the whole foods and processed foods concept.

If you consider fresh fruit, packaged in nature's container with no preparation necessary, one could qualify it as the original "convenience food." Often, the more processed a convenience food is, the higher its price and the lower its food value.

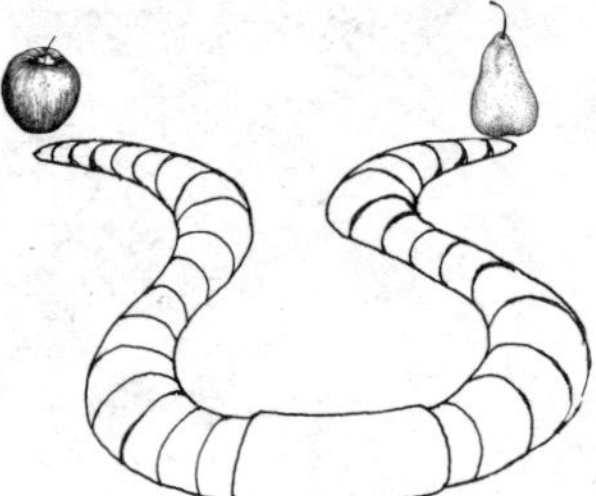

How to Do It

Begin by asking students, in their own words, to state the differences between, for example, an orange and various processed orange products; a tomato and various processed tomato products. (You could do this activity with many different foods.) Brainstorm a name and definition for these various classes of foods. ("Whole foods" or "natural foods" are ways that unprocessed foods are often described. Processed foods contain one or more "whole foods" that are altered in some way and may contain additives, preservatives, dyes, etc.) Have students think of more ways oranges and tomatoes are processed and make a list. Explain that all foods fall somewhere along a spectrum from no or low (minimal) processing all the way to totally processed with no original food contained in the product. Have them arrange the orange or tomato and the associated processed foods listed on a no/low processing to totally processed scale. Discuss what criteria they used to place the foods.

Next, see the nutrient information chart below (more information in Appendix). Have students fill in the blank categories, using package Nutrition Facts labels, and compare with other processed foods that contain oranges or tomatoes. Use nutrition labels from other foods the students brought in to make similar charts—starting with a basic whole food. (i.e., the grain, vegetable, fruit)

* University of Arkansas Division of Agriculture, Cooperative Extension Service.

Then, ask: What do students notice about minimally v. highly processed foods in terms of nutrition? What are the pros and cons for eating the different kinds of foods? How does convenience fit into the equation? Discuss how whole foods help the body to build and maintain health, growth, energy, and stamina, and increase attention for learning. Create graphs based on the charts that visually compare the nutrient amounts. Encourage students to brainstorm ways to consume a variety of fruits and vegetables, preferably at least five servings a day with minimal to no processing.

Classroom Conversations

- Examine the completed chart(s). Ask the students: What do you think about the numbers? If you were trying to eat a high salt (sodium) diet (probably not wise, but what if . . .) based on the chart, what would you choose to eat? If you needed to reduce calories in your diet, what foods would be a good choice for you? If you needed vitamin C? Continue with similar questions on other nutrients.
- Are whole foods available in all communities? What about kids who have access only to lesser quality, processed foods instead of fresh produce or "whole foods"?
- What about communities whose stores do not sell fresh produce or "whole foods"?

Want to Do More?

- Invite students to survey the food in their home kitchens, counting the number of products that contain the top two food additives (sugar and sodium). Explain the variety of names by which sugar appears (dextrose, maltodextrin, high fructose or regular corn syrup, sucrose, cane juice, etc.).
- Taste-test products made with whole grain ingredients such as breads, crackers, pasta, and other snack items.
- Make a display showing the amounts of sugar, sodium, and/or fat in common foods. Post near cafeteria.
- Have students research some common additives or newly created food substances (such as "Olestra" or "Quorn"). Have students invent their own additives along with functions they would add to future foods.

Lesson Links

French Fries and Couch Potatoes
Read the Small Print
Dear Diary lessons
Sugar Detectives
What If All I Ate Were Potato Chips?
Dollars and $ense
Global Staff of Life

Did you know that supermarkets have more shelf space filled with snacks than with fresh produce?

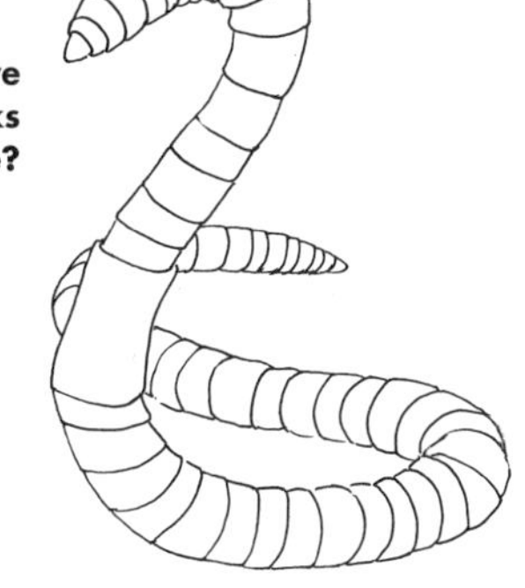

Literature Links

Good Enough to Eat: A Kid's Guide to Food & Nutrition by Lizzy Rockwell
The Sacred Harvest: The Ojibway Wild Rice Gathering by Gordon Regguinti
A Kid's Guide to: How Flowers Grow; How Vegetables Grow; How Fruits Grow; How Herbs Grow; How Plants Grow; How Trees Grow, all by Patricia Ayers
Fiber by Jane Inglis
Eat Up! Healthy Food for a Healthy Earth by Candace Savage
Oliver's Vegetables by Vivian French

Resources

- Center for Science in the Public Interest's *Healthy Eating Pyramid;* www.cspinet.org
- For nutrient composition data, see USDA's Nutrient Data Laboratory www.nal.usda.gov/fnic/foodcomp/search/
- Local life skills or family and consumer science teacher, or USDA Cooperative Extension educator for nutrient information.
- See *Bowes & Church's Food Values of Portions Commonly Used*, 18th ed. by Jean A. T. Pennington and Judith S. Douglass. Lippincott,

Williams & Wilkins, 2004, a nutrient reference guide for commonly eaten foods.

- *The Food System: Building Youth Awareness through Involvement* by Alison Harmon, Penn State College of Agricultural Sciences, 1999.

Benchmarks

The Human Organism: 6E—Physical Health, p. 144

Grades K-2

"Children should explore ways in which good health can be promoted."

Grades 3-5

"Food provides energy and materials for growth and repair of body parts. Vitamins and minerals, present in small amounts in foods, are essential to keep everything working well."

TOMATOES: From Seed to Soup & ORANGES: From Grove to Grocery

Comparing various tomato and orange products for for calories, total fat, carbohydrate, and sodium

Product	Energy, in calories	Total fat, in grams	Carbohydrates, g	Sodium, mg.
Tomatoes, 1 large, whole, ripe	38.2	0.6	8.4	16.4
Canned tomato sauce 1 cup	78.1	0.9	17.6	1,482
Canned tomato soup, made with water, 1 cup	85.4	1.9	16.5	695.4
Ketchup, 1 tablespoon	____	____	____	____
Other processed tomato products?	____	____	____	____
Orange, raw 1 fruit (2 5/8" dia.)	61.6	0.2	15.4	0.0
Orange juice, from frozen concentrate, 1 cup	____	____	____	____
Carbonated orange soda 1 can or bottle	____	____	____	____

HAVE STUDENTS FILL IN THE BLANKS

Handout from *Healthy Foods from Healthy Soils* by Elizabeth Patten and Kathy Lyons, Tilbury House, Publishers.

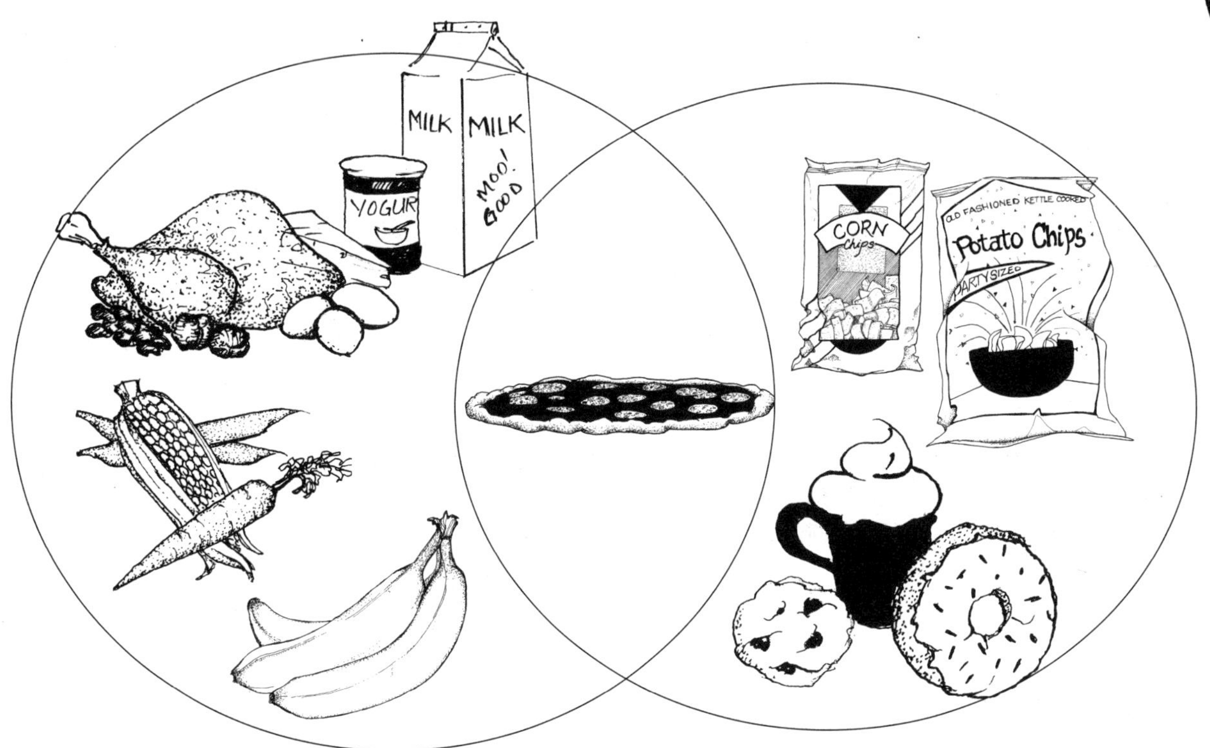

Pick a Food, Any Food

Classify a "typical" diet using a Venn diagram

Recommended Grades: K–6

- **Language Arts**
- **Health**

Goals

Use a common math tool to reinforce healthful food selections and to help make nutritious food choices. This activity is a hands-on introduction to classifying foods according to what they do to promote healthy growth.

Key Point

- Foods can be grouped by how well they help our bodies to grow and stay healthy: those to be eaten anytime, sometimes, or seldom.

Background

This activity uses Venn diagrams—a mathematical tool that relies on intersecting circles to help with sorting and classifying.

What You'll Need

Yarn of different colors for two or three approximately 24-inch-diameter (minimum) circles, or a sheet with overlapping circles drawn on it, or two hula hoops (additional circles may be needed with large classes); paper food models (enough for all students) depicting food from all food groups—available from the National Dairy Council (or you can use pictures of food from magazines, photos, or names of food written on cards); paper grocery bag; and the Center for Science in the Public Interest's *Healthy Eating Pyramid*. You'll find resource details in the Bibliography under Nutrition Sources.

How to Do It

In preparation for this lesson, review materials on the food pyramid. The Venn model can be made on the floor with yarn circles or two large circles drawn on a sheet—the larger the better. If you have a choice, use green and red for the circle colors and designate the intersecting area yellow.

Begin by reviewing with students what all creatures need to live (water, food, oxygen, shelter, space, TLC). Explain that the class will use a large Venn diagram to explore nutritious choices for humans. Lay out overlapping circles on the floor and have children sit around them. Depending on the size of the group, the class may need to be in sections, with a set of Venn circles for each group.

Explain that one (GREEN) circle is for foods that help you grow, ones you could eat anytime. The other (RED) circle is for foods that are best eaten seldom.The space that is created by the green and red circles overlapping is (YELLOW if you can draw it that way) for foods that are good for you if eaten sometimes.

Next, you may want to define, with students' help, what anytime, sometimes, and seldom mean for food choices. Depending on students' familiarity with food pyramids, ask them to which food groups items belong. Don't forget to include water as a beverage that *should* be consumed *all* the time.

Then, have students, in random order, select a "food" from the bag, show it to the class, identify it, and place it in whichever part of the circles they feel is appropriate. Ask them not to look at the foods in advance and encourage them to make independent decisions without help from their neighbors. Reinforce questions as students pick paper food models from the grocery bag: Would this food help us to grow? Would it give us energy? Does it have a lot of sweets or fats? Is it a food we could eat anytime? Sometimes? Seldom?

Classroom Conversations

- When all the foods have been placed face up in the circles, ask if there are any changes that students would recommend making. If so, have them explain why.
- Were there any foods that were hard to place? Why?

Want to Do More?

- Have students make posters with good eating tips to put up in their homes.
- Ask students to identify foods they eat routinely (in their lunches/snacks) to see in which anytime, sometime, seldom food group they'd fit.
- If you're familiar with vermicomposting, make the green circle be foods that are healthful for humans, the red circle would apply to what foods the redworms like, and the overlapping area in the middle would represent foods that are good for both humans and worms. The area outside of the two intersecting circles would be for "seldom" foods—ones that would not be considered nutritious for either humans or worms.

Lesson Links

Sugar Detectives
What If All I Ate Were Potato Chips?
The Global Staff of Life
Bark and Seeds for Breakfast
Pyramids Near You
What Are "Whole Foods"?

Literature Links

Health Matters: Food and Your Health by Jillian Powell

Food Rules! What You Munch, Its Punch, Its Crunch, and Why Sometimes You Lose Your Lunch by Bill Haduch

Down the Hatch: Find Out About Your Food by Mike Lambourne

The Healthy Body Cookbook: Over 50 Fun Activities and Recipes for Kids by Joan D'Amico

Resources

- Paper food models #0012N with leader guide (created by the National Dairy Council). Go through the national office to locate an affiliate near you. 847-803-2000; www.nationaldairycouncil.org
- Send home the reproducible snack handout: www.fns.usda.gov/tn/Educators/yrslf07.pdf
- *We Are What We Eat: Ethnic Food and the Making of Americans* by Donna Gabaccia, Harvard University Press, 2000.
- The USDA has an extensive listing of resources about nutrition issues and different ethnic groups in the U.S.: www.nal.usda.gov/fnic/pubs/bibs/gen/ethnic.html and click on ethnic and cultural food pyramids.
- CSPI Center for Science in the Public Interest's

Healthy Eating Pyramid for classification of anytime, sometimes, and seldom foods. www.cspinet.org

Benchmarks

The Human Organism: 6E—Physical Health, p. 144

Grades K-2

"Eating a variety of healthful foods and getting enough exercise and rest can help people to stay healthy."

Grades 3-5

"Food provides energy and materials for growth and repair of body parts. Vitamins and minerals, present in small amounts in foods, are essential to keep everything working well."

Grades 6-8

"The amount of food energy (calories) a person requires varies with body weight, age, sex, activity level, and natural body efficiency."

Common Themes: IIB—Models, p. 268

Grades 3-5

". . . diagrams . . . can be used to represent objects, events, and processes in the real world. . . ."

Who Am I? Game

What You'll Need

Paper or fabric food model cards (see Resources) or photos of foods; tape.

Note: This activity is simple to do and needs very little teacher involvement. It can be interrupted for "teachable moments" and is easy to start back up again. You may use the suggested rules or invent your own, depending on the class—the degree of difficulty can be varied according to how unusual the foods are and how in-depth your questions are. The object of the game is for participants to figure out what food image is on their backs—what food they represent by the card they wear—by guessing some of the food's traits such as food group, color, texture, plant part, etc. ("Am I green?")

How to Do It

1. Describe the game of "Twenty Questions": you pose questions that can be answered only by *Yes* or *No.* No cheating! Have someone pin or tape a food model (cloth or paper or drawn by students) on your back, without you knowing what it is.
2. Ask other classmates at least five questions before making your first guess.
3. If your guess is incorrect, ask three more questions.
4. When you guess correctly, remove the card from your back and put it on your front.
5. Once you've determined what food you are, answer these questions (have these listed on the board):

- Where does it fit in the food pyramid? (If applicable, why?)
- Is this an anytime food, a sometimes food, or an seldom food?
- Would it help me to grow and be strong? Why? Do you know any of the nutrients in the food?
- Where does this food come from? Is it grown locally or in this state? Have you grown it before? Do you know what plant part it is or comes from?
- Can you think of a way to eat or prepare this food?
- If you're composting in the classroom or outdoors, is this a food worms would like to eat?

Variations

- Pull food photos or models out of a grocery bag to make the "food" idea more realistic.
- Have the teacher "be" the food and thus the class asks the questions.
- Have participants work in pairs doing the game. Then switch to other foods from other partners, always keeping them hidden from one another.
- Try having one participant know the food and others ask him/her questions.
- Make it a game with contestants, and time how long it takes for a person or group to determine the "mystery food."

Action

Prepare a recipe using the select foods that people have "discovered" through this game. Make it as a snack in class, or create recipe cards to take home.

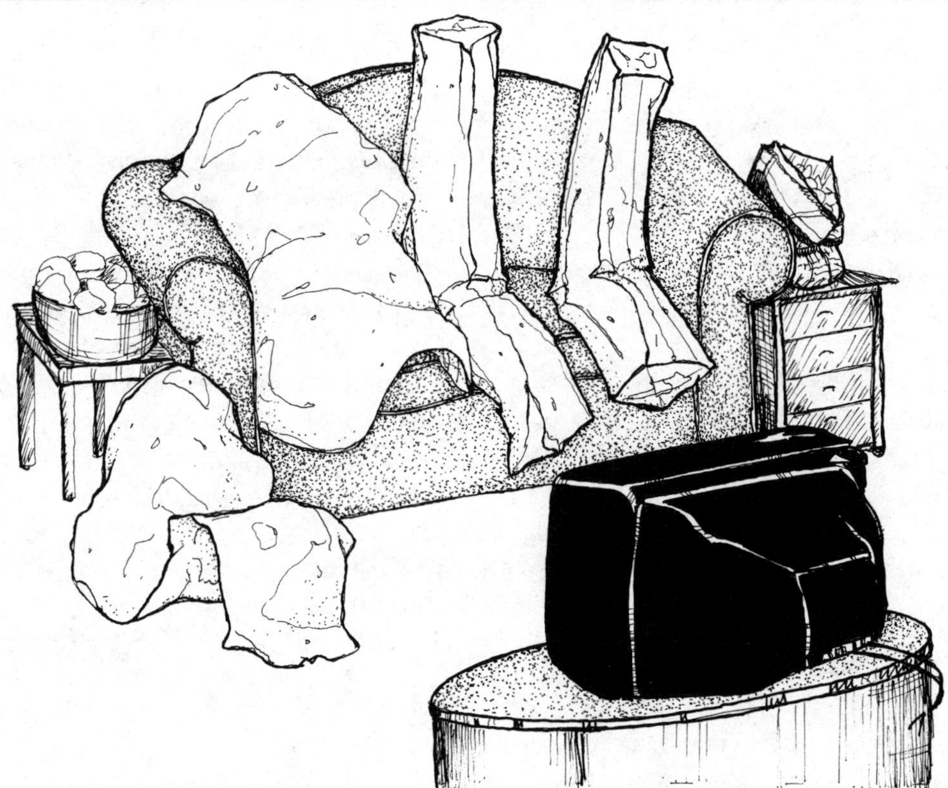

French Fries and Couch Potatoes[1]

Analyze television's influence on food choices

Recommended Grades: 3–6

- **Language Arts**
- **Social Studies**
- **Health**
- **Math**
- **Life Skills**

Goal

Being able to think critically about the role of advertising will help us evaluate our buying habits.

Key Points

- Television is a powerful sales tool to children.
- Ads played during prime time (for children) often sell unhealthful foods and drinks.
- Careful watching, listening, and reading of the media helps us learn about selling tactics.
- We can have an effect on TV and media advertisers by our actions: "To buy or not to buy?" (That IS the question.)

Background

TV is the major source of consumers' nutrition and health information, and advertisements are a fact of everyday life, coming at us from many directions, not only TV, but also radio, printed and electronic media, in-school clubs or promotions (even textbooks!), sporting events, movies, clothing, vending machines, and signs. Advertisers target children with gimmicks such as "free" merchandise, snazzy music, colorful popular theme characters, and/or celebrities. The average child sees more than 40,000 commercials each year during 1,460 hours of TV viewing.[2]

Dr. Michael Jacobson of the Center for Science in the Public Interest (CSPI) states: "Consistently, experts have found that kids who watch the most TV have the worst diets and the lowest levels of nutritional knowledge."[3] According to a National Science Foundation report, "Research has shown

1 Concept adapted with permission from *How to Teach Nutrition to Kids* by Connie Liakos Evers, 24 Carrot Press, 2006.
2 The Center for Science in the Public Interest; Washington, DC, and www.tvturnoff.org and American Academy of Pediatrics: "Television—How It Affects Children."
3 *What Are We Feeding Our Kids?* by Michael Jacobson and Bruce Maxwell, Workman Publishing, 1994.

primary negative health effects from television viewing on nutrition, dieting, and obesity."[1] CSPI states that 65 percent of commercials during that "prime kid time" are food-related, and 96 percent of those ads are for non-nutritious (read "junk") foods.[2]

Excess "junk" foods combined with a passive lifestyle lead to obesity and/or ill health, which can lead to poor self-esteem. Some experts say that there are no "good" and "junk" foods—that it's only the totality of the diet that matters. We respectfully disagree. Indeed, children do need to learn that while there are many different types of food available, they should not all be given equal weight in terms of a healthy diet. The sheer amount of foods from the "extras" part of the pyramid that are so commonly available and promoted in ever-increasing portions, combined with the increasing rates of childhood obesity, are indicators that we need to acknowledge that this approach of "all foods fit" has not been successful. Exercise is also crucial, of course.

Note: This is a two-part class which begins with a homework assignment, followed by a class discussion and graphing of data. For the initial assignment, ask students to define "media" and watch at least one hour of children's programming on Saturday morning (excluding public television). Send home a letter inviting parents to participate in the television study.

What You'll Need

TV or other media (printed or electronic); stop watch or timer; worksheet.

How to Do It

Begin by explaining their TV-viewing assignment: to become more media-savvy (to think about why ads are trying to sell us certain products), they will observe one hour of commercial children's TV on Saturday. Based on what they know about nutrition, ask them to estimate whether the food in commercials they see advertised are mostly healthful or not. Guide students in developing criteria, such as: Is the food in one of the five healthy food groups? Is it moderate in fat and sugar? Is it primarily "fats, oils, and sweets"—from the "extras" part of the pyramid? Have them make a note whether there were any public service announcements or "ads" that promoted healthful eating. Have students brainstorm a checklist or use sample provided.

Next, before they embark on their assignment, ask them to also keep in mind some of these other advertising techniques: What sound effects or music does the commercial use to make it more exciting? How do the actors using the product look? Do you think that if you consumed the product that you would be happier or more popular? If there are celebrities in the commercial, do you think the celebrity really uses the product?

Finally, using a worksheet they've created themselves (or the following one as a guide), have students record the number of food commercials they see and categorize them according to the criteria they chose.

Classroom Conversations

Following the TV-watching assignment:

- What are most of the ads for?
- What ads appealed to you most and why?
- What were the advertisers selling beyond the food (that is, what images did they use to spark your desire for that product)?
- What were some specific techniques that advertisers used?
- Will you make your food choices based on what you saw, or ask your families to buy these foods?
- Did any ads, promote healthy eating or a healthy, active lifestyle?
- What if you ate only the foods and drinks that were advertised on TV?

The food industry spends over $26 billion per year on marketing its products. McDonald's alone spends $1 billion for advertising and promotion which is 1,000 times the budget the 5-A-Day nutrition education campaign ($1 million). It's no wonder the big advertisers get more attention than the healthy messages!

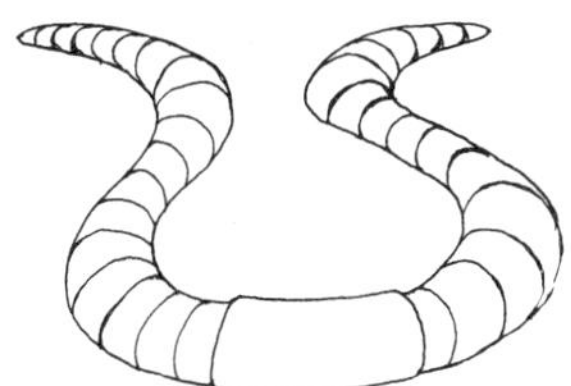

1 American Academy of Pediatrics, 2001.
2 The Center for Science in the Public Interest, Washington, DC.

- Review some of their other observations: What sound effects or music were used? How did the actors appear?
- Would buying the product make you happier or more popular? Did you think the celebrity really used the product?
- How would you describe the people in the commercials? Are they representative of the people we know?
- What other aspects of ads don't reflect real life?
- Were there any promotions for physical activity?

Actions

- Use the advertisers' tools to your advantage. Form your own advertising company. Create commercials as well as slogans, logos, storyboards, or videos for a healthy food or drink.
- Come up with an invigorating antidote to sitting in front of the TV becoming a couch potato—a short walk or exercise routine that gets physical activity into every day. Promote the activity through a local-access cable station or demonstrate to younger students during an assembly or physical education class (arranged with the help of the physical education teacher).
- Videotape your commercial to show to other students, along with TV "study" results. Try the commercial out on students during a school assembly.
- Write to a food company or television network to show the results of your informal "study" and to express your opinion about what you'd like to see instead: for example—ads promoting more healthful foods; fewer food ads and marketing aimed at children; examination of sponsorship of scholastic activities and professional nutrition organizations linked to product promotion.

Want to Do More?

- Ask students to count the number of advertisements they encounter in school throughout one day on all the possible media (clothing, signs, vending machines, vehicles, posters, publications, etc.). Make a chart and discuss their findings and impressions.
- A good way to begin evaluating food advertising messages is to point out products in television and magazine ads, and ask students to describe the similarities and differences.
- While discussing the ads, ask: What methods (e.g., animation, music, bright colors, or celebrities) do the manufacturers use to sell their products?
- How do these methods affect students' thoughts on these products? Do the props make the products more interesting to them?
- What is the message? (e.g., You'll be stronger, smarter, have more fun if you eat/drink the product.) Do students believe it?
- A product's packaging is another way to draw attention to the product. Have your children examine an apple then ask them to look at the packaging, or labels, on apple juice, apple "snacks," applesauce, or apple pie.
- Ask them to explain the similarities and differences between each product, as well as what they find attractive.

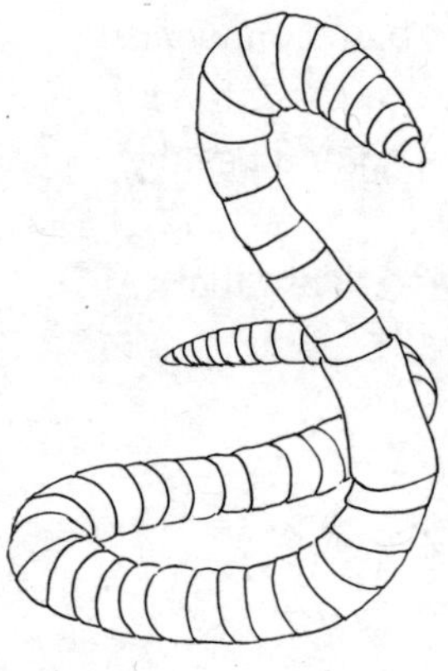

Surveys have shown that children's favorite brands remain favorites into adulthood—advertising promotes brand loyalty. Where are the ads for carrots? We rarely see enticing commercials for whole grains, fresh fruits, or vegetables. What do we all pay for convenience?

Ad Outing

Look beyond the television for advertisements in the real world. Take a pen and paper and go on an outing with your students. Make a list of all the different advertisements you see, such as billboards, logos, advertising on cars, in bus shelters, etc. Talk about the companies behind these advertisements and what they are trying to sell.

Lesson Links

Pick a Food, Any Food
Read the Small Print
Sugar Detectives

Literature Links

Junk Food, Fast Food, Health Food: What America Eats and Why by Lila Perl
Advertising: Information or Manipulation? (Issues in Focus) by Nancy Day
Arthur's TV Trouble by Marc Tolon Brown
Media Wizards: A Behind-the-Scenes Look at Media Manipulations by Catherine Gourley

Resources

- *How to Teach Nutrition to Kids* by Connie Liakos Evers. 24 Carrot Press, 2006; for additional related activities.
- *What Are We Feeding Our Kids?* by Michael Jacobson and Bruce Maxwell, Workman Publishing, 1994.
- TV-Turnoff Network, formerly TV-Free America, is a nonprofit organization that encourages children and adults to watch much less television in order to promote healthier lives and communities. www.tvturnoff.org/
- The Center for Research on the Effects of TV: www.ithaca.edu/cretv/research/tv_lives.html for information and related links.
- Commercial Alert, a nonprofit organization that helps families, schools, and communities defend themselves against commercialism, advertising, and marketing. www.commercialalert.org/ 4110 SE Hawthorne Blvd. #123, Portland, OR 97214.
- Food origins, from tea to potato chips! This site links visitors to information about the origins of many of the most popular foods we eat: www.asiarecipe.com/foodline.html

Benchmarks

Habits of Mind: 12A—Values and Attitudes, p. 286

Grades 3-5

"Keep records of their investigations and observations and not change the records later."

"Offer reasons for their findings and consider reasons suggested by others."

Grades 6-8

"Know why it is important in science to keep honest, clear, and accurate records."

"Know that different results can be given for the same evidence, and it is not always possible to tell which one is correct."

Habits of Mind: 12C—Manipulation and Observations, p. 293

Grades 3-5

"Keep a notebook that describes observations made, carefully distinguishes actual observations from ideas and speculations about what was observed, and is understandable weeks or months later."

Habits of Mind: 12D—Communication Skills, p. 296

Grades 3-5

"Use numerical data in describing and comparing objects and events."

Your Name ____________________

Add Up the Ads![1]

Your assignment: Watch about one hour of TV on Saturday morning. Every time you see a food ad, put a mark beside the food that is being sold.

Channel__________

Time__________

TYPES	
Fast food	
Soda	
Sweetened drinks (not 100% juice)	
Sweetened cereal	
Chips—corn, potato, other fried snack foods	
Cakes, cookies or pastries	
Sweetened fruit snacks	
Candy or other sweetened foods	
Combination meals (such as pizza)	
FOOD GROUPS Grains	
Fruits	
Vegetables	
Protein	
Dairy	
Extras	
OTHERS Public service announcement (promotes good nutrition or physical activity))	

How many total for healthy foods? ________

How many total for non-healthy foods? ________

TOTAL number of food advertisements: ________

Did any ads promote physical exercise? ________

Even sitting and reading or talking with friends burns about 35 calories more per hour than watching TV does!

Think of some physical activity you would like to do today. ____________________

1 Adapted with permission from *How to Teach Nutrition to Kids* by Connie Liakos Evers, 24 Carrot Press, 1995.

Sugar Detectives

Find the sources of hidden sugar in a common foods

Recommended Grades: 2–6
- **Math**
- **Science**
- **Health**

Goals

Many of us are not aware of the quantities of added sugar that are part of the foods we buy and consume. Track the sugar in our diets to make healthier choices.

Key Points

- Sugar is a common (and sometimes hidden) additive.
- When eaten too often or in large amounts, sugar can harm our bodies.

Background

It might surprise some children to learn that sugar comes originally from plants such as sugar cane or sugar beets; the plants make sugar and store it in their roots, stems, or trunks. The average American consumes the equivalent of a five-pound bag of sugar every two weeks—in the form of sucrose, honey, high-fructose corn syrup, molasses, and white and brown sugars, not including artificial sweeteners. Less well-known forms may be labeled: cane sugar, dextrose, fructose, lactose, maltose, mannose, sorbose, xylose, etc. While we have doubled our sugar intake during the last hundred years, the use of household sugar has dropped 50 percent. What accounts for this paradox? Large quantities of sugar are added to processed foods (such as baked goods and breakfast cereals). One-quarter of our sugar intake now comes from soft drinks. According to a recent USDA survey, some adolescents drink the equivalent of 870 twelve-ounce (over 80 gallons) sodas annually, with each drink averaging 10 teaspoons of sugar—coincidentally the maximum amount of sugar the USDA recommends we consume daily. Is there a problem with this?

The connection between sugar consumption and tooth decay is well documented. The phosphoric acid in soda causes tooth enamel to wear down so the sugar and bacteria can create cavities. Sugar also aggravates diabetes and certain forms of heart disease. In the body, sugar releases insulin and increases appetite, leading to "unconscious eating," or consumption based on "wants" rather than "needs." Sugar provides only energy—no nutrients other than calories.

Ways to reduce sugar consumption include: careful label reading when buying food; cutting the

Drinking just one can of soda every other day contributes enough calories to add about four pounds in a year!

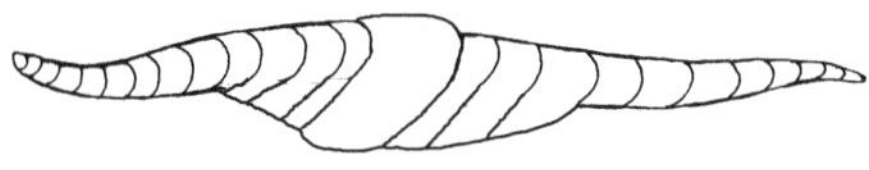

sugar levels in recipes by half; quenching thirst with plain water, juice, and non- or low-fat milk in place of soft drinks.

What You'll Need

Packages of foods from students' homes; pictures, illustrations, or actual foods taken from chart below (no nutrient labels showing); sets of measuring spoons (1/8, 1/4, 1/2 tsp., and Tbs.); sugar (granules or cubes); paper plates (or recycled lids from plastic food containers) or cafeteria trays; one can of regular soda; tooth from a student (or use a rusty nail or dull penny if need be); small transparent plastic or glass cups; labeling marker.

Note: Invite a dental hygienist to provide a class presentation—in some areas, these health presentations are paid for with state health education monies.

Getting Ready

Set up sweet stations. Refer to label reading lesson, Read the Small Print.

How to Do It

Begin by dividing the class into three groups, each of which will go to one of the following workstations: (one) for estimating teaspoons of sugar in common foods; (two) an experiment to determine effect of soda on tooth enamel and other substances; and (three) an examination of how many grams of sugar are in common packaged foods from their homes. *Note:* For simplicity, you may choose to do only one of the three stations, or to do them over a period of class sessions. Note that #3 is a long-term experiment.

- Station One: Students will try to match the correct amount of sugar with the actual product. Show them (a) the list below (or photos of foods or the actual foods themselves) but with the list of teaspoons of sugar on a separate card (in a different order). Their job is to match the food to the average amount of sugar in that food. Do as a group and try to get the group to agree on amounts before they discover the right answer. Then, using measuring spoons or sugar cubes, show how much sugar is in each food. Use as a display for the classroom.

Sample Chart for Station One

Food Serving	Teaspoons of Sugar (average)
Chocolate Bar (2 ounces)	7
Chewing Gum (1 stick)	1/2
Chocolate Cake (with frosting)	15
Soda (1 can) 12 fluid oz.	10
Breakfast Cereal (1/2 cup, brand dependent)	2–3

- Station Two: Students will examine the food labels of common foods from their homes and assess how many teaspoons of sugar are in each serving. Since each teaspoon of sugar represents about four grams of carbohydrate in the form of a simple sugar (glucose or dextrose), then each 1/4 teaspoon of sugar is one gram. Have them make a chart or graph—assign one person to measure, one to record, one to report, etc. They will share results with the whole class at the end of the activity.
- Station Three: This activity will take several weeks to get final results. Use a can of regular soda. Set up an experiment to see what happens over time to a tooth, a penny, and a rusty nail in the soda. (For the tooth experiment, put some saliva in the container along with the soda to provide bacteria for tooth decay.) Assign tasks to group members: recorder, daily monitor, presenter, etc. Ask: What will happen? How much time will it take? Have them do estimates and write up the experiment. Check it daily until results are reached. They will report to the entire class when finished. (Take "before" and "after" photos for dramatic effect.)

Next, have students spend time at each activity; do not rotate from station to station.

Classroom Conversations

Once students are all together, have each group's designated spokesperson present what his or her group did during its activities.

- Discuss as a class. Were there any surprises? Did you find sugar in products you didn't expect it to be? Why would a company put sugar in that product?
- If there are habitual soda drinkers in the class, how much sugar might s/he consume in one

year? What would be the effect on their teeth?

- Are the effects the same for diet soda?(Diet soft drinks have fewer calories but their acid levels still damage teeth, and drinking any type of soda, especially caffeinated ones, displaces healthier choices—thereby increasing osteoporosis and other health risks. Foods and drinks containing artificial sweeteners such as aspartame (Nutrasweet) are not recommended because the long-term health effects remain unknown.)

Actions

- Have students prepare, print and illustrate a colorful and appealing chart of "Sweet Substitutions." For example, in one column, list or show soda, in the opposite column, list or show healthier substitutions. Check chart with the school's Food Services director when finished, then have students brainstorm the best location to post—in the cafeteria, at local businesses, at a hospital or health care facility, at a dentist's office, etc.
- In many communities, soft drink companies are providing school equipment in exchange for advertising in the schools. Debate the pros and cons of doing this. What would you do in your school? Let your school board or local school administrators know what you think.

Want to Do More?

- Make a video advertisement with reasons to eat less sugar as a promotional message.
- Make bar graphs showing amounts of sugar and fiber in some of your class's favorite brands of breakfast cereal. Before you display your graphs, ask others (such as your family) to estimate which cereals they think would have the most and least sugar and fiber, then show them how their estimates match with reality.
- Look at the amount of packaging used for a typical box of cereal. Can any of the box or bag material be reused, recycled, or composted? (See the Recycled Art lesson on page 143.)
- Research where sweeteners are grown and/or produced. Learn about sweeteners other than sugar: honey, maple sugar and a variety of alternatives found in grocery stores and health food stores. (Stevia is an example of a recently popularized alternative sweetener.) How are these sweeteners the same or different from sugar? (For example, forms of sugar such as maple syrup, honey, molasses, or rice syrup are absorbed in the body similarly to other more processed forms of sugar, but may contain varying amounts of nutrients such as iron, some B vitamins, calcium and magnesium.)

Lesson Links

Read the Small Print
Anatomy in Action
Taste Buds Rule

Literature Links

Mr. Sugar Comes to Town/La visita del Sr. Azucar by Harriet Rohmer
Sugar by Elaine Landau
Food Rules! What You Munch, Its Punch, Its Crunch, and Why Sometimes You Lose Your Lunch by Bill Haduch
Sugars by Rhoda Nottridge
Ininatig's Gift of Sugar: Traditional Native Sugarmaking by Laura Wittstock
Raising Cane: The World of Plantation Hawaii by Ronald Takaki

Resources

- Ask your school's Food Services director for assistance with set up, nutritional advice or dietary guidelines materials.
- Ask a local dentist's office for help with material on tooth decay, or a hygienist willing to do a presentation.
- *Good for Me! All about Food in 32 Bites* by Marilyn Burns, Econo-Clad Books, 1999, is an updated resource with fun facts and activities that teach about nutrition and food.
- Center for Science in the Public Interest (CSPI) website for resources and labeling information about sugars, fats, and salt; www.cspinet.org (Ask about their *Healthy Eating Pyramid*.)

Benchmarks

The Nature of Science: 1B—Scientific Inquiry, pp. 10-11

Grades K-2

"People can often learn about things around them by just observing those things carefully, but sometimes they can learn more by doing something to the things and noting what happens."

Grades 3-5

"Scientific investigations may take many different forms, including observing what things are like or what is happening somewhere . . . and doing experiments. Investigations can focus on physical, biological, and social questions."

The Human Organism; 6E—Physical Health, pp. 144-45

Grades K-2

The background section states, "Children should learn how to keep healthy, although they may not understand why certain diets . . . help."

Grades 3-5

The background section states, "Children should explore ways in which good health can be promoted.

Grades 6-8

The background section states, "Students should extend their study of the healthy functioning of the human body and ways it may be promoted or disrupted by diet."

The Mathematical World: 9A—Numbers, p. 211

Grades K-2

"Numbers can be used to count things, place them in order, or name them."

"It is possible (and often useful) to estimate quantities without knowing them exactly."

Grades 3-5

The background section states, ". . . if students are to learn about the meaning of numbers and to use them properly, much of what they do must be based on solving problems in which the answers matter and the numbers used are measured quantities."

"When people care about what is being counted or measured, it is important for them to say what the units are. . . ."

Habits of Mind: 12B—Computation and Estimation, pp. 290-91

Grades K-2

"Use whole numbers . . . in ordering, counting, identifying, measuring, and describing things. . . ."

Habits of Mind: 12D—Communication Skills, p. 296

Grades 3-5

"Use numerical data in describing and comparing objects and events."

Grades 6-8

"Organize information in simple tables and graphs and identify relationships they reveal."

What If ALL I Ate Were POTATO CHIPS?

Examine the consequences of food choices in a "typical" diet

Recommended Grades: 4–6
- **Math**
- **Science**
- **Health**

Goals

Understand the benefits of a variety in the diet. Brainstorm a list of nutritious snacks and create a health-promoting exhibit.

Key Points

- All of our actions have "logical consequences," including what we choose to eat.
- Eating a variety of foods makes us healthier.

Background

We'll look at a "typical" food pattern for a modern child living in the United States, and what can happen if unhealthful childhood food choices grow into a lifetime of poor eating habits.

Sometimes we aren't motivated to make changes in our behavior until something significant happens—here, students look at some consequences of eating poorly and decide if they want to make any changes. This is another look at "What if . . . ?" What are the consequences of eating in extremes, as many people do? Common examples of extreme eating are liquid diets, many weight-loss diets, or an all-junk-food diet.

This class is not intended to instill fear of certain foods but to demonstrate the long-term consequences of actions that may appear innocuous in the short term. You can emphasize that incorporating foods from the "extras" of the pyramid is okay SOME of the time. Also, the word "diet," by itself, is intended here to mean a way of eating— in this case it does not connote a weight-loss regimen.

What You'll Need

Favorite snack foods of several students (choose at least one that is sugary and one that is fatty/greasy); Center for Science in the Public Interest (CSPI) *Healthy Eating Pyramid* (with foods grouped according to how often to eat: anytime, sometimes, or seldom); photos or websites with images of bad dental caries and clogged arteries (ask at local physician's and/or dentist's office, or at nearest American Heart Association affiliate).

How to Do It

Begin by discussing definitions of moderation and variety. List synonyms and antonyms on the board. Talk about extremes in eating patterns (eating all foods from the extras part of the pyramid, or eating only fruit, etc.) and the importance of variety in eating. More variety means more energy, more stamina, and better health because it gives us more nutrients. (More energy for recess!)

About Hunger

Having enough food to eat should be a basic human right everywhere, however it is more common around the world, and even in wealthy nations, to find a great disparity between the "haves" and the "have nots" in terms of food. In many places, not enough food is available or it isn't accessible to the people who need it. Consider the paradox: worldwide, there are enough calories available to adequately feed all of Earth's citizens, but still **one billion** people remain hungry. For more information on the issues behind food abundance and scarcity, refer to resources such as Stephanie Kempf's *Finding Solutions to Hunger* and contact organizations like World Hunger Year, Kids Can Make a Difference, and Food First: The Institute for Food and Development Policy. These and others are listed in the Bibliography and Appendix; see also Food Security in the Appendix.

Then, ask students about the possible effects of extreme diets (acknowledging that no one really eats this way). What if you ate sweets for every snack, and didn't brush your teeth? Write down students' answers. Guide at least one of the answers to dental caries. Show examples of severe dental cavities. What are the long-term consequences of eating too many sweets and poor dental health? See the Sugar Detectives lesson, page 83.

Next, ask, What if you ate potato chips (recommended only as an "eat seldom" food) with every meal, and never had any fresh fruits or vegetables? Record students' answers. Guide at least one of the answers to heart disease and hardened arteries. What are the long-term consequences of eating too many fatty foods? Show images of obstructed arteries, or draw a cross section of a tube filled with a clogging substance. (You might stuff a wad of toilet paper into a paper tube to show the same effect.) Make an analogy to a blocked drainpipe. How can the liquid get through the pipe if it's plugged up? (Blood needs room to move through arteries.) The body reacts with an overworked heart and possibly a heart attack. Point out that even thin people can have heart disease and that heart disease is something that happens over a lifetime . . . what you eat when young can contribute to heart disease later in life. Eating in extremes, such as regularly eating high-sugar and high-fat foods, can lead to health problems.

Look for labels of potato and processed potato products. Use them to fill in this chart and add to it. Make predictions of different fat content for the different ways foods are prepared. Make a chart to compare grams of fat and sugar in different potato products.

Food	Fat in Grams	Added Sugar in Grams
Potato, baked	< 1	0
Potato chips-1 oz.	10	
French fries (large fast food order)	31	

Finally, have students brainstorm the most effective way to promote the message: "Eating a variety of foods is important" by creating their own poster or exhibit—choosing to draw or make a representation of either dental caries or a clogged artery, or another "logical consequence" of eating in extremes. Display the posters at school or at the local doctor's/dentist's office or hospital.

Classroom Conversations

- What could we expect to happen in the long run to an individual who ate most of his or her meals at fast-food restaurants, where most of the choices are high in fat, sodium, and sugar?
- Cycle back to the discussion of variety. What could you add into your healthy snacks to provide more variety? Compare the importance of variety in what you eat to the importance of variety in garden plants. Why is plant diversity important?
- Compile a classroom list of "Favorite Health-Filled Snacks" and make copies for each child to take home.
- What are ways that health-filled snacks could be made easier to find, and less nutritious ones could be made to cost more?
- What do you think about paying extra for "junk" foods if that extra money paid for something you believed in? (Even cigarette sales go down when

cigarettes are taxed.)

- This lesson is all about an overabundance of foods. What happens on the opposite side of the spectrum, when there are not enough nutrients to fuel a body? (Malnutrition—too few calories or protein results in disease.)

Action

Choose to raise awareness about the other side of the coin—that in a land of bounty, there are many people who do not get enough to eat. Investigate why over 35 million Americans have inadequate nutrition. Overweight or obese people may actually have a form of malnourishment if they are not getting adequate nutrients for the amount of calories they are consuming.

Want to Do More?

- Bring the message home to the family by having the student and family create a chart showing: (1) Current snacks; and (2) Snacks that would make my body healthier.
- "What if all I ate were.. . . .?" is a good question to ask for a variety of foods. You could also ask: "What if I didn't have enough food to eat?" The What if . . . ? question can also be taken to the extremes of What if I never brushed my teeth? What if I never took a bath? etc. Have students choose one other food or health topic and extrapolate to the logical consequences, referring back to the themes of moderation and variety.

Lesson Links

Taste Buds Rule
Sugar Detectives
Anatomy in Action
Sow Many Seeds!
What are "Whole Foods"?
Food Security (Appendix)

Literature Links

Early Stores and Markets by Bobbie Kalman
Grossology and You: Really Gross Things About Your Body; and *Grossology: The Science of Really Gross Things* by Sylvia Branzei
The Berenstain Bears and Too Much Junk Food by Stan Berenstain
Food Pyramid by Joan Kalbacken
Down the Hatch: Find Out About Your Food by Mike Lambourne
Tooth Decay and Cavities by Alvin Silverstein, Virginia Silverstein, and Laura Silverstein Nunn

Resources

- A local dentist's or physician's office, or the local American Heart Association or American Cancer Society affiliate can provide assistance with class presentation or graphic materials.
- Center for Science in the Public Interest (CSPI) website for resources and labeling information about sugars, fats, and salt; www.cspinet.org (Ask about their *Healthy Eating Pyramid*.)
- For nutrient composition data, see Nutrient Data Laboratory www.nal.usda.gov/fnic/foodcomp/search
- Your local Life Skills or Family and Consumer Science teacher, or USDA Cooperative Extension educator can help with nutrient information.
- See *Bowes & Church's Food Values of Portions Commonly Used*, 17th ed. by Jean A. T. Pennington and Judith S. Douglass, Lippincott, Williams & Wilkins, 2004, a nutrient reference guide for commonly eaten foods.
- The Food Timeline is a collection of related web sites for parents and teachers on food history and traditions across cultures. This site links to multiple lesson plans; www.foodtimeline.org/
- Food origins from tea to potato chips! This site links visitors to information about the origins of many of the most popular foods we eat. www.asiarecipe.com/foodline.html

Benchmarks

The Living Environment: 5E—Flow of Matter and Energy

Grades 3-5

"Some source of 'energy' is needed for all organisms to stay alive and grow."

Grades 6-8

"Food provides molecules that serve as fuel and building material for all organisms. Plants use the energy in light to make sugars out of carbon dioxide and water. This food can be used immediately for fuel or materials or it may be stored for later use.

Organisms that eat plants break down the plant structures to produce the materials and energy they need to survive. Then they are consumed by other organisms."

The Human Organism: 6C—Basic Functions, pp. 136–37

Grades 3-5

"From food, people obtain energy and materials for body repair and growth. . . ."

The Human Organism: 6E—Physical Health, pp. 144–45

K-2

"Eating a variety of healthful foods and getting enough exercise and rest help people to stay healthy."

Grades 3-5

"Food provides energy and materials for growth and repair of body parts. Vitamins and minerals, present in small amounts in foods, are essential to keep everything working well. As people grow up, the amounts and kinds of food and exercise needed by the body may change."

Grades 6-8

"The amount of food energy (calories) a person requires varies with body weight, age, sex, activity level, and natural body efficiency."

"Toxic substances, some dietary habits, and some personal behavior may be bad for one's health. Avoiding toxic substances, such as tobacco, and changing dietary habits to reduce the intake of such things as animal fat increases the chances of living longer."

Habits of Mind: 12B—Computation and Estimation, p. 290

K-2

"Use whole numbers and simple, everyday fractions in ordering, counting, identifying, measuring, and describing things and experiences."

"Readily give the sums and differences of single-digit numbers in familiar contexts where the operation makes sense to them and they can judge the reasonableness of the answer."

"Give rough estimates of numerical answers to problems before doing them formally."

Grades 3-5

"Judge whether measurements and computations of quantities such as length, area, volume, width, or time are reasonable in a familiar context by comparing them to typical values."

Habits of Mind: 12D—Communication Skills, p. 296

Grades 3-5

"Use numerical data in describing and comparing objects and events."

Grades 6-8

"Organize information in simple tables and graphs and identify relationships they reveal."

Feast for the Eyes

Design food for beauty—

way beyond ants on a log!

Recommended Grades: K–6
- **Visual Arts**
- **Health**

"Discovery consists of looking at the same thing as everyone else and thinking something different."
—*Nobel Prize winner Albert Szent-Györgyi*

"It's simple; you just take something simple and do something to it and then do something else to it and keep doing this and pretty soon you've got something." —*Artist Jasper Johns*

Goals

The way foods look influences the choices we make! Encourage an appreciation of beauty (and good hygiene) as we express ourselves artistically with a variety of ingredients.

Key Points

- The way foods look influences their appeal to us.
- If it is beautiful as well as edible, it is appropriate for this class.

Background

This is an exercise that is fun, easy, and creative. You can emphasize what's beautiful, even if the combinations don't at first seem edible—a tomato slice fan topping peanut butter on a tortilla—you just never know! The trick here is to start with good hygiene practices and have a variety of simple healthful ingredients on hand. Limit your "palette" (the number of ingredients) so they aren't overwhelming to the students. This activity can be used in many ways: discuss various moods using the *Play with Your Food* books; introduce unfamiliar fruits and vegetables; for younger children, identify colors; or simply for tasteful art's sake. Remember to take photographs!

Teacher Tip

Ask a local restaurateur, culinary arts student, or art teacher to provide guidance with this activity, or join in the fun. Make sure that children know ahead of time that they are making edible art, that whatever they create is for eating.

What Is Needed

Chopped fruits and vegetables; "glue" such as lowfat cream cheese, hummus, tomato sauce, dip, yogurt cheese (made by letting the yogurt whey drip though a coffee filter, leaving the "cheese" curd behind), jam or jelly, mustard, honey, peanut butter (if no peanut-allergic or sensitive children); "substratum" material (preferably whole grain) such as tortillas, potatoes, bread, bagels, rice, etc.; tool (plastic knife); toothpicks; plates; camera; imagination.

How to Do It

Begin by asking children if they've ever been told "Please do not play with your food!" Here, that's exactly what you're asking them to do! Emphasize that they're not playing with it just for fun—it will be eaten, not wasted. Explain that they'll be making edible art ("Can you define edible?") Show photographs of different beautifully arranged foods. The books listed in Resources are inspiring—as are many images of edible art on the Internet.

Then, do a thorough job cleaning everyone's hands and asking that each artist/chef work individually. They will eat their own creation at the end of the class. Demonstrate one example by showing how the different ingredients might be used. Give them 10-15 minutes to work on their creations. Encourage them to make only as much as they can eat and use ingredients that are not only pleasing to the eye, but also tasty to the artist! Display their creations together before eating, if possible, and invite guests to see (and perhaps taste) the art.

After eating, ask for everyone's help with clean up; that is part of cooking and creating art, after all.

Classroom Conversations

- Ask students, How did you come up with your ideas? Ask for a few volunteers to describe how they made their edible sculpture and perhaps tell a story or give it a name.
- How many food groups did they use—can they name them? Did they enjoy the eating part?

Want to Do More?

- Invite school nutrition staff to pARTake—as well as parents or family members.
- Use this exercise to introduce new foods.
- Choose some particularly pleasing "edible art," develop a production plan, and create enough hors d'oeuvres for an appropriate function.

I'm doing a little weight training with my olive-and-celery dumbbells!

Lesson links

ART in AgRiculTure
Recycled Art
Oodles of Noodles

Literature Links

Fanny at Chez Panisse by Alice Waters
Play with Your Food by Joost Elffers and Saxton Freymann
How Are You Peeling?: Foods with Moods by Joost Elffers and Saxton Freymann
Cooking Art: Easy Edible Art for Young Children by Mary Ann Kohl

Resources

- *Can We Eat the Art? Incredible Edibles and Art You Can't Eat* by Paula Guhin. Incentive Publications, Inc., 2001. Edible art for older children.

Benchmarks

The Human Organism: 6D—Learning, pp. 140–41

Grades 3-5

"Human beings tend to repeat behaviors that feel good or have pleasant consequences and avoid behaviors that feel bad or have unpleasant consequences."

Grades 6-8

"Human beings can detect a tremendous range of visual and olfactory stimuli. . . ."

Choosing for Taste

Lessons in this section examine taste in two ways—how we sense the taste of various foods and how our food tastes develop (our food preferences). These activities should help students reflect on their own preferences and needs in food taste, and gain an appreciation for the diversity of personal and cultural/ethnic expressions in this realm.

Taste (and the related sense of smell) strongly affects our choice of food. Preference for flavors such as salty, sour, bitter, sweet, or *umami* stems from personal experience as well as genetic programming. As infants, for example, we have an instinctual hunger for the sweet nourishment of breast milk. Yet, a craving for candy is not innate or necessary but a learned preference due to the proliferation of refined sweets in this culture.

Taste in the larger sense—our partiality for certain types of foods—may be influenced by family culture, ethnic upbringing, childhood experience, friends' preferences, and/or religious dictates. These factors can be interwoven and powerful in ways we don't always comprehend rationally. Our taste in food (both as children and adults) also is affected by today's plethora of food choices—fast food restaurants, microwaveable meals and advertising tend to emphasize quick "fun" foods that are high in sugars, salt, and fat.

The Global Staff of Life

Bake with whole grains

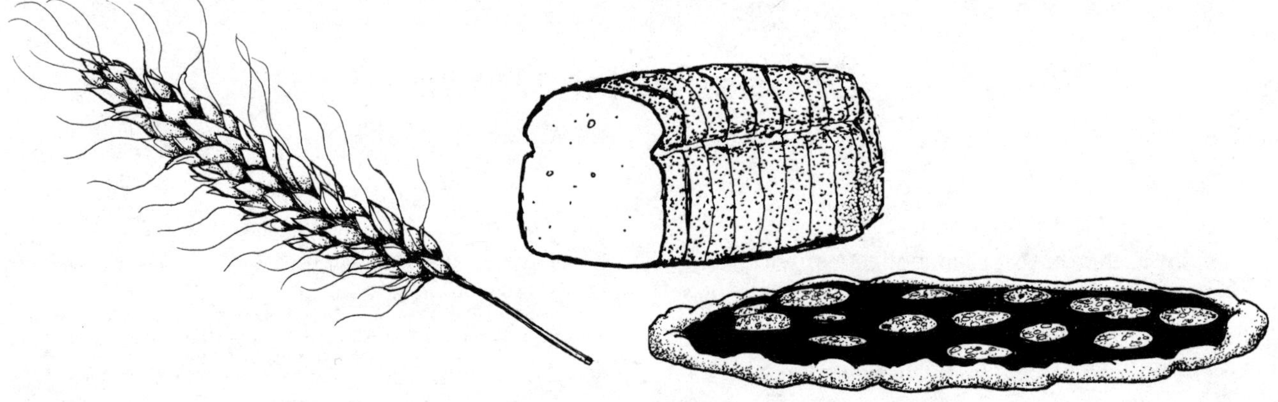

When you have only two pennies left in the world, buy a loaf of bread with one, and a lily with the other. —*Chinese proverb*

Recommended Grades: 1–6

- **Life Skills**
- **Social Studies**
- **Health**
- **Science**
- **Math**

Goals

Bread-making is a skill that many people depend on all over the world and one that children enjoy doing. The health benefits of eating whole grains (and fiber) are explained in this activity.

Key Points

- It's not as complicated as you might think to bake foods made with freshly ground grains.
- Grains are prepared in many ways throughout the world.
- There are many differences between refined and whole grains.
- Your health benefits when you choose a diet with plenty of whole grain products.

Background

The New Oxford Book of Food Plants states that grain crops, or cereals, are by far the most important sources of plant food for the human race. On a worldwide basis, they provide two-thirds of the energy and half the protein of the diet. These crops are: wheat, rice, maize (corn), oats, barley, rye, sorghum, and millet.[1]

In many countries around the world, people consider grain foods (rather than meat) the centerpiece of meals. Grains, also called cereals, are the seeds of grasses such as wheat, rye, oats, corn, rice and barley. Lesser known grains include buckwheat, millet, quinoa, and amaranth. Because grains supply most of the world's protein, they are often called "the staff of life." This lesson allows you to explore the role of grains in civilizations around the world— it could be an adjunct to various social studies units. Americans are counseled to eat six to eleven daily servings of foods from the bread, rice, and cereal group, yet few of us are accustomed to planning meals around grains, much less whole grains.

Many people are unaware of nutritional differences between whole grain flour and refined flour, other than obvious color variations. A whole grain kernel has three parts—the outer husk or "bran," which largely consists of fiber; the inner germ,

[1] *The New Oxford Book of Food Plants* by J. G . Vaughan and C. A. Geissler, Oxford University Press, 1999, p. xvi.

which is filled with protein and vitamins B and E; and the remaining inside portion, which is the endosperm or starchy part of the seed. Whole grains supply large amounts of B vitamins compared to other food groups. When flour is processed into white flour, it is generally stripped of the husk and the germ—leaving primarily the starch. About twenty nutrients are lost when grains are milled and refined. The flour is often bleached and usually enriched with several of the minerals that were removed—some B vitamins, iron, and folacin. Some foods are fortified to add vitamins and minerals that didn't exist there in the first place.

Because most of the nutrients that are removed from whole grains are not fully replaced, processed flour can be less nutritious, especially as far as fiber is concerned. When reading labels and teaching your young consumers about label-reading, seek out products whose ingredient lists contain the words "whole" grain or "100% whole" in the top three ingredients.

Graminae (members of the grass family) are found all over the earth. That's important because without grass, soil erosion would be enormous. Consider that grass provides food directly to humans in the form of cereals and indirectly in the form of meat and dairy.

"Staff" comes from a word meaning "staple" or "support." Called "the staff of life," bread has long been regarded as an essential part of the human diet. The root of the word "cereal" comes from the name Ceres, the Roman goddess of agriculture.

What You'll Need

Foodstuffs:

For the bread recipe: 2 cups warm water; 3 T sugar or honey; 2 t salt; 1/4 cup or more of vegetable oil for greasing your pans and for recipe; raisins (optional); 7 cups of flour: 2 cups whole grain and 5 cups white unbleached flour (could include small amounts of corn meal, spelt, oats, etc.); a handful or more of wheat berries for grinding into flour (available at a whole foods store or by mail); some extra whole wheat flour or white flour for handling your dough.

For the yeast "sponge" demonstration: 1 T. honey; 1/2 tsp. salt; 1 pkg dry yeast;

Plus: A sheaf of grain (you may be able to request this from your local supermarket or craft store); small amounts of different types of flours, such as whole-wheat pastry flour, white flour, and rye, corn meal, or spelt flours (available at most health food stores).

Optional: Purchase frozen bread dough from your supermarket—and use it to compare (ingredients, taste, texture) with the whole grain variety.

Utensils: coffee grinder or (preferably) grain mill; clipboards and writing tools; toothpicks; trays (cafeteria trays or cookie sheets); baking tins; sample grain-based food products with labels (some having whole grains, others having refined flours); a medium-size bowl, measuring cups and spoons; clean damp dishcloths; wooden spoon; rolling pin; knife; aprons; (optional) camera and film to document the process and the results.

Volunteers to help with centers and measuring. *Note:* Solicit help from your students by having them "volunteer" to bring in some equipment from home: toaster ovens, especially, if you do not have a kitchen facility at school.

Getting Ready

So that you'll have enough bread dough for all your students, prepare the simple bread dough recipe below ahead of time. Store it overnight in the refrigerator, or freeze but have it thawed in advance of your class time.

Go over classroom and cooking hygiene: make sure everyone's hands are washed. Caution: Some people are gluten sensitive and cannot eat wheat products—parents would generally alert you to such a health issue. You may choose to have students wear food-service gloves or work only their own small amount of dough to keep germ transfer to a minimum. (See Making Food with Children in the Appendix.)

How to Do It

Begin by recalling that for many centuries bread of some sort was made in almost every home around the globe. Show your students what a sheaf of grain looks like—how it is a grass. Find out what students know about wheat. Ask the students to describe the process themselves, from field to table. What did it

Basic Bread Recipe

Use for pretzels, breadsticks, loaves, buns, etc.

1 package dry yeast
2 cups warm water
3 tablespoons sugar or honey
2 teaspoons salt
1/4 cup oil
7 cups flour: 5 cups white unbleached flour and 2 cups whole grain (possible substitutions could be corn meal, spelt, oats, etc.)

Start yeast in warm sweetened water. Let stand 5 minutes to start yeast working. Add salt, oil, and enough flour to make it the consistency of pancake batter. Set aside for 5 to 10 minutes. Add flour, a little at a time, until you can work dough with your hands. If sticky, add more flour. Knead and make into "worm pretzels," breadsticks, or other small forms on cookie sheet. Let rise 10 to 20 minutes. If you're making bread, let it rise until doubled (about one hour). Bake at 350° for 20 to 25 minutes or until slightly browned. (Depends on the size of the worm!)

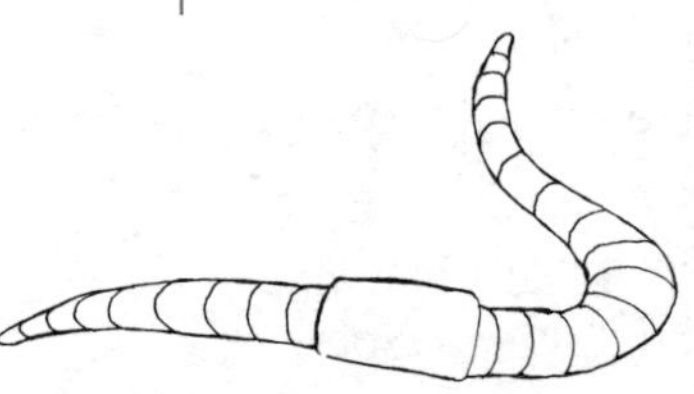

What is yeast? Animal, mineral, or plant? (None of the above! It is a one-celled fungi, and is the oldest domesticated life form on Earth! Like all living things, it needs the right habitat—air, temperature, climate, adequate food, room to grow, and water.)

Fast Bread/Rolls

1 cup warm water
6 teaspoons fast-acting yeast
1/2 cup brown sugar
2 cups whole wheat flour
4 to 6 cups white flour
1/4 cup oil

Add yeast and sugar to warm water to proof. Mix in oil and flour gradually until dough can be handled. Add extra flour as needed. Knead bread dough. Microwave bread 3 minutes on low. Take it out to rest for 6 minutes. Microwave 3 more minutes on low. Punch down and let rise 45 minutes to 1 hour (until doubled). Roll into cylinders and make knot rolls. Bake at 350° for 12 minutes.

Pizza Dough

4 cups white flour
2 cups whole wheat flour
2 cups warm water
2 tablespoons honey
2 tablespoons yeast

Add honey and yeast to warm water. Stir and allow to sit.
Stir in flours gradually until dough can be handled. Turn onto board and knead.
Allow to rise in greased bowl for 1 hour.
Roll dough out thinly to place on greased cookie sheets sprinkled with corn meal.
This recipe makes three cookie sheet-sized pizzas. You will also need 1 pound of grated mozzarella cheese and at least 25 ounces of tomato sauce for traditional pizza.

take to create one loaf of bread? (Help guide them: First the fields are tilled. Wheat is planted, watered, weeded, and maintained. After months of waiting, wheat is harvested, threshed (beat to separate the edible grains from the straw), then ground into flour. Dough is made, kneaded, and baked. This process involved a lot of physical labor over the course of a year, just to make a loaf of bread—the staff of life.

Next, ask what they know about fiber. (Look up the distinction between natural fibers that are used to make clothing, and dietary fiber, found in grains, beans, etc. There are many different kinds.) Why is fiber important? Describe the process of refining flour (see Background). Grind wheat berries and/or other whole grains using a hand mill or coffee grinder and compare it with your flour samples.

Then (refer to "yeast" recipe), ask a student team to measure and mix honey, salt, and yeast into

2 cups of warm (not hot) water in a bowl. (Do all the mixing and kneading and shaping on floured cafeteria trays or cookie sheets, to limit a migrating mess.) Stir in enough flour to make it the consistency of pancake batter. Set aside in a warm place to let the yeast bubble and grow.

Divide class into two centers—have each group analyze different features of yeast/dough. One group can watch the yeast sponge "proof," and compare the various flour samples for color, texture, and aroma. Another group can be kneading and forming the pre-prepared bread dough (optional). If you put raisins in the bread dough, when the gluten has developed enough they will start to "pop."

In 5 to 10 minutes, the first group can add more flour to form dough from the sponge (not too much—just enough so that you can handle it), knead, and form the dough into "breadsticks" or "pretzels," which bake quickly! Size your creations so that they will easily fit your oven, especially if you are using toaster ovens. Put the "breads" on greased baking pans, lightly covered with a damp dishcloth, and set them in a warm place to rise until about doubled before baking.

Finally, bake! Use this time to discuss/sing and clean up. Hand out recipe for kids to take home and try out with their families.

Classroom Conversations

- Has anyone made bread before?
- What was something new you learned about bread or yeast?
- One-fourth of the food eaten in the U.S. is cereal grain, but most of the grain we grow goes to feed livestock.[1]
- What are some of the differences between the whole grain and refined grain breads?

Want to Do More?

- Compare ingredient labels on frozen bread dough with your own bread ingredient list. What are the differences? Do a cost comparison between making bread from scratch, buying frozen dough, and purchasing whole grain bread from the market.
- Do a yeast/balloon experiment to demonstrate how yeast gives off carbon dioxide. Put a balloon over a bottle holding a yeast mixture—wait 15 to 30 minutes.
- Brainstorm and then research the various forms that bread takes around the world: chapatis, tortillas, crackerbread, soda bread, frybread, baguettes, biscuits, ashcakes, johnnycakes, focaccia, pitas, bagels, etc. Try as many samples of these as possible.
- Investigate other grains besides wheat: barley, buckwheat, corn, millet, oats, quinoa, rice, rye, etc. Look at their history, nutritional differences, common recipes or products made from them, where they're eaten in the world, and finally, taste test in class.
- Compare labels for fiber on various bread packages from the store—ask kids to check the fiber content of the bread in their house and make a graph.
- Discuss gluten, the protein that binds wheat bread. It makes dough elastic, and enables it to rise by trapping gas. (Not all flours have gluten—and are not used as much for rising bread dough.)
- Experiment! Let one of the shaped breads overproof to see what happens. (It will not hold its shape as well and will tend to flatten out.)

Lesson Links

Go to Seed!
Bark and Seeds for Breakfast
What Is Locally Grown?
Old-Fashioned Food
What are "Whole Foods"?
Read the Small Print!
Sow Many Seeds!

Literature Links

The Little Red Hen: An Old Story by Margot Zemach
The Little Red Hen and the Ear of Wheat by Mary Finch
The Tortilla Factory by Gary Paulsen
The Sacred Harvest: The Ojibway Wild Rice Gathering by Gordon Regguinti
Loaves of Fun: A History of Bread in Action and Recipes from Around the World by Elizabeth Harbison
Hold the Anchovies! A Book about Pizza by Shelley Rotner
Wheat (Natural Science Series) by Sylvia A. Johnson

[1] United States Department of Agriculture.

Fiber

Fiber is plant material that doesn't break down in our digestive tracts. Therefore, it is not absorbed into the body, but stays in the gastro-intestinal tract and passes out in the feces. It occurs naturally in vegetables, fruits, grains, and legumes, but not in animal products, fats, or oils. While not technically a nutrient, fiber is a component essential to good digestion and health.

- It slows absorption of digested food into the bloodstream, helping to stabilize blood sugar. (This is important for people who have diabetes because their internal mechanism is not able to regulate blood sugar.)
- Fruit and vegetable fiber helps reduce the amount of cholesterol absorbed in the bloodstream—protecting against high blood cholesterol and heart disease.
- Fibers like bran found in grains help decrease the risk of colon cancer.
- Fiber adds bulk to diets, displacing more energy-dense foods, and thus helps with weight loss.
- Substituting high fiber grains, fruits, and vegetables in the diet for more expensive meat products, may help you save money.

In shopping for whole grains (those that still include their fiber), don't be misled by labels. What is called "wheat bread" may simply be white bread with coloring. Look for labels that say "whole wheat," "100% whole wheat," or "stoneground whole wheat." A rule of thumb: the more substantial (less fluffy) a bread is, the more likely it is to contain fiber.

Resources

- Check the Internet (if no natural foods store is located in your area) for mail order sources for wheat berries and other grains.
- *Six Thousand Years of Bread: Its Holy and Unholy History*, by H. E. Jacob, Independent Publishers Group, 1997. An historical and philosophical history of bread.
- *The Laurel's Kitchen Bread Book* by Laurel Robertson, Carol Flinders, and Bronwen Godfrey, Random House, 2003.
- Children's Health and Nutrition is a site designed for kids with bright graphics and good information on many subjects related to their own health; www.kidshealth.org/kid

Benchmarks

The Physical Setting: 4C—Processes that Shape the Earth, p. 73

Grades 6-8

"The composition and texture of soil and its fertility and resistance to erosion are greatly influence by plant roots. . . ."

The Human Organism: 6E—Physical Health, p. 144

Grades 3-5

"Food provides energy and materials for growth and repair of body parts. Vitamins and minerals, present in small amounts in foods, are essential to keep everything working well. As people grow up, the amounts and kinds of food and exercise needed by the body may change."

Human Society: 7G—Global Interdependence, p. 176

K-2

Background: "Children should be encouraged to ask where various products they use come from."

"For many things they need, people rely on others who are not part of the family and maybe even part of their local community."

Grades 3-5

Background: "A variety of activities can familiarize (and fascinate) students with products grown or manufactured elsewhere in the world—many of which they see and use in their everyday lives."

"Many of the things people eat and wear come from other counties, and people in those countries use things from this country. . . ."

The Designed World: 8A—Agriculture, p. 184

K-2

Background: "Some of the earliest stories to be read to and by small children can tell about life on the farm and what happens to food between the farm and the store."

Grades 3-5

Background: "Where possible, students should visit markets, farms, grain elevators, and processing plants . . . and as many other parts of the 'technological food chain' as possible."

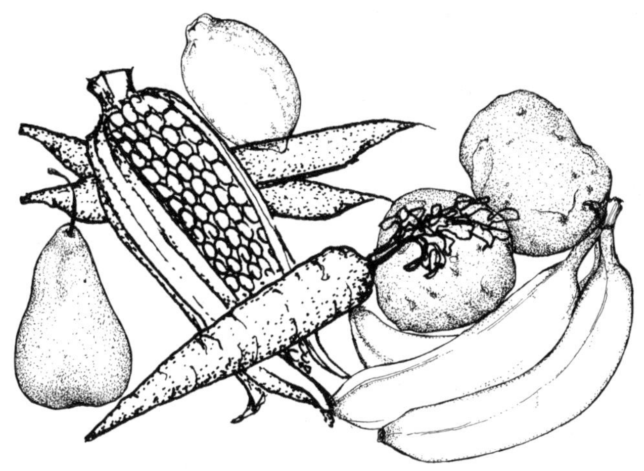

Guess with Gusto!

Play a guessing game to experience the range of senses

Recommended Grades: K–6

- **Language Arts**

Goals

Exploring foods using just a sense of touch or a sense of smell is a lively way to open our minds to a range of foods that we might ordinarily ignore.

Key Points

- Food can be explored and identified in ways other than by sight or by taste.
- The food pyramid can help students plan good meals and snacks.

Background

Some chefs say that we eat "with our eyes." Just looking at a photograph of a scrumptious-looking meal can start us salivating! Our sense of smell was the first to evolve, though, and it is directly linked to our taste buds; the aroma of a dish contributes greatly to our meal enjoyment. Doesn't the kitchen smell good when something's cooking? Note that smells are complicated, made up of numerous compounds (chemical parts). Their appeal can vary from one individual to another.

Combine these two investigations of the senses or use each option separately: (A) is a touch guessing game; (B) is a game using the sense of smell. Older children can use these ideas to develop a lesson on smell for younger kids.

Teacher Tip

The food pyramid can help students with identifying the hidden foods. Providing clues by food group can be helpful, especially for younger children.

What You'll Need

"Mystery Cans" or a large "Mystery Blanket" or kneesocks (for game A); several small baby food-sized jars (for game B); handouts; "Mystery Foods"; imagination. *Note:* Avoid foods that are potentially allergenic—such as nuts. Use some familiar and some less familiar foods (avoid any that are slimy or gooey). Select local foods if possible: Examples might be apple, winter squash or a small pumpkin, potato, pumpkin seeds, popcorn, oats, garlic, onion, parsnip, carrot, radish, turnip, celery, cranberry, leek, shallot, sweet potato, or beet. Try to include foods from as many food groups as possible, with contrasting textures.

Getting Ready

For game A—the touching game—make "Mystery Cans" or find a" Mystery Blanket." *Note:* Older students could create these materials. The "Mystery Cans" are large plastic opaque canisters (ask your Food Service director for empty mayonnaise or relish jars) which hold the hidden foods. Other methods of hiding foods can be used as well—cardboard shoebox or cardboard oatmeal containers (attach a tube sock top to make a sleeve extending from the container). For game B—the smelling game—cover baby food-type jars to conceal what's inside. Select foods with a variety of aromas so students can identify foods by smell. Use cotton balls or tissue soaked with such foods or essences as lemon, tomato juice, cinnamon, peanut butter (if no allergic students), vanilla, orange, mint, or almond.

Make a handout for recording students' "Mystery Foods" (optional).

How to Do It

Begin by reviewing the food pyramid.

Next, ask students to name all of their senses. Which ones do we use when eating? Can they identify foods without seeing them or smelling them?

A) Guessing by Touch

- Ask students (in groups of four or five) to identify a variety of foods by touch, using the "Mystery Cans" or "Mystery Blanket."
- Have them write down or name what they think the foods are. When all students have recorded their guesses, discuss the students' sensory reactions. Elicit descriptive adjectives by asking them to describe what they felt: Was it large or small, smooth or rough, round or uneven, squishy or hard? Design a handout (optional) according to the ability of the students and the particular topic you want to emphasize (texture of food, shape, part of plant it comes from, what they think food tastes like, etc.). For older students, encourage them to categorize the food objects (by food group, plant part, description, etc.), or incorporate the activity into an experiment testing how accurate students' senses are, for instance.
- Review their guesses and have students remove food from hiding to show the class. Were their guesses accurate?

B) Guessing by Smell

- Follow basic procedures described in game A, but instead of identifying the food by touch, ask students to describe the smells and name or write down what food they think matches that aroma.
- Can they tell how it tastes from the smell? Have them make predictions—would it be salty, sweet, sour, etc.? Does the aroma make them hungry? Discuss how smells affect decisions about eating. Ask them to describe some of their favorite and least favorite food smells and how their body responds to these aromas.
- As a writing activity, older students could describe a food experience.

Next, using the food pyramid, children identify where the foods fit on the pyramid.

Finally, have a snack that incorporates as many of your senses as you can create—foods that have texture, color, flavor, visual appeal, and that the children choose to eat together. It can be a simple fruit or vegetable platter, vegetables and dip, warm bread and toppings, etc.

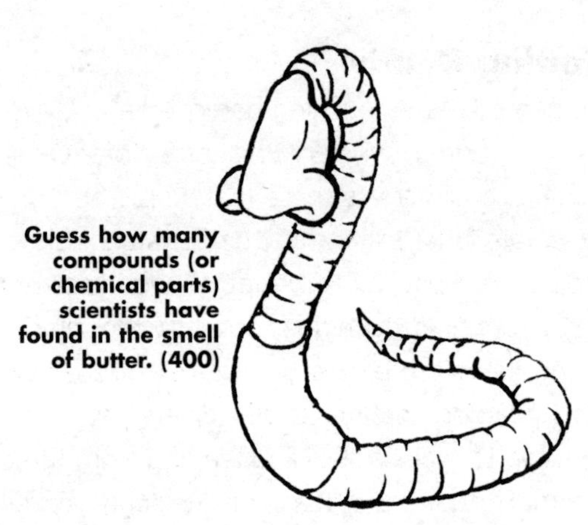

Guess how many compounds (or chemical parts) scientists have found in the smell of butter. (400)

Super Sniffers

Your nose is a very sensitive part of your body—it works better than any aroma-detecting machine ever invented! You can detect flavors of foods (mostly using your sense of smell) even if a VERY small amount of flavoring is in the food. Your nose can sense aromas in the air in amounts as little as a few parts per trillion. For an example, it is estimated that the main flavor of bell pepper can be tasted in amounts as low as .02 parts per billion; one drop would be sufficient to add flavor to five average sized swimming pools.[1]

[1] *Fast Food Nation* by Eric Schlosser, Perennial, 2000, p. 125.

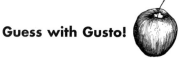

Classroom Conversations

- What senses did they use during the activity?
- Did the exercise make them pay more attention to the color, texture, taste, and aroma of what they ate?
- How does the touch and/or smell of food affect what you choose to eat?
- Do all people experience smells the same way?
- What would eating be like without the smell of food? (People without a sense of smell cannot taste their food.)

Want to Do More?

- Students can illustrate what they imagine the Mystery Foods to look like. Ask students to guess what their classmates' drawings represent.
- Bring in a food unfamiliar to your students such as taro or starfruit (found in the produce section of larger markets). Ask students to name the food item or make up a name. Ask them to identify it as a grain, fruit, or vegetable. Have them predict its taste by its appearance, texture, and smell. Have a taste test if appropriate.
- Have students devise a way to do this at home to share with their families as a game.

Lesson Links

Taste Buds Rule
Feast for the Eyes
Traditions at the Table
What's for Lunch?

Literature Links

Discover Your Senses: Feeling Your Way; Follow Your Nose (Five Senses Series) by Vicki Cobb

Explore Your Senses: Touch; Hearing; Sight; Smell; Taste (a series) by Laurence Pringle

The Magic School Bus Explores the Senses by Joanna Cole and Bruce Degen

Jamberry by Bruce Degen

Resources

- See *Project Seasons* by Deb Parrella for additional ideas on this activity. Shelburne Institute, 1995.
- See www.mypyramid.gov and www.sne.org/mypyramid for dietary guidelines and pyramid information.
- For examples of traditional eating patterns in many cultures, see www.oldwayspt.org
- "Follow your nose" with David Masumoto, farmer and writer, as he appreciates the sights, smells, sounds, and textures of life on a farm. *Four Seasons in Five Senses: Things Worth Savoring,* W. W. Norton & Co., 2003.

Benchmarks

The Human Organism: 6C—Basic Functions, pp. 136–37

K-2

"The human body has parts that help it seek, find and take in food when it feels hunger—eyes and noses for detecting food. . . ."

Grades 3-5

"The brain gets signals from all parts of the body telling what is going on there. The brain also sends signals to parts of the body to influence what they do."

The Human Organism: 6D—Learning, pp. 140–41

Grades 3-5

"Human beings tend to repeat behaviors that feel good or have pleasant consequences and avoid behaviors that feel bad or have unpleasant consequences."

Grades 6-8

"Human beings can detect a tremendous range of visual and olfactory stimuli. . . ."

The Human Organism: 6E—Physical Health, p. 144

K-2

"Eating a variety of healthful foods and getting enough exercise and rest help people to stay healthy."

Grades 3-5

"Food provides energy and materials for growth and repair of body parts. Vitamins and minerals, present in small amounts in foods, are essential to keep everything working well."

Taste Buds Rule

Explore the sweet, the sour, the bitter, the salty, and "umami"

Recommended Grades: K–6

- **Life Skills**
- **Health**
- **Science**

Goals

"Teach through the taste buds." Differentiate between various flavors and identify our own taste preferences. The sense of smell plays an important-role in taste. (Crunch, chew, swallow, smile!)

Key Points

- Flavors are currently classified into five basic groups: salty, sour, sweet, bitter, and "umami" (savory).

Background

Taste has shaped history—consider Columbus coming to the new world in search of spices and gold, and the trade that evolved from his "discoveries." Around the world, everyone seems to have different taste preferences—some cuisines, such as in parts of Thailand, Mexico, or the Caribbean, prefer hot, spicy foods, while others use few spices and rely on many salted foods—such as in Scandinavia, for example. Coffee, one of the most bitter-tasting beverages in the world, is consumed by adults everywhere, but it's a flavor most children dislike. Many factors influence our individual sensory differences: genetics, age, gender, experience, and the environment. Our ultimate choices of foods and beverages are actually made through a combination of personal taste, smell, and flavor and are established early in life.

We humans taste food mostly with our tongues—but along with other animals, we have taste buds all over our mouths. Many fish have their taste buds all over their bodies (catfish can taste their surroundings just by swimming!). The tongue sends a message to the brain to accept or reject food by sampling its taste, texture, and temperature. As we age, our taste buds decline in number and sensitivity so that by the age of seventy-five most people have lost two-thirds of the taste buds they had at thirty. Consider how this affects elders' ability to taste foods!

Taste sensations have traditionally been divided into four categories—sweet, salty, bitter, and sour—but scientists still debate about additional tastes such as astringent and fat. The most recently recognized and least known taste, called *umami* (pronounced "Ooh-Mommy") by the Japanese, has been described as the "savory" taste in meat, seafood, and some dairy products that are rich in an amino acid called glutamate. It is commonly marketed in a flavor-enhancer product named monosodium

glutamate or MSG. (*Caution:* Some people may be sensitive to this substance.)

For years, we have thought that we could "map" the tongue to get an adequate idea of which taste buds corresponded to particular flavors. In reality, though, while certain parts of the mouth are better at perceiving specific tastes than others, each taste quality can be sensed on any region of the tongue where taste buds are found.

Smell plays a significant role in how we taste: up to 90 percent of what we think is taste is actually smell! Our noses are so sensitive that we can detect molecules as small as a few parts *per trillion*—far better than any sophisticated machine can do.

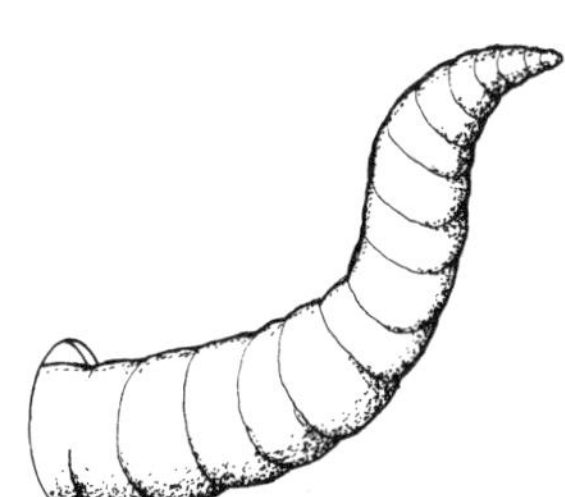

How does a fly taste? (Besides "not very good"!) The real answer is "With its FEET!" It walks all over a food to find out if it's good to eat!

Getting Ready

Refer to Making Food with Children in the Appendix. In the interest of good hygiene, devise a system where each child will have his or her own container of taste-test samples.

What You'll Need

Vanilla extract; small mirrors; foods with varying tastes (powdered sugar, cold tea, lemon juice, miso [Japanese broth] or soup broth from a bouillon cube); blindfolds; two drinks of the same consistency but different flavors, such as apple juice and grape juice or orange juice and grapefruit juice; drinking straws; taste-test containers (i.e., muffin cups or tins small cups, clean bottle caps, etc.).

How to Do It

Begin by asking students: How do we taste our food? (With the tongue and with our noses.)

- Smell a bottle of vanilla extract. How do you think it will taste? Taste one drop on your fingertip—is it what you expected? How does it taste?
- This next activity is best done with a partner, and particularly fun when done blindfolded. Begin by having students wash hands well and rinse their mouths with water. Have a one child put his or her partner's blindfold on and help him or her taste test foods.
- Give each student these instructions and hand out taste-test containers. *Note*: Remind each child that s/he will use only his or her own finger in his own mouth to minimize germs. Dip a finger in powdered sugar (each child using his/her own small pinchl). Dab it on one side of your cheek, lips, and the back and center of your tongue. Then dab it on one side of the tongue, then the other, and finally the tip. Where do you taste its flavor? How does it taste? Rinse your mouth and hands with water.

Next, test cold tea in the same places. Where can you taste the flavor—can you identify it? (Bitter.) Do the same with lemon juice (sour) and with broth (savory and salty). What do you notice? Invite younger students to use a mirror to see the tiny bumps (papillae) on the tongue's surface where taste buds are located.

Then, try tasting food without your sense of smell! Use the blindfold and test two drinks (using straws). With blindfold on, hold your nose (this is hard!) and taste one drink, then the other. Can you tell which is which? (Your tongue can tell you only that both drinks are sweet. It cannot tell them apart.) Try the test again without holding your nose. Ask: Is there a difference? Have you ever "lost" your sense of taste when you have had a cold?

Classroom Conversations

- Discuss conclusions as a group. Why do we have taste buds? (Scientists believe it was a way for us to avoid being poisoned.)
- What would happen if we couldn't taste food? (We might lose interest in eating, as happens in some illnesses, or be more vulnerable to spoiled food or environmental toxins.)
- Do we all identify food tastes the same way?
- Why do our mouths water when we sense food nearby? (The taste, sight, and aroma of food sends a message to our brains that prepares the

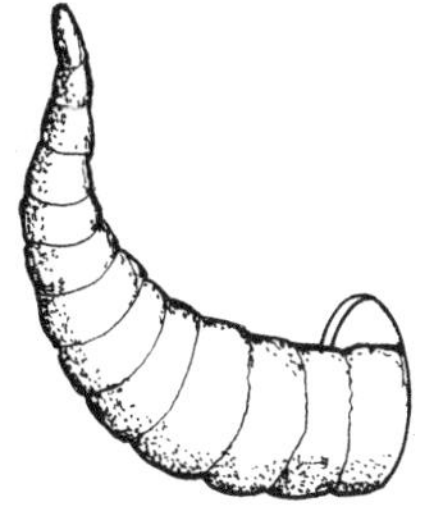

body to receive nutrients—helping us digest and absorb food better.)

Want to Do More?

- Make a chart for taste testing. On one side list five foods you want to taste. Along the top, draw in columns for "salty, sweet, bitter, umami, and sour." Taste the foods one at a time and fill in the chart with check marks. Compare the results of the individual charts. Were they all the same? Summarize and put the results up on the wall. (This exercise demonstrates that foods have a variety of tastes and each child perceives them differently.)
- Have the class make "Take-Home Taste Kits" to test family members and write up the results. (Materials: rating sheet and a variety of foods.)
- Choose one item for the whole group to taste. Describe the flavor with adjectives but do NOT use the words "sweet" or "salty" (or whatever word is usually used to describe that specific flavor).

Lesson Links

Guess with Gusto!
Sugar Detectives
What If All I Ate Were Potato Chips?
Oodles of Noodles

Literature Links

It's Disgusting and We Ate It by James Solheim
Experiment with Senses by Monica Byles
Explore Your Senses: Taste by Laurence Pringle
Discover Your Senses: Your Tongue Can Tell by Vicki Cobb
Food Fight: Poets Join the Fight Against Hunger with Poems to Favorite Foods edited by Michael J. Rosen

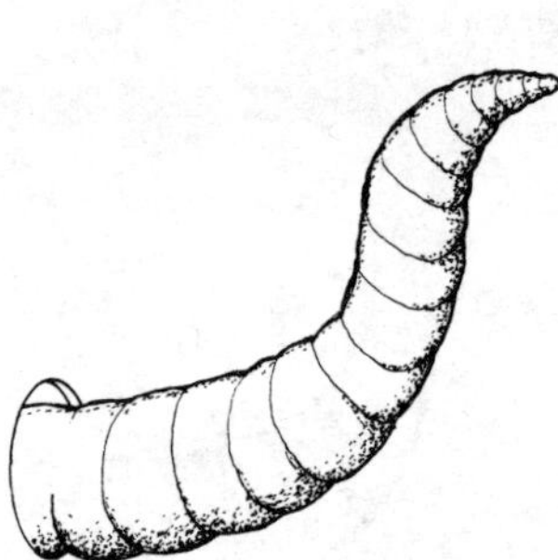

How many taste buds does the average human have? (5,000!) Chickens are believed to have only about 24, and catfish have close to 300,000 taste buds. Why is that, do you suppose?

Resources

- For additional activities and background on taste and the senses, see: *Good for Me! All about Food in 32 Bites* by Marilyn Burns, Econo-Clad Books, 1999; *Gardening Wizardry for Kids* by Patricia Kite, and Y. Banek, Barrons Juveniles, 1995; and *How to Teach Nutrition to Kids* by Connie Liakos Evers, 24 Carrot Press, 2006.
- An extensive account of the role of spices and taste in history can be found in *Dangerous Tastes: The Story of Spices* by Andrew Dalby, Univ. of California Press, 2000.
- For information on the flavor industry and flavorings in food, see *Fast Food Nation* by Eric Schlosser, Harper Perennial, 2002, pp. 122-28.
- The USDA has an extensive listing of resources for adults wishing to learn more about nutrition issues and different ethnic groups in the U.S. at www.nal.usda.gov/fnic/ —click on Food Guide Pyramid, then click on ethnic and cultural.

Benchmarks

The Human Organism: 6C—Basic Functions, pp. 136–37

K-2

"The human body has parts that help it seek, find, and take in food when it feels hunger—eyes and noses for detecting food. . . ."

Grades 3-5

"The brain gets signals from all parts of the body telling what is going on there. The brain also sends signals to parts of the body to influence what they do."

The Human Organism: 6D—Learning, pp. 140–41

Grades 3-5

"Human beings tend to repeat behaviors that feel good or have pleasant consequences and avoid behaviors that feel bad or have unpleasant consequences."

Grades 6-8

"Human beings can detect a tremendous range of visual and olfactory stimuli. . . ."

Oodles of Noodles

Compare, then prepare, a pasta meal

I always say, "Vermicelli to fill the belly!"

Recommended Grades: 3–6

- **Social Studies**
- **Math**
- **Science**
- **Life Skills**
- **Health**
- **Geography**

Goals

Compare pasta meals from different cultures, develop recipe and measurement skills, reinforce sensory evaluation, and prepare a recipe to eat in class.

Key Point

- Pasta (made from grain) is popular around the globe, but preparation of this basic food is different everywhere.

Background

Favorite meals develop in different kitchens around the world according to local taste and custom, religious or cultural preferences, family habits, economy, climate or geography, and history. A society's daily and seasonal living requirements also affect its food: couscous, invented from semolina wheat by Moroccan nomads, requires little water and only a pair of hands to create the small quick-cooking granules, as opposed to the Italians' wheat flour invention—the development of pasta—which wouldn't have been as compatible with nomadic living!

Pasta or noodles are found worldwide in various forms, and are many children's first-choice meal. We'll look at a variety of ways to prepare them.

In this activity, you may choose to make pasta "from scratch," which is fun and rewarding to do: lots of smiling kids and noodles hanging around the room! See the following recipes. Or, use purchased noodles and add your own variety of toppings. *Note:* This activity may be done over several class times: a different pasta dish can be prepared each time.

What You'll Need

Access to stove or cooktop; large cooking pot; ingredients for the pasta recipe you choose; serving and eating utensils; bowls; sauces; aprons; tablecloths and decorations if desired; clean-up sponges and towels. Optional: world map or globe; food-service plastic gloves.

Getting Ready

Purchase or get donated ingredients in advance. Refer to Making Food with Children in the Appendix. Solicit assistance from school nutrition staff or a local restaurateur, and arrange for adult volunteer helpers. Also, let your custodian know you'll be creating pasta, too. . . .

How to Do It

Begin by discussing food traditions from other cultures and brainstorm about foods that might be familiar to some students but atypical or perhaps even unknown, to their classmates. Have they had pasta? Noodles? Spaghetti? What do they call it at home? Have they made it before themselves? If possible, have one student describe the process of making noodles "from scratch", or have them guess how it's done.

Talk about how some of the foods we eat commonly are eaten around the world in very different ways. Examples: macaroni and cheese or spaghetti and tomato sauce in the United States; rice or buckwheat noodles in Asia; spätzle noodles in Germany ("Diet of Worms"—this pasta is also worm-shaped!); fresh-made vermicelli in Italy (homemade is called *fatto a mano* in Italian!); couscous in the Middle East/North Africa.

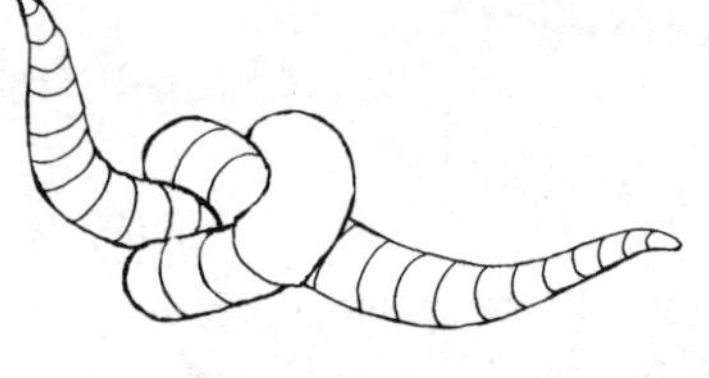

In Japan, rice (including rice noodles) is such an important part of meals and life that the Japanese word for rice, gohan, also means food.

Next, divide the class into teams and ask each team to investigate how a pasta or noodle recipe is made and consumed, and to explain the customs of the country in which it is typically eaten. Provide adequate time for the teams to research "their" dish and country, and then present them to the class as a group. Select one or more that you'd like to make in your classroom for a "Noodle-fest." (There are also some sample recipes at the end of this activity.) Students may choose to make travel posters, or a map of the country or region where the pasta dish originated. This can be used later to decorate the classroom during the meal.

Then (later class period), it's time to cook! Start with clean hands and a good hygiene reminder. It might be best to have students handling just their own pasta to minimize germs—or use plastic gloves. Review rules for safety in the kitchen. (See Making Food with Children in the Appendix.) Prepare the pasta dish that the class chose and researched. (You might prepare any baked noodles in advance for ease of preparation). *Caution:* Have adult helpers, especially near pots of boiling water and the oven.

Finally, eat, enjoy! Invite parents or community members—or the Food Service staff! Clean up.

Classroom Conversations

- Why is pasta such a universal meal?
- What are some of the ways that you've found people eat and enjoy pasta?
- Why do you think that the same ingredients (wheat and water mostly) are prepared in so many ways around the world?

Want to Do More?

- What is the word "pasta" or "noodle" in different languages? Look up the word "vermicelli." Using different "root" and "suffix" words, create your own noodle name and explain the meaning.
- Compare the cost of commercial and packaged noodles to those made in class.
- Send home the pasta recipes and ask who can come up with an interesting variation on what was created in class. Test it on family members and bring recipes back to class for a "Chef Noodlehead Innovation Day." (Come up with your own fun name!)
- Have younger students dictate their own "Favorite Noodle Recipe" directions, including the ingredient list, to you. Type up and publish an *Oodles of Noodles* big book for school. Make smaller copies to send home to families.

Action

Ask if classroom creations could be incorporated for a day into the school lunch or breakfast program. Have other students do taste tests to determine if it's a food that could be added to the regular menu.

Lesson Links

The Global Staff of Life
Taste Buds Rule
Traditions at the Table

Literature Links

Passport on a Plate: A Round-the-World Cookbook for Children by Diane Simone Vezza
Family Dinner by Jane Cutler
Strega Nona by Tomie de Paola
Everybody Brings Noodles by Norah Dooley
From Wheat to Pasta by Robert Egan
Everyone Eats Pasta by Jillian Powell
Daddy Makes the Best Spaghetti by Anna Grossnickle Hines

Resources

- Local community members, especially classroom families, who would be willing to share their culture's foods.
- School food service for sources of ingredients and utensils.
- *Creative Food Experiences for Children* by Mary Goodwin and Gerry Pollen has recipes, nutrition information, and global celebrations with food. Center for Science in the Public Interest, 1980.
- Wheat producers are usually willing to share their educational materials with classrooms.
- The Food Timeline is a collection of related sites for parents and teachers on food history and traditions across cultures. This site links to multiple lesson plans: www.foodtimeline.org/
- Food origins from tea to potato chips! This site links visitors to information about the origins of many of the most popular foods we eat: www.asiarecipe.com/foodline.html

Benchmarks

The Human Organism: 6E—Physical Health, p. 144

Grades 3-5

"Food provides energy and materials for growth and repair of body parts. Vitamins and minerals, present in small amounts in foods, are essential to keep everything working well."

The Designed World: 8A—Agriculture, pp. 183-84

The background section for all the *Benchmarks* across grade levels states, "Projects to trace locally available food . . . back to their origins are helpful. . . ."

Grades 3-5

"Some plant varieties . . . have more desirable characteristics than others, but some may be more difficult or costly to grow. The kinds of crops that can grow in an area depend on the climate and soil. Irrigation and fertilization can help crops grow in places where there is too little water or the soil is poor."

Habits of Mind: 12C—Manipulation and Observation, p. 293

Grades 3-5

"Measure and mix dry and liquid materials (in the kitchen . . .) in prescribed amounts, exercising reasonable safety."

Did You Know?

Pasta comes in an amazing number of sizes, shapes, and forms! It is usually made from *semolina—a* refined flour from hard spring durum wheat—which is unsuitable for breads and cakes as it won't rise. A cup of this seminolina-type of pasta contains some protein, potassium, phosphorus, calcium, and a little fat. When buying pasta, you can also purchase whole wheat, spinach, buckwheat, Jerusalem artichoke, egg noodles, rice, or many other exciting types. From a nutritional standpoint, whole grain pastas will provide more nutrients—some brands are tastier than others. Try a new one each week! Whole grains (look for "whole" on the label) and pastas made from them have a more full-bodied flavor.

As you know, pasta belongs in the grain (bread, cereal, rice, and pasta) food group, which forms the basis of the food pyramid. Figure out how many servings you are eating in a day from this food group and compare it to the recommended amount (6-11 half-cup servings daily).

Pasta is a tasty and economical choice for breakfast, lunch, dinner, or snack, and especially helpful for athletes. Go beyond the usual spaghetti sauce, and create some of your own toppings: mixed sautéed vegetables; garlic and grated parmesan cheese; peanut butter and a little tamari (soy) sauce; beans or tofu; or any fresh garden vegetable.

For fun, estimate how many pounds of pasta your family eats in a week/month/year!

Pots and Pots of Pasta for Oodles of Noodles!

Annelida's Favorite Vermicelli

Here is a recipe for making pasta from scratch. You don't need a pasta machine to do this. Make your vermicelli pasta with semolina flour (available at some supermarkets, health food stores, or Italian markets), referring to the recipe that follows.

Materials: Bowls; drying racks or clean place to hang pasta; wooden spoons; pastry cutter; rolling pins; pizza cutter or table knives; colander; plastic bags; sponges; aprons or lab coats (use shirts from a thrift store); sifters (optional); pasta makers (optional); camera (optional).

Ingredients:

3 cups semolina flour or you may also use a combination of white and whole wheat flour
1 teaspoon salt
2 tablespoons oil
warm water
extra flour for rolling out dough

Instructions: Sift flour with salt into large bowl. Add oil and enough warm water (slowly) to the dry ingredients and stir to form into a ball.

Knead gently for 5 or 10 minutes. (If using whole wheat (or any other flour besides semolina), it may not hold together as well in the cooking pot).

You may let it sit for 10 minutes to several hours.

Roll out to a thin layer, about 1/8 inch. If you're using a pasta machine, just roll to flatten and run through machine. If you're not using the pasta maker, cut into desired shapes.

Hang until dry. Time varies depending on shape.

The pasta can be kept dried for a few days or cooked immediately. Bring a pot of water to a rolling boil. Add pasta. After 4 to 7 minutes, check to see if it's done by removing a piece from the water and cutting it in half; it should be the same color throughout. If your pasta chef made small pieces, they'll cook quicker, so check early. If done, drain in a colander. Return to cooking pot or serving dish and toss with a small amount of oil. Enjoy plain or with your favorite topping.

Spätzle[1]

These are fun to make with children! This coarse egg noodle dish from the Germany's Alsace area can be used in place of potatoes or rice. The noodles make worm shapes while they cook!

Ingredients:

2 large eggs, beaten
1/2 cup milk
1 1/2 cups all-purpose flour
1/4 teaspoon salt
1/8 teaspoon ground nutmeg
2 tablespoons butter
OR
Whole grain version:
3 large eggs, beaten
1/4 cup milk
1 1/4 cups whole wheat flour
1/4 teaspoon salt
1/8 teaspoon ground nutmeg
2 tablespoons butter

Instructions: Bring a large pot of lightly salted water to boil. Lower to a simmer.

Combine eggs and milk; stir in flour, salt, and nutmeg and whisk until smooth.

Using the back of an 8-inch-square cake pan or a cutting board, pour 1/2 cup of batter onto it. Take a long spatula and shave 1/4-inch-wide ribbons into the simmering water.

As soon as the spätzle float to the top, they're done! Use a slotted spoon to remove and rinse under warm water.

Keep going until batter is gone, then season with salt and pepper and desired topping: fresh herbs such as parsley, olive oil, butter, garlic, paprika, grated cheese, lemon and poppy seeds, bread crumbs, etc. (More traditional is to melt butter in a skillet and gently fry spätzle until browned, about 3 to 4 minutes.)

Serves 4 to 6.

[1] Provided by chef and author Rebecca Reilly.

Simple Couscous

Ingredients:

1 1/2 cups couscous (whole grain if available)
2 cups water
1/2 teaspoon salt

Instructions: Boil water, then add salt and couscous. Bring to a second boil, and then remove from heat. Cover and allow to rest for 5 to 8 minutes. Fluff with a fork before serving. For additional excitement, add any small, fresh chopped vegetable or herb after removing from heat: tomatoes, carrots, celery, cucumber, mint, scallions, cooked garlic, parsley, peas, salt and pepper, toasted seeds or nuts.

Soba with Sesame and Ginger

"The Japanese feel that their traditional 'fast food' must be eaten immediately, before the piping hot broth has made the noodles limp. This means you must take in a cooling breath with each bite. The resultant slurping sound can be strange to Western ears, but it is a sign of enjoyment in Japan. In fact, eating noodles slowly and quietly is offensive to the cook."[1]

Soba means buckwheat noodles in Japanese. These noodles are made with wheat and buckwheat flour, and no eggs. They're available at Asian markets, and many large grocery stores. You may substitute *Udon*, Japanese whole wheat noodles. More noodles are eaten in Japan than any other food except rice. These are excellent for a main dish, snack, or served as a side dish.

Ingredients:

1 package soba noodles
2 tablespoon tahini (sesame paste—you may substitute other nut butters)
1/4 teaspoon salt
1/3 cup grated fresh ginger (squeezed) or 1/2 teaspoon dried ginger
1/2 pound tofu cut into 1-inch cubes
1 teaspoon sesame (or vegetable) oil
1 teaspoon tamari (soy sauce)
parsley (optional)

Instructions: Boil noodles in 3 quarts water for about 8 to 12 minutes. Remove and rinse under cold water. Add the tahini, ginger, and salt. If using fresh grated ginger, wrap it in a clean cloth and squeeze the juice onto the noodles, mixing well.

Sauté the tofu in oil and season with tamari before tossing with noodles.

Eat as is or chill for an hour before serving with parsley sprinkled on top for garnish.

This is wonderful when peanut butter is substituted for the tahini, but be cautious about potential peanut allergies.

Clear Rice Noodles and Vegetable Broth

Many Japanese people start their day with a steaming miso soup. Miso is a salty fermented soybean paste and can be roughly compared to the bouillon often used as a broth base in western soups. There are many varieties of miso: dark types have a meat-like flavor (labeled "red," "brown rice," or "barley"), and the lighter-colored sweet types ("mellow," "sweet," or "white") are almost like a dairy food. Typically, the choice of which miso to use is based on the season—lighter for warmer months, darker and heartier in colder months.

Two common types of thin transparent noodles made from rice flour are *bifun* (with some potato starch added) and *saifun* (with mung bean starch). They are easy and fast to prepare, and contain no wheat or salt.

Ingredients:

1 medium onion, thinly sliced
2 carrots, cut in small strips
3 to 4 tablespoons sweet miso, or to taste
1 package rice noodles
1 tablespoon wakame flakes or one 4–6-inch kombu strip (dried seaweed). This is optional.
1 green onion, thinly sliced

Instructions: To prepare broth: Put kombu or wakame into 4 cups water and bring to a boil. Add onion, carrot, and simmer for about 10 minutes. Remove kombu and turn off heat. (The kombu may be reused in cooking beans, vegetables, or for other stock.) Dissolve miso in 1/4 cup of the soup stock, then return to broth to steep before pouring over noodles. (Miso should not be boiled.)

To prepare noodles: Boil a large pot of water and add rice noodles, boiling for 5 to 6 minutes, no longer. Once done, remove, and rinse immediately in cool water. Drain.

Put in bowls, and pour broth on top. Garnish with green onion.

[1] *Cooking with Japanese Foods* by Jan and John Belleme, East West Health Books, 1986.

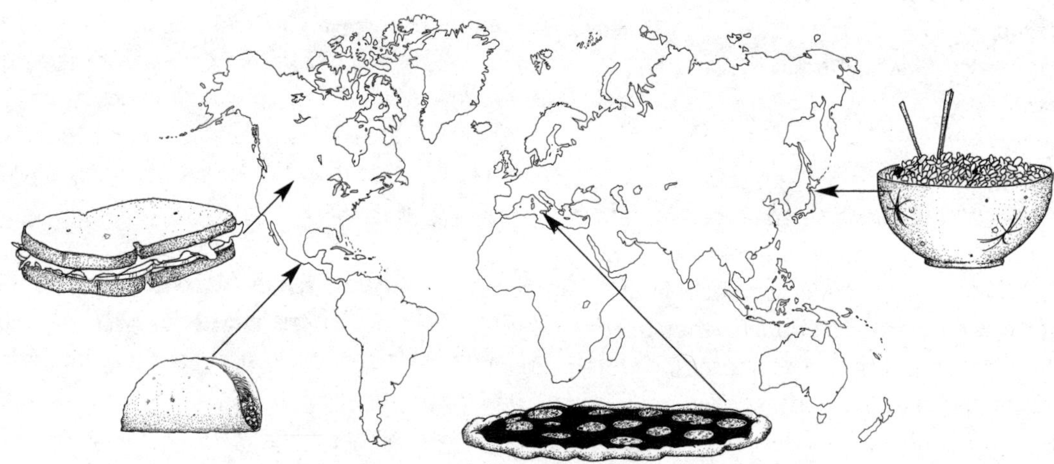

What's for Lunch?

Travel the Internet to learn about lunch around the globe

Recommended Grades: 3–6

- **Social Studies**
- **Geography**
- **Language Arts**
- **Health**

Goals

Food preparation and the customs surrounding meals vary greatly. Help students learn about different practices in other countries and compare them to what they consider to be "normal."

Key Point

- The lunch customs and habits of children all over the world are similar to and different from our own lunch customs and habits.

Background

Did you know that the average French student has a minimum of one and sometimes two hours to eat lunch? In the Middle East, daily breaks are commonly at least that long. North American schools usually do not have an extended mid-day break devoted to meals.

In this investigation, students explore differences and similarities between their school lunches and those of students in other regions by comparing types of foods, amount of time provided for lunch, and particular customs. If possible, connect with other students via the Internet or e-mail. Electronic correspondence permits a potentially rich exchange of stories about customs, rituals, and cultures.

Consider that there are many places in the world where you cannot find out this information by computer, or letters, or library research—where children may not even be attending school due to their living situation or poverty level. In such cases, the basic human right of adequate food is not being met. You may choose to compare food and calories consumed by children in developed versus developing countries.

What You'll Need

Contact information for potential teacher correspondence; e-mail or postal pen pals or web sites. (See Resources.) Your students or their parents may have contacts.

How to Do It

Begin by having students describe typical school lunches where they live. Then designate three states or countries where they might have a pen pal or a

classroom contact (in areas that are likely to have a different cuisine). Divide class into thirds by designated state or country.

Help students create a short series of questions to guide their inquiry into "What's for lunch in your school?" Their aim will be to produce a list that encompasses a daily experience of a peer living elsewhere. Some topics they might cover include: family and school life, local popular culture and pastimes, foods, climate, and environment.

Specific questions that students might ask: What does their "lunch" meal consist of? How do they like the food? How much time are they given to eat? Where does eating take place? Is there music during lunchtime? What are the seating arrangements? How many students purchase lunch versus bring their own?

"Lunch is the most important subject we teach our kids during the school day. If there's one thing we can be sure they'll be doing the rest of their lives, it's eating."
—Katherine Musgrave, Professor Emerita, University of Maine, in *The Penobscot Times*, May 2002

Each group contacts its "pen pals" to introduce this project—"Doing Lunch"—to learn about another school's food lunch period and contrast it with its school. Prepare and send letters.

Next, using responses received, compare their lunches with those of the other regions/cultures, within their own group. Each group makes a chart so the three groups can be compared side-by-side.

Finally, present results to class members.

Classroom Conversations

- Discuss the differences and similarities with students. How does this comparison change their own perspective?
- What would they like or dislike about the other students' daily lives?
- What might be some changes they'd like to see happen in their own school as a result of this experience?
- What about students in parts of the world who may not get lunch, or children who are unable to go to school or have a safe home due to poverty and extreme living conditions?

Want to Do More?

- Create placemats that illustrate a lunch scene in another region or culture. Laminate and sell as a fundraiser or use for the home meal table.
- Have students survey their parents, neighbors, or relatives about their lunch breaks as children or at work.
- Encourage students to look for demographic patterns in lunch traditions. What are the similarities between rural and urban populations? Or between those living in northern versus southern climates? Or between countries?
- Research how lunch was eaten 100 or 200 years ago compared with today.

Action

Do you have enough time to eat lunch? If not, is it a school or system-wide issue? What might change the lunch timetable? If you seek more time for lunch, draft a letter to your school principal/superintendent/school board. If you don't care for the school lunches, discuss with the school Food Services director (first praising what you like best about the meals!).

Lesson Links

The Global Staff of Life
Oodles of Noodles
Traditions at the Table
Old-Fashioned Food

Literature Links

The Multicultural Cookbook for Students by Carole Albyn
Hey Kids! You're Cookin' Now! A Global Awareness Cooking Adventure by Dianne Pratt
Fanny at Chez Panisse by Alice Waters
Family Dinner by Jane Cutler
Everybody Cooks Rice by Norah Dooley
Food Watch: Protecting Our Planet by Martyn Bramwell and Catriona Lennox
Let's Eat! Ana Zamorano
Children Like Me: Celebrations! Festivals, Carnivals, and Feast Days around the World by Barnabas Kindersley and Anabel Kindersley
Uncle Willy and the Soup Kitchen by DyAnne DiSalvo-Ryan

Resources

- For pen pal resources, see www.epals.com/ "world's largest online classroom community and leading provider of student-safe e-mail."
- Consult with foreign-language teachers in your district to connect with schools in other countries.
- *Healthy School Lunch Action Guide* by Susan Campbell and Todd Winant, EarthSave, 1994.
- Center for Science in the Public Interest, a non-profit advocacy organization, has resources to help schools create better lunch meals: www.cspinet.org

Benchmarks

Human Society: 7A—Cultural Effects on Behavior, p. 154

Grades 3-5

Background: "The curriculum should broaden the perception that students have of cultural diversity . . . . Contrasting the common national culture of the United States with other national cultures . . . can be particularly helpful."

"People can learn about others from direct experience . . . and from listening to other people talk about their . . . lives."

"What is considered to be acceptable human behavior varies from culture to culture."

The Designed World: 8A—Agriculture, pp. 183-84

Grades 3-5

Background: "To appreciate the rigors of agriculture, students should learn about life in earlier times and the great effort that went into planting, nurturing, harvesting and using crops." [As students will learn in this activity about lunch around the globe, some cultures are still engaged in the more rigorous aspects of agriculture.]

". . .The kinds of crops that can grow in an area depend on the climate and soil. Irrigation and fertilization can help crops grow in places where there is too little water or the soil is poor."

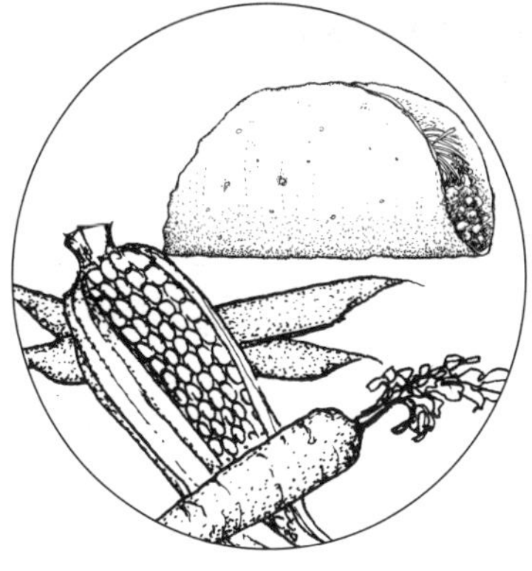

Traditions at the Table[1]

Trace the roots of different food traditions and customs

Recommended Grades: 3–6

- **Language Arts**
- **Social Studies**
- **Life Skills**
- **Health**

Goal

Reflect on different families' styles at mealtimes, share traditions with classmates, and be inspired to try new ways to celebrate.

Key Points

- Food rituals from different traditions may influence your own or your family's eating habits.
- What, how, and when people eat varies from house to house, culture to culture, and country to country.

Background

Food has always been a key element of family and community life. Some contemporary holidays are still based on agricultural cycles. Thanksgiving, for example, was first celebrated to commemorate the colonists' harvest made possible through the contributions of Native Americans. The traditions of eggs and lamb during Passover and Easter date back to a historic celebrations of springtime birth. Unfortunately, many of these agricultural roots have been lost in what tend to be today's commercially oriented celebrations.

Even in everyday routines, though, food continues to hold an important symbolic significance to people. Food is woven through the passages of life, a part of gatherings with friends, families, and community members at events marking births, marriages, deaths, anniversaries, and birthdays. Conversely, food can exclude us from some groups, if religion, preference, or health requires avoidance of certain foods.

Food rituals from our ancestors may involve foodways or practices that don't adhere to modern dietary recommendations—such as those limiting fats and saturated fats. Indeed, historically, fat and meat were prized (and often rare) foods. In addition, our culture's emphasis on dieting for weight loss is a potent reminder that while food nourishes us physically and emotionally, it can be hard for people to consume in moderation. Food practices from other cultures are often based on lifestyles that are more active than the sedentary lifestyles that most of our own citizens live today, and also based on foods without the detrimental additions of so much saturated fat and refined sugar.

In this activity, children can easily select some of their favorite foods and may even be able to describe why they made those particular choices. Popular and traditional culture, familial food customs including family influences, and ethnic as well as religious considerations may be identified.

[1] Adapted with permission from *How to Teach Nutrition to Kids* by Connie Liakos Evers, 24 Carrot Press, 2006.

How to Do It

Begin seated in a circle. Ask students: Think about some favorite foods you and your family enjoy—especially foods that might typically be eaten in other cultures. Are there any foods that are special to your family or that may have come from your grandparents' recipes? Are there certain foods that you or your family eat on special days? Can you describe a meal or celebration with food that was especially fun or meaningful? (You might consider sharing an example from your own ancestry.)

Next, make a list of their ideas on the board and choose one or two which the class could try for a tasting the following week. Encourage family involvement by inviting parents to help prepare or join in the eating. Ask them for ideas about a potential addition to their family's eating traditions. Provide examples such as: eating breakfast together on the weekend; trying food from a different culture occasionally; lighting candles with a special main meal; allowing kids to plan a menu.

Then, have students write a few sentences to complete the following: One food tradition that I would like my family to begin is. . . . Ask students to illustrate if possible, and to share their ideas with their families.

Classroom Conversations

- Guide the class to think about why there is such a variety of food customs and rituals around the world (history, farming requirements, religious practices, lifestyles, cultural traditions, food availability, economics).
- Emphasize that we all have different food preferences and tastes, and that we need to: (1) *first* have food available; and (2) try to eat as healthfully as we can from what's available to us.
- Discuss traditions at the table beyond food—for instance, who cooks and who cleans up? Are there specific rules around the table (show up at a certain time, no elbows on the table, etc.)? Ask: Do you set the table? Do you eat out? Where?

Want to Do More?

- Invite students to design and share a project based on the culture whose food they'll be tasting. Ideas: writing and illustrating a story; designing a skit; creating drawings, flags, or posters; learning a song or dance. Discuss with a music or art teacher if possible. Have students share with the class or school.
- Create a drawing, painting or collage of a new custom they'd like to introduce.
- Invite the food services director or a local restaurant chef to come and talk about different food customs, ingredients, or preferences and how these affect what they serve.

Lesson Links

Oodles of Noodles
What's for Lunch
Pyramids Near You

Literature Links

Moon Cakes to Maize: Delicious World Folktales by Norma J. Livo
The Kids' Multicultural Cookbook: Food and Fun around the World, Vol. 10, by Deanna F. Cook
How My Parents Learned to Eat by Ina Friedman
Everybody Cooks Rice by Norah Dooley
Family Dinner by Jane Cutler
Uncle Willie and the Soup Kitchen by Dyanne DiSalvo-Ryan
Children Like Me: Celebrations! Festivals, Carnivals, and Feast Days around the World by Barnabas Kindersley and Anabel Kindersley
Food Rules! What You Munch, Its Punch, Its Crunch, and Why Sometimes You Lose Your Lunch by Bill Haduch
Amelia's Road by Linda Jacobs Altman
La Mariposa by Francisco Jimenez

Resources

- For more ideas about teaching nutrition and food, including food rituals, see Connie Liakos Evers' excellent book: *How to Teach Nutrition to Kids,* 24 Carrot Press, 2006.
- For examples of traditional eating patterns in many cultures, see www.oldwayspt.org.
- *We Are What We Eat: Ethnic Food and the Making of America* by Donna Gabaccia, Harvard University Press, 1998.
- Combine diverse cultural foods with activities and reading with *Holiday Storybook Stew: Cooking Through the Year with Books Kids Love* by

Suzanne I. Barchers and Peter J. Rauen, Fulcrum Pub., 1998.

Benchmarks

Human Society: 7A—Cultural Effects on Behavior, p. 154

Grades 3-5

Background: "The curriculum should broaden the perception that students have of cultural diversity . . . . Contrasting the common national culture of the United States with other national cultures . . . can be particularly helpful."

"People can learn about others from direct experience . . . and from listening to other people talk about their . . . lives."

"What is considered to be acceptable human behavior varies from culture to culture."

The Designed World: 8A—Agriculture, pp. 183-84

The background section for all the *Benchmarks* under the agricultural section recommends teaching students ". . . how modern-day U.S. agriculture compares with agriculture in other places."

Grades 3-5

Background: "[Students are urged to] study what crops are found in different environments. . . ."

"The kinds of crops that can grow in an area depend on the climate and soil. Irrigation and fertilization can help crops grow in places where there is too little water or the soil is poor."

Choosing for Costs

When we wheel our carts down the grocery store aisles we aren't likely to think about ALL the "costs" associated with our food purchases. We may look at the price we will have to pay, but are we thinking about all that's necessary to bring food from farm to table: a farmer's investments in equipment, crop maintenance and harvesting, food processing, packaging, distribution, marketing, and the disposal of food wastes? Every step in our food system carries real economic, environmental, and social costs. When we choose one food over another, we are voting with our wallets, showing support for whatever goes into the production of the items we buy.[1] Are you voting for sustainable farming practices and local farmers, or for food grown outside your area/country which may be more processed and travels longer distances?

As consumers, we now expect a "seasonless market" where we can buy any food at any time of year. We value the fact that our food system provides:

- variety and abundance of foods;
- convenience; and
- generally safe products, especially given the distances traveled.

But we consumers are often less conscious of the costs involved:

- increased length of time since harvest means fewer nutrients;
- hidden transportation costs for fuel, roadway maintenance, and refrigeration en route;
- increased economic pressure on local growers, causing loss of small, family farms;
- increased air, water, and soil pollution;
- pesticide residues from chemicals banned in our own country that are still used on imported foods;
- loss of habitats abroad for plantation crops which feed consumers in our country;
- global inequities where poor people are displaced from land used to grow luxury crops for affluent consumers;
- low wages, unsafe working conditions, and pesticide poisoning for farm laborers and migrant workers;
- the unknown consequences of genetically modified food technology;
- continued vulnerability due to dependence on foreign oil.

The lessons in this section help students appreciate the range of hidden costs that should be factored into food choices. Ultimately, many of these "costs" are borne more by children. Per pound of body weight children ingest more food and beverages, and inhale more air than a larger adult. So exposure to substances such as pesticides, and air, soil, and water pollution translate into higher doses for children than for adults.

[1] Gary Hirschberg, Stoneyfield Farm Yogurt, Keynote Address at Common Ground Fair, Unity, Maine.

Dollars and $ense

Calculate and compare prices based on nutrients

Recommended Grades: 5–6
- **Math,**
- **Life Skills**
- **Health**

Goals

"Do the math" to learn how to buy the most healthful food with our money.

Key Points

- Food products can be compared in many ways.
- Shopping by price and for convenience are ways many people choose food, but shopping "by nutrition" is better for you and doesn't have to cost more.

Background

"The costs of making food *quick and convenient* probably are no less than the cost of making food *cheap.* Nearly eighty cents of each dollar Americans spend for food goes to pay for marketing services—processing, packaging, transportation, storage, advertising, etc. All of these costs are associated with making our food convenient—getting it into the most convenient form and package, getting it to the most convenient location, at the most convenient time, and convincing us to buy it. . . . So, we pay far more for the convenience of our food than we pay for the food itself. In fact, we pay more to those who 'package and advertise' our food than we pay to the farmers who produce it. So by far the greatest part of the total cost of food is the cost of convenience."[1]

Now, more than ever before, consumers eat more processed, ready-to-eat food products. Generally, this type of food costs more per bite than fresh food or food that is less processed. Not only might it cost more per portion, but it has fewer nutrients than "whole" foods. As we've all heard, "You are what you eat." Regularly eating food with fewer nutrients means your body will be less nourished. And, conversely, healthier bodies come from eating nutritious foods.

In this lesson students evaluate side-by-side the costs and nutrition of a typical processed lunch/snack product such as Oscar Mayer's Lunchables® with the comparable ingredients if the food were made at home.

Teachers and parents have been asking for education about this latest trend in snack and lunch fare. Marketed as a "complete meal" in a package, Lunchables is one of the more common examples of a new breed of convenience foods. How do they rate? Is the convenience worth the cost? How does the nutritional value stack up? This activity is included as much for the educators and parents as it is for the kids! (Here's a short answer: This is a food to eat only occasionally, not as an everyday snack. Oscar Mayer Lunchables contain heavily processed meat, cheese, and mostly white-flour crackers; you're paying more for convenience and getting less nutrition in return.)

There are many different varieties of Lunchables—some contain only two to three ingredients such as cheese, crackers, and ham, or crackers, peanut butter, and jelly, while others offer additional enticements such as candy, a high-sugar fruit-flavored drink, or a toy. For this exercise, we'll compare nutrition facts from one of these snack

[1] "The High Cost of Cheap Food" by John Ikerd, published in "Sustaining People through Agriculture" column, *Small Farm Today,* July/August, 2001.

products with the corresponding separately purchased items. Your class will need to research the prices and do the calculations.

Smart Snacks

Fruits and vegetables are "good buys," in terms of nutrient value. Many snack foods we buy in place of produce—such as pretzels, chips, crackers, etc.—offer fat and sodium instead of the vitamins, minerals, and fiber that fruits and vegetables provide. Here are some ways to reduce the costs of fruits and vegetables even further:

- Buy fresh produce in season when it's less expensive but also at its height of flavor and peak of nutrition. (Help children note that foods are "in season" at different times in different parts of the country/world.)
- Pick fresh fruit at pick-your-own farms and pay less than the farmstand or grocery price.
- Watch local grocery advertisements for reduced prices on your favorite fruits and vegetables.
- If you purchase frozen or canned produce or juices, compare prices of different brands and select the least expensive, as long as it's 100-percent fruit or vegetables. Clip money-saving coupons if you like canned and frozen fruits, vegetables, or juices.

What You'll Need

A package from a common small Lunchables or similar processed snack; package of Swiss cheese; label from ham package or deli; and package of snack crackers. For each product, have (1) the Nutrition Facts label or nutrient information from a reference guide (see Resources); (2) price of each item; and (3) price per unit; calculators. Obtain the foods themselves, not just the packaging, if you'd like the students to sample the various foods.

Getting Ready

Gather food item packages, prices, and unit prices ahead of time. Try to get boxes/labels donated from class members or local retail stores instead of purchasing them yourself. It is easiest if you're able to put all of the price and nutrient facts in a large easy-to-read format for several students to observe at once (or use overhead projector).

How to Do It

Begin by asking what the words "best buy" or "value" mean. Then, introduce the concept of unit pricing (price per pound, per ounce, per gram, per 100 count) as one way to figure out the best value.

UNIT PRICE
You pay 11.8¢ per oz. / $1.89 for 16 oz.
Rich chunky peanut butter

Hold up the Lunchables (or similar) products alongside the packages of cheese, ham, and crackers, and ask which one they estimate is a better buy or value.

Ask: Is price the only thing we should look at? Guide the class to notice that one food might cost less, but the nutrition it contains is also less; therefore, it's not as good a value for building a healthy body. Since "You are what you eat," eating less nutritious food means your body might be less healthy.

Next, focus on one product at a time to make an even comparison. Looking at the label, ask:

- How many ounces of the cheese (product) are contained in the Lunchables?
- How many ounces of ham are contained in the Lunchables?
- How many crackers or pretzels are contained in the Lunchables?
- If the average cost of one pound of Swiss cheese is $4.99, how much would one ounce cost?
- If the average cost of one pound of ham is $4.99, how much would one ounce cost?
- The average cost of a one-pound box of crackers is $3.29. How much would one serving of crackers cost? (Be sure to check serving size; it may not be what you think!)

Calculate the TOTAL price of the three separately purchased foods using the same size portions of cheese, ham, and crackers as are found in the prepackaged snack. Compare that price with the Lunchables price. Which is higher? What might explain the fact that they don't cost the same?

Then, look at the nutrition information for the separate items to demonstrate another type of "value" in this exercise. Divide the class into three

groups, and assign one of the following foods to each group: cheese, ham, or crackers. Each group's task is to determine three facts: the fat, the saturated fat, and the sodium content per unit of food for the food their group is checking.[1] (These are the foods purchased separately, not the Lunchable components.)

Use the chart below to help with calculating nutrients (and see Resources for more information).

Note if there are any other items contained in the prepackaged snack (such as a fruit drink, sweet treat or toy). If so, calculate what the price and nutrients of those items would be if purchased separately and figure those in when comparing overall price and nutrition of the Lunchables to the "homemade" snack foods.

After the calculating, have each group report its findings to the reconvened class: How much fat, saturated fat, and sodium is in the prepackaged versus the packaged food? You may want to record all the results on the list.

Finally, do a (blindfolded?) taste test of the various foods. Consider texture, saltiness, and flavor.

Afterwards, share the What to Munch for Lunch? handout (page 122) with your students and send a copy home with them.

Classroom Conversations

- In terms of money and nutrient value, what's a better way to spend your money: Lunchables or home-packed? Is there any problem with fat, saturated fat, or sodium? (Not per se; the quantities, types, and frequency make all the difference.)[2]
- Think about how the flavor, texture, and nutrition of your lunch would improve if you added some orange sections, an apple, or a carrot.
- Ask: What is the point in comparing the price and the nutrients contained in various foods? What if you are given $20 and are asked to get the best nutrition value for your money at your favorite supermarket? Besides comparing prices of products and the nutrition they contain, discuss the pros and cons of convenience foods. Guide the conversation to include packaging and marketing. Have students define the Latin phrase: *caveat emptor* (buyer beware).

[1] The Center for Science in the Public Interest states that children typically eat five to ten times more sodium than they need. National studies show that 5 percent of our children have high blood pressure. High-fat and saturated-fat food consumption (combined with sedentary lifestyles) play a considerable role in the skyrocketing rates of childhood obesity and diabetes.

[2] Ibid.

Best Buy?

Prepackaged food product (Lunchables: You may calculate separately or use total amounts listed on Lunchables label.)

	Total fat (in grams)	**Saturated fat** (in grams)	**Sodium** (in milligrams)
Cheese product			
Ham			
Crackers			
OVERALL TOTAL:			

Separate food products per serving	**Total fat** (in grams)	**Saturated fat** (in grams)	**Sodium** (in milligrams)
Cheese			
Ham			
Crackers			
OVERALL TOTAL:			

- (Optional) Ask students to recall the taste of the selected foods—which do they prefer? This is subjective, of course, but demonstrates that we value foods for different reasons: cost, taste, culture, health, and convenience are some of the aspects that influence our choices. How much value are they getting from this item?
- How would this information make you reconsider what foods you choose?

Want to Do More?

- Compare the price of the following snacks: one medium banana, one medium apple, two packaged cookies, a serving of chips—investigate which snack would be the least expensive, looking only at price. Then look at the value—how do the nutrients compare (e.g., are there any vitamins in the chips or cookies)?
- In small groups, students select a type of food, visit a grocery store to collect data, and then produce a chart identifying various brands and the best buy available. Charts are then displayed in the classroom. Have students present findings to peers and family. Compile findings into a handout to take home to families or to a local community center.

Action

Connect to parents and families by having students help with food purchases, using unit pricing as one criteria.

Lesson Links

Read the Small Print
Farm to Table
What Are "Whole Foods"?
Sugar Detectives

Literature Links

Kinder Spirits: Children Helping Children in the Fight Against Hunger by Vicki Hubbard and Nancy Killion

Uncle Willie and the Soup Kitchen by Dyanne DiSalvo-Ryan

Food Watch: Protecting Our Planet by Martyn Bramwell and Catriona Lennox

In the Supermarket by Henry Pluckrose

Resources

- Families or local grocery store for product donations.
- For nutrient composition data, see USDA's Nutrient Data Laboratory www.nal.usda.gov/fnic/foodcomp/search/
- See *Bowes & Church's Food Values of Portions Commonly Used*, 18th ed. by Jean A. T. Pennington and Judith A. Douglass. Lippincott, Williams & Wilkins, 2004. A nutrient reference guide for commonly eaten foods.
- For indexes of retail food costs, farm value, the farm-to-retail prices, and the farm value share see www.ers.usda.gov/briefing/foodpricespreads/basket/
- *The Food System: Building Youth Awareness through Involvement* by Alison Harmon, Rance Harmon, and Audrey Maretzki, Penn State College of Agricultural Sciences, 1999. This guidebook introduces the concept of the food system, emphasizes interactive learning, skill building, and using the community as a classroom. For parents and educators of youth in grades 4-12.
- Local life skills or family and consumer science teacher, or USDA Cooperative Extension educator for nutrient information or classroom speaker on topics of thrifty meal planning and "stretching" your money.
- For additional lessons see *Leader Activity Guide: How to Teach Nutrition for Kids* (see "Label Logic," page 32) by Connie Liakos Evers; 24 Carrot Press, 2006.
- For an in-depth and historical examination of our current societal patterns, including food, see *Battleground of Desire: The Struggle for Self-Control in Modern America* by Peter Stearns; New York University Press, 1999.

Benchmarks

The Human Organism: 6E—Physical Health, p. 144

Grades K-12

The background section for Physical Health for all the *Benchmarks*, K-12, states, "Knowledge of science can inform choices about nutrition . . . children should learn how to make and graph health-relevant measurements."

Grades 3-5

"Food provides energy and materials for growth and repair of body parts. Vitamins and minerals, present in small amounts in foods, are essential to keep everything working well."

Grades 6-8

"Some dietary habits . . . may be bad for one's health."

The Mathematical World: 9A—Numbers, p. 212

Grades 3-5

The background section states, ". . . if students are to learn about the meaning of numbers and to use them properly, much of what they do must be based on solving problems in which the answers matter and the numbers used are measured quantities."

"When people care about what is being counted or measured, it is important for them to say what the units are. . . ."

Habits of Mind: 12B—Computation and Estimation, p. 290

Grades 3-5

" . . . divide whole numbers mentally, on paper, and with a calculator."

"Use . . . decimals."

"Judge whether . . . computations of quantities . . . are reasonable in a familiar context. . . ."

Habits of Mind: 12D—Communication Skills, p. 296

Grades 3-5

"Use numerical data in describing and comparing objects and events."

What to Munch for Lunch?

Here are some of the facts about lunch options!

Oscar Meyer Lunchables® are a convenient "meal in a package" that are showing up in lunchboxes a lot lately.

- How do they rate in terms of value?
- If your family assembled its own "Lunchables," how would it look?
- Compare and decide what makes the most sense for your family.

	Lunchables	Packed Lunch	School Lunch
Price	High	Variable	Usually low
Nutrition	Low in nutrients but high in fat, sodium, and sugar	Variable, can be most nutritious choice	Conforms to USDA guidelines for national lunch program
Labor	Low, except for store trips	Variable—child can help or do alone	None, except by school lunch staff
Packaging	Excessive	Can reuse container	Variable
Waste	Some food often wasted	Can adjust portions to child	May be food waste—variable
Convenience	Very	Moderate	Very
Other	Use as an occasional food, not as regular feature	More control over selection, nutrition, cost	Generally balanced nutritionally if child eats full serving
Fill in what your family would pay for each type of lunch			

Farm to Table[1]

Calculate the travel costs for foods you consume

Recommended Grades: 5 and up

- **Math**
- **Language Arts**
- **Life Skills**
- **Health**

Goal

Trace the path of food production, and identify food's hidden costs from shipping, processing, advertising/marketing, packaging, pollution, fuel and energy use, and waste disposal.

Key Points

- A portion of the price we pay for food goes to the farmer, the bank, the seed company, the factory, the trucker, the store, etc. (contributing pieces of the profit "pie").
- Every year, farmers get paid a smaller and smaller share of that food cost "pie."

Background

Most of us take for granted being able to eat fresh produce from across the country and around the world all year long. Amazingly, just *getting* food from the farm to our plates now uses almost as much total energy as was used to grow it! Food prices are the sum of four costs: the raw materials; making it (production); moving and storing it (through all the stages of production and distribution); and marketing. Many of these four costs have additional features about them that we need to factor into the total, but which aren't counted now. Hidden costs such as health effects of highly processed products, and the environmental toll on natural resources by large-scale mono-cropping and controversial land-use practices, as well as production of more waste, make it difficult to calculate the actual cost of our food. The relative amount of money we pay for our food does not take any of these other factors into account; it is more determined by how much the consumer is willing to pay.

Long-distance food shipping is the norm today; most people live in coastal or urban areas and less than 2 percent of the U.S. population still works on farms. Everything that is done to a food—whether it is being grown, processed, or trucked—needs energy, and most of that energy comes from fossil fuels such as oil, coal, or natural gas. A little more than

[1] Activity inspired by "Food on the Move" in "Travelling Lunch" from *Project Seasons* by Deborah Parrella, Shelburne Institute, 1995. Used by permission.

half of U.S. transportation energy is consumed by cars, pickup trucks, utility vehicles, and vans; freight trucks accounting for another 23 percent.[1] There are at least two big problems with burning up large amounts of fuel to run our food system: one is that fossil fuels are nonrenewable—eventually they'll run out. The other problem is that burning these fuels causes pollution.

- Farmers receive less of every consumer dollar spent on food now than they did 50 years ago. In 1952, farmers received 47 cents of every consumer dollar compared to 21 cents in 2001.[2] Invert those numbers to see that 79 cents of every dollar spent at the market never makes it to the farmer, but to the various players in-between the farmer and you. This increasing loss of income explains why there are over 300,000 fewer farmers today than there were in 1979.
- If a typical loaf of bread in your area costs $1.50 to buy, how much would the farmer get if the farmer were paid 21 percent of its price?[3]

Getting Ready

Have students research a list of commonly produced foods and their sources. You may choose to have students bring in their own packaged foods from home.

What You'll Need

Various food packages with easy-to-read labels such as breakfast cereal, juice containers, cookies, crackers, snack foods, etc. (enough for all students in the class); map of the Western Hemisphere or a globe; mileage key; price per gallon/liter of diesel fuel in your area; Where Did My Food Come From? handout (page 126). You may choose to use yarn or string to measure from point to point on the map, and then measure the piece of yarn to calculate mileage.

Teacher Tip

Following the introductory parts of this lesson, 1) take a field trip to a grocery store to learn the origins of some foods or 2) send your students out with a homework assignment to locate the origins of some foods and the local price of diesel fuel.

How to Do It

Begin by describing the path food takes from seed to table in general terms. (See Background or Figuring Out Our Food System lesson on page 44.) Hold up a packaged food item that children often eat. Ask students: What is in this food—what do you think are its ingredients? Where did this food item come from? Using this product, have the group brainstorm the path of one specific, fairly common ingredient from the product, such as corn or wheat. Guide them to include planting, tending, harvesting, processing, transporting, packaging, wholesaling, and advertising. As students are figuring out how a food product is made, record their ideas. Then help them determine the sequence of steps in the process. (For example: which comes first, the packaging or the advertising, the addition of sugar or the raisins or the ____ ?)

Next, show them food items with labels depicting where the food was produced. (Note that not many foods list their place of origin. Ingredient labels list foods in order of highest to lowest quantity. The Nutrition Facts label lists nutrient and guideline percentages and amounts.) Discuss whether or not the farm that grew this food might be near the processing factory. How could we find out where a particular canned item (for example) was grown? (From the labels or information from the grocer or manufacturer, or websites listed in Resources below.) List the origins of as many of the food items as you can.

Then, locate on the wall map or globe the geographic origins of the foods and the route they may have traveled to get to your local market. Have students estimate mileage. (Use the Where Did My Food Come From? handout with them as they work in groups or pairs. Refer to Resources for additional help.)

Most of our food comes by truck, so figuring the local cost of diesel, and using the figure of approximately 6.5 miles per gallon (2.9 km/L) that a trucker gets from diesel fuel, what would be the cost just for shipping by truck? (The average mouthful of food is estimated to travel 1,500–2,500 miles,

[1] Office of Technology Assessment (OTA), *Saving Energy in U.S. Transportation* (Summary) 7-8 (1994).
[2] USDA Market Basket values, as of 2000. www.ers.usda.gov
[3] Ibid.

or 2,500-4,200 km. (So 1,500 miles/6.5 mpg = 231 gallons @ $2.75 per gallon = $635.25.) What are some of the other hidden costs you could include? (Pollution caused by truck exhaust, energy use in refrigeration, packaging, costs for disposal, etc.—all VERY hard to quantify.) What are some of their findings?

Try to figure out the food that has the least "frequent traveler" miles or kilometers and encourage having that food as a classroom snack, provided that it's healthful, which odds are it will be!

Classroom Conversations

- Is shipping food long distances an absolute necessity of life today? Why or why not?
- What if everyone in the world used as much energy as the United States does to produce food—how long would our fossil fuels last? (There is no consensus among the scientific and energy communities about how long current energy supplies will last.) Incidentally, the United States consumes about one-third of the world's transportation energy, however it accounts for only about 5 percent of the world's population.[1]
- Have students consider (and further research!) the amount of water used, waste produced, and energy consumed by an average U.S. student.[2]
- Discuss this statement by Albert Bartlett of the University of Colorado: "Modern agriculture is the use of land to convert petroleum into food."[3]
- What would life be like without oil or gasoline?
- Refer to the Dietary Guidelines for Sustainability (Appendix) and evaluate whether or not some of the foods the class has already discussed fit these particular guidelines.

Want to Do More?

- Have students complete the worksheet using foods in their homes and then share their findings with their families.
- Use various packages and take them apart, measuring actual area of packaging—including inner liners—to demonstrate how much packaging can add to cost/waste stream and energy usage.
- Figure out your class's fossil fuel savings by charting how many times you rode a bike, walked, skateboarded, or use some other non-motorized form of transportation over a specific time period. Make a chart including the activity, the distance traveled, and calculate savings based on the following pollutants or greenhouse gases: carbon monoxide, nitrogen oxides, and carbon dioxide. Get pollution and greenhouse gas figures from the Environmental Protection Agency: www.epa.gov/students/
- Take a tour of a food processing plant in your area. Ask the tour guide or manager where their product's ingredients come from.

With the amount of fuel that we use to produce one loaf of bread (to grow the wheat, grind the flour, bake the bread, and transport it), people in some countries could produce fifty loaves. The difference is that we use fuel to run machines and transport our bread over long distances. They use more muscle-power and eat bread that was produced locally. It takes the energy of approximately ten car tanks of gasoline to feed you for one year. That's about 130 U.S. gallons (or 500 liters). How much energy would our food system use to feed all 6 billion people on earth?

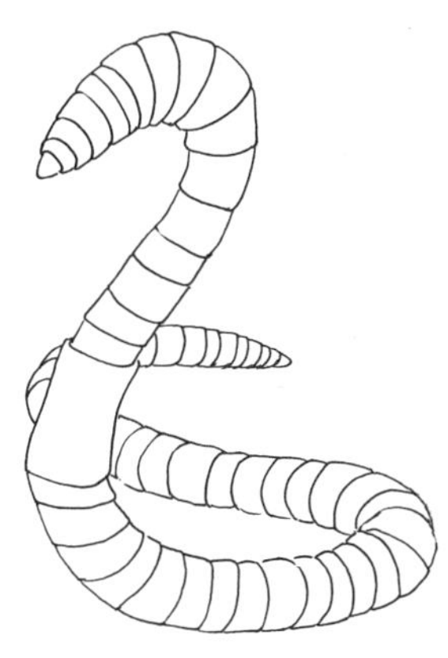

Action

Choose one product that the class deems to have the most unnecessary packaging. Write a letter to the manufacturer asking them why there is so much packaging, and whether they could reduce the amount of packaging they use.

Lesson Links

What Is Locally Grown?
Dollars and $ense
Once Upon a Farm
Figuring Out Our Food System
It All Adds Up

[1] Environment and Energy Study Institute Fact Sheet, "Oil and Transportation," cited in *Getting There*, Washington, DC: The Advocacy Institute; 14, 30; 1996. U.S. Census Bureau. www.census.gov/main/www/popclock.html U.S. population is 299,970,412 and the world population is 6,550,150,987 (as of 10-13-06).

[2] For those students born in the United States, by 75 years old they will have produced an average of 52 tons of garbage, consumed 10 million gallons of water, and used 5 times the energy of a child born in the developing world. National Wildlife Federation;. www.nwf.org as quoted in http://population.newc.com

[3] "Forgotten Fundamentals of the Energy Crisis," by Albert A. Bartlett, University of Colorado at Boulder; www.npg.org/specialreports/

Where Did My Food Come From?

Name ________________________________ Date _______

Look at the label of the food product you have. What is the food and its major ingredient?

Where does that major ingredient come from? Find that location on the map.

How far is that from your home? (Use map distance key.)

What steps did this food go through between being picked in the field and sold in the store? List as many as you can think of. (Consider examples discussed in class.)

How do you think this item was transported? Truck? Plane? Train? Other?

How much time do you think it took to get from field to table?

What resources might have been used in getting it here—topsoil, gasoline, diesel fuel, oil, water, coal, solar, other?

Is the container recyclable?

What happens to the waste products from making this?

Literature Links

Eat Up! Healthy Food for a Healthy Earth by Candace Savage
Feeding the World by Janine Amos
First Day in Grapes by L. King Perez
One Good Apple by Catherine Paladino
Supermarket by Kathleen Krull

Resources

- For color maps of commonly grown national agricultural commodities by county see the USDA National Agricultural Statistics Service site: www.usda.gov/nass/aggraphs/cropmap.htm
- See also USDA, Cooperative Extension Service for information on your state's crops.
- For rankings of major crops by state, see www.nass.usda.gov
- See American Farmland Trust for agricultural and conservation practices: www.farmlandinfo.org
- See *Project Seasons* by Deb Parrella, Shelburne Institute, 1995, for additional activities about food transportation. Note activity "Travelling Lunch."
- Ask school food service personnel for food origin information, particularly of commodity foods available to school districts nationwide.
- Hunger: The Community Food Security Coalition is dedicated to building strong, sustainable, local and regional food systems that ensure access to affordable, nutritious, and culturally appropriate food for all people at all times: www.food security.org

Benchmarks

The Designed World: 8A—Agriculture, pp. 183-84

The background section for all the *Benchmarks* states, "Primary-school children may have only vague ideas about where their foods . . . come from. So the first steps in teaching children about agriculture are to acquaint them with basics: what grows where, what is required to grow and harvest it, how it gets to the stores. . . . Projects to trace locally available food . . . to their origins are helpful in providing at least some personal experience."

Grades 3-5

The background section states, "Where possible, students should . . . examine trucks, trains, cargo planes, and as many other parts of the 'technological food chain' as possible."

The last *Benchmark* states, "Places too cold or dry to grow certain corps can obtain food from places with more suitable climates. Much of the food eaten by Americans comes from other parts of the country and other places in the world."

Habits of Mind: 12B—Computation and Estimation, pp. 290-91

Grades 3-5

"Add, subtract, multiply, and divide whole numbers mentally, on paper, and with a calculator."

Grades 6-8

"Estimate distances and travel times from maps. . . ."

Dear Diary . . . Again

Reviewing our food and health diary

Recommended Grades: 3–6

- **Health**
- **Math**
- **Language Arts**
- **Physical Education**

Goals

Take another look at our classroom health choices and relate them to our previous Health Diary records.

Key Points

- Doing another Health Diary will help us see if we've made any changes in our fruit and vegetable consumption over time.
- Comparing the two Health Diaries will help us see if our class has improved its activity level.

Background

Note: See original information about keeping a Health Diary in the earlier Dear Diary lesson on page 53.

Keeping a food diary is an intriguing exercise in and of itself: changes in behavior are much more likely to occur when the behaviors are being examined.

Changing habits is a personal choice: once the information is presented, it's up to an individual to choose what to do with it, or not. Remember to focus on both movement and food (physical activity AND not OR nutrition). We find health when we balance the two. If someone wants to lose weight, the exclusion of physical activity while only changing food habits is usually unsuccessful. Consider that physical activity and nutrition work together in more ways than weight management. Increasing the calories you use allows you to eat more, which makes it easier to get the nutrients you need. Physical activity and nutrition work together for bone health: calcium and other nutrients are needed to build and maintain strong bones, but physical activity has to be part of the equation.[1]

The National Association for Sport and Physical Education states "...school children are encouraged to be physically active at least 60 minutes, and up to several hours per day. Assure that your students are taught the joy and reasons for being physically active by a professional!"

What You'll Need

Copies of the Health Diary handout (page 55) for each student for the number of days you'll be recording foods; a variety of food pyramids for a refresher.

[1] U.S. Dietary Guidelines: www.health.gov/dietaryguidelines/dga2005/recommendations.htm

How to Do It

Begin by explaining to the class that they'll be comparing some of their current eating and exercise habits to the Health Diary they completed some time ago. Then they'll review how those class totals compare to general dietary guideline recommendations from the food pyramid.

Remind them that this is an opportunity for them to do a group (not individual) evaluation. Ask students to state some of the features of the food pyramid before beginning this lesson, including any serving sizes for fruits and vegetables. Review if necessary.

Next, do the Health Diary for a specified number of days. The longer the journal is kept, the more reliable the information may be.

Then, reassemble the group and have them collectively record responses on a large class graph. (They may keep their own tally private if they prefer.) You can use the same graph as the previous time, with marks in a different color for the newer totals. Tally the servings of fruit and vegetables, and then the minutes of activity. Each column represents a tally of the class's response as a whole. Add up the responses. Compare these to the original tallies.

Finally, have students compare their fruit and vegetable totals with the 5-A-Day recommendation (see Resources). Contrast physical activity class averages with the recommended amount. (Recommendations for adults are at least 30 minutes, or for children 60 minutes, of moderate physical activity, preferably daily— you can do it all at once, or spread it out over two or three times during the day.)

Classroom Conversations:

- What do you notice about eating patterns for the group?
- How was it different than the previous time?
- How do your food choices and physical activities fit within the USDA Dietary Guidelines and the Dietary Guidelines for Sustainability? (See Appendix, page 223.)
- What would you consider changing to help improve your class total?

Action

- Studies have shown that making stairs more accessible or more attractive increases their use. If your school or a local public building has underutilized stairs, here's a fun way to remind people that they have an easy free way to get in a few minutes of exercise.

Create an Activity Guide Pyramid using a 3-D pyramid shape. (Cut four equal triangles from stiff paper—with enough space for class to record their ideas) Brainstorm activities done daily, such as using

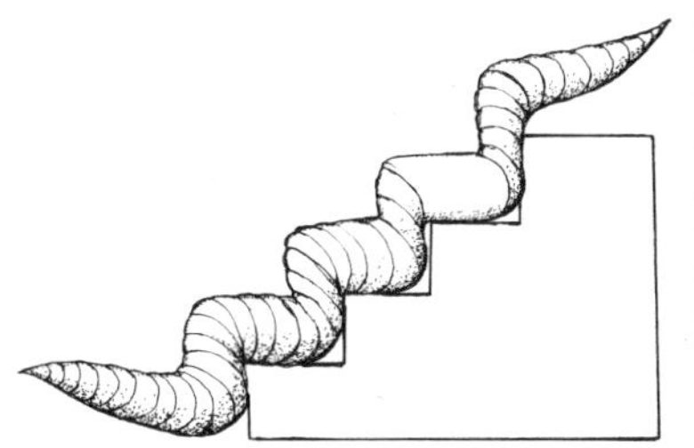

Researcher Kelly Brownell at Yale has estimated that walking up and down two flights of stairs just once a day for a year will keep off six pounds during that year.

stairs, walking to the mailbox or school, taking the dog for a walk, etc. and put these on one triangle. Another triangle could represent items you'd aim to do a few times a week. For example, playing sports, bicycling, physical education class, or dancing. The next triangle might be activities you'd do only a couple of times a week, such as going to the market, outdoor work, push-ups, etc. The final triangle (the fourth "side" of the pyramid) could represent activities that would correspond to the "extras"— the discretionary calories on MyPyramid, such as: watching TV, doing computer games, staying inactive for long periods of time. What are some ways you can cut down on those?

Want to Do More?

- Bring message home to students' families by having students encourage their families to eat at least five fruits and vegetables a day or to increase physical activity—how about using your chart on the fridge as a fun family competition?
- Make connections between food items in the Health Diary and concepts covered in other lessons—local food, miles traveled, packaging, processed and whole food, cost per nutrient, etc.
- Compare serving sizes of common food labels with the "supersized" portion sizes advertised for soda, snack foods, etc. What if you ate all "supersized" portions for all your meals? What if you "supersize" your daily activity—walk to and from school more often, etc.?

- Evaluate what nutrients are in the fruits and vegetables listed in the diary or the class chart using The Top Ten Fruits and Vegetables information (Appendix, page 224).

Penny Wise and Pound Foolish

"Americans are constantly induced to spend a little more money to get a lot more food. Getting more for your money is ingrained in the American psyche. But bigger is rarely better when it comes to food. . . . McDonald's actually charges customers more to buy a smaller, lower-calorie meal." *Margo Wootan, director of nutrition policy at the Center for Science in the Public Interest (CSPI).*

More Action

Speak up. Tell restaurants that are trying to sell you "more for less" that you'd prefer not to. Ask for small or half-sized portions. Suggest to a friend, "Let's share."

Lesson Links

Dear Diary
Pyramids Near You
What Is Locally Grown?
Read the Small Print
Farm to Table

Literature Links

Good Enough to Eat by Lizzy Rockwell
Food Fight: Poets Join the Fight Against Hunger with Poems to Favorite Foods edited by Michael J. Rosen
It's Disgusting and We Ate It! True Food Facts from around the World & throughout History by James Solheim
Elliot's Extraordinary Cookbook by Christina Bjork

Resources

- Ask school food service staff to assist with serving size and portion estimates.
- A local health professional can assist with evaluating the health diary.
- To order the 200 "paper food models" (includes a leader guide, Item #0012N), go through your state or regional affiliate of the Dairy Council. Call the national office (847) 803-2000 to find the Dairy Council nearest you. www.nationaldairycouncil.org
- Send home the reproducible snack handout: www.fns.usda.gov/tn/Educators/yrslf07.pdf
- See the USDA site for a kid-friendly Food Guide Pyramid and dietary guideline information: www.usda.gov/news/usdakids/index.html
- 5-A-Day Program National Cancer Institute: www.5aday.gov

Benchmarks

The Human Organism: 6E—Physical Health, p. 143-44

The background section for the *Benchmarks* states, "Knowledge of science can inform choices about nutrition . . . but that doesn't ensure healthy practices."

Grades 3-5

"Food provides energy and materials for growth and repair of body parts. Vitamins and minerals, present in small amounts in foods, are essential to keep everything working well. . . ."

Habits of Mind: 12A—Values and Attitudes, p. 286

Grades 3-5

"Keep records of their investigations and observations. . . ."

Habits of Mind: 12B—Computation and Estimation, p. 290

Grades 3-5

"Add, subtract, multiply, and divide whole numbers mentally, on paper, and with a calculator."

Habits of Mind: 12D—Communication Skills, p. 296

Grades 3-5

"Use numerical data in describing and comparing objects and events."

PUTTING "GARBAGE" TO WORK

"Waste not, want not."

Twentieth-century sociologists have labeled us the "throw-away society." These habits and our enthusiasm for "excess" have had dire consequences for our environment. In the area of food alone, Americans now throw away more than 96 billion pounds of edible "surplus" food, according to the Economic Research Service of the USDA.[1] That's more than 300 pounds of food a year per person! And while this waste is generated by farms, shippers, food-processing plants, and supermarkets, the largest source of food waste—91 billion pounds—comes from consumers and food service establishments such as schools, restaurants, hotels, fairs, and homes.

Just as we want to encourage children to manage their food world and make healthy choices, we want children to see that their "leftovers" don't have to be "waste." By learning about recycling, children can see different ways that the choices they make about their "garbage" can significantly affect their environment—and the pocketbook. The annual estimated cost of food waste in American households alone is about $43 million dollars.[2]

1 "Estimating and Addressing America's Food Losses," by Kantor, Lipton, Manchester, and Oliveira. *Food Review*, vol. 20, no. 1, January–April 1997. USDA.

2. "Clean Your Plate. There Are People Starving in Africa! The Application of Archaeology and Ethnograpy to America's Food Loss Issues," by Timothy W. Jones, Bureau of Applied Research in Anthropology. To be published in *Applying Anthropology: An Introductory Reader*, Aaron Podolefsky and Peter Brown, editors, 8th edition, McGraw-Hill, 2006.

In the generations that preceded ours, the saying "Waste not, want not" was commonplace. The natural world would benefit if we regained our skills at reducing, reusing, and recycling. That will happen only if we take the time to show children how to do so. Throwing away is easy to do. Reusing takes an imagination that needs to be cultivated.

Tracking Food Waste The activities in this section encourage children to act as detectives. They will identify where food waste is generated, examine the volume that is produced in the school setting, and discover ways to reduce the amount of garbage created.

A Worm's-Eye View of Composting If the earth's soil is the ultimate source of most of our food, what greater gift could there be than to "give back to the earth" by making compost? The activities in this section will introduce children to worms, nature's own recyclers. Whether children view worms at work on a small scale in a canister "vermi-condo," or on a larger scale in a classroom worm bin, they will be impressed by the efficiency of these wiggly creatures as they make "black gold" for use in gardens!

Tracking Food Waste

A joint USDA and U.S. EPA report states that 27 percent of the food available for human consumption in the United States is discarded somewhere between the farm and consumer.[1] For example, food is left in fields from natural disasters or missed harvests; it's spoiled or damaged in transit, or at wholesalers and markets; restaurants, cafeterias, etc. discard food before and after serving people; and families contribute a large amount of uneaten food as well as leftovers and plate scrapings. At each step of the way opportunities exist to "rescue," "recover," or recycle food residuals that would otherwise end up in the waste stream.

Thinking twice before wasting or discarding food can be the first step in solving a host of local and global problems associated with food. Since the largest contributors to this waste stream are food service facilities (like school cafeterias and restaurants) and individual consumers, kids are in a good position to personally make a difference in diverting food waste in school and at home.

Food waste follows a variety of paths:

Disposal

- **Incineration** is the process of burning waste in huge, high-temperature furnaces. Some incinerators generate electricity from trash burning. However, food waste is wet and very dense, so it gives a low-value burn. The by-product of incineration is considered toxic and must eventually be landfilled.
- **Landfills** (or open dumps) were a common place for towns to send their solid waste in the past. They are now highly regulated to reduce animal pests, odors, generation of methane gas (which is produced, in part, by rapidly decomposing food waste), and toxic leaching. Available landfill space has declined dramatically and many towns have sought other alternatives.

Recycling

- **Composting** is the human use of a natural process called decomposition. Organic materials are combined in such a way that microorganisms, worms, and other compost creatures can break down the waste into a valuable soil amendment. Composting at the residential and commercial level increases every year. In 2004 *Biocycle Magazine* reported there were 3,474 composting programs in the U.S., down from 3,846 in 2000.[2] Many towns encourage backyard composting and/or offer informational sessions for the beginner—a strategy to meet waste reduction goals and/or decrease waste disposal costs.
- **Processing** turns food waste into usable, valuable products. Some pet food comes from processed food waste. More directly, farmers use cafeteria food waste as animal feed. Rendering plants process liquid fats and meat by-products into soap, cosmetics, bio-diesel fuel, etc., but with reductions in rendering facilities, some meat processors are paying for waste removal. Composting is being considered as an alternative.

Rescue or Recovery

Simply put, "rescuing or recovering" is diverting edible and safe food from the waste stream to people in need. For example, food is gleaned from harvested farm fields; collected from wholesalers and retailers (excess non-perishable inventory, blemished produce, products past their expiration dates); and delivered from restaurants, fairs, airlines, cafeterias, etc. (perishable and prepared foods).

[1] "Estimating and Addressing America's Food Losses," by Kantor, Lipton, Manchester, and Oliveira. *Food Review*, vol. 20, no. 1, January–April 1997. USDA.
[2] "2004 State of Garbage in America Report," *Biocycle*, April 2006, Vol. 47, No. 4.

It All Adds Up[1]

Chart your lunchroom's food waste

Recommended Grades: 3–6
- **Math**
- **Science**

Goals

Take part in a "gloves-on" project that shows us concretely how much waste is generated and where it goes.

Key Points

- There really is no "away" when we toss out our trash; all garbage stays on earth and has to be dealt with in some way.
- Each U.S. citizen produces about 3–5 pounds (1.4–2.3 kgs) of trash every day. In 1960 it was 2.7 lbs (1.2 kgs) per person.[2] Why has the amount increased?
- A food waste inventory raises awareness of how much trash we make and can help us to create less of it.

Background

What do you know about your trash and the journey it takes once you're done with it? A waste inventory can help identify how much and what kinds of trash are produced by the classroom, the school, or at home. According to the United States Department of Agriculture Economic Research Service in 1997, "If 5 percent of consumer, retail, and food service discards were recovered, savings from landfill costs alone would be about 50 million dollars annually." Recovering only 5 percent of losses from these sources "could represent the equivalent of a day's food for each of 4 million people."[3] Since food waste is one of the largest component groups in the U.S. waste stream and it is the least likely to be recycled (currently we recycle just 2.7 percent of our food residuals), it would make sense to increase our efforts. Although the numbers of serious food waste reducers are small, the successes are inspiring. Food waste reduction programs in homes, schools, colleges, prisons, municipalities, and food markets are reporting a reduction of 50 to 100 percent of their food discards. This translates into a 33 to 85 percent savings in solid waste costs.[4]

What You'll Need

Inventory sheet (include collection dates, location, number of people included, and total weight); scale; rubber gloves; trash bags or pre-weighed plastic containers for collection; aprons or old shirts for protection; eye protection; Take Out the Trash Experiments handouts on page 137; and a large wall graph for data (optional). *Safety Tip:* Organize the waste audit to reduce as much direct contact with garbage as possible as trash may contain sharp objects or other hazards. Use protective clothing, gloves, and eye protection at all times. Most high school chemistry labs have eye-protection gear.

1 Adapted with permission from *Pathways to a Sustainable Future* by the Chewonki Foundation/Maine Waste Management Agency, 1999.
2 EPA, "Municipal Solid Waste in the United States: 2003 Facts and Figures.".
3 *Food Review*, vol. 20, no. 1, 1997.
4 "Don't Throw Away That Food!" EPA, September 1998, #EPA530F-98023.

Getting Ready

To minimize the amount of food waste students must handle, do some careful planning ahead of time. Discuss plans for the food waste audit with the principal, custodian, and food service personnel (have food trimmings from the kitchen included along with the leftovers, for instance). In cooperation with school nutrition service colleagues, develop a workable strategy, schedule, and work duty list. (Optional: Ask other classrooms to participate by collecting their food wastes each day of the audit.) It may help to prepare the school community by:

- Arranging time for students to speak to other classes about the project;
- Making posters that explain or illustrate why you want to collect the food waste and how students and teachers might help;
- Writing a letter to parents explaining the project and how it will be done—perhaps asking for old shirts or aprons, large plastic containers and/or volunteers;
- Explaining what food collection containers will look like (line with plastic bags to make disposal easier); where the weigh station will be located; and where the waste goes after weighing.

What to Do

Begin by asking questions about where food is discarded in their communities: "What do you do with it when you are through with it?" "What does it mean to throw something away—where IS away?" Offer examples as needed (dumpster ⟶ trash hauler ⟶ regional incinerator, landfill, farmer, etc.). Ask: If the school waste goes in the dumpster, where does the dumpster go? If it goes to a transfer station, then where does it go after that? Record their answers for types of food waste and places where it is thrown away. Ask: Is all of it waste or could any part be used?

Ask "How much do you estimate that you each throw away daily? Make a list and try to estimate the weight. Indicate that the class will conduct a food waste check (or audit) of the classroom (or whatever place you find best for your group) to see how accurate their estimates are.

Next, have students (wearing protective clothing, eyewear, and gloves) collect food waste over one day and weigh it all, subtracting out the weight of any containers. Pull out any non-food waste of appreciable weight. Weigh as soon as possible after discarding to diminish the "yuck" factor.

Continue this daily audit for two to five days; the longer you do it, the more accurate the numbers will be. Make classroom graphs; calculate the amount of food waste generated. (You might also calculate what weight or percentage might be compostable.) Figures you could calculate from your available numbers: waste generated per student, per classroom, per school—daily, weekly, monthly, and annually. Contrast the weights they derive with their own weight or that of comparable known objects—for example the average refrigerator weighs about 200 lbs (90 kgs); a sedan car weighs 2,000 lbs (900 kgs); an African elephant averages 11,000 lbs (5,000 kgs)—in fact, one elephant ear alone weighs almost 100 lbs (45 kgs)!

Classroom Conversations

Leave plenty of time to discuss your findings and make conclusions. Ask students how they feel about the activity and the results—are they surprised about the weight results? Did all this food have to be discarded? What other options might there be? What could students do to reduce the amount of their personal food waste? (See A Worm's Eye View of Composting on page 147 and the Taking Out the Trash handout for ideas.)

Want to Do More?

- Brainstorm a list of food waste generators (home kitchens, school cafeterias, businesses, restaurants, hospitals, etc.). Try to conduct audits from the waste generators on the list. Encourage students to do waste audits at home. Have students devise an easy-to-use form that they can explain to their parents.

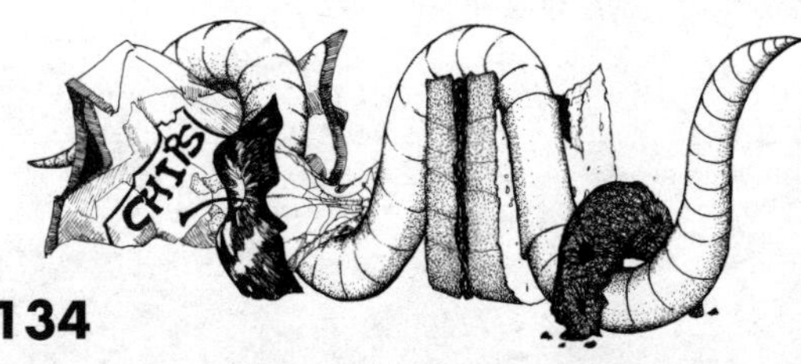

When explaining the concept of not wasting food, we should encourage children to take only as much as they know they can eat. We should not advocate membership in the "Clean Plate Club" (finishing their meal just for the sake of "saving" food) nor require that a clean plate will qualify them for dessert; these practices can be counter-productive.

- Explore the history of garbage disposal before modern landfills and incinerators. What did farmers do with food waste? What does the class know about specific waste disposal options locally: where does that local food waste really go? Do any places compost their waste? What is a modern landfill or an incinerator like? Use various methods to find out the answers: research, field trip, guest speaker, video, interviews, etc.
- Conduct a similar audit for food packaging waste—what is recycled, what is thrown "away" —and look at ways to reduce the waste.
- Survey local grocery stores, restaurants, food processing plants, farms, farmer's markets, and produce wholesalers to learn what they do with their food waste. Find out if they donate edible food (overstocked or discontinued items, blemished produce, day-old bread, surplus perishable food), to shelters and/or food pantries.

Action

Show what you know! Bring the results of your audit to your school and municipal community—choose the medium you think would be most effective for your audience: letter or speech, video, music, photographs, illustrations, or a skit. If you implement any waste reduction measures as a class or school, do another audit later to gauge the project's success and promote this information as well. One idea might be to work with your school lunch program to use reusable cafeteria trays and utensils, and to reduce their use of individual packaged products. Write a letter to your local legislator about your results—include an explanation of any steps you took to reduce food waste and if those measures were effective. Write up a short article for your local newspaper. If you're doing a classroom portfolio of **HEALTHY FOODS FROM HEALTHY SOILS** projects, include the article that you've written. (Or put together a newsletter, which could be called "Knowledge to Go: Here's What We Know!".)

Lesson Links

Lunch at the Dump
What Worms Want
Farm to Table
Recycled Art

Literature Links

Garbage by Robert Maass
Where Does the Garbage Go? by Paul Showers
Garbage by Eleanor Hall
Uncle Willie and the Soup Kitchen by DyAnne DiSalvo-Ryan
Kinder Spirits: Children Helping Children in the Fight Against Hunger by Vicki Hubbard and Nancy Killion
Feeding the World by Janine Amos
Trash Attack: Garbage, and What We Can Do about It by Steve Beinicke and Candace Savage
Cartons, Cans, and Orange Peels: Where Does Your Garbage Go? by Joanna Foster
The Throwaway Generation by Jill Wheeler

Resources

- Consult with administration, custodian, and food service personnel to advise them of your plan and enlist their support.
- A local solid waste director will be able to provide you with waste stream information pertinent to your district. S/he may also be willing to visit the class and discuss garbage issues for your area.
- A local historian or librarian may be able to describe waste disposal methods your region used before modern times. Compare modern and old-fashioned ways of disposing or re-using our discarded trash.
- Environmental Protection Agency: www.epa.gov/teachers/ for teacher resources concerning food waste: projects, community service ideas, and children's activities.
- *Stuff: The Secret Lives of Everyday Things* by John C. Ryan and Alan Thein Durning, Sightline, 1997. "If you don't know your stuff, you don't know your world." Life-cycle analyses (where stuff comes from, what it does, and where it goes) for common everyday items. You can download a pdf file of the "Stuff Curriculum Guide" as well as other teaching guides on consumption issues. www.sightline.org/publications/books/stuff
- *Affluenza* is a one-hour television special that explores the high social and environmental costs of materialism and overcomsumption. Also a sequel: *Escape from Affluenza*. www.pbs.org/kcts/affluenza/
- For an example of one state's waste reduction

campaign, including school ideas, see Minnesota's "Reduce Waste" program: www.reduce.org/

- *Pathways to a Sustainable Future* (1999) by the Chewonki Foundation for more ways to explore waste management issues with your students.
- Grass Roots Recycling Network: waste-reduction activists and recycling professionals dedicated to "building the next generation of informed, active citizens to change the world." www.grrn.org/ See "Kids Recycle!" for ideas, links, encouragement, and kid-to-kid suggestions.

Benchmarks

The Nature of Science: 1B—Scientific Inquiry, p. 11

Grades 3-5

"Investigations can focus on physical, biological, and social questions."

The Nature of Mathematics: 2A—Patterns and Relationships, p. 27

Grades 3-5

"Mathematics is the study of many kinds of patterns, including numbers and shapes and operations on them. Sometimes patterns are studied because they help to explain how the world works or how to solve practical problems, sometimes because they are interesting in themselves."

The Living Environment: 5E—Flow of Matter and Energy, p. 119

Grades 3-5

Background: "Students should begin to notice that substances may change form and move from place to place, but they never appear out of nowhere and never just disappear. Questions should encourage students to consider where substances come from and where they go. . . ."

Human Society: 7C—Social Change, p. 163

Background: "What is sought here is an understanding of what kinds of internal and external factors foster social change or influence character."

Grades 3-5

"Changes in social arrangements happen because some rules do not work or new people are involved or outside circumstances change."

Grades 6-8

Background: "Students can be helped to see that cultural patterns change because of technological innovations, scientific discoveries, and population changes."

The Designed World: 8B—Materials and Manufacturing, p. 188

K-2

Background: "It is not too early for children to begin to wonder what happens to something after it has been thrown away. They can monitor the amount of waste that people produce or take part in community recycling projects."

Grades 3-5

"Discarded products contribute to the problem of waste disposal. . . . Materials differ widely in the ease with which they can be recycled."

The Mathematical World: 9A—Numbers, p. 212

Grades 3-5

Background: ". . . if students are to learn about the meaning of numbers and to use them properly, much of what they do must be based on solving problems in which the answers matter and the numbers used are measured quantities."

"When people care about what is being counted or measured, it is important for them to say what the units are. . . ."

The Mathematical World: 9C—Shapes, p. 223

Grades 3-5

"Graphical display of numbers may make it possible to spot patterns that are not otherwise obvious, such as comparative size and trends."

Habits of Mind: 12A—Values and Attitudes, p. 286

Grades 3-5

Background : "Students should be required to keep written records in bound notebooks of what they did, what data they collected, and what they think the data mean. . . . The thrust of the science experience is still to learn how to answer interesting questions about the world that can be answered empirically."

"Keep records of their investigations and observations and not change the records later."

Grades 6-8

"Know why it is important in science to keep honest, clear, and accurate records."

Taking out the Trash Experiments[1]

Let's try to figure out how much garbage the average young person produces in a year. Record your estimate in a notebook.

CHIPS
I hate to see things go to waste!

Experiment A. This can be done in class or at home. You'll need a bathroom scale.

1. [Re]Use a grocery store plastic bag. For one day, put in it all the trash you discard. Ask your friends to do the same with their own bags, and compare.
2. Figure out how much you'd have (a) after one week at this rate, (b) after one month, and (c) at the end of a year. Make a bar chart or line graph if you wish!
3. What are some of the ways you could reduce your trash?

Experiment B. This is fun to do with your family. Ask their permission first, because it could get messy! You'll need a bathroom scale.

1. For one week, count the number of garbage bags your family fills. Maybe someone might help you weigh them. Write down what you discover. Was this an ordinary week?
2. Figure out how much garbage you'd have after (a) a month and (b) a year if you disposed of trash at this rate.
3. Where does the garbage go, and what happens to it after that? If you're not sure, try to find out.
4. What do you think might happen when there's no more space to put our garbage?

Experiment C. You'll need a bathroom scale again.

1. The next week, collect all the organic garbage (that is, wet food garbage not dry trash) in a separate covered pail or bag. It will start smelling before the end of the week, so keep the container closed when you aren't filling it. Compost or discard at week's end.
2. At the end of the week, count and weigh the regular garbage bags that your family has filled.
3. Compare the results to last week's garbage. Is there a difference?

Experiment D. Are you able to recycle any of the following materials where you live? Metal, aluminum, plastic, glass, newspaper, paperboard (such as cereal boxes), cardboard.

1. Separate out any of these items that you can't or don't recycle, and weigh them after a day or week's time.
2. Compare your numbers with students in your class or anyone else who'd like to try the experiment.

[1] Adapted with permission from *Backyard Magic: The Composting Handbook*, Communications and Educational Services/Department of the Environment, P.O. Box 6000, Fredericton, NB, Canada E3B 5H1; 506-453-3700; fax: 506-453-3843.

Lunch at the Dump[1]

Tour a landfill, transfer station, or recycling facility

Recommended Grades: 2–6

- **Science**
- **Math**

Goals

A "tour de garbage" field trip allows us to learn firsthand about where lunch refuse goes and synthesizes what we have learned about waste and recycling.

Key Points

- Americans recycle and compost about 30 percent of our garbage, and still throw away more than 236 million tons (214 million metric tons) a year.[2] (How many pounds or kilos do you throw away?)
- On average, a student's lunch can generate 67 pounds (30 kilos) of waste per year. Using this figure, how much would be generated by your class/group?[3]
- One person can reduce the amount of garbage he or she creates. Added together, every little bit makes a difference. In the natural world, ecosystems make no waste.

Background

At a solid waste facility near your school or locale, you can learn about where garbage and waste travel, from the sack itself to the plastic or glass contained therein. The tour is followed by a discussion.

A visual examination of the volume of waste is impressive for anyone to witness. "The waste generated annually in the US would fill a convoy of garbage trucks long enough to reach halfway to the moon."[4] Witnessing some of this "tonnage" on a trip to a local facility brings it "home," and can be extrapolated nationally for even more of an impact. It also allows children to see directly what they can do to make a difference in the amount of trash that leaves their own homes.

What You'll Need

Sack lunches or snacks for students; "Garbage-Less Lunch" handout; large plastic bag.

Getting Ready

Explain trip to students and arrange field trip to a landfill, recycling facility, waste separation station, or incinerator. Have an indoor plan for poor weather. Plan to divide class in two groups: the first group receives tour while the other group has lunch at the facility and plays the game.

Note: Discuss classroom goals ahead of time with local facility director or "tour guide."

How to Do It

A. Tour Group:

Begin with a tour of the facility. Ask the tour leader to show various methods of disposal and/or recycled materials at the facility. Describe types of trash recycled or disposed of, the weight or volume of various

1 Activity inspired by second-grade teacher Sarah Holman of Lewiston, Maine, and later adapted with permission from *Green Teacher* magazine, PO Box 1431, Lewiston, NY 14092; www.web.ca/~greentea

2 EPA: "Municipal Solid Waste Generation, Recycling, and Disosal in the United States," Facts and Figures for 2003.

3 www.wastefreelunches.org

4 www.pbs.org/kcts/affluenza/diag/diag.html

commodities, the price for material—one or two points about each to keep tour moving. Choose three or four commodities and ask the tour leader to discuss where some of these products commonly end up; try to make analogies in terms that students can understand (2 tons of paper is the weight of a big pick-up truck or large van, etc.). Examples of commodities (depending on the facility you can visit) and information to glean:

- Plastic—Which containers are accepted for recycling and which aren't? Yogurt? Milk? Detergent? Shampoo? #1 PETE? #2 HDPE? Etc. What happens to plastic after it's recycled? (Some becomes polar fleece clothing.)
- Cans and glass—Why don't they get refilled? What do you think becomes of these? (Some glass is used on highway construction.)
- Swap area—A fan, left by one person, is repaired and used by another. Remind them of the saying "One person's trash is another's treasure."
- Can you return bottles and cans in your state? If so, how many bottles or cans would you need to return in order to pay for a new scooter, a book, a meal? Why aren't there bottle deposits nationally?
- Scrap metal—How much is paid for each ton of scrap metal that leaves this site? Think of all the cars in our country and the scrap metal that results from them.
- Cardboard—Is there a cardboard crusher to compress cardboard in order to transport it—why? Can cardboard be reused?
- Paperboard—Think how many boxes of breakfast cereal are in this pile. Each box costs almost $3.00 in the grocery store. How much would this pile be worth if all the breakfast cereal boxes were full?
- Newsprint—It takes 50,000 trees to make one edition of the Sunday *New York Times,* published and distributed around the world. What happens to the paper after it is read? How is the paper reused?
- Composting area—Is there a composting area? What is composted, and how? Could composting be done here if it isn't? Can leaves be composted after they're raked and hauled to the facility? Is burning them better? If leaf composting or a large-scale outdoor composting area is available, compare indoor or backyard composting with facility-scale composting. How about composting food scraps? (See page 149 for ideas.)

Next, show students samples of recycled "end-products," if possible. Ask students to try to guess what the original material was. (For example: toothbrushes or lumber made from recycled plastic bottles; fleece pile clothing made from returnable bottles; dock pilings made from aseptic packages; corrugated cardboard made from other cardboard; paper made from post-consumer-waste paper; packing "peanuts" made from by-products of corn processing, etc.)

Later, provide a few facts particular to your area. For example: Our town/city sends ____tons off to the transfer station or landfill located in ________ __________. Do you know what happens to it after that? (Not all facilities will convert trash to energy.)

B. Lunch Group

Begin by gathering students at a suitable lunch spot (outdoors, in the facility cafeteria, staff area, or on top of the finished landfill pile, etc.). Discuss the site, when it was built, what it is used for, perhaps what the land used to be and what questions they might have. If you are on a landfill, ask: What's in there? Imagine what we're sitting on. Waste from your parents or grandparents may be buried here. What makes it safe for us to sit and picnic on it? How is it protected from leaking? Observe how many vent pipes there are. Why are they there—what purpose do they serve?

Next, have the students pile what they are throwing "away" on a piece of plastic (a flat garbage bag) in the middle of the group. Look at the contents and discuss where they go to be discarded. Quantify the amount of lunch trash created by the group for later classroom discussion. Ask the group if they think they could have lunches that created less garbage. Take notes on their suggestions. (Use this in the follow-up classroom conversation.) Winner of the "Least Waste" gets to _______ (maybe choose game to play outdoors, or receives a cloth lunch bag donated by the recycling facility, or an "I recycle" magnet, etc.) before walking over for recycling facility tour.

Classroom Conversations

- Ask the class for their impressions of the tour and the field trip in general.
- Find out what was new information and what they already knew. Review some of the commodities mentioned earlier and ask where they eventually end up.
- Ask if people have to discard all that trash.
- Challenge the class to reduce their total lunch trash over time. Discuss the option of creating a Garbage-Less Lunch. (Use handout, page 142.)
- Why don't we observe huge landfills or piles of nature's refuse in a field or forest, etc.?

Finally, after a discussion in the classroom, write a thank-you note for the tour to the facility director. Provide photographs if you took them (and send copies to the local media while you're at it!).

Want to Do More?

- Figure out how much waste is generated individually or collectively, and multiply by the population of the school. Write up results for the local newspaper.
- Use the "Taking out the Trash" handout on page 137 for your own experiment at home.
- Fill in the blanks: My state (or province) recycles ___percent of its waste stream, compared to the national average of ___? Our wet garbage comprises ____percent, of which ___is composted. (These numbers should be readily available from your local facility director.)
- Evaluate lunch trash in the cafeteria and discuss options to reduce the amount of it.
- Evaluate ways to reduce holiday waste. In the United States, we generate 25 percent more trash (25 million extra tons) between Thanksgiving and New Year's than at any other time of year. Be part of the solution—make your own gift wrap or make your gifts; be part of the "Use Less Stuff" movement!

Lesson Links

It All Adds Up
Farm to Table

Literature Links

Garbage by Robert Maass
Where Does the Garbage Go? by Paul Showers
The Nature and Science of Waste by Jane Burton
Too Much Trash by Fay Robinson
Compost! Growing Gardens from Your Garbage by Linda Glaser
Gardens from Garbage by Judith Handelsman
Recycle That! by Fay Robinson

Resources

- Local Solid Waste Facility Director will be able to provide you with information pertinent to your area.
- For free materials for teachers, students, and the community related to garbage, recycling, and landfills, see www.epa.gov/ (select "Education Resources" or "For Kids"); 800-424-9346.
- *The Archaeology of Garbage* by William Rathje and Cullen Murphy, University of Arizona Press, 2001. Information on "Garbology"—the study of garbage.
- *The Rotten Truth* (30-min. video/grades 4-6). See GPN Educational Media at http://gpn.unl.edu/ to preview the video (product code 671.001).
- See "Waste Free Lunches" at www.wastefreelunches.org/ for information, tips, encouragement, and more from moms who helped their local schools go waste-free. You can download a Waste-Free Lunch poster from the EPA at www.epa.gov/epaoswer/education/lunch.htm

Benchmarks

The Nature of Science: 1C—The Scientific Enterprise, p. 16
Grades 3-5
Background: "As student research teams become more adept at doing science, more emphasis should be placed on how to communicate findings."

The Living Environment: 5E—Flow of Matter and Energy, p. 119
Grades 3-5
Background: "Students should begin to notice that substances may change form and move from place to place, but they never appear out of nowhere and never just disappear. Questions should encourage students to consider where substances come from and where they go. . . ."

The Designed World: 8B—Materials and Manufacturing, p. 188
K-2
Background: "It is not too early for children to begin to wonder what happens to something after it has been thrown away. They can monitor the amount of waste that people produce or take part in community recycling projects."
Grades 3-5
"Discarded products contribute to the problem of waste disposal. . . . Materials differ widely in the ease with which they can be recycled."

The Mathematical World: 9A—Numbers, p. 211
K-2
"It is possible (and often useful) to estimate quantities without knowing them exactly."
Grades 3-5
Background: ". . .if students are to learn about the meaning of numbers and to use them properly, much of what they do must be based on solving problems in which the answers matter and the numbers used are measured quantities."
"When people care about what is being counted or measured, it is important for them to say what the units are. . . ."

Habits of Mind: 12B—Computation and Estimation, p. 288
Background: "In the real world, there is no need for people to make a calculation if the answer to their question is already known and easily available. . . . But in most situations, answers are not known and so making judgments about answers is as much a part of computation as the calculation itself."

Habits of Mind: 12D—Communication Skills, p. 295
Background: "There is an aspect of quantitative thinking that may be as much a matter of inclination as skill. It is the habit of framing arguments in quantitative terms whenever possible. Instead of saying that something is big or fast or happens a lot, a better approach is often to use numbers and units to say how big, fast, or often."

The Garbage-Less Lunch[1]

Try to pack yourself a lunch that won't leave garbage or trash behind

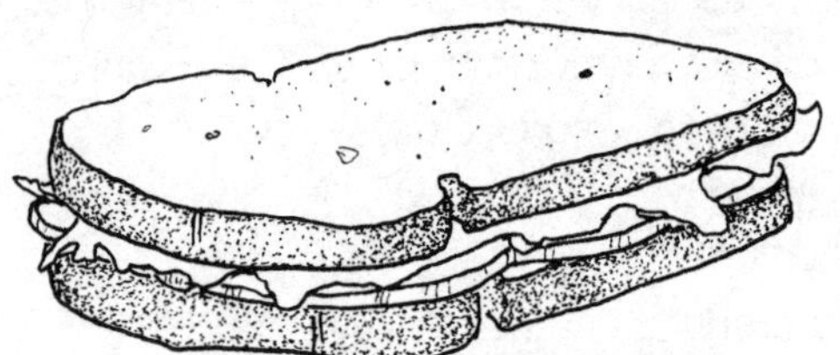

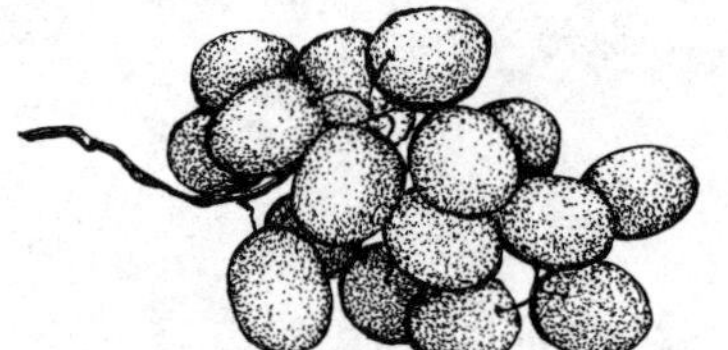

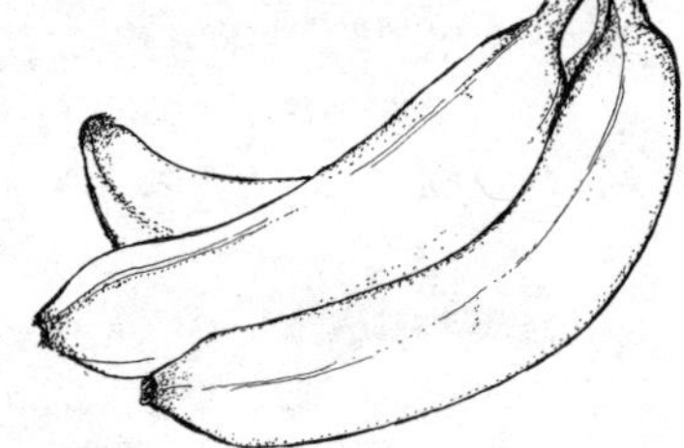

Take the challenge! Pack a Garbage-Less Lunch!
Now that you know what will break down in a compost pile or bin and what won't, here's a challenge for you. Think about:

- Will a chocolate bar make garbage?
- A banana?
- Should you choose waxed paper or a plastic bag for wrapping your sandwich? A hard plastic container?
- Do you eat all of your lunch each day? If not, what don't you eat?
- What scraps can be put into the compost bin?
- Is it better to use a paper napkin, even though it will decompose, or a cloth napkin that you can wash and use again tomorrow?
- What will you carry your lunch in?

You might want to go over this sheet with your family, to help in making "garbage-less" lunch(es)!

1 Adapted with permission from *Backyard Magic: The Composting Handbook,* Communications and Educational Services/Department of the Environment, P.O. Box 6000, Fredericton, NB, Canada E3B 5H1; 506-453-3700; fax 506-453-3843; www.gnb.ca

Now, play along with The Garbage Terminators!
At the end of morning announcements in an elementary school in Ontario, Canada, a member of the "Garbage Terminators" club rolls a pair of dice and announces the sum. If the sum is nine, all the students in the school who believe their lunches are garbage-free prepare to show them to a member of the "Garbage Terminators" club assigned to their classroom. Clipboard-wielding "Garbage Terminators" check off the student names who have qualifying lunches. End- of-the-day announcements include the total number of garbage-free lunches for that day. Year-end totals lead to individual awards. When the project began, "The Garbage Terminators" performed skits in each classroom and created posters to familiarize the school community. They also helped find reusable containers for students who needed them.

With permission from *Green Teacher,* Oct-Nov 1993 issue, "Garbage-Free Lunch Programs that Last." www.greenteacher.com

Recycled Art *Create puppets using recycled objects*

Recommended Grades: K–6
- Visual Arts

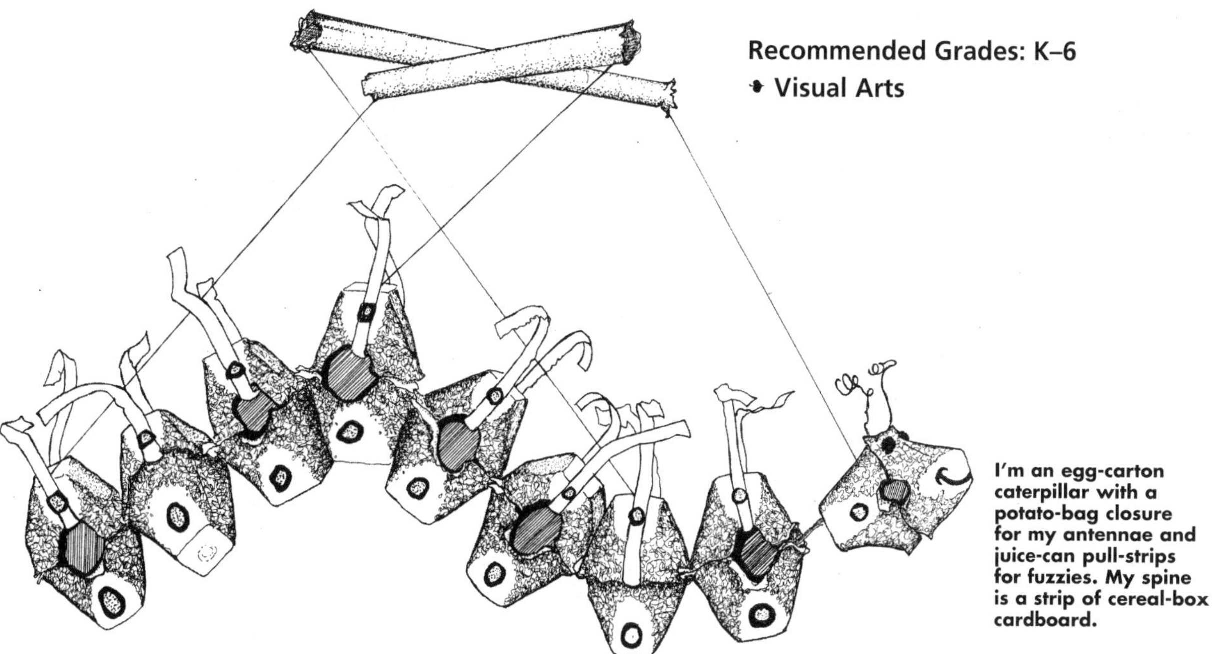

I'm an egg-carton caterpillar with a potato-bag closure for my antennae and juice-can pull-strips for fuzzies. My spine is a strip of cereal-box cardboard.

Goals

Move across the curriculum and create puppets using recycled food packaging materials. It's valuable for children to learn that art can be made with recycled supplies.

Key Points

- A puppet is any (inanimate) object brought to life by the puppeteer's imagination; it can take many shapes and forms.
- Reusing an item to create another changes something that used to be called "garbage, waste, or scrap" into a fresh, important resource.
- Food waste becomes usable when composted; food-packaging waste becomes usable as puppet-making supplies.

Background

Artists often use objects found at hand to create fresh pieces of art, some of which have become well-known. One example is the work of Louise Nevelson, a Russian-American sculptor who lived from 1899 to 1988. Among her many types of work, she took scrap wooden pieces and constructed them into elaborate forms which she usually painted either black or white. Spaniard Pablo Picasso is best known for his paintings but several sculptures he created after World War II are wonderful examples of "making something from nothing"; in these instances, he made animal forms from others' discards.

Children create this type of art naturally when they make snowmen, their own "junk-art," mud pies, beach castles, or "sculptures" from scrap ingredients. This lesson reiterates a HEALTHY FOODS FROM HEALTHY SOILS cyclic theme—all matter can be used and reused—in this case, one person's trash IS another person's treasure!

What You'll Need

Clean, discarded food packages (i.e., cardboard cereal boxes, egg cartons, corrugated cardboard, small-mouth plastic bottles, small aseptic juice boxes, plastic bottle caps—these materials are limited only by one's imagination and their availability!); washed clothing from thrift stores for puppet costumes; paint (acrylic works well); felt tip markers; thick black thread; string; yarn; scissors (utility knife—used with supervision); stapler; needles and thread; white glue (glue gun and glue sticks if you

have adult help and supervision); cellophane tape; masking tap; and duct tape (the universal tool according to Annelida). And finally, newspaper, a ground cloth, or a plastic sheet to protect work surfaces.

Getting Ready

Note: You may want to invite parents, art students, an art teacher, artist, or puppeteer to assist or be involved in this project in some way.

- You'll find more suggestions for using puppets in the classroom in the front of this guide, and instructions for making puppets in the Appendix.
- Ask students to bring in clean food packaging they think could be used to make puppets (This will start their imaginations going ahead of time!), as well as other supplies on the list. Emphasize using old or discarded materials. As materials arrive, sort into boxes for ease of use during puppet construction.
- Gather a few books on puppet-making to help inspire your future puppeteers. (See Resources.)
- Decide how best to use your available work space ahead of time: how and where to lay out supplies so they are accessible to many children at once, where you want them to use glue, or if you want them to bring supplies to their desks. An art teacher may provide helpful tips on managing a project like this.
- Find examples or photographs of artwork made from found objects to share and inspire your students. Pablo Picasso's sculpture *Bull's Head* (1943) or *The Little Owl (La Petite Chouette,* 1953), Louise Nevelson's *Rain Garden II* (1977), or the work of contemporary New York-based artists Sarah Sze and Tony Feher were created using discarded or "found'" materials.

I'm a cereal-box dog with egg-carton teeth and eyes, cereal-box ears, snipped foam whiskers, and brown paper streamers for fur. I had a bottle-top nose, but it fell off before the illustrator saw me. . . .

How to Do It

Begin by demonstrating how materials at hand can be used to create puppets. Remind students that a puppet is a creation limited only by one's imagination, as by definition it is *an inanimate object brought to life by the puppeteer.* They can start with an idea in mind and make the materials fit, or look at the materials and let them inspire a creation. Either way, their puppet construction will take time and they will probably find the final work of art comes about as a result of trial and error.

Then, introduce any classroom safety tips or rules they need to consider (i.e., no criticizing other people's creations), point out the available materials, and remind them to replace things they've used so others may find them. Encourage them to share ideas and materials and if a child finishes early, help keep the materials organized and available for others. (Or make another puppet!)

Finally, remind yourself and any other adults that children are quite capable of using their imaginations to create things. Children will need encouragement, positive reinforcement, and helpful suggestions as well as assistance with locating materials and solving a construction problem, but the puppet they are working on should be the result of their own ideas and creation.[1]

Classroom Conversations

- Invite students to share their reused-food-packaging puppets with the class. Ask them to explain what the puppet was in its former life (a cereal box, soda bottle, egg carton, etc.), how to operate it, and if it has a name. Some students may be comfortable enough to have their puppet

[1] *Puppets and Masks Stagecraft and Storytelling* by Nan Rump, Davis Publications, Inc., 1995.

speak or move. Help them realize the positive attributes of their individual puppets and encourage them to allow the puppet to express itself through movement and/or sound.

- Ask students to think of used or discarded materials that are reused or recycled on a regular basis. Examples of items often given another life (as opposed to being sent to the landfill, incinerator, or dump): scrap metal from discarded cars is melted down and formed into _____ (your class can research what happens!); recycled or returned plastic soda bottles are made into fleece fabric or plastic lumber; used glass bottles are broken and made into reflective bits of roadway or more bottles; leaves are broken down by micro-organisms and other decomposers into humus; and rocks are eroded by wind, freezing/thawing and water to become the mineral component of soil.
- How do they feel about creating puppets from their food packaging waste? What would happen if objects were never reused or recycled? Think of some items that get thrown away a lot and may have "another life" (examples might be computers, telephones, other electronic equipment, toothbrushes, plastic packaging, broken/damaged toys or baby equipment, etc.) What would be some ways to reuse those materials or get people thinking about how they could recycle them?
- Produce a puppet show with a "reduce, reuse, and recycle" theme and perform for other classes. Serve healthy snacks during intermission.

Want to Do More?

- Divide the class into small groups to create their own puppet plays using their puppets. Puppets want to move and perform!
- Brainstorm other art pieces you could create with the remainder of the food packaging waste. Consider building sculptures inspired by the artists mentioned in Getting Ready. Plan an exhibit of the pieces, labeled with title, materials, etc., called ARTrash?! Display printouts from the Internet of the artists used to inspire the work.
- Try creating puppets with other materials and in other forms. (See Puppet resources in the Bibliography.) Make a worm puppet out of discarded nylons (instructions in the Appendix).

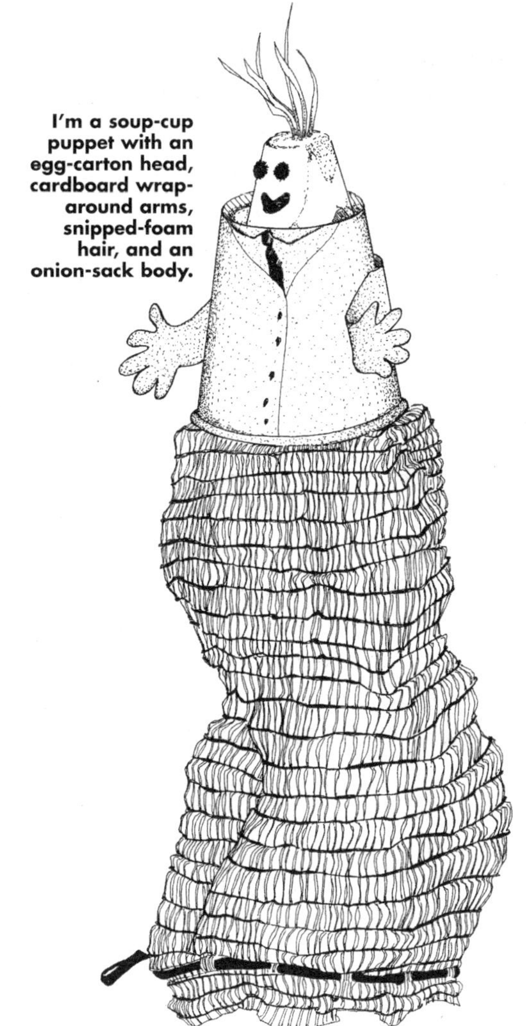

I'm a soup-cup puppet with an egg-carton head, cardboard wrap-around arms, snipped-foam hair, and an onion-sack body.

Lesson Links

Lunch at the Dump
It's a Small World
Soil Made My Supper!

Literature Links

Elizabeti's Doll by Stephanie Stuve-Bodeen
Galimoto by Karen L. Williams
Simple Puppets from Everyday Materials by Barbara MacDonald Buetter
Recycle Art: Look What You Can Make with Plastic Bottles and Tubs editor Kathy Ross
Ecology Crafts for Kids: 50 Great Ways to Make Friends with Planet Earth by Bobbe Needham
Good Earth Art: Environmental Art for Kids, by Mary Ann Kohl
The Most Excellent Book of How to Be a Puppeteer by Roger Lade

Resources

- A local art teacher, artist, or puppeteer familiar with using found objects.
- For student inspiration, refer to *The Muppets Make Puppets* by Cheryl Henson, Workman Publishing Company, Inc., 1994.
- *Puppets and Masks: Stagecraft and Storytelling* by Nan Rump, Davis Publications, 1995, for helpful information on making puppets with kids and using puppets in performances. The orientation is very child-directed.
- *Stories to Play With: Kid's Tales Told with Puppets, Paper, Toys, and Imagination* by Hiroko Fujita and Fran Stallings, August House, 1999.
- Artwork by Louise Nevelson, among other artists, can be found at: www.artcyclopedia.com/artists. For Nevelson's piece, *Rain Garden II,* see www.gihon.com/pages/artwork/nevelson.html
- Check your local recycling facility for materials for teachers.
- *Bottle Biology: An Idea Book for Exploring the World through Soda Bottles and Other Recyclable Materials* by University of Wisconsin, Kendall Hunt, 2003. Great ideas for "Recycled Science"! www.bottlebiology.org; 800-228-0810.
- Visit the web sites of Puppeteers of America www.puppeteers.org/ and UNIMA www.unima-usa.org for information, resources, listings of puppeteers in your area, and links to other puppet-related sites.

Benchmarks

The Living Environment: 5E—Flow of Matter and Energy, p. 119

K-2

Background: "An awareness of recycling, both in nature and in human societies, may play a helpful role in the development of children's thinking. Familiarity with the recycling of materials fosters the notion that matter continues to exist even though it changes from one form to another."

Grades 3-5

Background: "Students should begin to notice that substances may change form and move from place to place, but they never appear out of nowhere and never just disappear. Questions should encourage students to consider where substances come from and where they go. . . ."

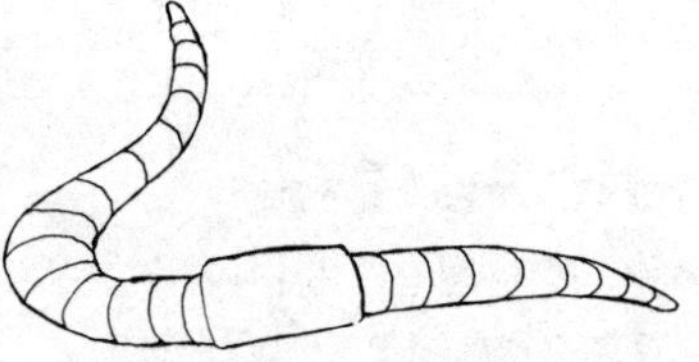

The original Kermit the Frog puppet "started out life as a green spring coat—by way of the ragbag!"* Lots of things deserve a second life! I know a puppet made out of a green, plastic ginger ale bottle named PETE. He's been talking about recycling with families and children since 1991. Even his clothes are made out of reused materials. PETE sometimes mentions that "It's not easy being green," (where have we heard that before?), but he never fails to mention how grateful he is to be given a second chance—especially as a puppet.

**The Muppets Make Puppets* by Cheryl Henson, Workman Publishing Company, Inc., 1994.

A Worm's-Eye View of Composting

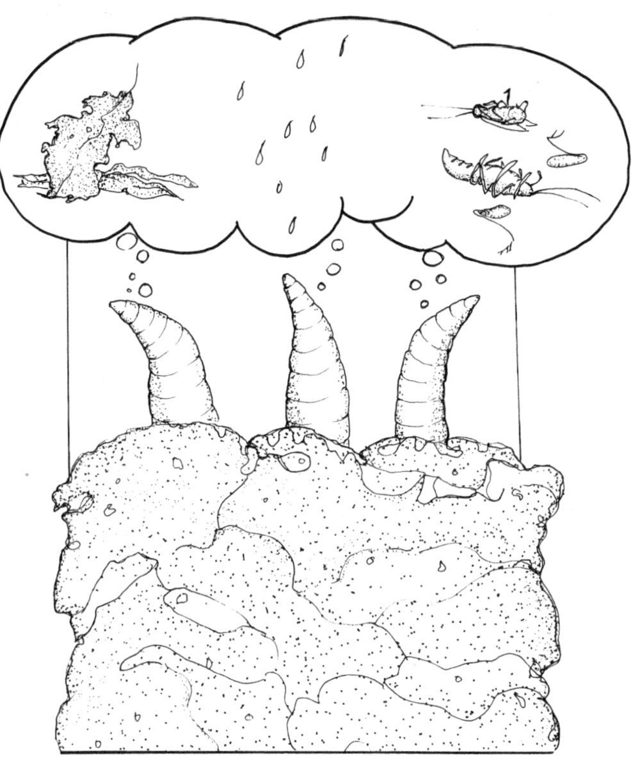

While visions of dead leaves, moisture, and dead insects danced through their heads. . . .

Show students some ways they can "be part of the solution," from diverting food waste from the incinerator or landfill and putting it back to work as compost, to finding ways to donate excess, edible food to people needing food in our communities.

Most kids at some point in life are fascinated with worms. Bringing them into the classroom is capitalizing on this enthusiasm. Decomposition is one of those things that appears as magic to children. Watching worms and micro-organisms decompose classroom snack waste (right under their noses) pulls them into the world of science. Every day in school, children consume food and dispose of what they don't eat. Using a composting bin allows them to be part of the solution—recyclers rather than disposers. And because kids like to feed classroom "pets" they sometimes change what they bring to school to eat so their scraps can be used to feed the worms. Creating vermicompost in the classroom allows you and your students to continue the important cycle of nutrients described in this book by using that compost to enhance soils used to plant our food.

Composting with earthworms, or "vermicomposting," is great for settings like apartments and schools where an outdoor compost pile may not be practical. The great advantage of worm composting is that it can be done indoors and out, thus allowing year-round composting—year-round recycling of food waste and year-round production of "vermicompost." Learning to compost at home and in the classroom provides lessons in decomposition as well as conservation. Vermicomposting is a naturally appealing and fun activity for most children (and adults), even those who may be hesitant at first.

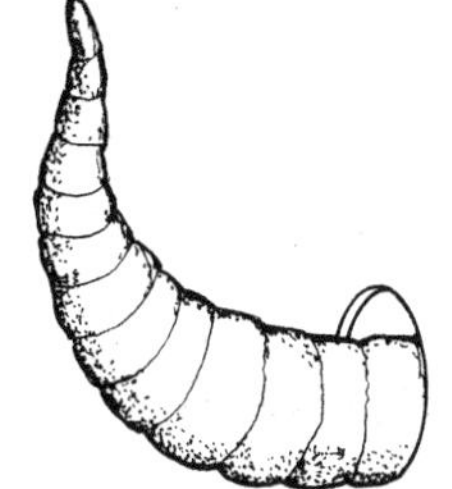

Vermicomposting Basics[1]

Container

Composting worms can live in a plastic bin or wooden box, with air holes punched in the sides and top. Holes in the bottom are generally needed for drainage, so you'll want a tray under the bin. Line the inside of the worm bin with fabric screening if the holes in the bottom are large. The size (surface area) of the box will depend on how much space you have and on the amount of food waste you generate. (In *Worms Eat My Garbage*, Mary Appelhof suggests weighing your food waste for one week, and providing one square foot of surface area per pound.) The container depth should be between 8 and 15 inches. You can use one large box or a number of smaller containers for easier lifting and more choice of location.

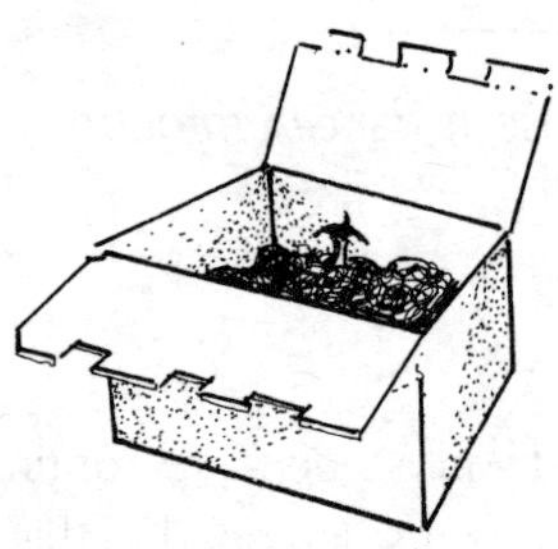

The bin needs a cover to conserve moisture and provide darkness for the worms. Worms move about in the darkness so a lid also helps to keep them in their composting home. For outdoor bins, a solid lid is preferable, to keep out unwanted scavengers and rain. Worms need air to live, so be sure to have your bin sufficiently ventilated. Worm bins can be used indoors year-round, and outdoors during milder months (as long as temperatures are between 40–80° F (5-30° C). Indoors, kitchens, closets, classrooms, and basements are excellent locations (warm, dark, and dry), but any spare space can be utilized. Outdoors, bins can be kept in sheds or garages, on balconies or patios, or in the yard. They should be kept out of hot sun and heavy rain, however.

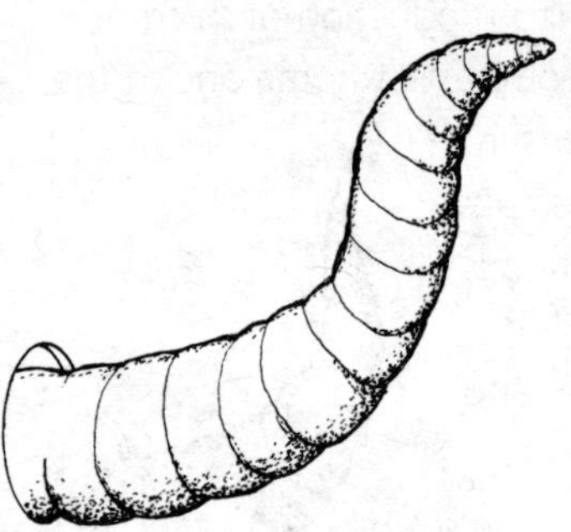
Worms like moist environments. We breathe through our wet skins so we are very unhappy if the worm bin is too dry or too wet.

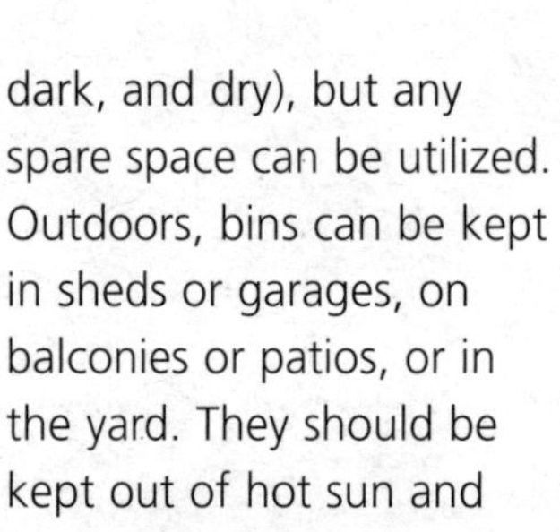

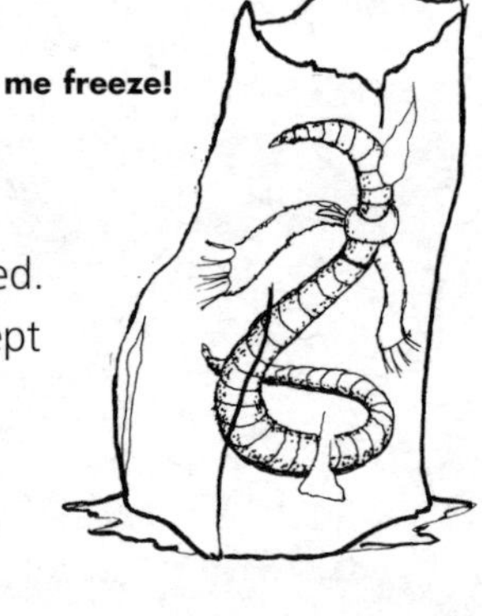
Please don't let me freeze!

You can build, buy, or recycle something like an old dresser drawer, trunk, or discarded barrel. Plastic bins hold moisture—an advantage in an arid schoolroom. Some composters prefer wood because it is more absorbent and a better insulator for the worms.

Bedding

The worms need damp bedding. Suitable bedding materials include shredded newspaper, cardboard, and peat. (We've had success with "peat-free" products—those using coconut husks for example.) Add a couple of handfuls of sand or soil to provide necessary grit for the worm's digestion. The bedding's overall moisture level should be like a wrung-out sponge. The bin should be about three-quarters full of moistened bedding. Lift the bedding gently to create air spaces that help to control odors, and give freer movement to the worms.

Worms

The two types of earthworm best suited to worm composting are the redworms: *Eisenia foetida* (commonly known as red wiggler or manure worm) and

[1] Adapted/edited with permission from *Composting with Red Wiggler Worms* by Gillian Elcock and Josie Martens, Canada's Office of Urban Agriculture, (City Farmer) 1995; www.cityfarmer.org

Lumbricus rubellus—often found in aged manure and compost heaps. Do not use dew-worms (large-size worms found in soil and outdoor compost piles), as they are not likely to survive. Several mail-order vendors can provide worms: shop around for the best price (see Bibliography). Mary Appelhof suggests acquiring two pounds of worms (roughly 2,000 wigglers) to digest one pound per day of food waste. If you start with fewer worms, simply reduce the amount of food waste accordingly while the population steadily increases.

Worms like a variety of foods—just like people! A class that ate mostly oranges for snacks gave the worm bins mostly orange peels for food. We don't know exactly what happened, but after just two weeks, the kids couldn't find one worm in the bin! Too much fruit produces acidic conditions in the worm bin. So give us some cucumber peelings, lettuce, even coffee grounds (which we love), and a regular diet of ground-up egg shells to help buffer the acidity. Otherwise you may find the worms trying to leave the bin or the fruit flies taking over.

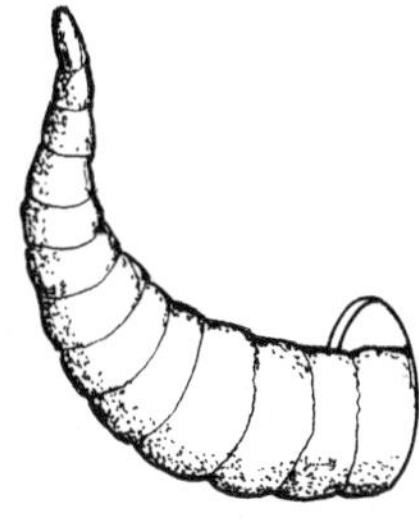

Food Scraps

You can compost food waste such as vegetable scraps, pulverized eggshells, tea bags, coffee grounds, and small amounts of fruit. Eggshells are essential to keep the bedding from becoming too acidic for the worms. For maximum benefit, dry them well, crush them, and sprinkle the tiny pieces over the top of the bedding. It is NOT advisable to compost meats, dairy products, oily foods, or refined grain products because of problems with smells, flies, and mold. Too much fruit in a worm bin can attract fruit flies.

Harvesting the Compost

The finished compost can be mixed with potting soil and used for houseplants and patio containers. It is an excellent mulch (spread in a layer on top of the soil) for potted or garden plants, or it can be dug into the soil.

It is important to separate the worms from the finished compost—otherwise the worms will begin to die. The quickest way to do this is to simply move the finished compost over to one side of the bin; place new bedding in the space created, and put food waste in the new bedding. The worms will gradually move over and the finished compost can be skimmed off as needed.

If you have the time or want to use all the compost, you can dump the entire contents of the bin onto a large plastic sheet and separate the worms manually. Most children love to help with this process and you can turn it into a fun lesson about worms for them. Watch out for the tiny, lemon-shaped worm cocoons which contain between two and ten baby worms! By separating the worms from the compost, you save more worms for your next bin. Mix some of the vermicompost in with the new bedding of the next bin, and store the rest in breathable bags for use as required.

Common Problems and Solutions

The most common problem is an unpleasant, strong odor caused by lack of oxygen in the compost due to overloading with food waste. If the food sits around too long, the bin contents become too wet. The solution is to stop adding food waste until the worms and micro-organisms have broken down what food is in there, to add dry bedding materials, and to gently stir up the entire contents to allow more air in. Check the drainage holes to make sure they are not blocked. Drill more holes if necessary. Worms will drown if their surroundings become too wet.

Worms have been known to crawl out of the bedding and onto the sides and lid if conditions are wrong for them. Even if the moisture level seems all

right, the bedding may be too acidic, which can happen if you add a lot of citrus peels or other acidic fruit. Adjust the pH by adding a little garden lime and/or crushed eggshell.

Fruit flies can be an occasional nuisance. Discourage them by always burying the food waste and not overloading with fruit. Keep a plastic sheet on the surface of the compost in the bin. If flies are still persistent, move the bin to an outdoor location, leaving the top off for a period of time to kill off the fruit fly larvae—or transfer it to a location where flies will not be bothersome. Flypaper in or near the bin can also help. Mary Appelhof has several additional remedies in *Worms Eat My Garbage.*

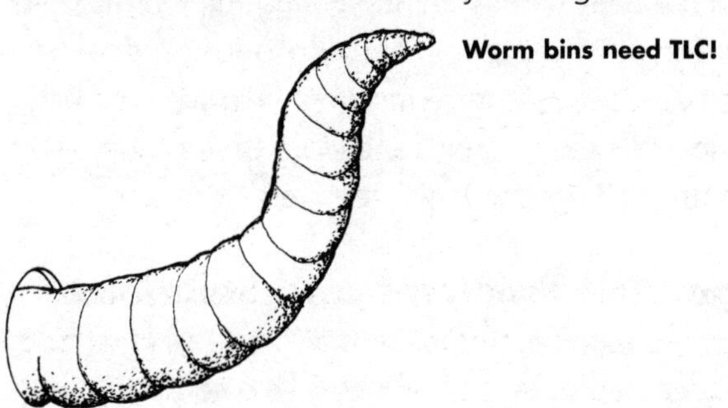

Worm bins need TLC!

- During school vacation in one class, an army of worms escaped from their parched bin and marched "en masse" *several feet* to find water in the classroom sink! The teacher found a path of dried worms from the worm bin to the sink on Monday.
- Food is made mostly of water. That water ends up in the worm bin. A class that was very enthusiastic put way too much food in the worm bin over a short period of time. Every day the class found worms escaping out the drainage holes in the bin—until things dried up a bit.

The Final Word

Taking worms out of their natural environment and placing them in containers creates a human responsibility. They are living creatures with their own unique needs, so it is important to create and maintain a healthy habitat for them to do their work. If you supply the right ingredients and care, your worms will thrive and make compost for you.

- It's a good idea to make a list of things to check each week. Be sure to put "feeding" on the top of the list! It's fun to check for worm cocoons and baby worms as well as other compost critters! See Compost Creatures and Friends on page 164.
- To get the most out of your experience with the worm bin, consider setting up a learning station with some or all of the following materials available to your students: plastic bucket or jar with tight-fitting lid (restaurants, health food stores, or your cafeteria may have extras), trowel or fork, sprayer/mister for adding small amounts of moisture to the bin, plastic (surgical) gloves for squeamish students, petri dishes/Styrofoam trays for worm or compost observations, measuring cups if you choose to measure food waste by volume, scale if you choose to measure by weight, paper towels for easy cleanup, magnifying glass, cutting board/knives, thermometer, clipboard and pencils, flashlight and colored cellophane, pH testers, humidity reader (hygrometer), untreated limestone, vinegar, reference books and materials, clever title for the worm center, and an observation chart.

Resources

For more information on worms and vermicomposting, see the Resources in the lessons that follow.

Earthworms . . .

- Improve the topsoil and enrich plants. That's why farmers and gardeners love them so much.
- Are not native to North America, believe it or not! They probably hitched a ride on plant material or soil brought over by European settlers in the seventeenth and eighteenth centuries.
- Make tunnels in the soil that benefit plants. These tunnels allow air and water to enter the soil. In

the process of digging their tunnels, earthworms mix soil layers.

- Eat soil—they actually are after the organic matter (dead plant and animal parts) of the soil and microscopic organisms living there. If you have earthworms, your soil has organic matter. When you add organic matter to soil, you invite more worms to your spot and they go to work to improve the soil that much more. It's a win-win situation.
- Excrete castings—a polite term for worm manure. Soil and organic matter that pass through a worm's digestive system is extremely rich in minerals.
- Can produce their own weight in castings every 24 hours at optimal conditions.
- Are segmented worms. There are many different kinds of earthworms on this planet. Garden earthworms are not the same worms as composting redworms. Night crawlers are another variety of earthworm. Some worms in Australia can grow to be several feet in length!!! It has been reported that these Giant Gippsland worms can be heard "munching and gurgling" during the night.
- In large numbers can do great things! The *USDA Yearbook of Agriculture* says that the worms in one acre of land can bring 20 tons of soil to the surface in one year.
- Have no eyes but can sense light, no teeth but they can grind food up in their gizzard, no feet or hands but they can move efficiently through soil, no antennae or nose but they can sense the presence of water nearby, no ears but they can sense the tiny vibrations of an approaching predator, no lungs but they can breath air through their moist skin, and have a brain about the size of a pinhead but are able to regenerate small sections of their tail.
- When cut in half do *not*—I repeat, do *not*—become two worms. It becomes two pieces of a worm wriggling in pain. Worms can regenerate only small sections of their tail.
- Are sensitive to chemicals and may not appear in great numbers where soil has been treated with pesticides.

More Wormy Ideas

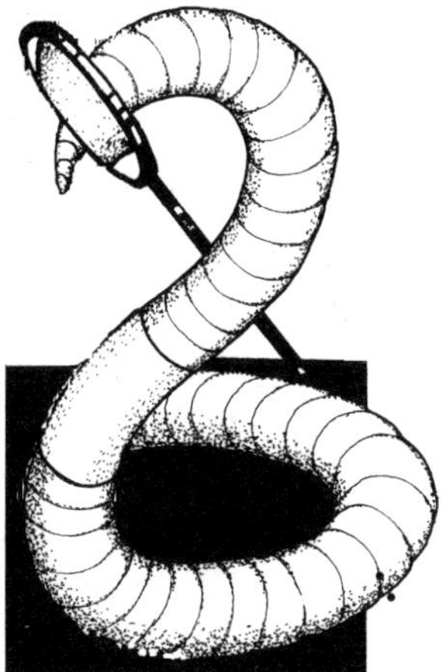

- Check out different soil samples for signs of worms.
- Find evidence of worms by looking for their castings around their worm tunnels.
- Write stories, songs, or poems about worms underground or in the worm bin.
- List all the adjectives you can think of to describe a worm.
- Look at the classification of animals and see where worms are listed (Annelids, segmented worms).
- Observe changes in the worm bin over time. Keep charts, records, and journals. Measure food waste going in.
- Classify or group food wastes that can be fed to worms. Use the food pyramid for categories or make up your own.
- Make a list of things you know about worms and another list of things you would like to know about worms.
- Build a large worm bin with wheels that you can wheel from classroom to classroom (collect leftovers, of course), sharing the fun and learning opportunities with other teachers who are interested but not committed to a full-time worm bin.
- Ask students to write about what it would be like if they were Annelida—how she lives, what she eats, how she moves, how she survives, good days and bad days, what she thinks about her predators, what kind of a burrow world she wants for her squirmy brood of baby worms, etc. Encourage "worm's-eye view" illustrations.

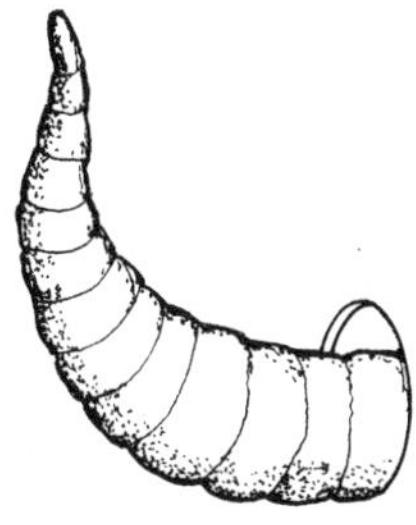

Starting Out Right with Worms

Grade Level: K-2

Teach students how to handle living things gently and to make some first observations with their worms.

- Begin by showing the class the bag of worms. (They are often shipped in paper bags or cloth bags inside a cardboard box.)
- Ask: Why cloth and not plastic? Explain how worms breathe. (Through their wet skin.)
- Next, give these directions: "Everyone close your mouth and hold your nose. Now breathe through your skin." Give them a chance to try. (We can't. We need to breathe through our mouths into our lungs. Worms don't have lungs, but like our lungs, the worms' skin needs to stay moist in order for them to get air through their skin.)
- Then hand out materials: one tray, a wet paper towel, and a small pile of wet, shredded newspaper per student or pair.
- Tell students: Now we are going to observe live worms. We have three rules:

1. Be kind to the worms;
2. Keep the worms moist (so they can breath);
3. At a designated signal, put down what is in your hands, freeze, and listen.

Ready? Hand out a few worms per student or pair. Allow observation and ask questions intermittently—for instance: How can you tell where the head and tail are? Show them how to find the clitellum; only adult worms have them. Clean up.

Sing "The Worms Go Marching Song" while putting things away

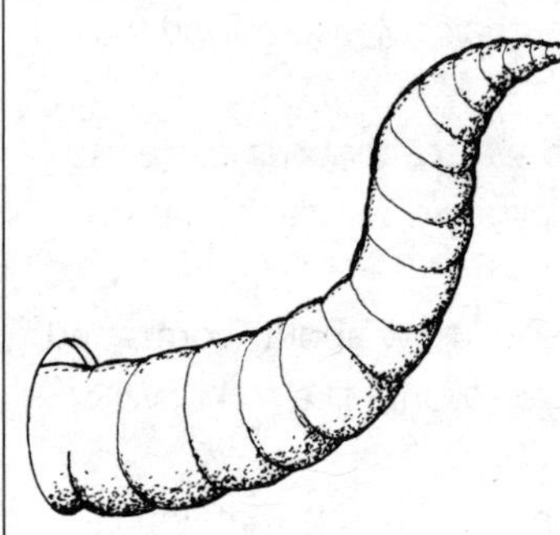

The Worms Go Marching Song

(Sung to the tune of "The Ants Go Marching," words by Kathy Lyons)

The worms go marching one by one,
Hurrah! Hurrah!
The worms go marching one by one,
Hurrah! Hurrah!
The worms go marching one by one,
We better go now, here comes the sun.

Chorus
And they all go marching down into the ground,
Where it's cool and it's wet.
Squirm, squirm, squirm, squirm
Squirm, squirm, squirm.

The worms go marching two by two. . . .
We are part of the garden, too.
Chorus
The worms go marching three by three. . . .
We eat your kitchen scraps for free.
Chorus
The worms go marching four by four. . . .
We'll happily eat your apple core.
Chorus
The worms go marching five by five. . . .
We help the soil, and that's no jive.
Chorus
The worms go marching six by six. . . . (make up your own words)

VERMICONDO[1]

Build a small-scale "worm farm" for classroom observations

Recommended Grades: 1–6
- **Science**
- **Math**

Goals

See firsthand what conditions help worms to reproduce and thrive.

Key Points

- Earthworms are "nature's own recyclers": they mix and fertilize soil layers and help decompose rotting plants—"organic matter."
- Worm castings ("wormanure") and vermicompost (a combination of decayed organic matter and castings) are rich in minerals and improve the soil for plants.

Background

This "worm condo" doesn't produce as much compost as a larger composting bin would, but it gives you an idea of the worms' actions, how they burrow, and what their castings look like—it's an ideal "hands-on" classroom project. Maybe if you're lucky, you'll see a cocoon or how a worm eats. Grab a magnifying lens for a closer look.

What You'll Need

Small plastic container (diameter about 3 inches, such as a tennis ball tube); small rocks or pebbles; spray bottle of water; "brown material" such as newspaper strips, dried leaves, sand, or peat moss; garden soil; sand; food scraps; redworms (some sources for worms are listed in Resources); paper or sock cover (see following "Cover Sleeve" handout). *Note:* You may want to precede this class with an activity that prepares children for bringing animals into the classroom, brainstorming care, feeding, and other responsibilities.

How to Do It

Begin creating this compost column or layered "parfait" by adding layers as noted below. (This can be done using only a single material, but the striped effect of different layers is fun and educational.)

- Start with 1 inch of rocks/pebbles/gravel. What for? Drainage!
- As you add each successive layer, spray gently with water to moisten.
- Each layer can be 1–2 inches—very approximate!

[1] Concepts for this lesson adapted with permission from *Bottle Biology* by the University of Wisconsin, Kendall Hunt Publishing, 2003; www.bottlebiology.org; 800-228-0810.

- Add shredded strips of newspaper. *"All the news that's fit to eat!"*
- Add soil or different types of "brown" material (soil is not necessary, but provides a "bio-boost" due to its micro-organisms).
- Add more newspaper strips.
- Continue alternating layers until you get close to the top.
- Add food: *"Vegetables work best; small pieces for small mouths!"*

Next, put a plastic cover on top, and aerate worm bin lid with poked holes. Add no more than five worms: two to four is probably best. Make a cover sleeve around the sides to give it darkness—you can use dark paper, a sock, or the handout provided to cover the sides of the tube completely.

Then, place columns in a dark place. **Make sure to feed and water regularly.** Remember they need a balance between dryness and moisture—too much of one or the other, and they'll be unhappy wigglers! Make an illustration or science journal entry documenting what you've done: encourage "worm's-eye view" illustrations!

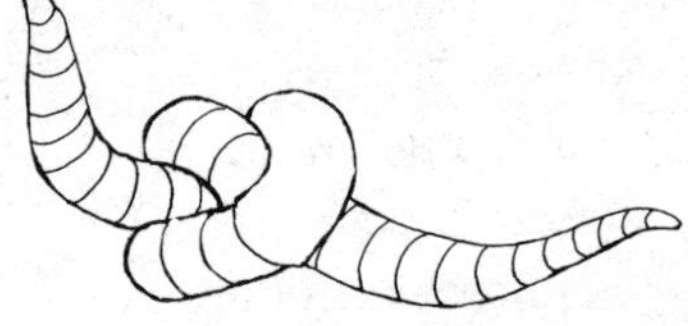

Q: What happens when you play Mozart backwards?
A: He de-composes. . . .

Classroom Conversations

- Think about how many worms you have at the start. Estimate how many worms you'll have before you dump out the tube. Will there be more or fewer? Why?
- What will the column look like after one day, five days, ten days? What will happen to the "parfait" layering or to the food scraps you added?
- What is the value of what these worms have done?
- How could worms be used to help reduce food waste?

Want to Do More?

- Test which foods your worms like best! Remember that they prefer to eat from the bottom of the food pyramid—vegetables, fruits, and grains. A tablespoon or two of leafy green vegetables (their favorites!) about once a week is usually sufficient. Check the drawer of your refrigerator for ideas—but don't use fresh food; they prefer "gently used" (decaying) food!
- Once the newspaper has completely disappeared in the container (six to twelve weeks), you have struck "Black Gold" (it's a safe, valuable fertilizer). To "harvest," layer a sheet or two of newspaper and empty out the container. Then, separate the worms from their vermicastings; this is a fun job for many kids and adults, if a bit messy. Save the "castings" (worm droppings) to fertilize your plants, and place the worms into another compost column or worm composting bin. Or, share them with a friend! Red wigglers may survive in a well-established outdoor compost pile, but they will generally not survive a northern winter as they do not naturally burrow below the frost line as cold-climate-adapted worms do.
- You'll notice that there are some castings stuck on the side of the tube. Fill the tube with water once the worms and paper are out of it—let the water sit in the tube for a few days—up to a week. This "compost tea" is excellent for watering your plants! Notice the difference in plants you water with this gentle fertilizer compared to those watered with plain H_2O.
- When you're done with the composting activity, you can use the tube (without the lid) to grow seeds in—watch root growth this time!
- See the instructions for making a Traveling Worm Bin in What Worms Want, page 162.

Lesson Links

Black Gold
What Worms Want
Compost Creatures and Friends
Are All Soils Created Equal?

Literature Links

Wormology by Michael Elsohn Ross
Earthworms (Nature Close Up) by Elaine Pascoe
Wonderful Worms by Linda Glaser
The Amazing Earthworm by Lilo Hess
Earthworms and Their Food, How Earthworms Live, and *How Earthworms Grow*, all by Inge Plater

HSRHEALTHYSOILREALTY

A Habitat for Wormanity

VERMICONDO

Name
Starting Date
Number of Worms Today
Draw What You See!

Handout from *Healthy Foods from Healthy Soils* by Elizabeth Patten and Kathy Lyons, Tilbury House, Publishers

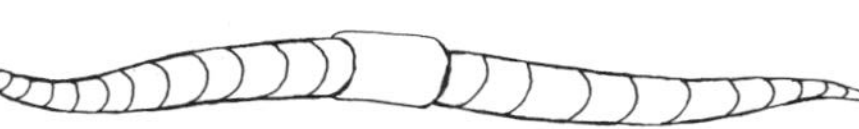

OBSERVE the action of nature's recycler—the redworm!

REMEMBER to keep this cover sleeve on to give it darkness—you can slide it off to do your observation.

MAKE SURE to feed and water regularly. They need a balance between dryness and moisture—too much of one or the other, and they'll be unhappy wigglers! Add more food only when you see that the worms have started munching what you gave them last time. Do NOT overfeed. Just one tablespoon to start.

IDEAS

- Draw a picture of how it looks now.
- Estimate how many worms you'll have at the time of harvest (when no newspaper or other starting material is visible). Will there be more or fewer?
- Test which foods your worms like best! Remember that they prefer to eat from the bottom of the food pyramid—vegetables, fruits, and grains. They *love* leafy green vegetables! Variety and moderation in everything.
- When you harvest, separate the worms from their vermicastings. Save the castings to fertilize your plants, and place the worms into another compost column or worm composting bin. Or, share them with a friend!
- When you're done with the compost column, use the tube (without the lid) to grow seeds in—watch root growth this time!

Squirmy Wormy Composters by Bobbie Kalman and Janine Schaub
Worms Wiggle by David Pelham
Keeping Minibeasts—Earthworms by Chris Henwood

Resources

- Mary Appelhof is the original "Worm Woman." Her books *Worms Eat My Garbage* (1997) and *Worms Eat Our Garbage* (co-authored with Mary Frances Fenton and Barbara Loss Harris, Flower Press, 1993) make an excellent starting point for any worm investigations you undertake!
- Books about worms: *The Worm Book: The Complete Guide to Worms in Your Garden* by Loren Nancarrow and Janet Hogan Taylor, Ten Speed Press, 1998; *As the Worm Turns: New and Easy Methods for Raising Earthworms* by Roy Fewell and Dianne Fewell. Shields Publications, 1998.
- For a basic composting primer, see www.gardening.cornell.edu/soils/factsheets.html and for more on vermicomposting, see http://compost.css.cornell.edu/worms/basics.html
- *Worm Digest* at www.wormdigest.org for answers to just about anything you want to know about vermicomposting.

Benchmarks

The Nature Of Science: 1B—Scientific Inquiry, p. 10–11

K-2

"People often learn about things around them by just observing those things carefully. . . ."

Grades 3-5

"Scientific investigations may take many different forms, including observing what things are like or what is happening somewhere. . . ."

The Nature of Science: 1C—The Scientific Enterprise, p. 15

K-2

"A lot can be learned about plants and animals by observing them closely, but care must be taken to know the needs of living things and how to provide for them in the classroom."

The Physical Setting: 4C—Processes That Shape The Earth p. 72

K-2

"Change is something that happens to many things."

"Animals and plants sometimes cause changes in their surroundings."

Grades 3-5

"Soil is made partly from weathered rock, partly from plant remains—and also contains many living organisms."

The Living Environment: 5D—Interdependence of Life, pp. 116–17

K-2

"Living things are found almost everywhere in the world. . . ."

Grades 3-5

"Insects and various other organisms depend on dead plant and animal material for food."

"Changes in an organism's habitat are sometimes beneficial to it and sometimes harmful."

The Living Environment: 5E—Flow of Matter and Energy, p. 119

Grades 3-5

"Some source of 'energy' is needed for all organisms to stay alive and grow."

"Over the whole earth, organisms are growing, dying, and decaying, and new organisms are being produced by the old ones."

The Living Envrionment: 5F—Evolution of Life, p. 122

K-2

"Different plants and animals have external features that help them thrive in different kinds of places."

What Worms Want

How to make authentic vermicompost in the classroom

Recommended Grades: K–6
- **Science**

Goals

Discover what is needed to maintain a worm compost bin at school and observe the action of nature's great recycler, the redworm. Demonstrate how we are connected to the food cycle by turning food waste into "fertilizer"; and learn skills for taking care of small creatures.

Key Points

- Three-quarters of the food discarded in schools is compostable, according to the EPA.[1] By composting food waste in school, we become an active part of the solution.
- Take a problem—food waste—and turn it into a compost for the school grounds. By taking these food scraps out of the waste stream, we can save money.
- Worms eat and digest food scraps with the help of soil creatures, bacteria, and fungi. Worms make castings and broken-down organic matter called vermicompost.

Background

Be sure to read Vermicomposting Basics on page 148 for valuable information, tips, tricks, and troubleshooting.

Composting provides kids with an empowering, hands-on way to learn science, math, the arts, and community service. Indoor worm composting works well in classrooms, apartments, or urban dwellings. Where outdoor composting is not allowed or is not practical, and in northern climates where outdoor composting goes "dormant" in winter, indoor worm composting is a good alternative.

Worm bins can be purchased or made. Important features of a worm bin are moisture, darkness, aeration, temperature and drainage. Size is determined by each classroom's needs. *Note*: Adding a small amount of garden soil helps the wigglers do their work better and brings on small critters that you can investigate later (as

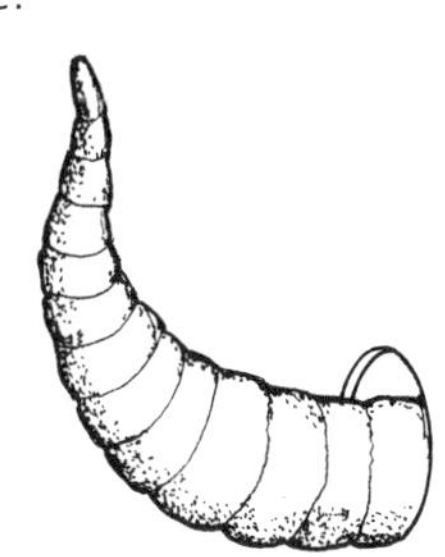

1 "Foods Residuals Management Issue Paper, 2000." JTR Recycling Market Development Roundtable.

well as beneficial micro-organisms), but the worms can make vermicompost without it.

Teacher Tip

The following analogies may be helpful in explaining the purpose of each part of a worm bin.

- The worm bin is the *habitat* (a place that contains the basic elements a worm needs to survive).
- The lid is the roof (keeps worms in, and sunlight and water out).
- The holes in the bin provide *aeration*, as do windows.
- Holes in the bottom of some bins provide *drainage,* as does a basement drain.
- The wet, shredded newspaper—called *bedding*—is the living space.
- The food scraps provide *nourishment.*
- The plastic bag over the bin is the covers to tuck them in (acting to keep *moisture* in).

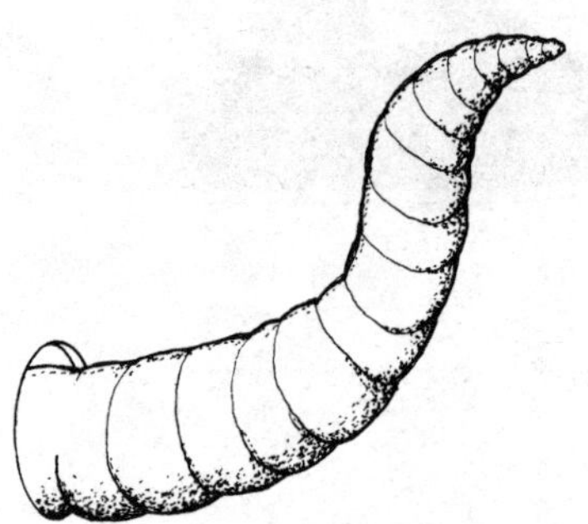

Newspaper has a "grain" and rips quite easily in one direction—in long, skinny strips—and not so easily in the other direction.

What You'll Need

Worm bin; newspaper; water; about a cup of garden soil; plastic bag large enough to cover the inside of the bin; about a pound of redworms; food scraps; plastic container with a tight-fitting lid; garden fork; water sprayer (for wetting newspaper); and food pyramid poster. Optional: peat or coir (coconut husk); rubber or latex gloves; magnifying lenses; cutting boards; knives. (For younger students—the Sequence Cards mentioned in How to Do It can help them prepare the bin.) Post a list of worm "gourmet" foods, and a list of "What Worms Need" for care. Be sure your students understand that worms are living creatures, deserving of kindness and good care!

How to Do It

Begin by telling students that they will be assembling a worm composting bin and introducing a pound of red wiggler worms to their new home. Draw a worm bin on the board or hold up an empty worm bin and discuss why the various parts are necessary. Ask students, What will be put in the bin for the worms? What will the worms need in their new home? The concept of habitat can be used here to explain the importance of the various features of a worm bin. You are creating an artificial habitat for the redworms. (Indicate that foods in the lower three food groups in the food pyramid are okay. The worms need eggshells, newspaper (wetted and shredded) as bedding, and soil. Explain that they will need a container with a tight-fitting cover to store food scraps.

Next (for grades K-2),[1] hand out the following set of directions for setting up a worm bin to teams of 2 or 3 students. Ask them to read the cards to each other and put them in an order that makes sense (more than one order will work).

Sequence Cards

- Save your snack scraps
- Cut the snack scraps into small bits
- Shred the newspaper
- Put newspaper in the worm bin
- Wet the shredded newspaper
- Add a cup of garden soil to the newspaper
- Bury food scraps in the newspaper bedding
- Add worms to the worm bin (It's nice to save this for last for dramatic effect!)

Then, gather the large group together again and ask them to help you put the sequence cards in order on the board. Tape the cards in the order the students suggest and then go back over them to see if any classmates have further suggestions. Keep the cards up for worm bin setup time.

Ask what they need to do to get ready and create a list. Make arrangements to gather materials and assign jobs.

Later, when the food scraps are saved and cut and the newspaper is shredded, put the worm bin in the middle of the circle. Follow the sequence cards. Review why each item is important for the worms as you add them to the bin. Gently dump the worms onto the bedding and have the children guess how long it will take for them to disappear into the bedding. Then just watch!

[1] Activity adapted with permission from *Worms Eat Our Garbage* by Mary Appelhof, Barbara Loss Harris, and Mary Frances Fenton, Flower Press, 1993.

Next (for grades 3-6), put the worm bin together either by giving groups of students specific tasks (cutting the food scraps, shredding the newspaper, wetting the newspaper, adding the food, adding the worms, etc.) or by having the entire class assemble in a circle around the worm bin.

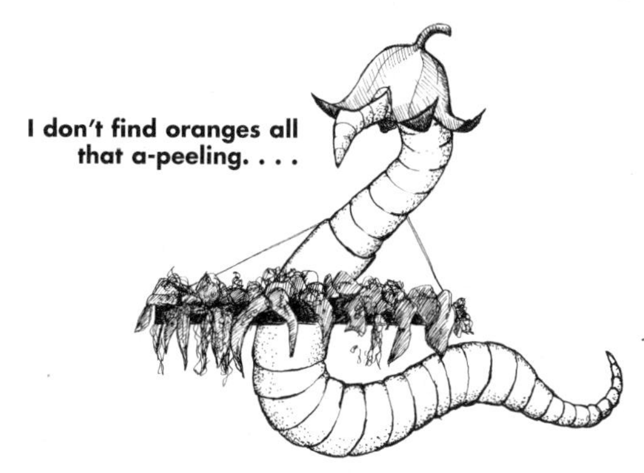
I don't find oranges all
that a-peeling. . . .

Classroom Conversations

(For grades K-6)

- Discuss why worms are important—for soil, for plants, for humans.
- Start predicting what will happen to the worm composting bin contents over time. List things the students would like to learn from their new "pets." Figure out what is known already in the group of students and start keeping a list of questions to answer as time goes along.
- Ask: Why are the best [classroom] foods for worms from the lower three food groups of the food pyramid? (The ones that we humans are told to eat more of.) They are the best foods for worms only because they are in the indoor worm bin. Worms are actually capable of working on meat and dairy and probably sugary items, but these are avoided to reduce the chance of pests and odors in a school worm bin.

Want to Do More?

- Make a chart of worm-care responsibilities and a schedule. Leave a place to list the persons responsible. (The book *Worms Eat Our Garbage* by Mary Applehof gives excellent suggestions.)

  Observer: Write down what you see in the bin: How moist is it? Are there lots of cocoons? Is it dry or moldy? What is of interest?

  Waterer: Check how moist or dry the bin is! Spray or squirt enough water into the bin to prevent newspaper from being dry. A common problem in classrooms is parched worms! If excess water collects on tray at bottom, save and use on plants as liquid fertilizer. If you overwater the bin, add in dry newspaper and mix into wet paper, to absorb excess moisture. Too much water is preferable to too little water.

  Feeder: Cut food into smallish pieces, bury in bin under paper, and feed regularly. Too much food will make bin smell; too little food and your wigglers will be hungry and won't reproduce. Aim for more vegetables than fruit. Avoid adding citrus peels.

  Worm Doctor: Look for mold or fungus, creatures other than worms (fruit flies, sow bugs) or unusual organisms that might affect the worms.

  Monitor: Make sure jobs get done in a timely manner.
- Use Annelida the puppet to host her own "Quiz Show." Write up questions and place in a container. Annelida directs students one at a time to come and pull out a question. She helps the student read the question and asks them to choose a classmate to answer. She uses each question as an opportunity to teach the children about worms. Incorrect answers are used as opportunities. Questions could include**:** Why are worms slimy? Do worms have eyes? If worms do not have teeth, how do they chew food? How do worms breathe? How do worms use their setae (bristles)? What color are baby worms? How do worms help the soil? Do worms have bones? Do worms like to be moist or dry? Do worms like to be in the daylight or the dark? Etc.
- Learn the words to "Take Me Out to the Compost" (page 162) and sing this fun song to your worms!
- Ask your local recycling committee to sponsor a Worm Com-Poster Contest to promote worm composting. A local business might donate money to purchase prizes for winners at each grade level, and the library could post the entries and choose the judges.
- Have students start their own "mini-garbage-bag": using a sealable baggie, place outdoor found objects or food refuse inside bags with a lit-

Worms, Inside and Out

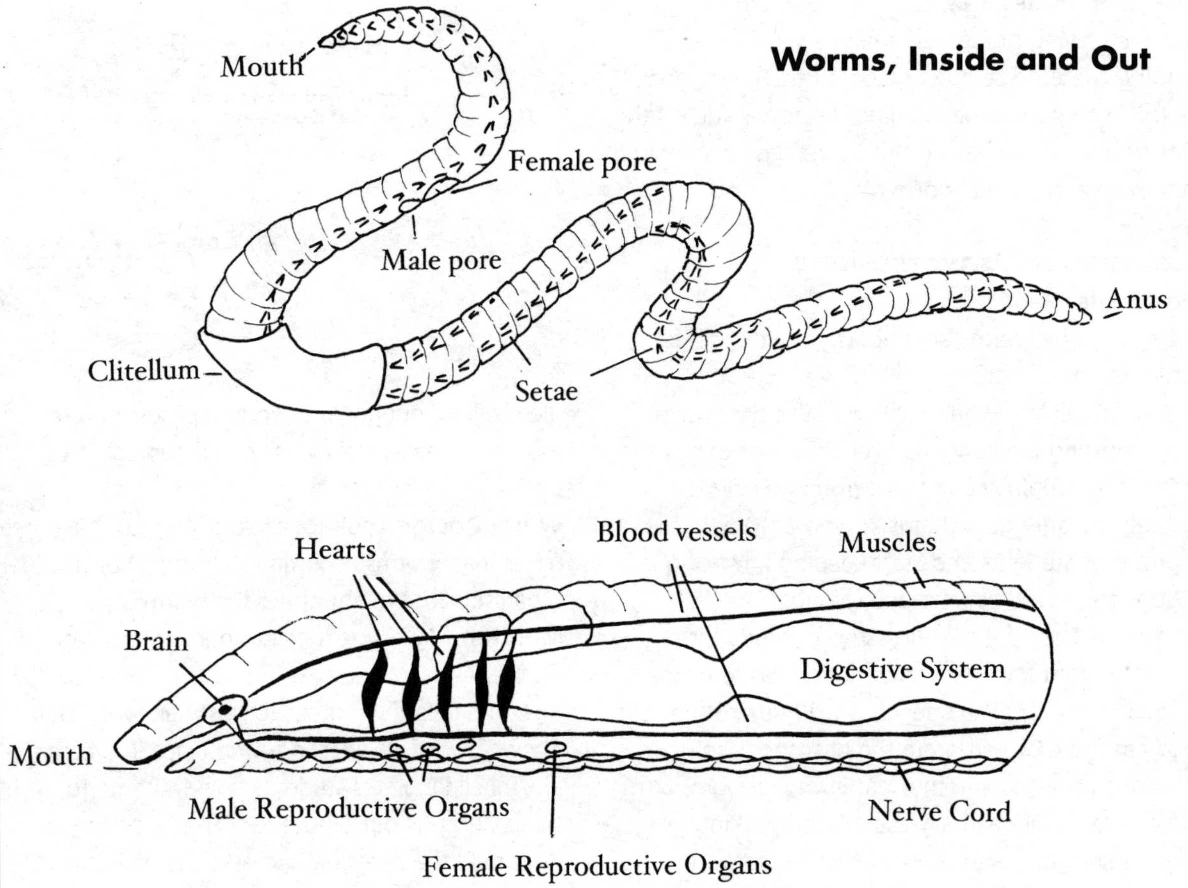

tle water, and observe what happens over several weeks. This "Decomposition Viewer" allows them to see what is harder to observe inside the worm bin. Follow up with documentation: ask how objects changed from when they were first placed in bag.

- Design a chart to measure the amount of food added to the worm bin.
- Make a "Worm Center" with tools and necessary equipment to care for and observe the worms.
- An adult worm will have 115 to 120 segments. Young worms have fewer. You can locate their internal organs by counting their segments. The mouth is between segment 1 and the knob end, the brain is under segment 3, and the heart is between segment 5 and 11. Food storage and the gizzard are under segments 15 to 19, and the intestines run from segment 20 to the worm's end. Worm cocoons are made in segments 32 through 37. Note that the worm does not have lungs or bones. This helps to illustrate why a worm cut in half does not become two worms. They can regenerate only a few segments near their tail. Look at a worm anatomy diagram and compare their anatomy to ours. What do they have that we do not? And, vice-versa?

Lesson Links

Vermicondo
Black Gold
It All Adds Up
Alive and Thriving!

Literature Links

Wonderful Worms by Linda Glaser
The Amazing Earthworm by Lilo Hess
Compost Critters by Bianca Lavies
Earthworms and Their Food, How Earthworms Live, and *How Earthworms Grow,* all by Inge Plater
Squirmy Wormy Composters by Bobbie Kalman and Janine Schaub
Worms Wiggle by David Pelham

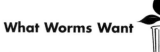

Keeping Minibeasts—Earthworms by Chris Henwood
Wormology by Michael Elsohn Ross
Wormania! (video) by Mary Appelhof

Resources

- *Wonderful World of Wigglers* by Julia Hand and Carolyn Peduzzi, Food Works, 1995. Stories, guided visualizations, many hands-on activities, cute illustrations. Activities more suited for younger children.
- *Worms Eat Our Garbage* by Mary Appelhof with Mary Frances Fenton and Barbara Loss Harris, Flower Press, 1993; *Worms Eat My Garbage,* 1997; and *Wormania!,* with Billy B., 1999, a lively and silly video (in a fun way) about worms and composting.
- *The Worm Café—Mid-Scale Vermicomposting of Lunchroom Waste* by Binet Payne, Flower Press, 1999. A teacher and her students developed a manual for schools, community groups, and small business—and saved their own school some money in the process.
- Musical tapes and CDs from the Banana Slug String Band: www.bananaslugstringband.com ("Decomposition" song).
- *The Farmer's Earthworm Handbook: Managing Your Underground Money-Makers* by David Ernst, Lessiter Publishing, 1995.
- *Worm Composting* by Joshua Nelson, Storey Books, 1998.
- *Worm Digest* at www.wormdigest.org for comprehensive information on anything you ever wanted to know about worm composting; also, a newsletter, and they sell back issues.

Benchmarks

The Physical Setting: 4C—Processes that Shape the Earth, p. 72

K-2

"Change is something that happens to many things."

Grades 3-5

"Soil is made partly from weathered rock, partly from plant remains—and also contains many living organisms."

The Living Environment: 5A—Diversity of Life, p. 102

Background: "All students, especially those who live in circumstances that limit their interaction with nature, must have the opportunity to observe a variety of plants and animals. . . ."

K-2

"Plants and animals have features that help them live in different environments."

The Living Environment: 5C—Cells, p. 110

K-2

"Most living things need water, food, and air."

The Living Environment: 5E—Flow of Matter and Energy, p. 119

Background: "In their early years the temptation to simplify matters by saying plants get food from the soil should be resisted."

K-2

"Many materials can be recycled and used again, sometimes in different forms."

Grades 3-5

"Some source of 'energy' is needed for all organisms to stay alive and grow."

"Over the whole earth, organisms are growing, dying, and decaying, and new organisms are being produced by the old ones."

Take Me Out to the Compost

(Sung to the tune of "Take Me Out to the Ball Game")

Take me out to the compost,
Take me out to the pile.
Add some soil and a few good worms.
I don't care if I'm turned and I'm churned.
'Cause it's root root root for the microbes;
If they don't live it's a shame.
For in two, four, six weeks, I'm out—
In the old garden!

Used with permission. By Pam Ahearn, Waits River School, East Corinth, VT, as published in *Project Seasons* by Deb Parrella (Shelburne Farms, 1995)

Make a Traveling Worm Bin

This mini-bin-within-a-box contains all your students need to help them learn about worms at home and demonstrate their knowledge to their families.

The outer traveling suitcase is a padded lunch-box, the soft kind that closes with a zipper. Inside is a plastic container which has tiny air holes in the top. A webbing strap runs all around the container and then overlaps on the top, fastened with Velcro. An instruction booklet fits in the zipper pocket, along with a letter to the student's family, some rubber or latex gloves, a magnifying glass, and a journal. The worms are snug in their bedding, of course!

Encourage students to reuse materials they might already have:

- Soft padded lunch container bag with zippered top; 2-3 inches of Velcro; rectangular plastic (microwave-type) container with removable lid (small enough to fit in soft bag); webbing (any width: enough length to go all around the plastic container); glue gun and glue; drill and tiny drill bit.
- Contents: Worms, bedding, instruction letter, gloves, hand magnifier, journal.

1. Drill tiny holes in the top of the plastic container.
2. Measure webbing to fit around and overlap the plastic container. (Keeps lid on snugly in transit!)
3. Glue or apply Velcro on the overlapping sections.
4. With a glue gun, glue the webbing to the bottom and sides of the container.
5. Make or purchase a small journal that fits inside the lunch container.
6. Develop an instruction letter to send home with the children (or use the one below).
7. With fabric paint, decorate your new, temporary, traveling worm bin!

Each student can take the traveling "worm and pony show" home on a weekend or vacation throughout the year. Develop a system for checking out the worm bin for the night or weekend. Fill the container half full with worms, compost, and bedding from the class worm bin. Each time the Worm Travelers come home, empty the Traveling Worm Bin into the classroom bin. Read the journal entries to the class upon the return of their worm friends! Encourage parents to write entries or illustrate the journal as well. Remind students to have fun and be kind to the worms!

Handout from *Healthy Foods from Healthy Soils* by Elizabeth Patten and Kathy Lyons, Tilbury House, Publishers.

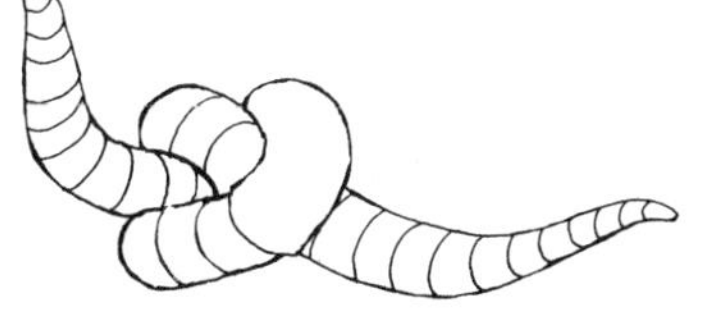

Dear Parents, Guardians, Grandparents, Brothers, Sisters, Friends, Aunts, Uncles, Cousins, and Pets:

This is a traveling worm bin. Our classroom "home" bin is much roomier and is full of shredded paper, healthy food scraps, soil, water, and hundreds of red wiggler worms. In this bin you will find just a few red wigglers—the adventurers from the class worm bin who want to see the world—and just the bare necessities to last the trip. Thank you for helping these wigglers "broaden their horizons"!

Red wiggler worms are very special. Outside, you might find them in a manure pile or a compost pile, and sometimes in a garden. They don't eat the soil as most regular garden worms do; that's why they are sometimes called composting worms! In the class bin, red wigglers are hard at work recycling food scraps into "vermicompost"—a rich soil amendment that plants love.

In the traveling worm bin, these red wigglers are doing some work, but also enjoying the ride. You can take some out of the bin to look at, but just be sure to keep them moist. Worms breathe through their skin! Replace the worms in their mini-worm bin when you are done. If you like, you may add a small amount of uncooked vegetable scraps (chopped into small pieces).

In this traveling worm bin you will find a few items to help you learn about worms: an instruction booklet, some gloves, a magnifying glass, and a journal. Please observe this mini-worm bin, learn about us worms, and write a note in the journal about our adventures at your home.

Please remember to put the cover on securely at night and when the bin is traveling. Replace all the equipment and get my red wiggler friends safely back to class for their next adventure!

Thank you for sharing your home with red wiggler worms. (Who would have guessed!) It will be fun to read about these worms' adventures at your home in the journal.

Sincerely,
Annelida
The **HEALTHY FOODS FROM HEALTHY SOILS** Spokesworm

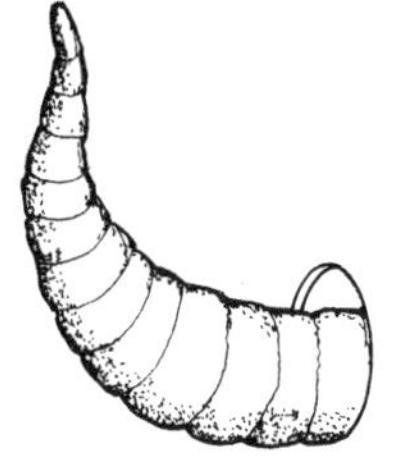

Handout from *Healthy Foods from Healthy Soils* by Elizabeth Patten and Kathy Lyons, Tilbury House, Publishers.

Compost Creatures and Friends[1]

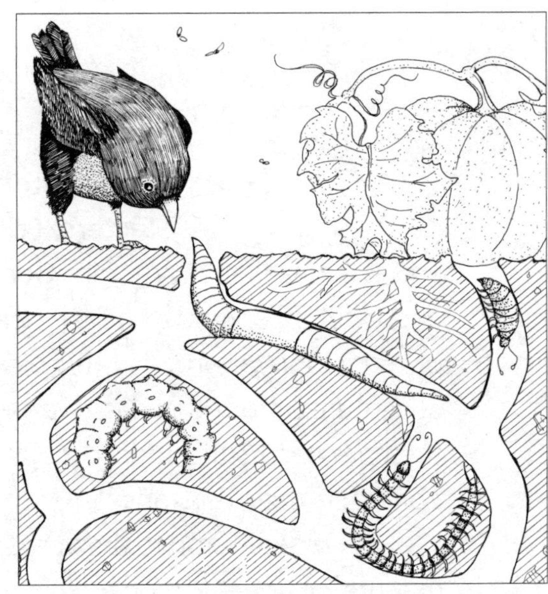

Play Worm Bin Bingo and make a Worm Bin Field Guide

Recommended Grades: K–6

- **Science**
- **Language and Visual Arts**

Goals

Learn about the inhabitants of the compost ecosystem and appreciate what is involved in creating healthy soils. Students research, locate, and identify the inhabitants of the world of decomposition ("creepy crawlies").

Key Points

- There is more to a worm bin than meets the eye; the closer you look, the more you will see.
- Every critter in the worm bin plays an important role in the composting ecosystem.
- Believe it or not, the largest number of organisms in vermicompost are too small to see without a microscope! Billions of bacteria, fungi, and actinomycetes are an "invisible" workforce in soils and compost piles.

Background

They're not officially invited guests, but after two to four months, a variety of compost creatures can be found scurrying and crawling around in what you thought was solely a home for composting worms. This is usually good news; for the most part, the uninvited guests are toiling away for their room and board—and aiding the worms in breaking down some of the hardest stuff in the process.

Who arrives in your bin will vary from bin to bin and how they get there seems like a bit of a mystery. However, bacteria and fungi are ever-present in our air, and foods contain organisms that naturally start the decaying process over time. If you added a handful of soil to the bin as recommended, it probably contained some eggs or larva of some of these unsolicited guests. Others may have just followed their noses, so to speak. The organisms you find in the bin can also be found in soils rich in organic matter and in outdoor compost piles. These creatures are basically decomposers or are the predators of decomposers!

While the other decomposer organisms may outnumber the earthworms in the bin, the worms are still essential. It is their digestion of organic material that creates the nutrient-rich worm castings that plants and gardeners love. *Note:* The activities in this lesson could be divided into projects for younger and older students.

A worm bin is a regular working neighborhood—an ecosystem all its own.

[1] Worm Bin Bingo Game inspired by and adapted with permission from *The Microcosmos Curriculum Guide to Exploring Microbial Space,* edited by Douglas Zook, Kendall Hunt, 1994.

What You'll Need

For the Worm Bin Field Guide: books on soil and compost organisms; drawing paper; pencils; microscope if available (ask high school science teacher).
For Worm Bin Bingo: large plastic containers (recycled from home) or trays; magnifying lenses; copies of the Worm Bin Field Guide and Compost Creature Bingo Cards (see Getting Ready); worm compost, outdoor compost, or organic-rich soil.
Optional: prizes for bingo.

Teacher Tip

For younger students, just taking time to search for and identify compost inhabitants from illustrations is probably enough. For older students, this could take several class periods, depending on your goals.

Getting Ready

For the **Bingo Game**: Duplicate the Worm Bin Bingo Cards for handouts.
For the **Worm Bin Field Guide**: List living organisms the students have noticed in the worm bin so far—redworms, cocoons, etc. Add names of potential worm bin visitors from Meet Some Compost Creatures on page 167. Divide class into small groups and distribute worm bin inhabitant names evenly among the research groups. They are to create identification pages for the assigned organisms. (Be sure they include an illustration and four important facts for each organism.) When their research is complete, compile the pages together in a Worm Bin Field Guide. Make copies for each group if desired. This Field Guide will be helpful in the bingo game to follow. You may want to enlist a parent or older student helpers for these activities.

How to Do It

Begin by explaining the rules of the game.

- Groups work together finding compost organisms. (They can use the Worm Bin Field Guides made earlier for help.) Explain the rules/procedure. When they find a compost creature, they must identify it by name and record an observation about it—what it was doing, how it looked, where it was, etc. For each organism they identify and observe, they must receive verification from the teacher. If the teacher is satisfied with their description, and their observation, they can "X" out that organism's square on the bingo game or draw it in a blank square and "X" it out, and then start looking for another.
- A group gets "bingo" when four blocks, vertically, horizontally, or diagonally are "X"ed out.
- All searching must stop when the teacher gives a pre-determined signal—for additional instructions, to ask questions, or to share a special observation in the classroom.

Next, hand out bingo cards, trays with compost samples, magnifying lenses, and Worm Bin Field Guides, if available. Allow groups to start. Monitor success among the groups. Allow one sample swap of compost from the bin per team if locating creatures is slow.

Then, stop when either a certain amount of time has passed, or there's a bingo. Clean up.

Classroom Conversations

- Ask the groups to describe what they observed in the worm bin. Did each group find the same things? Discuss how these organisms got into the worm bin.
- Encourage students or groups to report any interesting behavior or sights during their investigations.
- Ask them if they played the game in a month or so from now, would anything be different?

Want to Do More?

- Dig into some leaf litter or an outdoor compost pile in search of the same compost creatures. Play the bingo game as you locate specific creatures. For indoor exploration, take a shovelful of soil from outdoors and place it on a white sheet to look for creatures.
- Have older students teach younger kids about compost creatures using the Worm Bin Field Guide they created.
- Write a story from the point of view of one of the organisms found in the compost.
- Arrange the organisms according to where they fit in the compost food web.

Worm Bin Bingo Card

	Draw What You Found	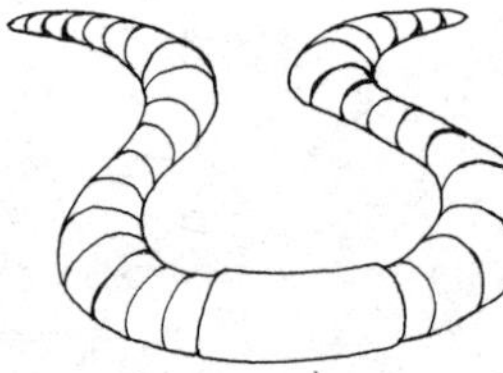	
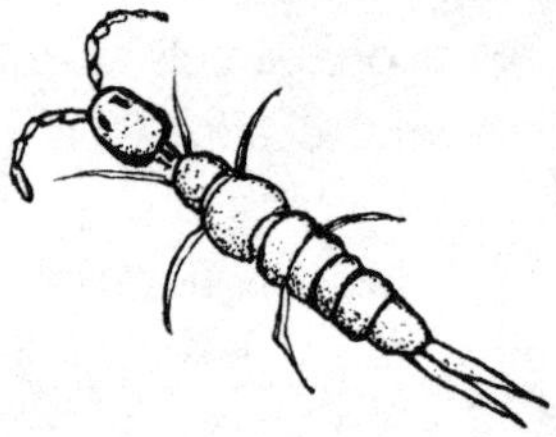	Draw What You Found	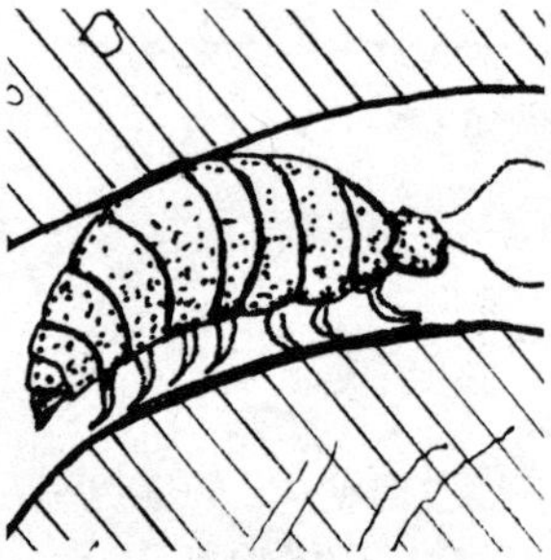	Draw What You Found
Draw What You Found	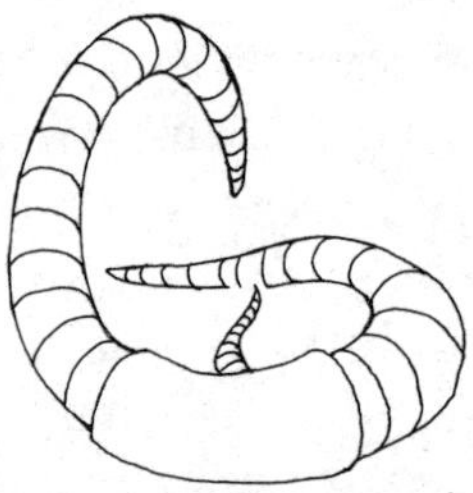	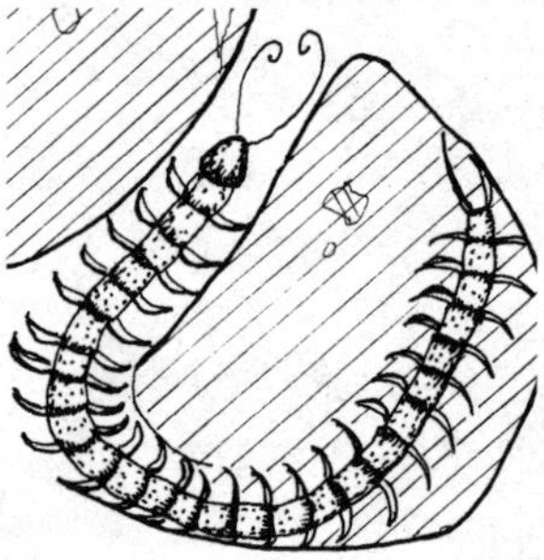	Draw What You Found
		Draw What You Found	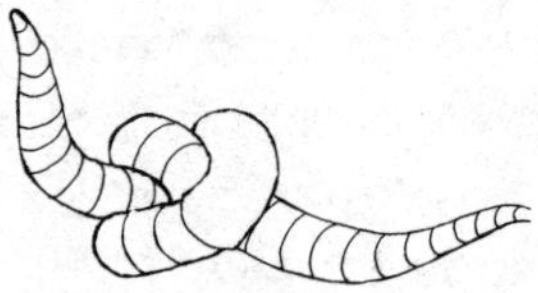

How to Play: Teams work together finding compost organisms. (You can use your Worm Bin Field Guides to help identify compost creatures.) When you find a compost creature, identify it by name and record an observation about it—what it was doing, how it looked, where it was, etc. For each organism you identify and observe you must get an okay from the teacher. If the teacher is satisfied with your description, and their observation, you can "X" out that organism's square on the bingo game or draw it in a blank square and "X" it out, then start looking for another. A team gets "bingo" when four blocks, vertically, horizontally, or diagonally are "X"ed out. All searching must stop when the teacher gives the signal.

From *Healthy Foods from Healthy Soils* by Elizabeth Patten and Kathy Lyons, illustrated by Helen Stevens, Tilbury House, Publishers.

Meet Some Compost Creatures

With the exception of the centipede and spider, all the organisms listed below are decomposers. They help break down vegetable matter.

Springtails are numerous in nature and are impressive in how they hop. However, they are so tiny (1/16 of an inch—small enough to fit on the head of a pin) that their huge leaps don't look like much to us. Only if they appear in large numbers in the bin will their jumping draw some attention.

Spiders like dark places and they like to eat, so it's not uncommon to find one or two making themselves at home and dining on the tiny insect life living in your bin.

Sow bugs are related to pill bugs. They also have armored plates but do not roll up into a ball like the pill bug does.

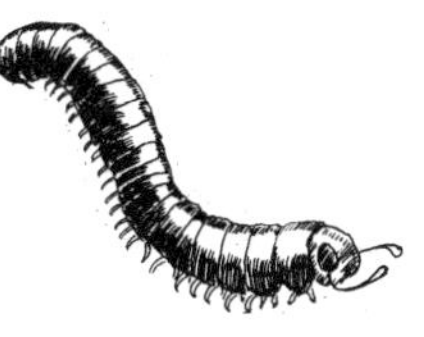

Mites are related to ticks but most of the species in the bin are vegetarians. You may find them in large numbers on the surface, but you'll have to look closely. They have eight legs and are quite tiny.

Millipedes don't really have one thousand feet but some may have as many as one hundred. Fossils indicate they appeared on earth roughly 400 million years ago—long before dinosaurs walked the earth. Like pill bugs, they curl into balls when disturbed.

Pill bugs have ten pairs of legs, making them "isopods" and they have flattened plates that make them look like mini-armadillos. They roll up into a ball for protection.

Snails appear once in a while in a worm bin. They are quite delicate and tiny.

Fruit flies are not harmful but they do reproduce quickly! They are small but if you look closely, they are somewhat stout for their size (as compared to skinny fungus gnats, below).

Enchytraeids (en-kee-tray-ids), also called white worms or pot worms, can be confused with "baby worms." These tiny worms can appear in large numbers and are white.

Fungus gnats are often confused with fruit flies and can also appear around potted plants as they love soil, fungi, and tender plant roots. They are daintier looking, resembling tiny mosquitoes.

Centipedes are predators of the compost and they do eat earthworms, so you don't want too many of them, if any, in your worm bin! They have longer legs than millipedes.

Redworms (wigglers) are found in compost piles, decaying manure or leaves, and worm bins. They are more slender than the garden-variety worms, have a reddish hue, and sometimes yellow stripes along their segments.

Slugs are basically snails without their shells—but they start out shell-less. If you look closely at a side, you might see their breathing hole.

Worm Cocoons (egg cases) are smaller than an apple seed, lemon-shaped, and vary in color from yellowish tan to dark brown. These cases hold two to ten worms!

Worm "Babies" are not to be confused with enchytraeids (pot or white worms), as they are small and whitish. They do have color, though, as you can see their insides (a red line) running from head to tail.

Lesson Links

Are All Soils Created Equal?
Vermicondo
What Worms Want
Black Gold

Literature Links

Compost Critters by Bianca Lavies
What Rot!: Nature's Mighty Recycler by Elizabeth Ring
Worm Bin Creatures Alive Through a Microscope (video) by Warren A. Hatch
The Magic School Bus Meets the Rot Squad: A Book about Decomposition by Joanna Cole
Annelida the Wonder Worm by Katie B. Diepenbrock

Resources

- *Invertebrates of the Compost Pile* http://compost.css.cornell.edu/invertebrates.html Part of Cornell University's compost site is devoted to exploring the food web of the compost pile and includes images of the "critters."
- *Worm Digest* www.wormdigest.org for comprehensive information on anything you ever wanted to know about worm composting. Also a newsletter, and they sell back issues!
- *The Microcosmos Curriculum Guide for Exploring Microbial Space* by Dr. Douglas Zook, Kendall Hunt, 1994. For student-centered observations and activities involving organisms like yeast, one-celled pond organisms, and other tiny inhabitants of this planet.
- A worm's-eye view of soil and its micro-organisms on http://school.discovery.com/schooladventures/soil

Benchmarks

The Physical Setting: 4C—Processes that Shape the Earth, p. 72

K-2

"Animals and plants sometimes cause changes in their surroundings."

Grades 3-5

"Soil is made partly from weathered rock, partly from plant remains—and also contains many living organisms."

The Living Environment: 5A—Diversity of Life, p. 102

Background: "They [scientists] came to understand the living environment first through observations, then classifications, then theories. It's a useful model for students to follow in learning about the environment."

K-2

Background: "All students, especially those who live in circumstances that limit their interaction with nature, must have the opportunity to observe a variety of plants and animals in the classroom. . . . The students should have reasons for their observations—reasons that prompt them to do something with the information they collect. . . . Some students may enjoy displaying, with drawings . . . all the living things. . . ."

"Some animals and plants are alike in the way they look and the things they do, and others are very different from one another."

"Plants and animals have features that help them live in different environments."

Grades 3-5

Background: "Students should have the opportunity to learn about an increasing variety of living organisms, both the familiar and the exotic, and should become more precise in identifying similarities and differences among them."

"A great variety of kinds of living things can be sorted into groups in many ways using various features to decide which things belong to which group."

The Living Environment: 5E—Flow of Matter and Energy, p. 118

K-2

"Plants and animals both need to take in water, and animals need to take in food. In addition, plants need light."

Grades 3-5

"Questions should encourage students to consider where substances come from and where they go. . . ."

"Some source of 'energy' is needed for all organisms to stay alive and grow."

"Over the whole earth, organisms are growing, dying, and decaying, and new organisms are being produced by the old ones."

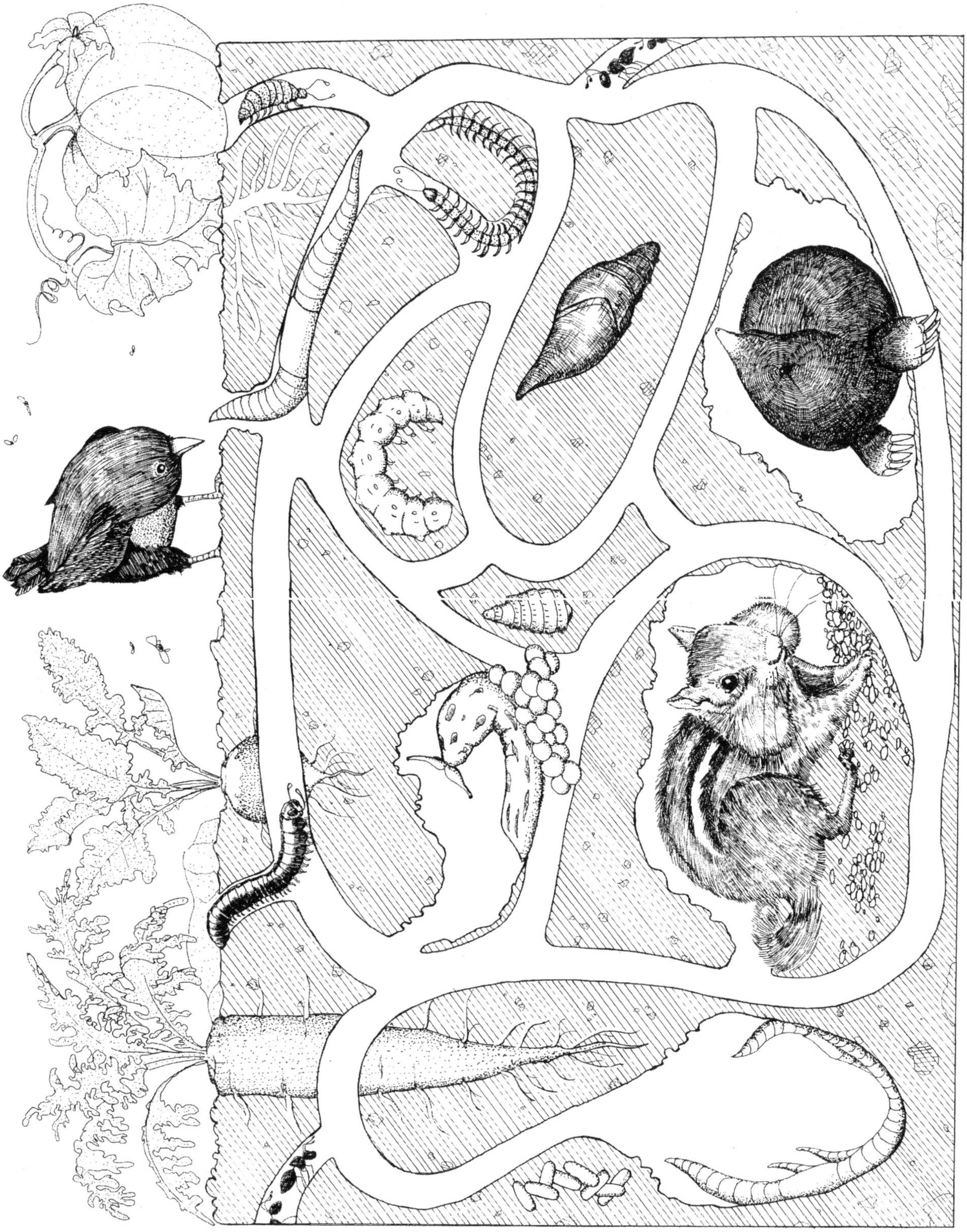

Annelida's A-Mazing World

Handout from *Healthy Foods from Healthy Soils* by Elizabeth Patten and Kathy Lyons, illustrated by Helen Stevens, Tilbury House, Publishers.

Contents are guaranteed to be: 100% pure organic vermicompost

**Carefully crafted by red wigglers and ________________________.
This gentle fertilizer may be used directly on house or garden plants, or soaked in water (1/4 cup : 1 gallon) for one week to make compost tea for watering plants.**

A Small Business Lesson[1]

Composting for change!

Recommended Grades: K–6

- **Science**
- **Math**

Goals

Knowing that compost is valuable and others will pay for it may serve as an additional incentive to vermicompost. In this activity children work cooperatively to "harvest" their vermicompost and raise money for their group. They will enjoy marketing their plant "health product."

Key Points

- Compost is sold as a fertilizer in stores. If you have a worm bin, you don't have to buy compost and can use vermicompost instead. You can even use it as a fundraiser. (This is a true "trash to treasure" cycle.)
- Vermicompost contains decomposed plant material, bedding, and worm castings (worm manure). The presence of worm castings makes vermicompost even more "nutritious" for soils and plants than outdoor compost because waste passed through a worm's gut contains even more minerals.

What You'll Need

"Ripe" worm bin; tarp or large spread of newspapers; drying area; small paper bags (coffee bags work best—see if a local store might donate them); snap-lid plastic quart-sized containers; trays (optional); labels (make your own labels or reproduce the one above).

How to Do It

Note: Let custodial staff know of your plans beforehand.

Begin by familiarizing yourself with the harvest tips offered by Mary Appelhof in *Worms Eat My Garbage* or *Worms Eat Our Garbage* and used here. (See Vermicomposting Basics, beginning on page 148.) Dump the contents of the worm bin onto a large tarpaulin or area covered with newspaper. (If the worm bin is very moist and you are indoors, use a waterproof barrier on the floor!) This is best done outdoors (preferably in the shade for the comfort of both students and worms), but can be done indoors.

Divide the contents into six to ten piles, according to the number of students: two or three students to a pile. Each pile should be a cone shape (mini-vermicompost mountains) so that as light comes from above, worms migrate to the base of the cone. Remove vermicompost from the tip little by little, and spread it thinly on several layers of newsprint or paper bags. Place these on trays for easier transport.

[1] Adapted from *Worms Eat Our Garbage* by Appelhof, Harris, and Fenton, Flower Press, 1993.

Next, place worms and worm cocoons into a container with moist newspaper. Separate out worms for sale into small, labeled containers with air holes. These are perfect for other vermicomposting enthusiasts. Extra worms can be used to start a new composting bin. (Red wigglers may be released into the wild, but will likely not survive northern winters as they are surface dwellers and not capable of burrowing below the frost line as cold-climate earthworms and night crawlers do—and most gardens do not contain enough food in the form of decomposing food or plant matter).

Then, when the vermicompost is dried (but still moist to the touch, having a nice "feel" and texture, but not thoroughly dried or dusty), put 2–3 cups into lined paper or breathable plastic bags with labels "Black Gold." Sell at a school function such as conference time, or along with a seedling sale in the spring, or at a farm stand, nursery, or greenhouse. On the sale table, show the difference between a plant fertilized with "Black Gold" and an unfertilized plant (optional). Make sure that unsold wigglers are returned safely to a bin in a timely manner.

Classroom Conversations

There will be lots of informal conversations among students as they separate the worms from the vermicompost and make observations about worms, cocoons, the texture of the compost, etc. After clean-up, gather together to discuss their impressions.

- Decide what kind of label to use on the worm and vermicompost containers for sale.
- Figure out how much to charge for your packages of "Black Gold" (could be called "Compost Tea Bags") and "Fresh Wigglers," based on local price demand. You may want to decide ahead of time what you will do with the profits.
- Assign students to the final-stage jobs: bagger, labeler, seller, marketer, etc. Have students make a plan to test out the fertilizer themselves first in order to be able to make personalized recommendations.

Want to Do More?

Make marketing or sales slogans. Use money to purchase next year's seeds.

Lesson Links

What Worms Want
Vermicondo
Are All Soils Created Equal?

An Ice Cream Social!

We had a plant sale and sold "Black Gold" and "Fresh Wigglers" in conjunction with our Ice Cream Social (!) and School Spring Art Show. We sold small, snack-size bags with one cup of "Black Gold." We consulted with my assistant and decided that given the labor, we should charge one dollar.

It had basically been the work of two girls who hand-wrote out the tags. They dictated the process of how to make the "Black Gold," I wrote it down, and they wrote a second draft and included that information with the bags. It describes how to use it with plants.

Counting out 500–1,000 worms was fun and more financially successful than the "Black Gold." The students decided to give the money they raised to UNICEF. I suggested going to the market and buying food for our local food pantry, but they were familiar with UNICEF from Halloween, and that was their choice. —Jane Weinstein, 2nd Grade Teacher

Literature Links

Recycle! A Handbook for Kids by Gail Gibbons
Recycle That! by Fay Robinson
Compost! Growing Gardens from Your Garbage by Linda Glaser
Compost, By Gosh! by Michelle Portman
Compost Critters by Bianca Lavies

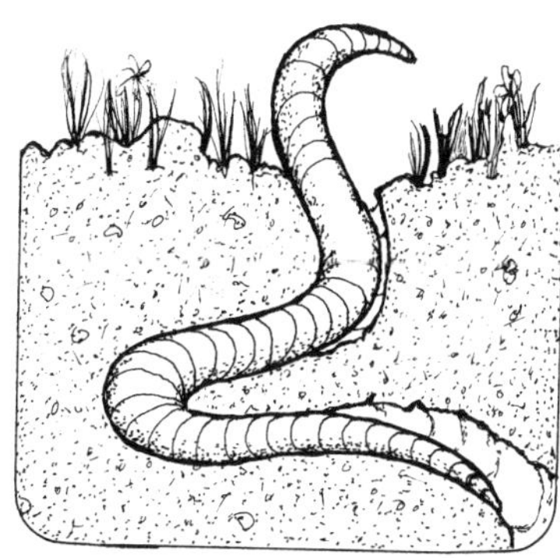

The average earthworm produces its own weight in castings every 24 hours. Just think of all the black gold they are producing right now!

Resources

- See books by Mary Appelhof, "Worm Woman" extraordinaire: *Worms Eat Our Garbage* (with Mary Frances Fenton and Barbara Loss Harris, Flower Press, 1993) or *Worms Eat My Garbage* (Flower Press, 1997).
- *The Farmer's Earthworm Handbook: Managing Your Underground Money-Makers* by David Ernst, Lessiter Pub., 1995.
- Vermicomposting Frequently Asked Questions at www.oldgrowth.org/compost/wormfaq.html

Benchmarks

The Physical Setting: 4C—Processes that Shape the Earth, p. 72

K-2

"Animals and plants sometimes cause changes in their surroundings."

The Living Environment: 5D—Interdependence of Life, p. 116

Background: "Students should investigate the habitats of many different kinds of local plants and animals, including . . . worms."

K-2

"Living things are found almost everywhere in the world. There are somewhat different kinds in different places."

Grades 3-5

"Their [students'] studies of interactions among organisms within an environment should start with relationships they can directly observe."

"Insects and various other organisms depend on dead plant and animal material for food."

The Living Environment: 5E—Flow of Matter and Energy, pp. 119–20

K-2

"Many materials can be recycled and used again, sometimes in different forms."

Grades 3-5

"Over the whole earth, organisms are growing, dying, and decaying, and new organisms are being produced by the old ones."

Grades 6-8

"Over a long time, matter is transferred from one organism to another repeatedly and between organisms and their physical environment. As in all material systems, the total amount of matter remains constant, even though its form and location change."

The Designed World: 8A—Agriculture, p. 184

Grades 3-5

"Some plant varieties . . . have more desirable characteristics than others, but some may be more difficult or costly to grow. . . . Irrigation and fertilizers can help crops grow in places where there is too little water or the soil is poor."

Habits of Mind: 12B—Computation and Estimation,p. 290

K-2

"Use whole numbers and simple, everyday fractions in ordering, counting, identifying, measuring, and describing things and experiences."

Grades 3-5

"Add, subtract, multiply, and divide whole numbers mentally, on paper, and with a calculator."

LET'S GROW OUR OWN!

Options for Urban and Rural Classrooms

"Ripeness is all." —*Shakespeare*

Children benefit from witnessing nature's cycles—especially as they are embodied in plant growth. Unfortunately, the growing cycle is at odds with the school cycle in some parts of the country, making it difficult for many teachers to incorporate outdoor gardening into their curriculum. In this final section of the book, we've developed a set of simple garden activities that will enable you to actually grow your own food with students in the classroom, whether your school is urban or rural, whether you're growing indoors or out. If you can't get involved with "real dirt," we've even included several activities such as Room to Grow and Pop-Up Puppets, which require only your imagination: they mimic nature through the arts.

We encourage growing and gardening because the lessons they offer students are so uniquely powerful. We hope you will go for the "real thing." The garden projects presented here include growing sprouts, raising lettuce under lights, planting a theme garden (and exploring seed diversity) with an ABC garden, starting a Grow a Row project to help those less fortunate than ourselves, and more. If you have never gardened before, we have included a list of helpful hints for school garden projects in The Real Dirt.

In the end, a celebration of knowledge is called for! Having a festive gathering as students and teachers reflect and share the fruits (and vegetables) of their labor and learning is a valuable and fun tradition. We wish you all a full and bountiful harvest with your students!

Room to GrOW

Imaginary play activity provides a review of garden basics

Recommended Grades: K–2

- **Science**
- **Performing Arts**
- **Math**

Goals

Experience the growth and harvest of a garden through our imaginations and bodies. Introduce the concept of planting seeds with sufficient room to grow.

Key Points

- Plants have needs as people do and will grow healthy when their needs are met.
- It's fun to experience the planting, growing, and harvesting of a garden with our bodies and minds.
- All plants need room to grow.

Background

Farming and gardening take a lot of planning. Long before the seeds are planted, a farmer or gardener has already made many important decisions: when and where to plant, what to plant, what is needed. This can also be a very creative part of farming/gardening. Like all enthusiastic gardeners, you and your students can make the most of the non-growing time of the year in your region—planning, scheming, and dreaming. Whether "planting" an imaginary garden or getting ready for the real thing, it's a valuable and fun activity to explore ideas and plans. The later lesson—What Does Your Garden Grow?—can also be used to plan the imaginative garden of your dreams, but if you plan to garden outside this school year, get the kids involved in this dreaming and scheming early on.

Note: For those planning The Real Thing, be sure to read The Real Dirt—Gardening with Children, starting on page 184.

What You'll Need

A grid on the floor (make with tape, string, chalk), with each cell large enough for a child to stand or sit in; a flashlight to represent the sun; a mister to represent the rain; a small fan to represent air/wind; and an *imaginary* blanket of soil.

Teacher Tip

Provide a background in seed anatomy and growth by doing the Go to Seed! lesson first.

How to Do It

Note: You can choose the plants for this imaginary vegetable soup garden based on suggestions below, student-inspired garden ideas, or selections from what you might actually plant later in your garden.

Begin by saying, "We are going to plant a garden in this classroom today. The floor will be the garden and you will be the plants. There will be a row of (for instance) carrots, a row of onions, and a row of potatoes for our Vegetable Soup Garden. I need my carrot seeds!" (Take some seed volunteers and place them in the carrot row. Do the same with the potatoes and onions so all students are included.) Instruct the seeds to curl up if they haven't already.

Next, take on the role of the gardener and act out the following. (Use your own script and ideas if you prefer.)

Let's Plant Our Garden

"These seeds are so tiny all lined up in the garden! I must put a blanket of soil over my seeds to protect them from the sun, cold and wind. [Spread the imaginary blanket.] Now it is dark underground for these seeds, but they are warm and ready to sprout. [Turn off the lights.]

"Every seed is equipped with food, but they need rainwater to help them shed their seed coat. [With a fine plant mister, spray each row of seeds.] Now their seed coats are softer and their little roots are making their way into the soil. Ohhh! Tiny shoots are coming out of the ground just in time to get food from the sun. [Shine the flashlight on the plants and encourage your "seeds"—if they haven't already begun on their own to start growing.]

"My garden is growing and growing! The carrots are big underground with feathery leaves on top. The onions, too, with spiky green leaves reaching to the sky. The potatoes look like bushes above the ground, but below they have lots of tubers called spuds!

"I think it's time to pick them for my soup! [Walk through each row and pull your produce, asking them to return to their seats.] MMMmm—the soup is going to be delicious!"

Continue, shortening or lengthening as needed. Include putting waste into a compost pile if students are familiar with this step. You can continue the activity by making "pretend soup," if it feels right.

Then, use the grid to explain how gardeners and farmers often plant their crops in rows. When "planting" your "student seeds," emphasize the space they will need when they are grown. They will need room for their roots and leaves.

Classroom Conversations

- Take time for the children to share what they enjoyed about being a carrot growing into the ground (or whatever plant they were), what happened when it rained, what was it like to be picked, etc. Thoughts and impressions from this discussion can lead to many topics related to growing gardens. Other potential questions: Ask students what plants look like as they sprout from seed. How large are they? How much space will they need? What would happen if the seeds were planted too close together?
- Have children act out any of the above scenarios.
- What other vegetables would you imagine putting into an imaginary vegetable soup or planting in the garden? (If there's the enthusiasm, act out the garden growing again with the new plants.)
- Revisit the harvest part with your students for more specifics on harvesting vegetables and more opportunity to use their bodies. (This is especially helpful to do before harvesting an actual garden.)

For carrots, onions, turnip and beets, place two to three students standing in a row. They will be the root crops. Ask them to put their arms and feet out at an angle to show roots holding onto the soil. The teacher pulls on their imaginary green leaves, demonstrating that you must hold close to the top of the vegetable (the person's head) so it won't break off. Wiggle the head if you can or loosen the soil around it. Wiggle some more and pull out of the ground.

For potatoes, get two to three students to huddle under a blanket, holding hands. The teacher digs around the edges, loosening the soil, then digs with her hands so she doesn't stab her beautiful potatoes. She finds them under the blanket and pulls them out, removing them from the roots (the children's hands).

For squash, pumpkins, and cucumbers, ask three students to roll up into balls on the floor. Arrange four or more students kneeling near the three, with their arms out and hands spread to cover and hide the fruits. The teacher puts on gloves, carefully spreads the leaves and vines aside to find what's hiding underneath, then cuts the stem and lifts out the harvest.

Following the discussion, create garden designs using grids on paper. For older students, you can use a scale, i.e.—each square on the grid is a foot. Encourage colorful garden plans and post them together on the wall as a "Vegetable Soup Garden Patch Quilt."[1]

Want to Do More?

- Sing "The Soup Garden Song" (page 177) after eating a vegetable snack.
- Sing "This Is the Way We Grow the Plant" (page 178) and perform for another class. Or use the words to create an illustrated book on gardening.
- Make vegetable soup in the classroom with a crock-pot. The children could prepare the vegetables the day before and refrigerate them. Hint:

[1] Idea from Beedy Parker, organic gardener.

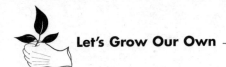

Start crock-pot first thing in the morning and you may have soup ready for lunch. To prepare: Add all soup ingredients and then pour *boiling water* into the pot to speed things up.

"Every day of the year, a harvest is being gathered somewhere in the world. Where there's a successful crop, people hold a festival. Harvests take place at various times of the year depending on the crop, the climate, and whether the people live in the North or South hemisphere. In India, there are rice harvests in January, and in Europe wheat in September and grape harvests in November. In tropical areas, where there is plenty of rain and sunshine, fruit and vegetables can be harvested throughout the year." From *Harvest Celebrations* by Clare Chandler, Millbrook Press/Wayland Publishers, 1997.

Lesson Links

What Does Your Garden Grow?
Vegetable Pop-Up Puppets
Go to Seed!
The Classroom Is Sprouting!
Alive and Thriving! (especially concept of "space")

Literature Links

Stone Soup by Marcia Brown
Jack's Garden by Henry Cole
How Flowers Grow; How Fruits Grow; How Herbs Grow; How Plants Grow; How Trees Grow; and *How Vegetables Grow,* all by Patricia Ayers
The Gardener by Sarah Stewart
The Maybe Garden by Kimberly Burke-Weiner
Planting a Rainbow by Lois Ehlert
Christopher's Harvest Time by Elsa Beskow
Growing Vegetable Soup by Lois Ehlert

Resources

- *Earth Child 2000: Earth Science for Young Children* by Kathryn Sheehan and Mary Waidner, Council Oaks Books, 1998 (ISBN 15717805480). A thick resource for parents or teachers of young children. Activities, resources, and songs in many different categories, including a gardening chapter.
- *Storybook Stew: Cooking with Books Kids Love* by Suzanne I. Barchers and Peter J. Rauen, Fulcrum, 1997 (ISBN 1555919448). Additional story and cooking-related activities.
- *All New Square Foot Gardening* by Mel Bartholomew for a garden method that "uses less space with less work," Cool Springs Press, 2006; www.squarefootgardening.com

Benchmarks

Human Society: 7E—Political and Economic Systems, p.. 168

K-2

"Money can buy things that people need or want. People earn money by working at a job making or growing things, selling things, or doing things to help other people."

The Designed World: 8A—Agriculture, p. 184

K-2

"Most food comes from farms either directly as crops or as the animals that eat the crops. To grow well, plants need enough warmth, light, and water. Crops also must be protected from weeds and pests that can harm them."

The Living Environment: 5E—Flow of Matter and Energy, p. 119

K-2

"Plants and animals both need to take in water, and animals need to take in food. In addition, plants need light."

Habits of Mind: 12B—Computation and Estimation, p. 290

K-2

"Use whole numbers and simple, everyday fractions in ordering, counting, identifying, measuring, and describing things and experiences."

"Readily give the sums and differences of single-digit numbers in familiar contexts where the operation makes sense to them and they can judge the reasonableness of the answer."

"Give rough estimates of numerical answers to problems before doing them formally."

"Make quantitative estimates of familiar lengths, weights, and time intervals and check them by measurements."

The Soup Garden Song

(Sung to the tune of "Home on the Range")

My garden is full
Of ripe vegetables
That are tasty and nutritious to eat. *(rub tummy)*
I planted each seed *(pretend to plant seeds)*
And I pulled every weed *(pretend to pull weeds)*
The cool rain was water to drink. *(let fingers rain down)*

Oh, my garden so green!
There's corn and peppers and beans. *(count on fingers)*
The bright sun did shine *(make ball with hands over head to represent sun)*
On this garden of mine
That will soon be hot vegetable soup!

Slurp! Mmmm! *(pretend to eat soup)*

Handout from *Healthy Foods from Healthy Soils* by Elizabeth Patten and Kathy Lyons, Tilbury House, Publishers

This Is the Way We Grow the Plant

(Sung to the tune of "Here We Go 'round the Mulberry Bush")

This is the way we plow the ground,
Plow the ground,
Plow the ground,
This is the way we plow the ground, to make our garden grow.

This is the way we plant the seeds,
Plant the seeds,
Plant the seeds,
This is the way we plant the seeds, to make our garden grow.

This is the way we water the plants,
Water the plants,
Water the plants,
This is the way we water the plants, to make our garden grow.

This is the way we pick the plants,
Pick the plants,
Pick the plants,
This is the way we pick the plants, to give us food to eat.

Used with permission from *Growing with Plants,* by Linda Watts and Steven Garrett MS, RD: Washington State University Pierce County Cooperative Extension, 3049 S. 36th Street, Suite 300, Tacoma, WA 98409; 253-798-7180; www.pierce.wsu.edu

Handout from *Healthy Foods from Healthy Soils* by Elizabeth Patten and Kathy Lyons, Tilbury House, Publishers

Vegetable Pop-UP Puppets

Make vegetable puppets that "grow"!

Recommended Grades: 1–4

- **Visual and Performing Arts**

Goals

Making small stick "pop-up" puppets allows us to role-play the steps necessary for growing our food, using vegetable characters of our own creation. If you can't make a real garden, this gives the kids a chance to experience growth through the dramatic arts. If you are making a garden, it can prepare them for the steps ahead.

Key Points

- The food we eat starts as a seed and grows with the help of sunshine, fertile soil, clean water and air, and lots of TLC from the farmer or gardener.
- In pop-up pots you can "grow your own food" by creating a puppet vegetable and acting out the many steps it takes to grow our food.

What You'll Need

Felt (use construction paper if you don't have felt) in appropriate colors (cut into vegetable shapes for younger children—carrot, pepper, broccoli, potato, tomato, celery, corn, beans, cucumber, etc.); cardboard vegetable-shape patterns for older students; green paper raffia (available at craft stores; cut in various lengths 4-6 inches); pipe cleaners cut in half; fabric paint (or glue gun with adult supervision); fabric glue; sticks (about one foot long—or chopstick-size); plastic googly eyes (optional); paper cups; construction paper; scissors.

For one puppet, each child will need one felt vegetable shape (finished size about 5" x 3"; pattern pieces are cut on the fold, making a small hole for the neck), one raffia section, one stick, one piece of pipe cleaner, googly eyes, and a paper cup.

Teacher Tip

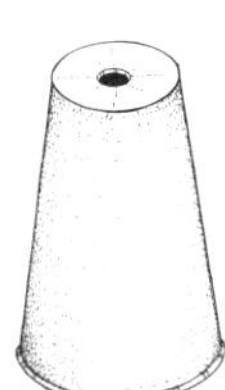

Reuse small yogurt or instant soup "cups" for this activity. To make the pop-up hole, nest a number of them together and gently drill a large hole through the bottoms.

Getting Ready

Gather needed materials. Either cut out individual felt vegetable puppet pieces or make multiple cardboard patterns, then make a sample puppet. Ask for parent volunteers. *Note:* Some children may need help using the materials. Fabric paint takes many hours to dry, so if it is used, the puppets must rest a day before they will be ready to perform.

How to Do It

Give a synopsis of these instructions, then send children to tables where supplies are set up to make their puppets.

1. Choose the vegetable you want to make and gather together the materials. You'll need a felt piece for the vegetable body; stick; pipe cleaner arms; paper, plastic, or cardboard cup; paint, or eyes.
2. Cut a piece of raffia to the size you desire for "hair" greenery. Open it and cut slits into one end.
3. Glue the unslit end on the top of your stick, curling it around to make festive-looking "hair."
4. Put the vegetable body onto the stick from the bottom. Push all the way up to the raffia.
5. Wrap the pipe cleaner arms around the stick just under the felt piece and up to the edge of the

raffia. (The pipe cleaner keeps the felt piece up and holds the body in place on the stick.)

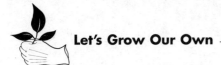

6. Put fabric glue on the inside portion of the felt bodies and press together, keeping the stick in the middle. Wait to dry.
7. Cover your cup with construction paper and make a hole in the bottom for the stick. This will slide on from the bottom with the open end at the top to resemble a plant pot. Decorate your "pot" if you like.
8. Paint a face or glue eyes onto the puppet.
9. Slide your puppet into the pot and start growing! As the puppeteer slides the stick up, the plant will "grow up."

Performance Suggestions

- The whole class works their puppets to a planting, growing, harvesting, eating story the teacher tells.
- In small groups, the children write their own vegetable soup garden plays and perform for their classmates. Afterwards, discuss the story line. Suggest variations—what would happen if. . . ?
- Have puppets ask each other riddles. (How can you tell if an apple is organic? Look for a healthy worm! What did one tomato say to the other tomato? You run ahead and I'll catch up.) Make up some riddles of your own.

Lesson Links

Alive and Thriving!
What Does Your Garden Grow?
Sow Many Seeds!
Go to Seed!
Sprout Yourself!
Bark and Seeds for Breakfast

Literature Links

Growing Vegetable Soup by Lois Ehlert
Potato by Barrie Watts
Vegetables by Susan Wake
Stone Soup by Marcia Brown
How Flowers Grow; How Fruits Grow; How Herbs Grow; How Plants Grow; How Trees Grow; and *How Vegetables Grow,* all by Patricia Ayers
The Ugly Vegetables by Grace Lin
Gardening Wizardry for Kids by Patricia Kite

Resources

- For more resources and ideas for puppets see these books: *Leading Kids to Books through Puppets* by Caroline Feller Bauer, ALA, 1997; *Puppet Games and Projects (Rainy Day)* by Denny Robson, Gloucester, 1991; *Simple Puppets You Can Make* by Jennifer MacLennon, Sterling, 1988.
- Visit the web sites of Puppeteers of America www.puppeteers.org/ and UNIMA www.unima-usa.org for information, resources, listings of puppeteers in your area, and links to other sites.

Benchmarks

The Designed World: 8A—Agriculture, p. 184

K-2

"Most food comes from farms either directly as crops or as the animals that eat the crops. To grow well, plants need enough warmth, light, and water. Crops also must be protected from weeds and pests that can harm them."

The Living Environment: 5E—Flow of Matter and Energy, p. 119

K-2

"Plants and animals both need to take in water, and animals need to take in food. In addition, plants need light."

Common Themes: 11B—Models, p. 268

K-2

"Every opportunity should be taken to get students to talk about how the things they play with relate to real things in the world."

"A model of something is different from the real thing but can be used to learn something about the real thing."

"One way to describe something is to say how it is like something else."

Grades 3-5

Background: "As students develop beyond their natural play with models, they should begin to modify them and discuss their limitations. . . . Students also can begin to compare their . . . constructions to the things they portray or resemble. . . . What they are learning in the arts and humanities can supply analogies."

"Stories can be used to represent objects, events, and processes in the real world, although such representations can never be exact in every detail."

What Does Your Garden Grow?

A review of practical, hands-on gardening basics

Recommended Grades: 3–6

- **Life Skills**
- **Science**
- **Math**
- **Language Arts**

Goals

Planning a garden helps us practice research, discussion, cooperation, communication, decision-making, and troubleshooting.

Key Points

- A garden takes a lot of planning and preparation.
- It can be a lot of fun to take on a project of this size!

Background

There are many ways to garden with children. You can plan the entire garden through classroom conversations, using group research and community gardeners' advice—and include the kids in all the actual work: selecting the site, preparing the soil based on class-run soil tests, drawing up a garden plan, starting seedlings, and planting the garden. Everyone is involved from the beginning—that's one end of the spectrum.

The other end is for you/volunteers to prepare everything (site selection, soil preparation, garden layout, and purchased seedlings) in advance until the day the children plant the garden. They would not be involved in the planning—just the planting. Where you end up along this spectrum will depend on your comfort, the amount of class time you are willing to devote to the garden, your students' interest, AND your support system. The moral is: choose your own garden "path"!

Note: If you are excited and committed to this project, your students will be, too. Explain right from the start how they will be involved and what kinds of things are expected. If any of your students have a parent (or grandparent, etc.) who loves gardening, invite that person to join! If you aren't an experienced gardener, just know that you will be learning with the kids and you will need a good support system.

Getting Ready

This project can be a real community-builder—many hands are needed. Involve parents, friends, community members, and professionals. Don't be afraid to ask for advice or assistance. Read The Real Dirt (in the following pages) and decide how extensive (or not) you'd like your class garden to be. Look at the major headings and decide at which point you want to get your students involved. Also, check out Ten Steps for Taking Action in the Appendix and switch the word "issue" or "project" in the text to "garden" for ideas on how to proceed.

What You'll Need

Butcher paper for a large-scale plan; crayons or markers; gardening books for student research; seed catalogs; garden theme ideas; garden magazines, etc.

> **Cultivating Decision-Makers: Butterfly Gardeners Take Charge**[1]
>
> A second-grade teacher decided to totally involve her students in the garden planning and decision-making. An important and very powerful aspect of her approach was to close every discussion and meeting by asking, "What do we need to know?" "What is our next step?" This seemed to provide a structure for the conversation that helped students move forward, she adds. After a committee of students learned about garden design concepts, they were inspired to try a butterfly garden. "What do we need to know next?" led to research on butterflies. She let them take the lead whenever and wherever she could. She found that because everyone was encouraged to share his or her opinion and work together to reach a compromise, students at all ability levels were engaged in sharing and defending their ideas. Although the process was sometimes slow and tedious, the kids really did work through issues themselves. They learned that the responsibility for democracy can be challenging, but the gains are great.

How to Do It

Begin by presenting the opportunity to plant a garden during the school year. Explain what kinds of

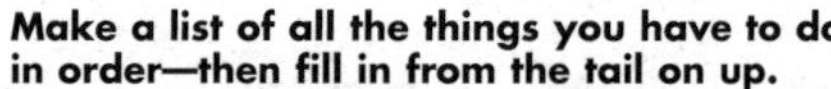

Make a list of all the things you have to do in order—then fill in from the tail on up.

things they will be doing as a class. **Next**, make the process of decision-making (at whatever place in the planning process you feel your class can join in) as democratic as possible. Start by asking, What do we need to think about as farmers or gardeners here? (What to plant, seasons, garden site, etc.) Ask what some of the kids' favorite vegetables are. Have they ever grown them or do they think that they could be grown locally? Consider this the garden brainstorming session: Start a list! You might see groups of vegetables that lend themselves to a theme garden (see page 198). Would their suggestions make up a "Vegetable Soup Garden" an "Appetizer Garden," a "Pumpkin Patch"? Would matching the garden to a book appeal to the class? Winnow down the choices by selecting a theme with them, which focuses students and avoids having a patchwork of personal favorites. At the same time, emphasize that there is NO one right way to do this, but as a group they'll need to compromise in order to make this garden work smoothly. Put your four or five selections to a vote! Tally results. Now that you've chosen what to plant, what will be your next step? (Getting the seeds or seedlings, planning out where they're all going to go.) Guide them in doing research, encourage them to seek outside information and advice, or present them with some options to investigate.

Then, form student teams for each section of the garden, and ask them to draw a plan for the garden on large sheets of paper. If you have the floor space, go full-size! Encourage them to make this colorful and fun.

Classroom Conversations

- At each juncture in the process, have them ask: "What do we need to know to do this?" Answer that with the question: "What is the next logical step?" Evaluate progress as you go.
- When it is time to transplant seedlings, you may find that in some cases, children want to take their plants home, instead of planting them in the school garden. Those can be grown as indoor

[1] *Growing Ideas: A Journal of Garden-Based Learning,* vol. 10, no. 2, April 1999, page 11. National Gardening Association.

seedlings and not transplanted until they are ready to join the family garden—so almost everyone can be accommodated if need be.

Want to Do More?

- Visit a farm, garden, greenhouse, community garden, etc., for inspiration and ideas.
- Join a number of people concerned about green space and "Green map" your urban area: www.greenmap.com

Lesson Links

Room to Grow
Go to Seed!
The Classroom Is Sprouting
Alive and Thriving!
Visiting a Grower

Literature Links

Roots, Shoots, Buckets, and Boots: Gardening Together with Children by Sharon Lovejoy
The Garden in Our Yard by Greg Henry Quinn
Linnea's Windowsill Garden by Christina Bjork
The Gardener by Sarah Stewart
My Indoor Garden by Carol Lerner
Sunflower Houses by Sharon Lovejoy
The Garden in the City by Gerda Muller
Container Gardening for Kids by Ellen Talmage
One Good Apple: Growing Our Food for the Sake of the Earth by Catherine Paladino
The Edible Italian Garden (also Asian and Mexican—*Edible Garden Series*) by Rosalind Creasy

Resources

- See excellent garden-based learning resources by Marcia Eames Sheavly at Cornell Cooperative Extension: www.hort.cornell.edu/gbl/ And for dry, southwestern climates—*Learning Oasis in the Desert* by Guy, Cromell, and Bradley, Arizona Master Gardener's Press; http://ag.arizona.edu/maricopa/garden/html/pubs/sch-bk.htm
- "Children's Participation: The theory and practice of involving young citizens in community development and environmental care" by Dr. Roger Hart, *Earthscan,* 1997.
- For great indoor gardening ideas and support, see the National Gardening Association's books, newsletter, and web site, www.kidsgardening.com
- City Farmer website for school-based garden projects. They have dedicated a portion of their web site to provide opportunities for students to explore such gardens on their own: www.cityfarmer.org/subchildren.html#children
- Join many school garden enthusiasts through e-mail on the School Gardening listserve: majordomo@ag.arizona.edu (put "subscribe school_garden" in message).
- The Green Schools site, hosted by the Center for Environmental Education, hopes to help interested teachers learn how to start and sustain a "green" school: www.cee-ane.org/systemic.html; 603-357-0718.
- Nutrition and School Gardens web site from Texas A & M University for lesson plans and slide shows illustrating how and why gardening and composting projects in schools are valuable: http://aggie-horticulture.tamu.edu/kindergarden/index.html A Step-by-Step Guide to Starting a School Garden is also available.
- Theme garden ideas: (schoolyard wildlife habitat) www.nwf.org/schoolyard/; (butterfly garden) *Grow a Butterfly Garden* by Wendy Potter-Springer, Storey Publishing Bulletin #A-114; (square-foot gardening) www.squarefootgardening.com; (three sisters garden) *In a Three Sister's Garden by Joanne Dennee,* FoodWorks, 1995, and *Gardens That Children Will Dig* by Jane Hogue, The Prairie Pedlar, 712-668-4840.

Benchmarks

The Designed World: 8A—Agriculture, p. 184
Grades 3-5
"Some plant varieties . . . have more desirable characteristics than others, but some may be more difficult or costly to grow. The kinds of crops that can grow in an area depend on the climate and soil. Irrigation and fertilizers can help crops grow in places where there is too little water or the soil is poor."

The Mathematical World: 9C—Shapes, p. 223
Grades 3-5
Background: "Concepts of area and volume should first be developed concretely, with procedures for

computation following only when the concepts and some of their practical uses are well understood."
"Scale drawings show shapes and compare locations of things very different in size."

Habits of Mind: 12D—Communication Skills, p. 296
Grades 3-5
"Make sketches to aid in explaining procedures or ideas."

The Real Dirt—Gardening with Children

from Penobscot County Master Gardeners, Maine[1]

A garden: "It's never done, it's never perfect, but it's always okay."

You'd like to start a school garden?

Congratulations! We hope the following information, checklists, and suggestions will help prepare you, without seeming too daunting:

- At the beginning the task may seem insurmountable, so take one step at a time. Know your limits and work within them.
- Pick and choose from these lists what fits for your situation, vision, and community.
- Speak to the school administration and school board to find out what your support base will be.
- Start planning four to five months ahead to ensure success. Like gardens, worthwhile projects take time to germinate, grow, and blossom.
- Answer these questions:

Why have a garden?

An overall vision or objective is essential; every project needs common goals to be successful. Find out what the other future garden users are thinking. Your vision might include any or all of this.

The garden could:

- Enhance or complement nutrition education and physical activity;
- Provide a food source for the school and/or the community;
- Be used in multidisciplinary activities and serve as a laboratory for science/environmental education;
- Beautify the landscape and be a place of respite and observation;
- Enrich the special education program by meeting special needs;
- Involve parents and/or senior citizens from the community;
- Provide food for people in need ("Plant a Row" for hungry people);
- Be grown sustainably and/or organically using integrated pest management;
- Help acquire social consciousness by developing stewardship skills such as responsibility, pride, and critical thinking;
- Start a lifelong gardener;
- Help develop nurturing skills;
- Provide a habitat for pollinators;
- Offer inspiration.

How big a garden or project are we talking about?

When you plan to garden it's a good idea to start small. The reality is that even a small garden takes time and work—although the rewards are usually worth it! Consider the options below:

- Use a grow-light unit and garden indoors, only.
- Use the school greenhouse, if you're lucky enough to have one.
- Plan a school year garden. (Your options will vary depending on your climate.) That means choosing plants with growing requirements to fit your region, schedule, and temperatures typical in your area over the school year.
- Plant a garden in an already established area, like a farm or community garden. This will be even more advantageous if there will be people there to do summer maintenance.
- Start a strip garden or container garden in front of your classroom window.
- Plan a workable small or medium garden for one or more classrooms and team up with a few teachers and volunteers.

[1] Adapted with permission from *The Real Dirt* by Penobscot County Master Gardeners Mary Turner, Ellen Port, Allison Keef, and Kathy Lyons.

- Tackle the "whole enchilada"! You are game to start a school-wide gardening project. If this is your aim, still start smaller than the size you ultimately want the garden to be. Carefully go through these lists! And, good for you!

Do I have to be a garden expert?

No. (Although it can be helpful to have one on board.) All experienced gardeners start out with a bare patch of earth and their first seed. Gardening is one of those things you learn best by trial and error. If you know too much, you might get in the way of the children's learning.

- Consider taking a Master Gardener course from your state Cooperative Extension. You will learn a lot and may find folks willing to help you with your project.
- Read some of the great gardening resources in the Bibliography.
- Locate parents, volunteers, or school staff who "know a thing or two."
- Research what you need to do with your students and you will all greatly benefit!
- Invite senior gardeners to help. They may have a lifetime of experience to share.

When do we start?

- The earlier the better! Start planning long before planting time for adequate scheduling and involvement of participants. Believe it or not, starting at the end of the previous growing season is not too early—no matter where you live.
- Learn about your region and its climate in regard to plant needs.

Where will we put the garden?

Identify potential sites based on your vision, accessibility, and plant needs. Things to consider:

- Accessibility to the garden from the classroom and for volunteers.
- Visibility from classroom windows.
- Full sunlight for at least 6-8 hours each day.
- Access to a water source.
- Soil with good drainage. Get a soil test.
- Safe from foot traffic and lawn mowers.
- A spot that will enhance the beauty of the school.

What do we need to do to ensure successful integration of the garden in our learning environment?

Every aspect of gardening has potential for learning an amazing array of topics and skills. Lessons that are taught at the garden site are limited only by one's creativity and imagination.

- Set doable goals the first year and plan with a multi-year vision in mind.
- Map out garden spaces for each garden user long before planting day.
- Decide what topics or projects you want to do with your class.
- Schedule garden time to avoid conflicts with other garden users.
- Structure your garden time to coincide with related units or lessons.

Let go of any concept of perfection when it comes to growing things with children. Even when things go "wrong" we still learn and have fun.

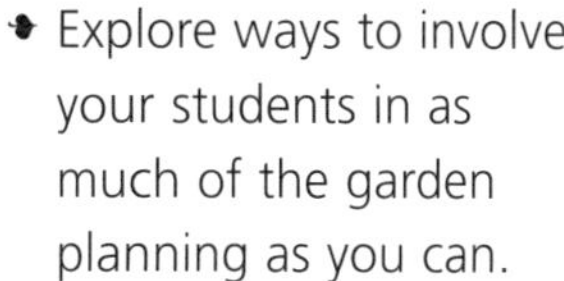

- Explore ways to involve your students in as much of the garden planning as you can.

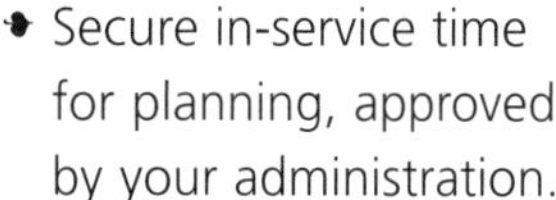

- Secure in-service time for planning, approved by your administration.
- Provide for staff and enrollment changes.
- Plan for school vacations right from the start—watering, weeding, etc.

Who will help with the garden?

Make sure there are enough people committed to the project. Every step of the way, think how to instill ownership, allowing people to shape the program: broad-based support ensures long term success.

- **Children** should be involved in the details as often as possible.
- **Teachers** are extremely busy people and a garden may seem like just another responsibility. Those who want a garden need to be committed to its year-round maintenance in some way.
- **Seniors** can benefit any garden program, as many have a lifetime of experience.
- **Classroom parents** interested in gardens can

become your greatest allies and may volunteer to help maintain a garden over the summer.

- **Custodial staff** need to know what's happening with the project every step of the way. Some may even be willing to help with regular maintenance.
- **Cafeteria staff** may be very supportive of using garden produce if involved in the process right from the start.
- **Principal and administration** are an important and supportive part of your long-term success as they can connect you with the right resources and people when you need them.
- **Parent Teacher Organizations** are often willing to go to bat for you in the fund-raising arena or in gathering equipment. Be sure to involve them.

How are we going to ensure success?

Know what needs to be done and who is going to do it. Identify community partners such as students in local horticulture programs, garden clubs, seniors, or the Cooperative Extension Service as community involvement is crucial. Some specific areas that could use committed individuals include:

- **Coordinators**—a person, but preferably a *small* group or committee to initiate the project; secure ownership; keep committees on task; establish a method for securing volunteers; orient volunteers to the vision of the garden.
- **Fundraisers**—grant writing; approaching area businesses for donations; making it easy for everyone to contribute.
- **Maintenance**—schedule volunteers to water, weed, mulch, transplant, clean up.
- **Publicity and community relations**—maintain photographs and journals; recognize community supporters; keep supporters updated.
- **Communications**—create database of volunteers for distribution; develop a communication system—newsletter, bulletin board—to keep everyone in the loop.
- **Curriculum developers**—develop multidisciplinary activities that utilize the garden, using this guide, of course!
- **Detail people**—set up regular meetings to share progress and direct efforts; establish a time line with specific goals; have a year-round garden plan; keep communication available and frequent; make classroom assignments; plan parallel events to maintain enthusiasm (for instance, hold a spaghetti dinner fundraiser to highlight a garden theme using tomatoes, basil, and parsley—or hold a photography contest for a pollinator garden); improve the soil every year. (Right, Annelida?)
- **Volunteer participants**—provide orientation to the project and training for the task. Make them a knowledgeable part of the team. Discuss their goals and meet their needs as well as yours, matching them to what they want to do and making the best use of their time and talents. Make work easier by providing hospitality for volunteers—food and drinks. Show your appreciation through regular encouragement; supervise supportively, give feedback and suggestions, and share the garden bounty!

Garden safety

- Set and follow garden rules right from the start.
- Start with good quality tools/kid-sized tools.
- Teach kids how to use, take care of, and store tools.
- Maintain a safe distance between workers in the garden.

Common garden concerns (and pests)

- Teach that not all "pests" are to be feared and not all insects are "pests."
- Plan and plant garden to avoid the most common problems.
- Use companion plantings to help avoid some pests and diseases.
- Your Cooperative Extension has handouts on many common pests.
- Carefully monitor the garden.

Vandalism

- The more kids and community members are involved, the better. More local "ownership" means more oversight.
- Discuss this topic with the kids for their suggestions.
- "Protect the garden with beauty." A well-tended garden is a less likely target for vandals.

Harvest time

- Make plans well in advance of the harvest—honor the fruits of your labor!
- Eat what you grow—celebrate!
- Participate in a farmer's market.
- Enter agricultural fairs/garden shows.
- Save seeds for next year or to sell as a fundraiser.
- Dry, can, or freeze foods: preserve the harvest.
- Evaluate for next season.
- Put the garden to bed/plant a cover crop.
- Share your bounty with others: Join with the Plant a Row for the Hungry. Launched in 1995, PAR is a public service campaign of the Garden Writers Association of America (GWAA) and Home and Garden TV (HGTV). Its goal is to help to feed hungry people nationwide: www.gwaa.org/par/

What about summertime?

If your school does not hold classes year-round, summer care and maintenance of the garden can be a challenge. Some possible solutions include:

- Run a summer class through the local recreation or community education program. You could call it something like "Summer Garden Wizards." Incorporate garden care, education, composting, eating, tasting, artwork, music, and crafts.
- Enlist the help of the local community. Perhaps through the PTO or garden club, organize a "Friends of the Garden Club" to schedule work in the garden at certain times.
- Sign up families from the classes that planted the garden.
- Get grant money to run an at-risk youth gardening program. While this may sound ambitious, one Maine community was able to do this through the Americorps program.
- Find a group willing to take on the garden as a summer project—Boy or Girl Scouts, 4H Club, local camp, childcare program, or Master Gardeners.
- Work with elders in your community who may wish to lend their gardening experience.

Grow a Row

Your students might already know that not everyone in their community has enough food to eat. After exploring some of the reasons why, the class can get involved in a community service project to take fresh local produce to a nearby food pantry. The students either plant a garden themselves, grow greens under grow lamps, or put in an extra row at a local community garden or area farm to grow vegetables for donation.

Note: This activity requires planning and coordination over several months and involves students in the growing cycle from planting to harvest. It may be that one group of students does the first part and another class completes it, or you may be able to invite students from the spring planting to assist with the fall harvest.

Background

Food pantries are one place where people may get food when they can't afford to buy it at the grocery store. Unfortunately, too many people need to rely on this source of food far too often, or, perhaps, they don't have enough land or time to grow food for themselves. Help children understand that no one should feel ashamed if s/he needs to get food from food pantries. At the same time, help them explore ways that would allow everyone to be able to choose the foods they need and want by going to a grocery store or farmers' market or community garden. Why can't everyone do this? A discussion about this deals with "food security," a term that encompasses hunger but includes larger problems within the food system (such as how distribution may be skewed making quality food less accessible to poor people). Refer to the Resources below and Food Security and Food Recovery in the Appendix.

Getting Ready

If you haven't already contacted any local growers or a community food services organization (such as

a general assistance office or local church which runs a food pantry), this is your opportunity to collaborate as partners. It involves the children in the community and brings community spirit into your school. A local food pantry can provide you with suggestions for foods they'd love to have donated—often it's "long-term keepers" such as winter squash, pumpkin, cabbage, potatoes, beets, carrots, or turnips—or sometimes "short-term keepers" like cucumbers, tomatoes, summer squash, lettuce, spinach, broccoli, and beans.

Caution: Remember that some students may be sensitive to discussing the "hunger problem," especially if they experience hunger or have families who don't want others to know that they're in need. Remind the class that we all need help at different times and depend on one another; it's important to be able to ask for help. A food pantry is one way of getting that necessary help. You might ask them to reflect on the meaning of this anonymous quote: "Remember, we all stumble sometimes. That's why it's important to walk hand in hand."[1]

Part 1: Planting

- Arrange for a field trip to a community garden or farm willing to donate a plot for children to plant a "food pantry crop."
- Brainstorm with your students: How do they define hunger? Write their answers on the board. For older students, discuss the concept of "Food Security" (see Resources below and page 215 in the Appendix). How does that differ from hunger?
- Explain that one emergency measure to help families get through times of inadequate food and to help provide decent nutrition is a "food pantry."
- Ask students to estimate how many children in their state go hungry every night. (Check with World Hunger Year, state welfare departments, or food pantries for state and/or local statistics.) Depending on your class circumstances, you might do a simulation where the class is divided to represent those who have enough food and those who don't. Have older students research statistics on hunger in America.[2]
- Discuss: Is this a lot or a little? Is it acceptable for anyone to feel hungry? What happens when a body doesn't get enough food and nutrients? How do our bodies react? Think about plants or animals—what happens to them without enough food?

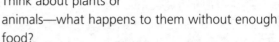

Every day perfectly safe and good food that someone could eat gets thrown away. Some places make sure this food is donated to soup kitchens, etc.

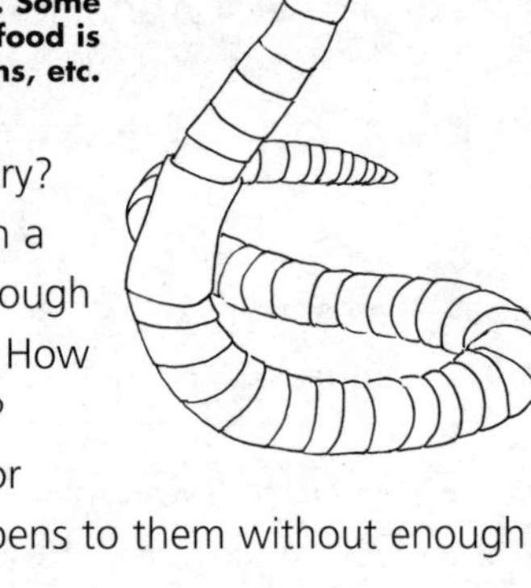

- Go on field trip. Ask a grower to provide seeds and guidelines for planting. Have students plant according to the grower's plan and water if possible. Gather in a circle after planting and ask if anyone has any "well wishes" for the planting.
- Once back in class, ask students about their farming or gardening experience. How do people get food if they don't have land or resources to purchase food? Older students can brainstorm about the meaning of food supply terms such as: access, income and affordability, nutrition information, food safety and security, culturally appropriate choice, and sustainable food production. Ask: How are those terms related to one another?

Part 2: Harvesting

- Arrange the timing of your field trip with the farmer and food pantry operators.
- Discuss (prior to harvesting) what was done for planting, what is now growing in the garden/farm and what will be harvested. Find out what children know about how these things grow (on a vine, underground) and how to harvest them (for instance, the whole carrot plant, just the potato). Explain how to harvest different vegetables. See ideas for younger students in Room to Grow, page 175, Classroom Conversations.
- Assemble boxes or baskets for the harvest and recipes or food preservation information for the food pantry (optional). Explain to students that they'll be revisiting the farm for a special harvest day. They are being good neighbors by gathering foods that won't be for them to enjoy, but for other people in the community. There are many people that don't always have access to fresh

1 *Finding Solutions to Hunger: A Sourcebook for Middle and Upper Schoolteachers* by Stephanie Kempf, World Hunger Year, 2005.
2 Ibid.

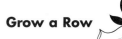

food or the money to buy it. This is a way of helping others just as they'd appreciate being helped if they were in the same situation.

- Take a field trip to harvest with the grower's help, and then return to the food pantry. Sing a harvest song or read a poem in field or to food pantry director. Afterwards, discuss the excursion.
- Initiate a group discussion: Why doesn't everybody eat fresh healthy food all the time? Review what hunger means and what the purpose of a food pantry is—an emergency measure which is only one part of society's larger effort to make all households "food secure." Thank each other for this community service. And don't forget to thank your partipating growers with a letter and perhaps photographs from the class.

Want to Do More?

- Students can write about and illustrate the experience in their journals and/or appoint class historians to document the trip on a display board, with drawings and/or photos. (Submit to a newspaper or newsletter.)
- Discuss hunger issues in your area, the U.S., and around the world.
- UNICEF has an extensive collection of videos covering the issues of hunger and other preventable diseases (for older students): www.unicef.org/broadcast/vidcat.htm
- Invite local media to celebrate and document your harvest and contributions.

Resources

- Local food pantry or community services director.
- Local University, Cooperative Extension, and Master Gardeners—for farmers and emergency food services in your area. In many states, Cooperative Extension administers "Plant a Row"—a national campaign sponsored by the Garden Writers of America and Home & Garden TV to assist in feeding homeless and hungry people in one's own community—through backyard and community gardens. Initiated in 1995, the program has raised more than one million pounds of fresh produce for hungry people. 703-257-1032; www.gwaa.org
- America's Second Harvest is a national network of food banks and food-rescue programs that distribute donated food through 50,000 charitable agencies to hungry Americans; serves all 50 states and Puerto Rico. 35 E. Wacker Dr. #2000, Chicago, IL 60601; 800-771-2303.To find your local food bank or food rescue program, www.secondharvest.org/zip_code.jsp
- Community Food Security Coalition, P.O. Box 209, Venice, CA 90294; 310-822-5410; www.foodsecurity.org
- Food First/The Institute for Food and Development Policy, 398 60th Street, Oakland, CA 94618; 510-654-4400; fax: 510-654-4551. www.foodfirst.org whose purpose is to eliminate the injustices that cause hunger.
- Kids Can Make a Difference. This educational program developed by Jane and Larry Levine focuses on the root causes of hunger and poverty, and how students can help. Their major goal is "to stimulate students to take some definite follow-up actions as they begin to realize that one person can make a difference." www.kidscanmakeadifference.org
- *Finding Solutions to Hunger: A Sourcebook for Middle and Upper Schoolteachers*, Stephanie Kempf, World Hunger Year, 2005.
- World Hunger Year, 505 Eighth Ave, New York, NY 10018-6582; 800-5 HUNGRY. WHY attacks the root causes of hunger and poverty by promoting effective and innovative community-based solutions that create self-reliance, economic justice, and food security: www.worldhungeryear.org

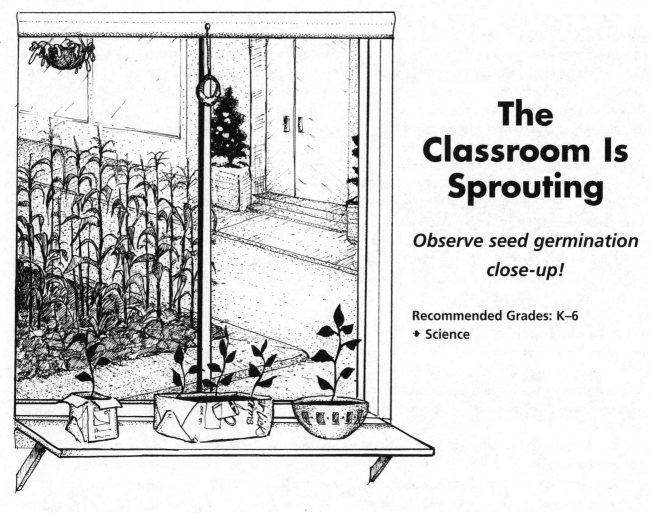

The Classroom Is Sprouting

Observe seed germination close-up!

Recommended Grades: K–6

- **Science**

Goals

Observe the growth of different kinds of seeds—find similarities and differences. Sprouts can be grown anywhere easily, and (when eaten) are an excellent source of vitamins and protein. This is a mini-gardening project that engages children quickly.

Key Points

- Sprouts are fun and easy to grow anywhere.
- When eaten, sprouts supply more nutrients than foods many times their size! Many animals, including humans eat sprouts for this reason.
- Growing sprouts for food requires practicing food safety and proper cleanliness habits.
- When you research an issue, you can learn about many different viewpoints.

Background

Note: Sprouts have long been enjoyed for their taste and nutritional value. Chinese people have consumed sprouted mung beans for over 3,000 years. We did this activity successfully for several years growing sprouts as a classroom "fast" food. However, due to recent outbreaks of illness associated with bacteria-contaminated sprouts, and the resulting warnings posted by the Food and Drug Administration, we felt it necessary to change the focus but still wanted to provide the information. (Contaminated seeds, when grown in a moist, warm environment as sprouts are, have become a potentially serious health risk. See FDA caution below.) Sprouts you intend to eat should not be handled for the observation exercise.

Caution: Eat Sprouts Safely.[1] The FDA advises persons in high risk categories (i.e., children, the elderly) to avoid eating raw or lightly cooked sprouts. No one should eat potato or tomato sprouts as they are poisonous members of the nightshade family. If you are a healthy adult, follow these tips:

1. Food and Drug Administration, sprout advisory as of October 2002. www.cfsan.fda.gov/~dms/fs-toc.html

Wash hands with warm water and soap for at least 20 seconds before and after handling raw foods.

Rinse sprouts thoroughly with water before use. Rinsing can help remove surface dirt. Do not use soap or other detergents.

Refrigerate sprouts at home. Store sprouts no warmer than 40° F (4° C).

If you purchase sprouts, buy only sprouts kept at refrigerator temperature. Select crisp-looking sprouts with the buds attached. Avoid musty-smelling, dark, or slimy-looking sprouts.

Any variety of sprouts can harbor harmful bacteria if they are grown in an unclean area. It's best to start with a sterilized jar, and make sure that the water you use is always fresh from the tap or a safe bottled source.

Cook sprouts. This significantly reduces the risk of illness.

Additional information, including FDA advice concerning sprouts, is available at www.cfsan.fda.gov

There are many people, organizations and sprout growers who believe that growing sprouts can still be very safe and that the warnings are out of proportion to the problem. Many organic growers point out that the contamination did not come from organically grown seeds. If you are interested in looking at this issue with your students, start with these two web sites: The International Sprout Growers Association www.isga-sprouts.org and The Sprout People www.sproutpeople.com

What You'll Need

A variety of seed types and sizes.[2] Try: parsley, watercress, mustard, soybeans, mung, or garbanzo beans, peas, lentils, flax, and cereal grains such as wheat, oats, barley, or rye; seeds for demonstration (such as sesame, poppy, sunflower, corn, or coconut); elastic bands; cheesecloth or clean mesh fabric for cover; small wide-mouth jars for each child or small group. For sprout journals: construction paper (blue and brown); drawing and writing paper; glue; paper punch; yarn or string; magnifying lenses.

[2] If growing sprouts for consumption, "Buy your started sprout seeds from a reputable source that sells the food-grade organic type meant for sprouting. Avoid agricultural seed, especially any that are coated with fungicide." (Edible seeds for sprouting are available through health food stores or some seed catalogues.).

Getting Ready

Cut the blue construction paper into 6" x 9" halves and rip the brown construction paper into fourths, approximately 3"x 9". (You will need the two blue half pieces and one of the brown quarter pieces per child.) Cut writing and drawing paper into halves (similar size to the blue construction paper). Arrange the seeds for sprouting in containers, labeled by type (i.e., lentil, oats, parsley).

Teacher Tip

Refer to Go to Seed! lesson on page 15 for names of seed parts. This activity requires one school week to complete, starting on Monday morning and finishing Friday afternoon.

How to Do It

Begin by passing out a sample of seeds (seeds for sprouting and demonstration) and allow children to examine them. Use magnifying lenses for close examination, if desired. Ask: Have you seen these beans/seeds before? Do you know their names? How many kinds of beans or seeds can you think of? Where do seeds come from? Do you know what food group they belong in? (Protein group.) How have you eaten beans or seeds before? How do seeds help us to grow? (By providing protein to help our bodies grow.)

Show a dry bean and explain that these seeds are from a bean plant. A seed is a small package with lots of stored-up energy ready to sprout. All it needs is water to start. Beans are rich in protein, vitamins, and minerals. What kinds of seeds do we eat? (Sesame or sunflower seeds, corn, peas, beans). Show them examples from the small (sesame or poppy) to large (coconut). Despite their different appearances, they all share similar features that help them grow. What are these features? (Seed coat for protection, embryonic leaves and roots and cotyledon(s) for food.)

Next, explain that they will sprout their own seeds, make predictions, study any changes over time. and record their observations in a sprout journal. To create the sprout journals, make a rough edge on the brown construction paper by ripping a small strip off the long end. Glue it to the blue piece so the brown (soil) is at the bottom and the blue (sky) is above. Arrange drawing and writing paper between the two covers. Punch two holes at one end through all layers and tie with yarn or staple through all layers to create a "journal."

Then, have students choose their seeds to sprout. Glue some of them in the "soil" on the cover of their sprout journals. (They can later draw plants rising from the seeds on their covers.) Place seeds in the jars, label seed types if desired, add enough water to cover the seeds, cover top with cheesecloth and fasten with rubber band. Ask for predictions of what they will see the next day. For the first night, soak seeds/beans in a dark place. The next day, ask students to observe any changes. Can they identify any seed parts? Do the different types of seeds look the same? What are the similarities and differences? Give them a chance to draw the sprouts and write about the beans in their journals. Demonstrate how to rinse seeds by first draining through the mesh fabric top, rinsing in the jar, then draining the water out, leaving sprouts moist. Place the jar on its side at a slight angle with the cheese cloth end down (for drainage) and keep it out of sunlight. Rinse and drain the sprouts 2 to 4 times per day.

Try to have children examine them every day or every other day and document what happens. On the final day, place the rinsed sprouts in the sun or under a grow light for "greening." Photosynthesis in action! Observe the differences from the seed prior to sprouting compared with the "full-grown" sprout!

Finally, decide what to do with the finished sprouts: compost them, plant them, feed them to a school pet?

Classroom Conversations

- What predictions did you make from day to day? How did these predictions compare with the actual results? Were some sprouts very different from the others? (Some seeds might be mono-cots (one-leafed sprouts) and some are di-cots (two-leafed sprouts).
- How does this activity relate to farming? To food?
- Why do the seeds grow without any soil? What will happen to them if we keep rinsing them and allow them to grow more?
- If you sprouted a variety of seeds, why did certain ones grow faster?
- What would happen if you grew sprouts in the cold? In total darkness? With salt water instead of plain?
- What part of the plant are sprouts? (The WHOLE thing!)
- Do you eat sprouts at home or in restaurants? Do you know anyone who got sick from food? What do you think about the food safety concerns?

Want to Do More?

- Use measurement, construct graphs, and make predictions about how the sprouts will grow.
- Research the food safety issue concerning sprouting seeds for consumption. Find the different sides to the issue and foster discussion. Look into other food safety issues and discuss how food gets contaminated (in production, in processing, in transport, at a store, in your home) and how you can protect yourself.
- Write a story about the sprouts—give them various names!
- Examine the sprouts closely under a microscope and identify the plant parts.
- Plant some of the sprouts in a pot or outside. If they go to seed, save the seeds for next year.

Lesson Links

Go to Seed!
Sprout Yourself!
Germ and Cinnamon Trick (Appendix)
Bark and Seeds for Breakfast

Literature Links

The Magic School Bus Activity Guide: Plants and Seeds/A Book About How Living Things Grow by Joanna Cole

The Jar Garden: Making Delicious Sprouts: A How-To Book for Boys and Girls by Don Berggren and Dorothy Weeks

Gardens from Garbage: How to Grow Indoor Plants from Recycled Kitchen Scraps by Judith Handelsman

Container Gardening for Kids by Ellen Talmage

Linnea's Windowsill Garden by Christina Bjork

Resources

- See the governmental sites www.FoodSafety.gov or your local Cooperative Extension for current sprouting guidelines and fact sheets.
- *The Sprout Garden* by Mark Mathew Braunstein. Book Publishers Company, 1999.
- *Sprouting for All Seasons: How and What to Sprout, Including Delicious Easy-to-Prepare Recipes* by Bertha Larimore. Horizon, 1997.

Benchmarks

The Nature of Science: 1B—Scientific Inquiry, pp. 10–11

K-2

"People can often learn about things around them by just observing those things carefully, but sometimes they can learn more by doing something to the things and noting what happens."

"Describing things as accurately as possible is important in science because it enables people to compare their observations with those of others."

Grades 3-5

"Scientific investigations may take many different forms, including observing what things are like or what is happening somewhere. . . ."

The Nature of Science: 1C—The Scientific Enterprise, p. 15

K-2

"A lot can be learned about plants and animals by observing them closely, but care must be taken to know the needs of living things and how to provide for them in the classroom."

The Designed World: 8A—Agriculture, p. 184

K-2

Background: "The basic experiences for primary-school children include seeing plants grow from seeds they have planted. . . ."

"To grow well, plants need enough warmth, light, and water."

Try Choy Sum! This one-bite-sized Asian vegetable, like a miniature Bok Choy, is delicious, easy to grow quickly, and is ideal for salads or a stir-fry.

Lettuce under Lights

Even if your space is limited, you can still grow your own tasty living salad in a variety of ways.

Where?

- Under growlights
- In (recycled!) containers indoors or out
- Windowsills
- Balconies (*not* fire escapes!)
- Hanging baskets
- Rooftops
- Patios or sundecks
- Under cloches (small structures which cover and protect plants)
- Solarium

What?

Most any vegetable—tomatoes, cucumbers, lettuce, peppers, garlic, onions, potatoes (these last three in deep containers), radishes, turnips, cress, clover, mustard, mesclun, carrots, sweet potatoes, nasturtiums; herbs such as chives, parsley, basil, oregano, thyme, lemon verbena, rosemary, and sage, or wheatgrass (from wheat berries); and other sprouts. To avoid investing too much in lighting or space, you may want to start out with herbs. For vegetables, choose naturally small plants such as cherry/grape tomatoes, miniature bush zucchini, finger carrots, small bush cucumbers, or miniature varieties. Root crops will need deeper containers.

(continued)

Why?

Besides the obvious advantage of efficient use of space, growing vegetables indoors or in containers is versatile, fun (less weeding!), economical, accessible to gardeners of all capabilities (including the elderly and disabled), and can be a beautiful addition to your school or home. The biggest boost, though, is that you'll have fresh food year-round, regardless of season or climate.

How to Do It

The most important consideration for plants grown indoors is adequate light, so using lighted grow-stands is the most reliable method. There are as many ways to accomplish this as there are plants to try!

- Grow-stand units can be built, purchased, or borrowed, and can be any size that suits your need.
- You can use special growlights or ordinary fluorescent lights. (Compact fluorescent-type bulbs work well and are more energy efficient, especially when left on for the 14-16 hours daily that indoor vegetables like.) Keep the light 2-6 inches above the top of the plants, adjusting it as the plants grow. Alternatively, if you have windowsill space in a south- or west-facing direction, you should be able to provide plants with 6-8 hours of natural light a day. (Plants grown with insufficient light become pale and leggy and may start to droop.)
- Choose a pot large enough to account for the full-grown plant's roots, about one-third as deep as the plant is tall. For lettuce-growing indoors, use a container roughly 4-6 inches deep and as long and wide as works for your space and light.
- Once you've decided on a container and put it in its eventual location, make sure it has adequate drainage in the bottom—use sand or small pebbles.
- Fill it to about 1 inch below the rim with soil mixed with vermicompost, or potting mix. Make sure that whatever growing medium you use is free of vermiculite, artificial fertilizers, or chemicals. (You can make your own organic recipe of coir or peat moss and about 20 percent vermicompost.) Plant seeds at recommended depth and spacing, and cover gently with more potting mix or soil and water lightly. To help keep the soil moist, cover with a clear plastic bag or clear plastic film.
- Indoor "beds" usually need more frequent watering and control than their outdoor counterparts, but the management is MUCH easier.
- With indoor vegetable growing, you need to think about the birds and the bees—some plant varieties will need your help with pollination. Tomatoes might need a tap on the stem to scatter pollen on the flowers, but others such as squash and cucumbers require you to play the part of a bee—hand-pollinating with a cotton swab or small paintbrush.
- If your new "greenhouse" isn't the right temperature for your plants (such as lettuce, which likes it cooler than room temperature), put them in the coolest spot you have. (If you have air conditioning, put it near a vent.)
- Sprinkle some vermicompost on the soil surface about once a week, or use "compost tea" for regular watering. (See Glossary.)

An excellent resource for purchasing, making, or using lighted grow-stands is the National Gardening Association, in Burlington, Vermont. Find contact information in the Bibliography or see their website at www.garden.org. See also *City Farmer* for an abundance of urban agriculture tips. "Urban Agriculture is a new and growing field that is not completely defined yet even by those closest to it. It concerns itself with all manner of subjects from rooftop gardens, to composting toilets, to air pollution and community development. It encompasses mental and physical health, entertainment, building codes, rats, fruit trees, herbs, recipes, and much more." From the *City Farmer* website, www.cityfarmer.org.

An alternative for "Lettuce under Lights" is "Lettuce in the Water" using hydroponics, a soil-less system using nutrients in water. Several companies sell hydroponics systems, or they can be constructed using directions from your local Cooperative Extension office.

Sow Many Seeds!

Celebrate diversity and variety in the garden

Recommended Grades: 3–6
- **Science**
- **Art**

Goals

Learn about the concept of biodiversity as it applies to seeds, plants, and our food supply by planning an ABC garden (a garden with plants starting with every letter of the alphabet). Students will develop familiarity with seed varieties available in seed catalogs.

Key Points

- There are many more kinds of edible plants available to eat than we find in our grocery stores. Seed catalogs sell many kinds of tomato, for instance.
- Biodiversity means "many different kinds of living things." Even though we usually use this word to talk about endangered plants and animals (and loss of habitat), in this lesson we are talking about the many kinds of farm-grown or edible plants.

Background

Farmers used to save seed from each crop so that they could plant it again. (Many traditional farmers still do.) By selecting seed from the most productive plants, they "improved" their crops. But more recently people have begun to "design" crops so that they'll taste better, be easier to harvest, or withstand shipping better. (Currently, commercial seed companies have often emphasized increased shelf life over improved flavor—which is why some packaged fruit and tomatoes are tasteless and as tough as car bumpers!)

"There are about 380,000 kinds of plants in the world. About a hundred kinds are regularly grown and eaten as human food. But more than half of the world's food from plants comes from only four crops. Three of them are grains, and one is a tuber vegetable. The powerhouse producers are wheat, rice, corn, and potatoes. More than one-third of the world's people use wheat as a main food and one-third use rice."[1]

Big-scale farming tends to use a limited number of high-performance varieties, but relying on just one variety—or one crop—can have its downside. Disease can wipe out an entire crop if only one variety is planted. Or if a population depends on just one crop as a food staple—as the Irish did with the potato in the 1800s—crop failure can lead to famine.

Some of the seed varieties that are ignored by today's huge farms might be needed again someday, either for agricultural reasons or because they might be useful in developing medicines. Seed banks have

[1] "The Big Four," *Agriculture* magazine, vol. 9, issue 2, 1994–95, page 3.

been set up to preserve thousands of species, and many gardeners themselves save and exchange seeds of old plant varieties, to keep them going. (Many people have discovered how tasty some of the old varieties are!)

How Do You Like Them Apples?

"By the end of the nineteenth century, the American Department of Agriculture listed some 8,000 growing varieties of apples: there were Red Astrachans; Golden Reinettes; Black Gilliflowers; Lodis; Fameuses; Roxbury Russets; Newtown Pippins; Jersey Blacks; Tompkins Kings; Gravensteins; Spitzenbergs; Sheep's Noses; and Maiden Blushes. If you haven't tasted them yet, you probably never will. As national transport and market chains developed, breeding for flavor gave way to breeding for looks and durability. Today, only about 100 varieties of apples are even available from American nurseries—the growth of the food industry has cost us the flavor of millennia. Most Americans now may bite into one of only three or four varieties of supermarket apples—its color brilliant red, its shelf life archival, its taste sleep-inducing—a direct descendant of the fruit that nailed Snow White."[1]

What You'll Need

Enough fruit and vegetable seed catalogs for at least one per student. Seed companies from your area may be more likely to carry varieties that are best suited to your conditions and may have some seeds that are native types, as well. If you plan to go ahead with planting an ABC Garden, you will need to work with your students to find varieties that will grow in your climate. Also decide whether or not you will plant some perennials (plants that die back at the end of the growing season, but return the next year).

[1] "What We're Up Against," *Quest Magazine,* June 1981, page 59.

Getting Ready

Put out the word via students, teachers, PTO, and garden clubs that you need fruit and vegetable seed catalogs—chances are you'll be wading in them in no time.

How to Do It

Begin by writing a list of fruits and vegetables in a row across the top of the board. Ask the students to come up with varieties of these foods. Most children may know a few varieties of apples, peppers, or grapes, but will be unaware of different varieties of corn, spinach, green beans, etc. List the varieties they know under each heading.

Next, hand out seed catalogs and ask them to find more varieties for the list on the board. Record their findings. When they have three to five for each category, stop them.

Then, describe an ABC garden. Assign a letter or two of the alphabet to students or groups of students to find potential plants for the garden. Keep the emphasis on food—ask them to find vegetables, herbs, or edible flowers when possible. Some letters require extensive searching and/or a bit of creativity. For example: planting cucumbers for the letter *Q*, extra-sweet corn for the letter *X*, or plant white alyssum in the shape of an *X*. (Choose by the variety name, not *C* for carrot.) Ask them to select and record five choices for each letter. Exchanging seed catalogs and helping other students with variety suggestions should be encouraged.

Following the activity, suggest constructing a two-dimensional model "collage" of the ABC Garden using the plants they selected. Draw up some plans with paths, vote on one the majority likes, map out where the plants will go (by letter), and "plant" the seed catalog pictures on the map (as in a real garden, be sure to label the plants!). Add color or drawings to enhance the look of the "paper garden." Post on the wall to admire!

So many kinds of seeds, so many plants, so little time to EAT!

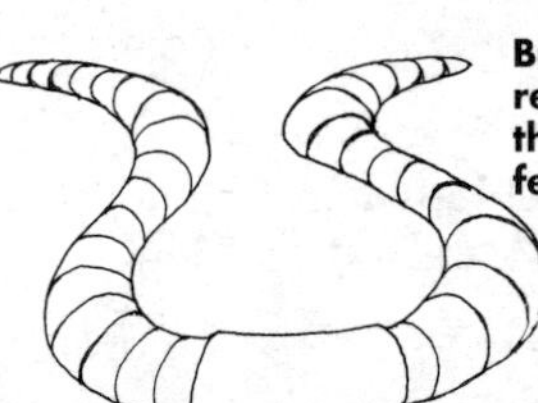

But all that "variety" in the grocery store doesn't reflect an equivalent biological variety—many of those products are made from the same relatively few raw food materials!

Plant the Alphabet

Be creative. Use this list for inspiration. Your students will come up with an entirely different list from the catalogs you provide!

Atlantic Broccoli
Baby Boo Pumpkins
Blue Corn
Chicago Red Delicious Tomato
Dill's Atlantic Giant Pumpkin
Early Golden Summer Crookneck
Early Jalapeño
Feher Ozon Paprika
Fresno Chile Pepper
Funbell Watermelon
Greek Oregano
Habanero Pepper
Honey Girl Charentais
Irish Tomato
Ibis Lettuce
Japanese Yellow-Hull Corn
Kohlrabi
Kentucky Wonder Pole Beans
Lady Godiva Pumpkin
Mini Yellow Beans
Moonbeam Watermelon
Novella Peas
Okra-Annie Oakley
Peppers: Red, Yellow and Green
Potato, Blue
Quadrato D'oro Pepper
Ring-O-Fire Chile Pepper
Rose Finn Apple Potato
Sunflower-Mammoth
Sugar Ann Snap Peas
Tepary Beans
Tomatillo
Ultra Boy Tomato
Velvet Queen Sunflower
Veronica Pinkshades
White Icicle Radish
World Record Tomato
Xeranthemum
Yellow Brandywine Tomato
Yard-Long Beans
Zucchini

Classroom Conversations

- Ask them about what they found. Were there any surprises?
- Why don't we know about these different varieties of food plants?
- What varieties are sold in the grocery store? Why are there so many varieties, but so few sold commercially?
- Why might we want different varieties?
- Do varieties make a difference to a farmer?

Want to Do More?

- Plant an actual ABC garden!
- Ask students to create a garden in their name—the plants start with each letter in their name.
- For older students, take some time to explore the definitions of species, variety, hybrid, heirloom, and open-pollinated varieties of plants. This will allow them to understand the biodiversity issue on a much larger scale.
- Look through seed catalogs devoted to preserving native seeds and heirloom or heritage seeds. Discuss the reasons behind saving seeds from native cultures and older days.
- Discuss the importance of diversity in seeds and farming practices, as a parallel for one of the dietary guidelines: Eat a variety of foods. If we rely on only a few foods in our diet, we are not only limiting our personal nutrition, but also potentially limiting our natural resources by not encouraging and supporting the diversity and abundance in the natural environment. (See the USDA Dietary Guidelines and the Guidelines for Sustainability on pages 223 and 224 in the Appendix.)
- Discuss the ramifications of these facts in terms of biodiversity and crop failure. "The world's population depends on a mere handful of species (30 to be exact) with four crops (wheat, rice, corn, and potatoes) contributing more tonnage to the world total than the next 26 species combined."[1] and "Seventy-one percent of the country's corn crop descends from a single plant."[2]
- Study the Irish Potato Famine.

[1] Joan Dye Gussow and Mary Schwartz Rose, Professor Emerita of Nutrition and Education, Teachers College, Columbia University.
[2] Ibid.

Lesson Links

Go to Seed!
Alive and Thriving!
Visit a Grower
What Is Locally Grown?

Literature Links

Blue Potatoes and Orange Tomatoes by Rosalind Creasy
Eating the Alphabet: Fruits and Vegetables from A to Z by Lois Ehlert
The Victory Garden Alphabet Book by Bob Thomson and Jerry Pallotta

Resources

- Seed Savers Exchange, 3076 North Winn Rd., Decorah, IA 52101; 563-382-5990. "A network of home gardeners growing and saving rare varieties of vegetable seed and some fruits for preservation and swapping with other members. This non-profit organization is also dedicated to educating the public about the role seed saving plays in preserving genetic diversity."
- *Epitaph for a Peach: Four Seasons on My Family Farm* by David Masumoto, Harper, 1996, for a farmer's account of trying to save the old varieties.
- *Seeds of Change: The Story of Cultural Exchange after 1492* by Sharryl Davis Hawke and James E. Davis. For a perspective on how old world and new world foods were traded and changed after European exploration of the Americas.
- *Seeds of Change: The Living Treasure* by Kenny Ausubel, HarperCollins, 1994. Background on biodiversity.
- *Rainforest in Your Kitchen: The Hidden Connection between Extinction and Your Supermarket* by Martin Teitel, Island Press, 1992. A look at how our eating practices can compromise plant diversity.

Benchmarks

The Living Environment: 5F—Evolution of Life, p. 123
Grades 3-5
"Individuals of the same kind differ in their characteristics, and sometimes the differences give individuals an advantage in surviving and reproducing."

The Designed World: 8A—Agriculture, p. 184
Grades 3-5
"Some plant varieties ... have more desirable characteristics than others, but some may be more difficult or costly to grow. The kinds of crops that can grow in an area depend on the climate and soil. Irrigation and fertilizers can help crops grow in places where there is too little water or the soil is poor."

More Ideas for Theme Gardens

A theme provides a focal point and lends itself to cohesiveness in planning.

- ABC Garden—Plant the alphabet! Find a plant that starts with each letter of the alphabet.
- Appetizer Garden—Foods that might be used for an appetizer party: summer squash, tomatoes, carrots, broccoli, string beans, peas, etc. (You'll have to make your own dip.)
- Companion Garden—Some plants protect each other if grown together. Research, plant, and test the hypothesis.
- Container Garden[1]—No space available? Plant your garden in containers!
- Cornucopia Garden—Plants that all begin with the letter "C": calendula, cherry tomatoes, carrots, cucumbers, corn, cauliflower, find more!
- Craft Garden—Raise plants for dyeing, drying, or weaving. Use large seeds for jewelry and plant gourds for making shakers and birdhouses.
- Cultural Garden—Dedicate your garden to a specific culture within the U.S. or from other countries.
- Edible Flower Garden[2]—Some examples include squash blossoms, nasturtium, marigold, bee balm, and the blossoms of dill, marjoram, oregano, and mint.

[1] *Container Gardening for Kids* by Ellen Talmage, Sterling Publications, 1997.

[2] Johnny's Selected Seeds (catalog), 955 Benton Avenue, Winslow, ME 04901; 877-Johnnys (877-564-6697); www.johnnyseeds.com

- Fairy Tale Garden—Plants mentioned in fairy tales or that conjure the image of ogres, pixies, gnomes, and fairies, i.e. catnip, garlic, ferns, witch hazel, Jack's magic bean (purple hyacinth bean).
- Grow a Row or Plant a Row Garden—Assign a portion of your edible garden to donate to local charities.
- Habitat Garden[1]—Research plants that benefit birds, butterflies, frogs, and native pollinators. Study what your garden attracts.
- Heirloom Varieties Garden—Research varieties grown traditionally that aren't found in most grocery stores.
- Historic Period Garden[2]—Choose a time and do some research. What seeds were brought here with different immigrants? What plants did Thomas Jefferson have in his garden?
- Literature Garden—Base the plants included in the garden on a children's book.
- Memorial Garden—Plant a garden in someone's honor. Include a plant they really like. If you plant perennials, your memorial will grow back next year.
- Patchwork Salad Quilt—Salad greens planted in a pattern to resemble a quilt.
- Peter Rabbit Patch Garden—What plants would Peter Rabbit and his friends like?
- Pizza Garden—A pizza-shaped garden with wedges of wheat, tomato, onion, garlic oregano, basil, parsley, green pepper, etc. Leave a small wedge out so you can "step into" the pizza and care for the garden. Use the harvest to make your own pizza sauce.
- Plant Parts Garden—Group your plants by the parts you eat! Roots, leaves, stems, fruits, flowers, seeds.
- Prehistoric Garden—Research and add living relatives of plants that have evolved from the days of the dinosaurs. (They would be all non-flowering plants).
- Pumpkin Patch Garden—Take time to explore the amazing variety of pumpkins available in seed catalogs. Construct a sturdy, wire-mesh tunnel through the middle of the patch for the pumpkins to vine on. By summer's end, you'll have a leafy tunnel with perhaps a pumpkin or two hanging through.
- Rainbow Garden—Get inspired by Lois Ehlert's book, *Planting a Rainbow* or Rosalind Creasy's *Blue Potatoes, Orange Tomatoes: How to Grow a Rainbow Garden.* Sort flower seeds by color. Use a rainbow book as a model for the color scheme, arranging plants by their hue. Plant a pot of gold marigolds at the end of the rainbow!
- Salsa Garden—plant tomato, cilantro, onion, hot peppers, etc.!
- Sensory Garden—Find plants fun to touch, smell, and taste. Some seedpods can rattle for sound.
- Shakespeare Garden—Take the plant references in Shakespeare's plays and you have a huge number of plants to choose from for a garden in his name.
- Square-Foot Garden[3]—This technique is based on grid planting—proponents say it conserves energy, seeds, water, and time.
- Stone Soup Garden—Read the story and plant what the townspeople add to the soup.
- Sunflower Clubhouse Garden[4]—Plant giant sunflowers in a circle. Add shorter ones on the outside for variety and beauty. Makes a cozy den.
- Three Sisters Garden[5]—A garden based on some Native American traditions of planting corn, beans, and squash together.
- Vegetable Soup Garden—Make up your own recipe or use a cookbook, then plant it.
- Zoo Garden—Plants with animal names like Hogs Heart Tomato, Bee Balm, Hens and Chickens, Lambs Ears, Cardinal Flower, etc.

Resources

- *Gardens That Children Will Dig* by Jane Hogue of the Prairie Pedlar. A booklet on theme gardens for children.
- *Planting a Rainbow* by Lois Ehlert. Mother and child plant bulbs, seeds, and seedlings, which result in a rainbow of flowers.
- *Roots, Shoots, Buckets, and Boots: Gardening Together with Children* by Sharon Lovejoy.

[1] National Wildlife Federation Backyard Wildlife Habitat Program, 800-822-9919; www.nwf.org/backyard
[2] The Thomas Jefferson Center for Historic Plants, Monticello, P.O. Box 316, Charlottesville, VA 22902; 434-984-9822; www.monticello.org
[3] Square-Foot Gardening at www.squarefootgardening.com
[4] Johnny's Selected Seed (catalog), Winslow, ME..
[5] American Indian Agriculture Project, 300 Caldwell Hall, Cornell Univ., Ithaca, NY 14853; 607-255-6587;www.nal.usda.gov/afsic/AFSIC_pubs/heirloom/srb9806.htm

How to Keep a Good Thing Going

Preserving food for later

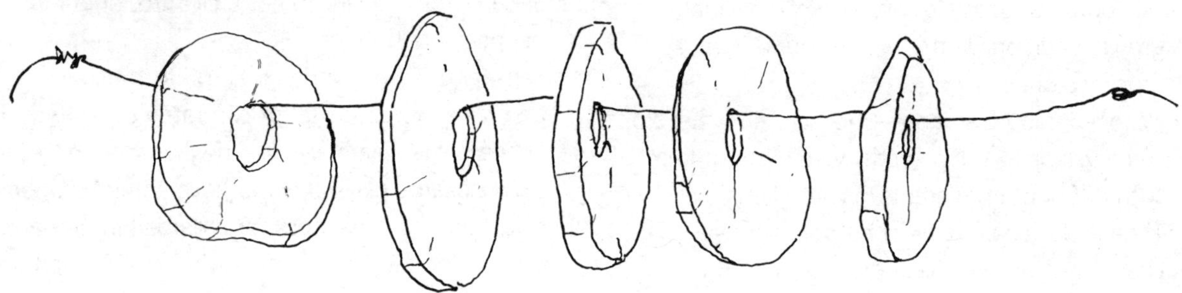

Recommended Grades: K–6

- **Math**
- **Science**
- **Life Skills**

Goals

Explore different methods of processing foods to preserve nutrients.

Key Points

- Food processing and preservation have been around since humans started growing food. Up until modern times, preserving foods through drying, salting, culturing, or pickling were typical ways to survive in temperate climates.

Background

The easiest way to eat locally grown foods year-round is to preserve them when they are in season. Involving children in this part of the food cycle exposes them to methods that have been used throughout history—drying, salting, or pickling—and "newer" methods such as canning, quick drying, and freezing. In this class, for ease and safety, we'll try the drying method.

Nutrients are preserved differently in various methods of conserving food: fresh from the garden is best, quick-frozen is next best, followed by dried, salted, and pickled foods.

Three Preservation Methods

Canning: Clean cooked food is placed in cans or jars and heated to a temperature that destroys micro-organisms that could cause the food to spoil. Heat causes the air to leave the can and creates a vacuum. As a result of the vacuum, covers are sealed, keeping micro-organisms out.

Freezing: Freezing is an easy modern way of preserving food, although it requires more energy use. It doesn't sterilize food but the extreme cold temperature prevents micro-organisms from growing. Generally, vegetables are blanched (dropped into boiling water) or steamed to kill external microbes, then plunged into cold water. Foods may be frozen in freezer-grade bags or in clean containers.

Drying: This is one of the oldest methods of preserving food—it's simple, safe, and easy to learn. Drying removes moisture from food so that bacteria, yeasts, and molds cannot grow. Dried fruits and vegetables taste sweeter than fresh, since removing the water concentrates the flavor. This method uses the least energy.

What You'll Need

Examples of various types of processed foods—canned, dried, salted, pickled, and frozen; a piece of rotting food (isn't that a lovely item for your materials list?!); fresh produce (such as peppers, tomatoes, apples); a food dehydrator (ask someone for a loan—low temperature oven-drying is another possibility); kitchen utensils: knives, cutting boards; tongs; cleaning supplies; aprons; labeling markers; labels; clean kitchen towels; directions at each station/center delineating tasks.

Getting Ready

See Making Food with Children on page 217 in the Appendix. Caution students about kitchen rules and the use of sharp kitchen utensils; prepare kitchen—cutting boards, adequate space, and labeling. If using a dehydrator, plan to do this activity on a day that will allow a 24-hour follow-up. Cooperative Extension staff are valuable resources and may be willing to help with this class if you contact them early enough.

How to Do It

Begin the activity by holding up a tomato (or other food) that has started to rot. Ask what's going on. Talk about micro-organism growth—rotting or decay is food's natural way of decomposing, and worms' gourmet choice! How are foods kept from spoiling? Pose the questions: How can we continue to eat local, seasonal foods when our growing season is over? What are ways to keep foods longer without adding salt, sugar, or other additives that are commonly found in canned foods? Explain that these additives are usually included in foods to allow the food to last longer before being eaten.

Discuss different methods of preserving food and show some examples. Ask: What foods do you have at home that have been preserved in some way? Have students describe ways they've helped their families preserve food or what they may have observed, read about, or noticed before. Explain that today they'll be drying foods as a method of preserving them for later consumption.

Next, divide the class into groups and discuss what will be happening at each workstation: washing and pat-drying; coring fruit and trimming as needed; slicing and arranging on trays or stringing. If desired, you may dip apples into pineapple or citrus juice to keep them from browning. If the classroom has low humidity, hang apple rings on string lines that can be covered with cheesecloth to prevent dust accumulation. Explain that dryer fruits, like an apple slice, will air dry, but a moist fruit, like a tomato slice, needs extra help, like the hot sun or a dehydrator. For tomatoes, wash, slice vertically into even thicknesses, place on racks. Start dehydrator (if using one). Prepare and label storage bags or containers. Clean up. Put refuse in compost. When your fruit or vegetables are dry, place them in prepared containers.

Classroom Conversations

Imagine doing this activity before modern times. How would it be the same or different?

Want to Do More?

- Ask a local senior citizen to contribute his or her experience and help to this activity.
- Study native or colonial history, focusing on food preservation methods as a way to learn about their day-to-day life.
- Research how different preservation/processing methods affect the nutrient content in foods.
- Make labels for selected preserved foods and give as gifts to school food service staff, teachers, or families, or use in a "Summer-in-Winter Tasting Celebration."

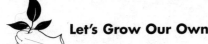

- Make "fruit leather" by spreading applesauce or any other fruit purée and baking on a cookie sheet for 2-3 hours. In some classes with low humidity, an oven for drying is unnecessary!
- Play the "Pioneer Apple Peel Game." To play, take a long peeling from an apple. Twirl the peel above your head and toss over your left shoulder. What letter does the peel resemble? (This is the initial of the person who will be your mate for life!)
- Set aside times to taste and inspect dried food during the process and to test for doneness.
- Visit a local food processing plant to observe how food is preserved there.

Lesson Links

Old-Fashioned Food
Pyramids Near You
Once Uupon a Farm

Literature Links

The Autumn Equinox—Celebrating the Harvest by Ellen Jackson
Itse Selu: Cherokee Harvest Festival by Daniel Pennington
The Sacred Harvest: The Ojibway Wild Rice Gathering by Gordon Regguinti
Early Stores and Markets (Early Settler Series) by Bobbie Kalman

Resources

- Community members for volunteers and background information.
- School nutrition director or staff for supplies or possible support with kitchen facilities.
- For current canning or preserving information, and educational assistance, contact your local Cooperative Extension.
- *Victory Garden Cookbook Putting Food By*, by Marian Morash, 4th Edition, Alfred Knopf, 1982.
- *USDA's Complete Guide to Home Canning* available through some land grant Universities (Cooperative Extension) or as a publication—*Complete Guide to Home Canning and Preserving,* 2nd rev. ed., Dover Publications, 1999, ISBN 0-48640-931-7. For up-to-date preservation techniques and information.
- *Ball Blue Book—Guide to Home Canning, Freezing & Dehydration.* Alltrista Corp., 2002. A comprehensive food preservation resource.
- Rural and urban people interested in supporting family size farms will find many helpful resources when they visit the Community Alliance with Family Farmers site: www.caff.org
- *Pickled, Potted, and Canned: How the Art of Food Preserving Changed the World* by Sue Shephard, Simon and Schuster, 2001, for a historical perspective on food preservation.
- *Putting Food By,* 4th ed., by Green, Hertzberg, and Vaughn, Penguin, USA, 1992.

Benchmarks

The Designed World: 8A—Agriculture, p. 184
Grades 3-5
"Heating, salting, smoking, drying, cooling, and airtight packaging are ways to slow down the spoiling of food by microscopic organisms. These methods make it possible for food to be stored for long intervals before being used."

How do you fix a cracked pumpkin? With a pumpkin patch.

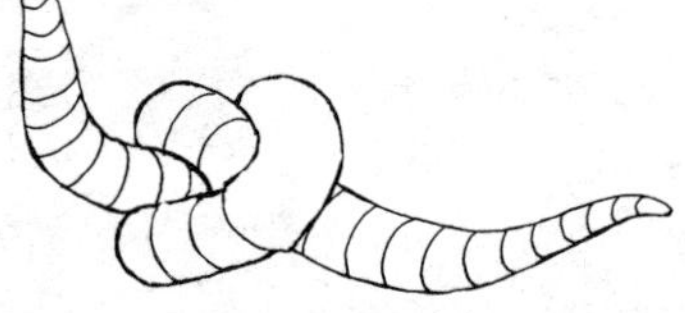

What does corn say when it's picked? Ouch! My ears!

Soil Made My Supper!

Dramatize the food cycle through a "Theater in the Round"

Recommended Grades: K–6

- **Performing Arts**

Goals

A review activity that completes the cycle! Reinforce the idea that our food system is a cycle—and that actions people take along the way contribute to the cycling of nutrients—from composting to humans and back again.

Key Points

- Many people say that our food travels "from farm to table" but that tells only a part of the story. Not only are there many steps along the way, but a food system should involve a circle, not a straight line as that phrase suggests—where food waste leftovers from the "table" part can be used back in the farm's soil.
- This lesson demonstrates several ecological principles: everything is connected to everything else; everything goes somewhere; everything is always changing; everything has limits. (See Appendix for "Commoner's Laws of Ecology.")

Background

This activity should occur at a point when students have experienced lessons from each of the **HEALTHY FOODS FROM HEALTHY SOILS** concept areas: agriculture, nutrition, and composting. It is best done outdoors or in a gymnasium with plenty of room, but a large classroom will suffice. Make this a physically active "theater in the round"! Students can use creative license to depict all the various components of the food cycle which they have learned through previous lessons: soil preparation → gardening → preparing food → eating → disposing of food waste → returning to soil. Use music to help with the rhythm of this activity; a round would be particularly appropriate, and even more fun if the verses were written by the children.

Getting Ready

For younger students, demonstrate the difference between a line and a circle. Show how a piece of string can be laid out in a line and then made into a circle when the two ends are joined. Use this as a conceptual basis for making a linear concept (the food system from farm to table) come alive as a continuous cycle (table waste is used in the form of compost to help build better farm soil). Also, reproduce the words to "The Nutrient Cycle Song" and prepare to teach your students the lyrics and tune.

What You'll Need

Props (from recycled materials?) to depict various parts of the cycle listed below (ideas: garden clothing such as a straw hat, gloves, boots or sneakers; potted plants to represent a garden; desks and chairs made into a food-processing factory; boxes for grocery shelves; food utensils; a large box for a compost pile; clock); food for a snack (fresh fruit or vegetables); and serving utensils; a large sheet of paper with *grow, harvest, sell, buy, prepare & consume,* and *compost* written on it—for outdoor or gymnasium use; instrumental music (example: one of Vivaldi's *Four Seasons,* or folk music). Optional: Student-created script to narrate cycle.

How to Do It

Begin by reminding students about previous lessons that involved different parts of the **Healthy Foods from Healthy Soils** nutrient cycle, encouraging them to list some of what they remember about food's journey, beginning at the farm. Explain that now they will become parts of the cyclic "flow" which takes nutrients from vermicompost into the garden soil, into the roots of the seedlings, then is assimilated into the growing plant, and is eventually eaten. Leftover scraps from that food are returned to the soil when the scraps are composted.

Then, discuss the detailed steps the food/nutrients travel in this cycle. Review that almost all food crops originate from a seed planted in farm soil. Choose a particular crop—tomatoes or carrots, for example (two popular homegrown vegetables!). Ask students to tell how the tomato/carrot grows—is it on a vine, tree, or shrubby plant, above ground or underground? (Tomatoes, which are considered fruits botanically, grow above ground on upright vines; carrots are roots, hence underground.) When the tomatoes/carrots are ready to harvest, they are picked, and loaded onto trucks. Next they are washed and packed so they can be shipped to markets or stored briefly in warehouses to be shipped later. They are sold wholesale to food processors, or to grocers. We consumers buy most of our tomatoes/carrots from the grocery store. After we prepare and eat them, we may choose to compost the food scraps. The "finished" compost is worked back into the soil in order to return nutrients to the soil. Inevitably some hardy tomato seeds end up there too (!), only to start the cycle anew when they sprout into "wee" tomato plants.

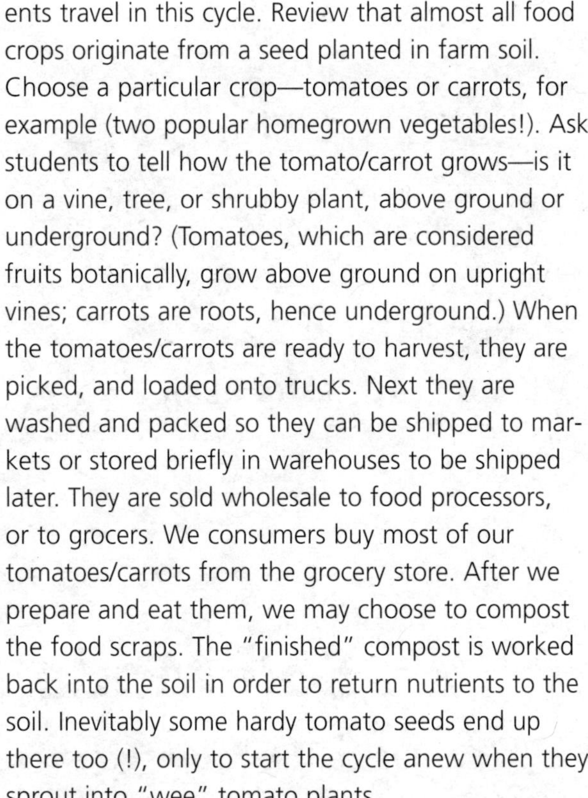

Next, write on the chalkboard the words *grow, harvest, sell, buy, prepare & consume,* and *compost* in a circle. Connect each step with an arrow. (*Note:* Class may adapt the **Healthy Foods from Healthy Soils** cycle drawing here.)

Choose or assign these roles to small groups of children. You may wish to have students wear signs to help identify them (necklace labels, paper "crowns," etc.).

Explain that they will now pantomime (using, for instance, movement, dance, gestures, sound, expression, interaction, and dialogue) each step and give each group some time to come up with their short skit. They may "jump in" at any point in the cycle, as there is no starting point here. To begin, give the group an object that represents the crop or nutrients being passed along from step to step. (Assign a food item or have the class choose the pantomime object.) Gather the groups together and perform the food cycle play.

Improvise with the activity for discussion's sake. Have one group sit down and run the pantomime again without them. Ask how this affects the entire process or cycle. Repeat the activity, choosing different students, a different path for the same crop

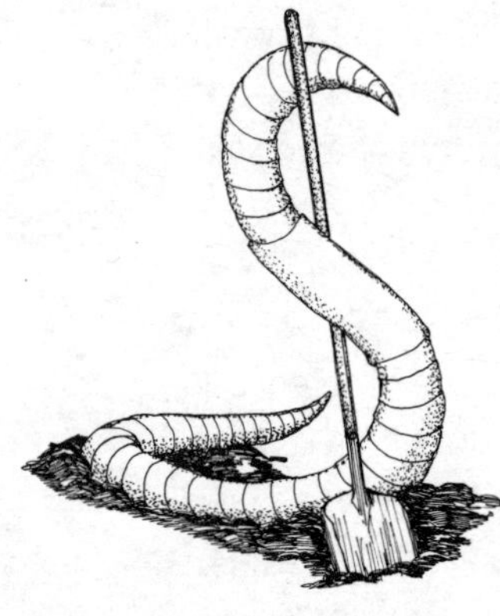

Here's another song, one I like to sing to the tune of "Wheels on the Bus Go Round and Round." The song starts and ends with:

What I eat goes round and round, round and round, round and round

The seeds that I plant all grow up tall, grow up tall, grow up tall

Etc. (*You* fill in the words here!)

Etc.

The compost I make goes back in the ground, back in the ground, back in the ground

What I eat goes round and round, round and round, round and round.

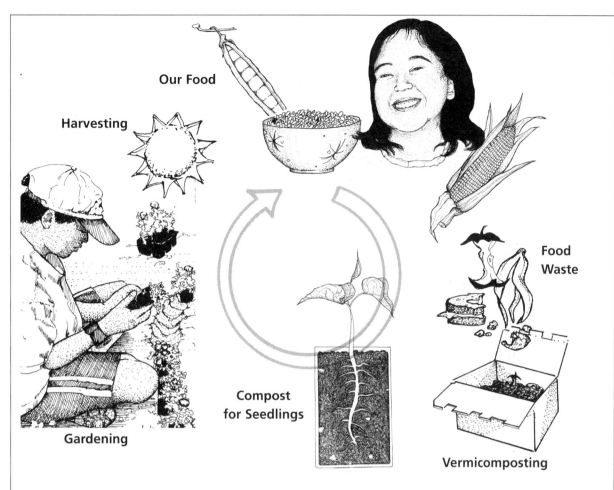

Our Food

Harvesting

Food
Waste

Compost
for Seedlings

Gardening

Vermicomposting

The Nutrient Cycle Song

(Sung to the tune of "The Farmer in the Dell." Words by Kathy Lyons and Elizabeth Patten.)

The kids eat the plants,
The kids eat the plants,
Hi ho the munching-o, the kids eat the plants.

They compost the waste,
They compost the waste,
Hi ho the cycle-o, they compost the waste.

The worms eat it up,
The worms eat it up,
Hi ho the burrow-o, the worms eat it up.

It goes in the soil,
It goes in the soil,
Hi ho the mixing-o, it goes in the soil.

The plants drink it up,
The plants drink it up,
Hi ho the thirsty-o, the plants drink it up.

The kids eat the plants,
The kids eat the plants,
Hi ho the way to grow, the kids eat the plants.

The nutrients go around,
The nutrients go around,
Hi ho the cycle-o, the nutrients go around.

Handout from *Healthy Foods from Healthy Soils* by Elizabeth Patten and Kathy Lyons, Tilbury House, Publishers.

(from farm to food-processing plant instead of to the grocery store) or add real-life complications to food systems like drought, insect damage, low prices, etc. Help students realize the importance of each step in the food production process.

Finally, enjoy a fresh snack using whatever food you chose for your skit—tomatoes if in season, carrots, or your pick! Prepare fresh cherry tomatoes—bursting right in the mouth; or make carrot "logs" into a log cabin?; or a slaw with finely grated carrots marinated in lemon juice and topped with a dash of black pepper (a traditional French carrot "recipe"!); or quartered tomatoes tossed with basil or mint.

Classroom Conversations

Gather the group together to discuss such issues as:

- Who really grows the food we eat?
- What do we eat that's produced locally?
- What changes in diet are important and will make us healthier?
- What happens to food waste if it's not composted?
- How do nutrients get into soil in the first place?
- What would prevent a nutrient from making it all the way through the cycle? (For example: if no one composted, artificial fertilizers would have to be used; if a family didn't have a way to buy food; if crops failed due to hurricane flooding; if soil was eroded; if children weren't eating healthy garden foods, etc.)
- What's your favorite part of the cycle and why?

Want to Do More?

- Sing "Dirt Made My Lunch" (page 4); have students take home words to songs to sing at home.
- At each point in the cycle, sing a verse of a song to celebrate that part of the cycle: a song at harvest ("Bringing in the Sheaves," "Zum Gali Gali"), a planting song ("Garden Song," "Oats Peas Beans & Barley"), an eating song ("All I Really Need," "Food Glorious Food," "Sweet Potatoes"), an ecology song ("The Earth Is My Mother," "Decomposition," "Sun Soil Water Air," "Down on the Farm"), etc.
- Make a video to show to other students or share with other schools. Include music.
- Create paintings to illustrate each cycle component and display around the cafeteria walls. Label.

Lesson Links

Figuring Out Our Food System
Farm to Table
Sprout Yourself!

Literature Links

The Tortilla Factory by Gary Paulsen
Itse Selu: Cherokee Harvest Festival by Daniel Pennington
Grandpa's Garden Lunch by Judith Casely
Thirteen Moons on Turtle's Back: A Native American Year of Moons by Bruchac/London

Resources

- Banana Slug String Band audiotape or CD *Dirt Made My Lunch* for songs: "Decomposition," "Plant Parts Song," "Solar Energy Shout," "Dirt Made My Lunch," etc.
- *Rise Up Singing—The Group Singing Songbook* (15th Anniversary Ed.) by Pete Seeger (Foreword), Peter Blood (Ed.), Annie Patterson (Ed.), and Kore Loy McWhirter. Sing Out Publications, 2004.
- See Traditional Diet Pyramids link at www.oldwayspt.org for healthy eating patterns in many cultures.

Benchmarks

The Living Environment: 5D—Interdependence of Life, p. 116

Grades 3-5

"Insects and various other organisms depend on dead plant and animal material for food."

The Living Environment: 5E—Flow of Matter and Energy, p. 119

Grades K-2

Background: "An awareness of recycling, both in nature and in human societies, may play a helpful role in the development of children's thinking. Familiarity with the recycling of materials fosters the notion that matter continues to exist even though it changes from one form to another."

"Many materials can be recycled and used again, sometimes in different forms."

Grades 3-5

"Over the whole earth, organisms are growing, dying, and decaying, and new organisms are being produced by the old ones."

APPENDIX

Glossary

absorption The passage of nutrients through the digestive tract walls into the bloodstream.

aeration The process of supplying something with air. In soils or compost bins: creation of spaces to allow air circulation.

agriculture The science, art, and business of farming.

annelida The phylum of organisms with tube-like segmented bodies, such as earthworms.

annual A plant that can complete its life cycle in one growing season from seed and back to seed.

arable land Land that can be used to grow food.

bacteria A large group of one-celled, microscopic organisms. Some are beneficial; others cause disease. Bacteria in soils help recycle nutrients.

bedding A moist, organic medium such as leaves or newspaper that can be used for vermicomposting.

beneficial species Plants and animals that make a positive contribution to a crop.

biosphere Where life is on our world, from deep caves and the bottom of the ocean, to as high in the air as a microbe can support itself; the ecosphere.

buckwheat An edible plant whose seed can be cooked as a cereal, main dish, or made into flour.

castings The undigested remains deposited by worms. Also called vermicastings or worm castings.

chickpea A small, round seed used as the main ingredient in hummus; a garbanzo bean.

cholesterol A type of fat found naturally in the body and in foods that come from animals.

cinquain A type of poetry consisting of five lines.

circulation The movement of blood through the body.

climate Temperature, annual precipitation, and length of growing season in a particular area.

clitellum The swollen saddle-like area that is the reproductive part of an earthworm.

cocoon A lemon-shaped, protective case formed by the worm's clitellum containing up to 10 embryonic worms; an egg case.

coir The fiber from coconut husks that can be used in place of peat moss in gardens and as bedding for a worm bin.

Community-Supported Agriculture (CSA) An agreement between a farmer and community members who purchase "shares" of seasonal crops to ensure continual income for the farmer.

compost The process and result of rotting organic wastes such as table scraps, straw, or manure for use as garden fertilizer; humus.

compost tea A nutrient-rich solution for plants made by soaking compost in water.

cotyledon The first leaf or leaves of a sprouting plant containing the endosperm: a plant's short-term food supply.

cover crops Plants specifically planted for protection and enrichment of the soil.

crop nutrition The feeding of plants by adding organic matter and minerals.

crop rotation The changing of crops grown in particular fields from season to season for the purpose of benefiting the soil over the long term.

decomposition The process of breaking down or rotting organic matter into basic elements that help enrich soil.

dehydration The process of taking moisture out of food to help it last longer.

dental caries Tooth decay; cavities.

diet The food that a person eats; commonly used to mean a weight-loss regimen.

dietary guidelines Recommendations for improving health through food and activity.

dietitian A health professional who specializes in the field of food and nutrition.

digestive tract The tube-like passage from mouth to anus through which food is passed and processed.

Dust Bowl The area in the south-central U.S. where topsoil eroded so much that residents were forced to leave (1930s).

ecology The study of the interrelationships between living organisms and their environment.

ecosphere Where life is on our world, from deep caves and the bottom of the ocean, to as high in the air as a microbe can support itself; the biosphere.

ecosystem A working system formed by a community of living and non-living parts and linked by cycles and systems unique to this grouping.

Eisenia foetida The Latin name for a redworm used in vermicomposting; found in leaf litter, compost, and manure.

electrolyte A substance in cells that helps balance body fluids.

embryo (the seed) A tiny plant with leaves, stems, and root parts waiting for the right conditions that will allow germination.

endosperm A part of the seed that contains a seedling's first, short-term food supply; stored in the cotyledon(s).

erosion Soil movement from the land surface by water or wind action.

esophagus The tube through which food passes from the throat to the stomach.

excretion The process of ridding the body of waste products.

farmers' market Usually an open-air market where farmers sell their wares directly to the consumer.

farming, diversified A farm growing and raising a variety of crops and animals.

farming, industrialized Usually a farm growing one or two crops over large tracts of land and relying heavily on machinery, technology, synthetic pesticides, and fertilizers.

farming, mixed The practice of growing crops and raising livestock on the same farm.

farming, organic The practice of growing food or raising animals by guidelines that emphasize avoiding synthetic chemical inputs and working the soil to create conditions favorable to plants

and soil organisms.

fertilizer The nutrients from natural or synthetic sources that are applied to plants (usually through the soil) to foster plant vitality and growth.

fiber The coarse, non-digestible parts of the food we eat that help our bodies with digestion and with cleaning the intestines.

flower The reproductive part of a seed-bearing plant designed to attract insects (sometimes bats and birds) to aid in pollination.

foliage The leaves of the plant.

food additive A substance put into food during production, processing, storage, or packaging to prolong shelf-life, add color, enhance taste, or add nutrients.

food bank A community facility for the collection and distribution of food to people in need.

food chain A "chain" starting with the sun (captured by green plants) and followed in turn by who eats whom next—for example, sunlight is converted by green plant, which is eaten by mouse, and the mouse is eaten by fox.

food label A list of food ingredients and the percentage of the Recommended Daily Allowance (RDA) of various vitamins and minerals.

food production The process of making or creating goods, i.e., food in a variety of settings including farms, greenhouses, factories, etc.

food pyramid A visual representation showing one person's daily recommended food choices and portions from the various food groups.

food recovery The process of saving and collecting edible food no longer considered usable or salable in one location and delivering it to people in need. For example, day-old bread, discontinued canned goods, etc.

food security People who are "food secure" do not feel vulnerable about where their next meal is coming from. Community food security means "all persons obtaining at all times a culturally acceptable nutritionally adequate diet through local non-emergency sources." (Community Food Security Coalition)

food supply The quantity and quality of the food that we need to survive and thrive.

food system A system that includes the food produced, processed, consumed, and discarded by people in a given area.

food web A complex, interlocking of food chains within an ecological community; includes more complex relationships than a linear food chain.

foodways Foods particular to a geographic area.

fortified Food containing added ingredients designed to improve its nutritional value.

fossil fuels Non-renewable resources like coal, natural gas, and petroleum produced from thousands of years of decomposed prehistoric plants and animals and used for plastics, medicines, heating oil, diesel fuel, and gasoline.

fruit The ripened ovary of a plant containing the seeds.

fungi A group of non-photosynthesizing plants—such as mushrooms and molds—that live on dead or dying organic matter; an important decomposer in soils.

garbanzo beans Small, round seeds used as the main ingredient in hummus; chickpeas.

gastrointestinal tract The tube through which food is processed and passed from mouth to anus; the digestive tract.

germ The innermost portion of the seed; contains protein.

germinate/germination The process of a seed becoming a plant.

green manure Legumes, such as peas, that are grown to "fix" nitrogen into the soil. When the crop is harvested or plowed back into the soil, the nitrogen remains in the topsoil, available for the next crop.

habitat A suitable environment for a living organism that includes the proper amounts of air, water, shelter, space, and food.

haiku A Japanese poem of a fixed, seventeen-syllabic form.

heirloom Something of value from the past, in this case, non-hybrid seeds grown and saved from long ago.

humus The part of topsoil that comes from rotted plants and animals and animal wastes.

hunger A lack of food, which can lead to sickness and death.

hybrid Of mixed origin; a plant produced from two different plants whose seeds do not necessarily

produce plants like the parent.

hygiene The practice of maintaining cleanliness.

industrial agriculture (also called factory farming) refers to large-scale, machine- and chemical-intensive farms designed to produce the highest output at the lowest financial cost, i.e., hundreds to thousands of (1) genetically similar animals tightly confined indoors; (2) acres of one high-yield, hybrid variety (monocropping).

inputs In the food system, inputs of natural resources include soil, water, seeds, fertilizers, pesticides, compost, and nonrenewable fuels. Farm machinery, factories, and transportation systems, as well as human resources are other examples of food system inputs.

landfill A large, outdoor area for waste disposal. Sanitary landfills provide liners and a layering system to reduce leakage of chemicals into ground water.

leaves The food-making factories of green plants, usually green, flat to catch light, and attached to a stem.

legumes Plants such as peas and beans with the ability to take in nitrogen through their roots; also called "nitrogen fixing" plants.

loam A rich, crumbly mix of fertile soil containing the right amounts of clay, silt, and sand. Organic matter contributes to its texture and water-holding capacity.

Lumbricus rubellus The Latin (or scientific) name for a red worm species used in vermicomposting.

malnutrition The lack of nutritious food or proper variety of nutrients in one's diet.

manure tea See compost tea—the same process, but using manure from farm animals.

metabolism The chemical activity that maintains living organisms.

micro-organisms Organisms too small to be seen with the naked eye.

migrant farm workers Farm workers and (often) their families who work on farms on a seasonal basis, traveling from farm to farm as the availability of work dictates.

millet A small yellow grain which can be cooked as cereal or ground into flour.

minerals Non-living substances that make up soils.

MSG Monosodium glutamate—a chemical added to food to enhance flavor.

mung beans Small round green or yellow beans native to Asia—used in sprouting, cooking, or dried.

natural food Food that does not contain artificial ingredients or preservatives; often used to refer to non-processed, whole food.

nutrient A nourishing substance, such as the minerals that a plant takes from the soil or the constituents in food that keep a human body healthy and help it grow.

nutrition The study of how food is used by a living organism.

obesity A condition in which a person's body weight is more than 20 percent above what is recommended for the person's height.

Olestra The brand name for an artificial fat substitute which has caused health problems in some consumers.

organic matter Naturally occurring plant and animal remains. Organic matter is an important part of soil, which improves moisture retention, soil structure, water drainage, and soil aeration.

outputs The work done or amount produced by a person, machine, production line, etc.

peat moss Decomposed sphagnum moss from peat bogs; used to add organic matter to soil.

percent daily values The percentage of a nutrient from one serving of a food in relation to everything an average person needs.

perennial A plant that lives over more than one year—it can grow, flower, and produce seeds for several years.

pesticide A chemical from synthetic or natural sources used to kill pests.

pH The relative level of acid (acidity) or base (alkalinity), as indicated by the presence of hydrogen ions.

phenology The study of seasonal, weather-influenced changes in plants and animals such as bird migrations, budding, etc.

photosynthesis The process by which cells in green plants convert light to energy. In this process carbon dioxide and water in the presence of chlorophyll (the green pigment) and light energy are changed into glucose (a sugar). This energy-rich sugar is the source of food used by most plants. Photosynthesis is unique to green plants and supplies food for the plant

and oxygen for other forms of life.

preservatives Additives to food that keep it from spoiling.

processed food Food that has been altered from its whole, natural state.

produce Farm and garden products—fresh fruits and vegetables.

quinoa A South American plant whose edible seed is high in protein.

recycling Processing waste products back into usable items.

recycling facility A place where "recyclables" are gathered, sorted, stored, and shipped for processing.

red wiggler worm A species of earthworm (Annelid) well suited to worm composting.

root The underground part of the plant that helps provide support by anchoring the plant and absorbing water and nutrients needed for growth. Roots also store sugars and carbohydrates the plant uses to carry out other functions.

seed A tiny plant (embryo) with leaves, stems, root parts, and temporary food storage inside a protective seed coat.

seed bank A place where heirloom seeds and other special seeds are saved and stored in such a way that they remain viable.

seed coat The protective outer layer of a seed; also called the bran.

soil The naturally occurring outer covering of the earth where plants grow. Soil is made up of minerals (sand, silt, clay), air, water, and organic matter.

soil organisms Literally billions of microscopic (bacteria) and macroscopic (earthworms, sow bugs, mites, etc.) organisms that thrive in soils.

soil structure The shape that soil takes due to its physical and chemical properties (examples are granular, blocky, columnar, etc.).

solid waste Discarded solids and liquids—anything determined to be no longer usable—from households and industry.

sorghum A cereal plant grown for its grain, as fodder, or for making syrup.

starch An abundant carbohydrate found in the endosperm of corn, wheat, and rice.

stems The part of the plant that provides support and carries water and nutrients from the roots to other parts of the plant.

stewardship The concept of being responsible to the land; ensuring its health for future generations through our current management of resources.

sustainable agriculture A farming system that conserves resources, is socially supportive, commercially competitive, and environmentally sound.

switchel A tangy, thirst-quenching drink made from apple cider vinegar, brown sugar, ginger, and water.

theme garden A garden based on a specific concept or subject, i.e., Shakespeare, Vegetable Soup, Pizza.

thresh The process of separating grain seeds from stems through beating.

till To cultivate or plow the land.

transfer station A facility for sorting and storing (solid waste) trash and recyclables until transport to processing or disposal sites.

umami The fifth recognized sense of taste; savory.

Venn diagram A mathematical tool which uses overlapping circles to demonstrate relationships between different items.

vermicelli A thin (worm-shaped) pasta; "skinny" spaghetti.

vermicompost A mixture of vermicastings and rotted organic matter.

vermicomposting The decomposition of organic wastes, such as table scraps, using worms.

vermiculite A lightweight, tan material that can hold water; often an ingredient in commercial soil mixes. Harmful if inhaled.

wheat berries The whole kernels of wheat.

wheat germ The vitamin-rich center (embryo) of the wheat kernel.

whole food Food that has not been processed.

whole grain The entire seed, including the bran, germ, and endosperm.

worm castings Vermicastings; worm manure; (worm poop).

Commoner's Laws of Ecology

In the 1970s the renowned biologist Barry Commoner drafted four "Laws of Ecology":[1]

- **Everything Is Connected to Everything Else.** There is one ecosphere for all living organisms and what affects one, affects all in some form or fashion.
- **Everything Must Go Somewhere.** There is nothing such as "waste" in the natural setting. What one organism produces as waste is taken up and used by another organism.
- **Nature Knows Best.** Major man-made change in a natural system is likely to be detrimental to that system.
- **There Is No Such Thing as a Free Lunch.** In Nature's equation both sides of the scale must balance—for every gain there is a cost.

When applied to the food system, one can view these "laws" through the integral relationships that link consumers with that cycle. The system of farming is another ideal place to observe the laws of ecology in action. As long as plants make food from sunlight and take in water and nutrients from the soil, the farmer will be tied to the earth. Therefore, as consumers we are also tied to the land. The farmer is affected by what happens to the land (drought, flood, pollution, famine, development) and the land is affected by how it is farmed (soil erosion, desertification, fertile topsoil, healthy crops).

Let's see how the Laws of Ecology fit with **HEALTHY FOODS FROM HEALTHY SOILS:**

- **Everything Is Connected to Everything Else**

We are organisms who rely on food; we actually eat what the earth creates. Therefore we must also feed and nurture the earth in return. We are inextricably linked to this planet by our intimate connection to the land. The cycle can't stop, the web can't be broken or there are consequences. Consider food chains and food webs, and how all living things are linked by them; predators and prey affect animal and plant populations and vice versa. This law also applies to soil health, water and air quality and ultimately, our personal health. Economic and social principles are likewise interconnected and interdependent, even more so now in the beginning of the twenty-first century.

It's not just that we recognize connections between all things, it's that we/they are all part of the same whole—like cells in a body, like drops in the water cycle—the very same water that circulates through our oceans, bodies, and plants. So, as with the land and farms, with animals and plants, and with the raw materials of sun, water, and air, we all must share.

- **Everything Has Limits and Has to Go Somewhere**

The earth is finite. Its minerals, water, soil, and air are all we'll ever have. These elements are continuously cycling through the ecosystem. Each individual or step in the cycle plays an important, specific role in the continuation of these cycles. These resources will not be available infinitely. We can better manage what we have available to us. "Where we put things" makes a difference. Through creativity, resourcefulness, and a degree of common sense, we can go a lot further with what we've been given. Composting, as discussed in this manual, is a specific example. Why bury food waste that can be naturally transformed into new, useful material?

This law applies also to soil management, water conservation, resource management, and innovative thinking about alternatives to current practices.

- **Everything Is Always Changing**

Nature is always changing. Children observe, relate, and document this dynamic process easily. Plants, animals, and land evolve over time. A field becomes a forest through succession and all organisms must adapt to survive (or not) and take advantage of an ecosystem's resources. As humans attempt to

[1] Commoner, Barry. "The Closing Circle: Nature, Man, and Technology," *Thinking About the Environment*, M.A. Cahn. and R. O'Brien, eds., Armonk, NY: M. E. Sharpe, Inc., 1971. Pages 161-66.

control Nature by managing plant species (and inventing ways to prevent tomatoes from ripening too quickly, for instance) we are paradoxically accelerating Nature's pace of change in other areas (example: rainforest destruction, etc.). The changes have been aggressive in the 1900s especially, to the point that our evolution may not keep up with them—-but the insects and micro-organisms will!!

This relates to plant and animal biodiversity, which is diminishing inexorably. If we humans can modify some of our current behaviors, we may be able to help preserve some of our precious and diverse ecosystems.

➧ There Is No Such Thing as a Free Lunch

All we eat, wear, and use during our lives exacts an environmental cost. This refers to the consequences of our actions and whether sustainability is a collective human goal. It leads us to ask the question that runs through this book, "What if . . . ?" Through contaminated water, loss of wildlife habitat, soil erosion, and extinction, we are paying for some of our ill-considered decisions. A balance needs to be sustained and improved between human consumption and natural resources for the benefit not just of humans but for all life. Hidden costs of everything from food and fiber to water and energy use make it seem as though we do get a "free lunch," especially in Western societies—but, the planet is "footing the bill."

Activities throughout this guide explore these concepts and provide some concrete examples for the upcoming generation.

Ten Steps for Taking Action[1]

No matter what problem or topic you're addressing, there are a few steps that will help you organize a successful project. Barbara Lewis describes these ten steps in *The Kid's Guide to Social Action* (1991).

Identify the issue. Choose a problem that is important to the whole group and everyone can support. Don't just consider a problem that is easy to solve, but at the same time don't choose something that would overwhelm the group.

Research the problem. Find out as much about the issue as possible. Use books, newspapers, and experts. Survey people to see how they feel about the issue, talk with public officials on the phone or in person.

Brainstorm possible solutions. Brainstorming is a creative group process. Think of all the different possibilities and discuss them to refine your plan of action. Choose one or a few solutions.

Get support for your project. Find people who agree with you and get their support; build a coalition. Talk with parents and relatives, neighbors, other students, town officials, or state agencies.

Identify the opposition. Who has different opinions or is against your solution? Listen carefully to find out how people really feel about the issue. Seek out your opponents and try to win them over. Listen to them to understand their side and appreciate their opinions.

Advertise. The media are usually enthusiastic about "kid action." Use press releases and public service announcements to express your concerns or get your message out.

Raise money. This is not always necessary, but often having money can help you accomplish parts of the project much easier.

Carry out the solution. After getting all the plans in place, get to work. List the steps, decide who is responsible for each, and when each step will happen.

Evaluate the progress. How is the plan working? Are there things you should change? Do you need to talk to more people? Make it work!

Don't give up. Don't just accept everything people say about why your plan won't work. Keep at it until you find a solution that *will* work. If the issue is important, stay with it.

"Food security is not just about how we "protect" our food supplies and guard them against terrorist attack. It is about how we grow our food and how people gain access to it. It is about how we organize our businesses and our communities. It is about what we value in the global human family and how we use planet earth's finite resources. It is about what we value in our food and our families."
—Fred Kirschenmann, Ph.D., Director, Leopold Center for Sustainable Agriculture, Iowa State University (New Perspectives on Food Security, 2004 Conference Proceedings) www.leopold.iastate.edu/pubs/other/files/food_security.pdf

[1] Used by permission. *Pathways to a Sustainable Future—A Curriculum Guide for Maine Schools Exploring Waste Management Issues* by the Chewonki Foundation and Maine Waste Management Agency. Revised by Tom Bertocci in 1999.

Handout from *Healthy Foods from Healthy Soils* by Elizabeth Patten and Kathy Lyons.

Food Security and Food Recovery

In teaching about the food system, we would be remiss in not discussing food security. This book introduces the topic of hunger and food security by encouraging students to reflect on some of the disparities in our food system: *How do people who don't have land get their food? What happens when a person doesn't get enough nutrients? Are whole foods available in all communities? How does food waste contribute to the hunger problem in the U.S.?* Discussing these questions helps students recognize the links between healthy food and a "healthy environment, economy, and community."[1]

We talk all through the book about the high numbers of children who are at risk or already overweight or obese. However, "overnutrition," while it affects the same *number* of people as does "undernutrition," roughly one billion, has nowhere near the same magnitude of health consequences. "Obesity [in the developed countries] is not as big a problem as hunger in developing countries. First, we need to make sure that people are eating enough food and the right foods."[2] In fact, even the right to an adequate diet is not universally recognized.

In harsh contrast to developing countries, nearly 90 percent of U.S. households were food secure in 2004. This means they had assured access at all times to enough food for healthy active lives. At the same time, a little more than 10 percent of households were food insecure. That means 13.9 million children were hungry at times during the year because there was not enough money for food.[3] Indeed, in the U.S., one of the richest countries in the world, 38.2 million people lived in households experiencing food insecurity, compared to 33.6 million in 2001 and 31 million in 1999.[4]

"Each year, around one fifth of America's food goes to waste annually, with an estimated 130 pounds of food per person ending up in landfills. The annual value of this lost food is estimated at around $31 billion. While food material is the second-largest component group in the country's solid waste stream, it currently is the type of material least likely to be recovered. Thus, there is a vast potential to dramatically increase the amount of excess food that is recovered and recycled. But the real story is that roughly 49 million people could have been fed by those lost resources."[5] This waste is not just an environmental problem, it is an unethical waste of a precious resource that we all need to live, and which many people lack.

What can students do?

- First, encourage (older) students to become aware of the magnitude of the issue. See Ten Steps for Taking Action, page 214, and Stephanie Kempf's *Finding Solutions to Hunger* (see Resources).
- Work with existing youth service groups and volunteer organizations to assist on-going food recovery efforts.
- Organize essay, speaking, or art contests for school children which focus on a child's view of hunger and its consequences.
- Sponsor a community garden that gives a portion of the harvest to food banks, soup kitchens, and other food recovery programs. (See Grow a Row, page 187.)
- Supply gardening tools and harvesting equipment for local gardening and gleaning efforts.

What can individual citizens do?

- Educate yourself about some of the reasons food insecurity exists.
- Suggest that organizations you belong to or businesses you work for help examine the root causes of hunger and poverty. (See Resources).
- Join or form a community walk/run to benefit an anti-hunger program.
- Volunteer at a local food recovery program. More than 90 percent of food pantries and soup kitchens rely on volunteers for food distribution.
- Call "1-800-GLEAN-IT," a toll-free hotline of the USDA and National Hunger Clearinghouse.

Thinking twice before wasting food or discarding food can be one step toward solving many worldwide problems. Here are a few options for taking uneaten food out of the waste stream.

1 Michelle Mascarenhas, "School Food Perspectives."
2 Dr. Prakash Shetty, Chief of FAO's Nutrition Planning, Assessment and Evaluation Service
3 www.ers.usda.gov/briefing/foodsecurity/ Also the Food Research and Action Center (FRAC), Economic Research Report, October 2005.
4 *Hunger in America 2001,* a study commissioned by America's Second Harvest.
5 *A Citizen's Guide to Food Recovery*, USDA, April, 1997; www.usda.gov/news/pubs/gleaning/two.htm

Food Recovery

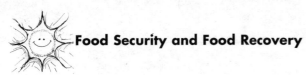

Food recovery is the collection of wholesome food for distribution to poor and hungry people. It follows a basic humanitarian ethic that has been part of societies for centuries. We know that "gleaning," or gathering after the harvest, goes back at least as far as biblical days. Today, however, the terms "gleaning" and "food recovery" cover a variety of different efforts. The four most common methods are:

- **Field Gleaning** The collection of crops from farmers' fields that have already been mechanically harvested or from fields where it is not economically profitable to harvest.
- **Perishable Food Rescue or Salvage** The collection of perishable produce from wholesale and retail sources.
- **Food Rescue** The collection of prepared foods from the food service industry.
- **Nonperishable Food Collection** The collection of processed foods with long shelf lives.

As an alternative to discarding unserved and/or unsold food, many businesses are working with food recovery programs, shelters, and human service agencies to get this food to people in need. Examples of food donations include produce wholesalers donating slightly soft or damaged blueberries or apples to a local food bank, a restaurant owner donating unsold pizzas to a lunch program at a community shelter, a farmer donating excess squash to a local shelter, a grocery store donating excess nonperishable food to a food bank, and a food manufacturer donating food overruns to hunger organizations. Food recovery programs offer numerous benefits to businesses, communities, and individuals. They can:

- heighten people's awareness about issues related to hunger, the environment, and personal choice and reduce waste;
- provide wholesome food to needy families;
- provide volunteer opportunities for people wanting to help;
- save businesses money on trash collection and disposal fees;
- help communities and businesses meet mandated waste-reduction goals; and
- help sustain local industries and jobs.

Composting

According to the EPA, about 72 percent of food scraps (10 million tons) are compostable. (Most compost facilities exclude meats, cheese, and oil.) Since food waste is a large component of municipal solid waste, backyard composting could make a huge impact on the amount of food waste handled by municipalities each year. Many public and private institutions are considering the benefits of composting; some record-setting food waste reduction programs are composting between 70 and 100 percent of their wastes. See the EPA web page "Don't Throw Away That Food" at www.epa.gov/epaoswer/non-hw/reduce/food/food.htm Composting offers many advantages:

- raising awareness of waste recycling in a low-impact/environmentally friendly way;
- avoiding trash collection and disposal fees;
- helping the community meet local and state waste reduction goals; and
- sustaining local industries and jobs.

In all of the above food recovery scenarios, food waste becomes a resource instead of a disposal problem.

Resources

- USDA on Gleaning and Food Recovery: "A Citizen's Guide to Food Recovery."
- *Finding Solutions to Hunger* by Stephanie Kempf. World Hunger Year, 2001.
- Kids Can Make a Difference (KIDS) Mission: "to inspire students to realize that it is within their power to help eliminate hunger and poverty in their communities, country, and world." www.kidscanmakeadifference.org
- For hunger and food insecurity data collected state-by-state by the Census Bureau and the U.S. Department of Agriculture: www.frac.org/html/news/foodinsecurity.pdf.
- Second Harvest, the nation's largest hunger relief operation at www.secondharvest.org

"While not all excess food is edible, wholesome, or appropriate for human consumption, much of it is . . . even if 5 percent of the food waste were recovered, four million additional people could be fed each day." (Economic Research Service, USDA)

Making Food with Children[1]

Safe Cooking in the Classroom

For safety and sanitation, review the following rules with your class. You may wish to make a laminated version of this for your classroom, or simplify it and have your students illustrate it as a poster for several classrooms or to take home.

- Wash hands with plenty of soap and water before cooking. Rub your hands well when washing.
- Keep food preparation surfaces clean.
- Clean up as you cook.
- Do not touch your mouth, nose, or hair when working with food.
- Avoid sneezing or coughing on food: cover your mouth with your arm if you have to sneeze or cough.
- It's better not to help if you have a sore throat or cold.
- Go over precautions about ovens, table-top griddles, or hot pans before starting.
- Be careful using sharp knives—use a cutting board and cut away from yourself.
- Keep handles of pans turned toward the inside of the range or table.
- Do not plug electrical appliances in or remove the plug with wet hands.
- Throw away (or compost) any food or wash any utensil that falls on the floor.
- Do not taste with the cooking spoon.

Tips for Safe Handling of Fruits and Vegetables[2]

- Wash hands with warm water and soap for at least 20 seconds before and after handling food, especially fresh whole fruits and vegetables and raw meat, poultry, and fish. Clean under fingernails, too.
- Rinse raw produce in warm water. Don't use soap or other detergents. If appropriate, use a small scrub brush to remove surface dirt.
- Use smooth, durable, and nonabsorbent cutting boards that can be cleaned and sanitized easily.
- Wash cutting boards with hot water, soap, and a scrub brush to remove food particles. Then sanitize the boards by putting them through the automatic dishwasher cycle. Always wash boards and knives after cutting raw meat, poultry, or seafood and before cutting another food to prevent cross-contamination.
- Store cut, peeled, and broken-apart fruits and vegetables (such as melon balls) in the refrigerator.

For more food safety information see: www.health.gov/dietaryguidelines/dga2005/document/ Look under Food Safety.

Germs and the Cinnamon Trick

This fun activity reinforces the importance of thorough handwashing. Use cinnamon, vegetable oil (1/4 cup oil and less than 1/8 tsp. of cinnamon is adequate for several students), a hand-washing area, towels, a 2" half-size steam table pan (available from your food services staff), or a large (9" x 13" or greater) pan with at least 1-inch sides; a timer.

Have students time each other, recording the typical amount of time they spend washing their hands.

Put about 1/4 to 1/2 inch of oil into the pan. Have the students put their hands in it, just to get oil all over their hands. Take their hands out and let some of the oil drip off. You may use an "oil pump" available from kitchen supply stores, which you can use to spray the oil onto their hands.

Shake cinnamon on their hands. You can even encourage them to scrape their nails in the cinnamon to illustrate the issue around cleaning under their fingernails.

Set a timer and have them wash their hands for the amount of time they did in step number one.

Evaluate the results. Are hands clean?

Then repeat the oil/cinnamon coating, this time

[1] Adapted with permission from *Pyramid Builders,* a collection of integrated nutrition education activities for grades K-6 developed by the Kansas Nutrition Education and Training Program, Nutrition Services, Kansas State Board of Education.

[2] Adapted from FDA's 5-a-Day website: www.fda.gov/fdac Search under "fruits and vegetables."

washing for 30 seconds. You might try the difference between hot and cold water, adding soap, or different amounts of time.

Have children clean their hands completely and then allow discussion time. How long did it take to remove all the "germs." Were they surprised? Can they "see" how invisible germs might be on their hands? Ask: What if . . . you never washed your hands?

Variations: Use hand lotion or vaseline instead of the oil, with or without the cinnamon. (Some teachers use glitter in place of cinnamon, but be careful not to clog the sink drain.) Show how, if you have oil and cinnamon on your hands, the germs can spread from one person to another, to the door knob, sink handle, table, utensils, etc. Germs are everywhere. We need them to live, but we don't need to pass them around quite so much!

This is excellent for all teachers and food service personnel to try.

One teacher related how, after having done this exercise in class, one of her students refused to eat cinnamon toast anymore. He'd mistakenly believed that the cinnamon *was* the germs!

Resource

- See also "Guidelines for Safe Classroom Cooking" in *How to Teach Nutrition to Kids* by Connie Liakos Evers, which includes food handling, work surface, and equipment safety tips. 24 Carrot Press, 2006.

Selected Nutrition Information

There are more than 40 different known nutrients; only some of their multitude of functions are understood. This guidebook focuses on garden and farm-raised plant foods; several significant nutrients found in those foods are discussed here. For more complete nutrient information, see *Bowes & Church's Food Values of Portions Commonly Used* by Anna De Planter Bowes, Helen Nichols Church, and Jean A. Pennington (nutrient data); *Jane Brody's Nutrition Book* by Jane Brody (good narrative section on nutrients); and *How to Teach Nutrition to Kids* by Connie Liakos Evers (overview of nutrition guidelines geared toward children).

Most dietary guidelines emphasize grain products, vegetables, and fruit. Those food groups are all excellent sources of many beneficial compounds, yet there are some distinct nutritional differences between these three groups. *Note:* The major nutrients (macronutrients) contained in our foods fall into six categories: proteins, carbohydrates, fats, vitamins, minerals, and water. In the field of nutrition, we think of energy as *kilocalories*, which are found in proteins, carbohydrates, and fats, not in the other three macronutrients. All foods on the food pyramid supply kilocalories for the body.

- **Fruit** contains the carbohydrate fructose (fruit sugar), which makes it especially appealing for snacks or dessert. This form of sugar is absorbed more slowly into the bloodstream, and combined with the fact that they contain fiber, fruits are therefore more gently assimilated in the body. Both fruits and vegetables are rich in carbohydrates, vitamins A and C, minerals, and fiber.

- In general, **vegetables** are even more "nutrient dense"—containing more nutrition per calorie—than fruit. They are considered nutritional superstars for having the broadest range of nutrients of any food group. Vegetables also contain protein, vitamins A and C, carotenoids, other beneficial phytochemicals associated with the color of the (fruit or) vegetable, and essential fatty acids. Vegetables may be consumed freely because their calories are offset by the energy it takes for the body to digest them. Did you know the Latin origin of the word vegetable, *vegetabilis,* means "to enliven or animate"?

- **Grains** are good sources of different nutrients than those found in vegetables and fruits. The complex carbohydrates found in grains are made up of long chains of simple carbohydrates, or sugars. These long sequences of sugar molecules must be broken down more slowly by the body, thereby better regulating insulin release, blood sugar levels, and appetite. Refined sugars, such as those in cakes or cookies, are more rapidly absorbed and do not provide the range of nutrients that less refined products do.

- **Nuts, beans, and seeds** are found in the high-protein group of the food pyramid along with fish, meat, poultry, and eggs. They are richer in this primary nutrient than any other plant food and are essential for growth, maintenance, and repair of body tissue. Protein (made up of amino acids) is required for a huge array of functions and uses, including hormone and enzyme manufacture. Next to water, protein is the most abundant element in the body.

Selected nutrients found in garden and farm plants:

- **Beta-Carotene** is found in fruits and vegetables and is converted into vitamin A in the body. This "pro-vitamin" keeps your skin and mucous membranes intact and aids in vision. Like vitamin C, it is an antioxidant that helps keep your cells healthy. You can see it in yellow/orange foods such as sweet potatoes, carrots, cantaloupes, winter squash/pumpkins, and apricots, but it stays hidden in green vegetables such as collard greens, kale, and spinach.

- **Vitamin C** helps us heal and fights off infections. It may help in preventing or reducing colds. Good sources are peppers (especially red ones!), oranges, broccoli, Brussels sprouts, and grapefruit.

- **Folic Acid** is a B vitamin necessary in blood formation. It makes healthy cells in your blood, and is super important during growth periods, especially in pregnancy. You'll find it in cooked beans, fresh spinach and other greens, oatmeal, asparagus, peas, wheat germ, and broccoli.

- **Niacin, riboflavin, and thiamine** are all part of the vitamin B complex, are necessary for carbohydrate, fat, and protein metabolism, and help the nervous system function. They're found in whole grains and nutritional yeast.

- **Fiber** isn't technically a nutrient, but you'd be unable to function without it! It helps the movement of food through your digestive tract, and slows absorption of digested food into the bloodstream, regulating blood sugar. It protects against high blood cholesterol and heart disease. (See also page 98.)

Some important minerals are **magnesium**, **calcium**, and **phosphorus**, which are also found in vegetables. They are critical for good bone mass, healthy teeth, and muscle (including the heart!) and nerve function. These three minerals have to work as a team inside the body. Look for calcium in many greens—collard greens, in particular—dairy products, and canned fish such as sardines and salmon (with bones). Magnesium can be found in almonds, hazelnuts, spinach, Swiss chard, sunflower seeds, halibut, tofu, brown rice, and wheat bran. Foods rich in protein are where you'll find phosphorus: fish, poultry, eggs, meat, whole grains, nuts, and seeds. Other important minerals are:

- **Iron**, found in many vegetables, is also abundant in legumes, along with B vitamins. This mineral is found in most dark green leaves. Iron is essential in blood formation.

- **Potassium**, another essential mineral, is found in all vegetables, especially potatoes and leafy greens, oranges, bananas, and whole grains. It assists with fluid balance, helps control heart muscles, the nervous system, and the kidneys.

- **Copper** is a trace mineral (found in much smaller amounts that the essential minerals) necessary for hemoglobin formation. It's found in whole grain products, almonds, leafy greens, and dried legumes.

What Do We Have in Common with Plants?[1]

(This activity is for older students.)

Plants require some of the same nutrients that humans do for growth, repair, and regular functioning. Plants get minerals from the soil (once they're dissolved in water) but require the food (sugars) produced in the leaves, which in the plant, as in humans, can be stored as carbohydrates, fats, and proteins. People and plants depend on some similar nutrients—in particular, nitrogen (N), phosphorus (P), and potassium (K). See the nutrient chart on page 222.

We can trace the journey a nutrient takes not only through humans (see Anatomy in Action, page 63), but through soils and plants as well. For the sake of simplicity, we use three elements that are necessary for both plants and humans. Have students pick one of the following three nutrients (and associated foods). Group students by the nutrient they choose.

- **Nitrogen (N)**, a component of all proteins, is found in the high-protein groups—seeds, nuts, and animal foods (including dairy).

- **Phosphorus (P)** is an essential element found in the walls of each cell. Good food sources of phosphorus include egg yolks and high-protein foods of animal or plant origin.

- **Potassium (K)** is a mineral which helps regulate all your cells' functions. It occurs in all vegetables, some fruits, whole grains, and sunflower seeds.

Give each group of older students the following tables to use in tracing what happens to the nutrients as they travel from plant to human. Guide students in following the nutrients through the cycle, allowing them to choose where they start—in plant, human, soil, or water. Have them describe each step using facts from the chart, but making a story line—with adventures that occur along the way. Example: Nitrogen "Ned" chooses to begin his trip in the soil and helps a spinach plant to grow and become leafy (using Table for Nutrients in Plants) which Ned likes because it provides him with shade. Then NitroNed finds himself airborne (being picked) and being placed in a sauna (steamer or cooking pot) that he doesn't much like. Later, he gets devoured by a giant (human) named "Ivan Appetite" or "I.M. Hungry", and after the long journey through digestion, absorption, and metabolism, finds himself being made into muscle tissue (using Table for Nutrients in Humans) that Ivan likes to use when he bikes to school, etc. Students can create a skit around the story.

See the charts on the following page:

[1] See Alive and Thriving on page 10 for a more complete answer.

Nutrient Functions and Deficiencies/Excess Symptoms in PLANTS

Nutrient	Function	Deficiency Symptoms	Excess Symptoms
N nitrogen	necessary for foliage, growth	yellowing of leaves, beginning with the youngest	long, weak stems and lush, thin foliage, failure to flower
P phosphorus	necessary for root growth, flowering, and fruiting	development of deep green or purplish hue on lower leaves	(not apparent)
K potassium	contributes to overall vigor and resistance	slow growth, stunting, and browning of leaves	(not apparent)

Adaped with permission from: *Growlab: A Complete Guide to Gardening in the Classroom*, National Gardening Association, 1994, p 50; www.kidsgardening.com; www.nationalgardening.com

Nutrient Functions and Deficiencies/Excess Symptoms in HUMANS

Nutrient	Function	Deficiency Symptoms	Excess Symptoms
N nitrogen	essential part of all proteins, necessary for synthesis and maintenance of tissue	growth abnormalities, protein malnutrition, anemia, hair loss, poor muscle tone	excessive protein may cause fluid imbalance and more calcium excretion
P phosphorus	component of all plant and animal cells, helps perform most basic life functions	stunted growth, poor quality bones/teeth, lack of appetite, irregular breathing, fatigue	disturbs calcium:phosphorus ratio, effects on bone controversial
K potassium	electrolyte which contributes to fluid balance, cell growth, and metabolism	general weakness, poor reflexes, neuromuscular impairment, skin disorders, irregular heartbeat	lethargy, muscle spasms, convulsions (cell-to-cell communication is disrupted)

Information reprinted with permission from *Nutrition Almanac* by Gayla J. Kirschmann and John D. Kirschmann, Nutrition Search, Inc., McGraw-Hill Education, 1996.
Handout from *Healthy Foods from Healthy Soils* by Elizabeth Patten and Kathy Lyons, Tilbury House, Publishers.

Dietary Guidelines

USDA Dietary Guidelines

The 6th edition of the *Dietary Guidelines for Americans* booklet was released in 2005. It may be viewed and downloaded at www.healthierus.gov/dietaryguidelines

The basic guidelines are:

Make smart choices from every food group

A healthy eating plan is one that:

- Emphasizes fruits, vegetables, whole grains, and fat-free or low-fat milk and milk products.
- Includes lean meats, poultry, fish, beans, eggs, and nuts.
- Is low in saturated fats, trans fats, cholesterol, salt (sodium), and added sugars.

Mix up your choices within each food group

- Focus on fruits
- Vary your veggies
- Make half your grains whole
- Get your calcium-rich foods
- Go lean with protein
- Know the limits on fats, salt, and sugars

Find your balance between food and physical activity

- Children and teenagers should be physically active for 60 minutes every day or most days.
- Increasing the intensity or the amount of time that you are physically active can have even greater health benefits and may be needed to control body weight. At least 60 minutes a day may be needed to prevent weight gain.

Get the most nutrition out of your calories

- Use the Nutrition Facts Label

Play it safe with food.

- Know how to prepare, handle, and store food safely to keep you and your family safe.
- If you are an adult and choose to drink alcohol, do so in moderation.

[1] Compiled from various sources, including *The Green Guide, Mothers & Others*, 40 W. 20th St., New York, NY 10011, and Joan Dye Gussow and Katherine L. Clancy "Dietary Guidelines for Sustainability," *Journal of Nutrition and Behavior Education,* vol. 18; no 1: 1-5, 1986.

Dietary Guidelines for Sustainability[1]

- Eat a variety of local, seasonal foods.
- Balance the food you eat with outdoor physical activity—maintain or improve your weight.
- Choose a diet with plenty of whole grains and fresh vegetables and fruits.
- Eat fewer and smaller portions of animal products.
- Choose a diet low in refined sugars.
- Choose minimally processed and packaged foods.
- Prepare your own meals at home.

Eating from the Food Pyramid

You'll find a food pyramid handout on page 56. As a rule of thumb, elementary-aged children should be eating in the lower-to-middle number of servings suggested for the five healthy food groups. Use the food pyramid to help you eat better. Start with a base of plenty of whole grains, and aim to get at least five servings of vegetables and fruits daily. Add a few choices from the protein strip, then go easy on the "extras" in the smallest part of the pyramid—the sweets, solid fats, and salty foods. Choose water anytime, exercise often, and take time to eat and enjoy a variety of foods.

- **Bread, Cereal, Rice, and Pasta Group 6-11 servings (look for whole grains)**

1 slice of bread
1 ounce dry cereal
1/2 cup of cooked rice, pasta, or cereal

- **Vegetable Group 3-5 servings**

1 cup of raw leafy vegetables
1/2 cup cut-up raw or cooked vegetables
3/4 cup of 100% vegetable juice

- **Fruit Group 2-4 servings**

1 medium fruit
1/2 cup dried fruit
1/2 cup fresh, frozen, or canned fruit
3/4 cup of 100% fruit juice

- **Milk, Yogurt, and Cheese Group 2-3 servings**

1 cup milk
1 cup yogurt
1 ounce of natural cheese

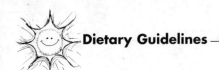

- **Dry Beans, Eggs, Nuts, Poultry, and Lean Meat Group 2-3 servings**

3 oz. cooked meats, poultry, or fish
1/3 cup or 1 1/2 oz. nuts, 2 Tbsp nut butter,
2 Tbsp or 1/2 oz. seeds
1/2 cup cooked dry beans or peas

- **Extras: solid fats, salty foods and sweets**. Use sparingly.

The Top Ten!

Here are some "Top 10" lists (plus a few more!) of the best fruit and vegetable choices you can make for your health. Aim for variety—and purchase as many locally as you can.

Try many colors and kinds. Choose any form: fresh, frozen, canned, dried, juices. All forms provide vitamins and minerals, and all provide fiber except for most juices—so choose fruits and vegetables most often. Wash fresh fruits and vegetables thoroughly before using. If you buy prepared vegetables, check the Nutrition Facts Label to find choices that are low in saturated fat and sodium.

In selecting your daily intake of fruits and vegetables, the National Cancer Institute recommends:[2]

- **At least one serving of a vitamin A-rich fruit or vegetable a day.**
- **At least one serving of a vitamin C-rich fruit or vegetable a day.**
- **At least one serving of a high-fiber fruit or vegetable a day.**
- **Several servings of cruciferous vegetables a week.**

High in Vitamin A
Apricots, cantaloupe, collards, carrots, kale, leaf (not iceberg) lettuce, mango, mustard greens, pumpkin, romaine lettuce, spinach, sweet potato, winter squash (acorn, hubbard).

High in Vitamin C
Apricots, bell peppers, broccoli, Brussels sprouts, cabbage, cantaloupe, cauliflower, chili peppers, collards, grapefruit, honeydew melon, kiwi fruit, mango, mustard greens, orange, orange juice, pineapple, plum, potato with skin, spinach, strawberries, tangerine, tomatoes, watermelon, 100% juices made from these foods.

High in Fiber or a Good Source of Fiber
Apples, bananas, blackberries, blueberries, carrots, cherries, cooked beans and peas (kidney, navy, lima, and pinto beans, lentils, black-eyed peas), dates, figs, grapefruit, kiwi fruit, orange, pear, prunes, raspberries, spinach, strawberries, sweet potato, cruciferous vegetables (means a plant whose four petals form the shape of a cross) such as bok choy, broccoli, Brussels sprouts, cabbage, cauliflower.

Canadians can get a copy of *Canada's Food Guide to Healthy Eating* from www.hc-sc.gc.ca/fn-an/index e.html. The Canadian *Food Guide* places food into four groups: grain products, vegetables and fruits, milk products, and meat and alternatives, Its emphasis on fruits, vegetables, and whole grains is similar to the US food guidelines. For dietary suggestions and nutrition materials for the Latino community, see the Latino Nutrition Coalition: www.latinonutrition.org

Resources

- For examples of traditional eating patterns in many cultures, see Oldways Preservation Trust, 266 Beacon Street, Boston, MA 02116; www.oldwayspt.org
- Center for Science in the Public Interest's *Healthy Eating Pyramid* differentiates between processed/less processed foods; www.cspinet.org
- The American Dietetic Association (ADA) offers food pyramid posters and other materials for a variety of ethnic and regional food patterns, including vegetarian, Latino, Chinese, traditional Southern/Soul, Native American, and others. Search for Diversity Resource List / Food Pyramids under www.eatright.org or contact ADA Customer Service: 800-877-1600, ext. 5000.
- www.nutrition.gov is a federal resource that allows easy access to all online government nutrition information: Food Guide Pyramid, food labeling, food safety (e.g,. foodborne illness), biotechnology, and food assistance, etc.
- www.dietitians.ca/ for the Canadian Dietetic Association.

Sock puppets can be made in many ways. One is to give kids a sock and allow them to discover their own way. Below are a few more structured ways.

[2] See www.5aday.gov.

Creating a Recycled Sock or Stocking Puppet

(Possibly your own Annelida!)

Thumb-in-the-Heel-and-Fingers-in-the-Toe Sock Puppet

For Both Methods:

Thread a needle before you start as you'll need it for sewing the extra sock fabric in place.

Put your hand in the sock so that your thumb is in the heel and your fingers are in the toe.

Extra toe fabric hanging off the fingertips will need some attention. (This is assuming the sock is longer than the child's hand—which is usually the case.)

Gather up or tuck in the excess toe fabric (you have a few options—see below).

Variation One (This style can have interesting snouts.)

Note the excess toe fabric flopping from your fingertips. This is tricky. With your free hand, push the toe inside of the sock—not into the mouthpart but over the top of your fingers, under the sock layer—until all the extra fabric is neatly tucked in.

The puppet's face will look funny at this point—almost like it has two mouths.

Either sew the extra layers together—as you would a seam—or take hold of the extra layers of fabric on the top of the puppet's head and use your imagination. You could double up the extra fold into a nose ridge. Maybe you have a better idea! Experiment.

Sew that entire sock nose ridge onto the top of the puppet and the upper lip. The puppet might look funny at first, but with the addition of features, it will take shape.

Variation Two (This is a less complicated, more traditional style.)

Follow steps above "For Both Methods."

Note the excess toe fabric flopping from your fingertips. (What you need to do is almost equivalent to a facelift!) Push tip of toe all the way to the tip of your fingers and tuck that big wrinkle into/under the sock all the way around.

Sometimes this fold can be used as an eye ridgeline. Sew in place (optional).

Variation Three (Make a big-nosed puppet!—harder to do with extra-large socks.)

Follow steps above "For Both Methods."

Note the excess toe fabric flopping from your fingertips. It will become the nose.

Stuff something light into the sock and push all the way to the toe. Tie some string around the sock, somewhere between the stuffing and your fingertips

Fingers-in-the-Toe-and-Heel-Resting-on-the-Knuckles-of-Your-Hand Sock Puppet (This method makes puppets suitable for smaller hands.)

Thread a needle before you do the next step, as it will need to be ready. Put your hand in the sock so that the heel is on your knuckles and the toe is hanging off your fingers. (The hand you write with needs to be free, so put your puppet on the other hand.) Open your puppet's mouth wide—your thumb is in the body of the sock.

Push extra toe fabric down into the puppet's mouth—that's between your fingers and thumb. Pull the excess fabric from each side of the mouth and bunch it up (or fold it up) where the tongue might go. Sew that excess fabric in place from side to side and through all layers. Add tongue.[1]

So You Want a Rigid Mouth! Here are a few ideas for that. You'll need some cardboard—cereal boxes work nicely.

One Way: Cut a rectangular piece that, when folded, will fit into your hand (fold rests in palm) or, if your puppet is completed, the length and width of the puppet's open mouth.

Use scissors to round the edges. Fold the mouthpiece. I like to make the thumb piece (lower lip) shorter than the fingers (upper lip).

Apply glue to the rough side of the cardboard mouthpiece. The glossy/printed part doesn't stick as well.

Fold the mouthpiece with the glue inside. This can be messy and tricky.

Carefully insert glued/folded piece into your puppet toward the mouth.

Open the cardboard inside the mouth and stick to the inside of the sock where mouth is. Press.

(Optional) Once the mouthpiece is inside, you can add a cardboard outer mouthpiece and glue felt to that.

This Way: Same as above, but place the glued cardboard mouth on the outside of the puppet (less messy).

Another Way: Before working on your puppet, place the sock on a table (the heel can be on top or below, but not out to the side). Cut out a rectangular piece of cardboard less wide than the sock's width, and at whatever length you want. Long pieces make alligator-like snouts.

Add Personality!

This is the fun part! Make eyes by sewing on buttons, felt, or fabric. Add eyelashes or eyebrows from felt. Glue pupils so your puppet can see you.

Sew on a felt, pom-pom, or fabric nose.

How about lips or a tongue for the mouth? Use felt, fabric, or cardboard.

Give your puppet hair or whiskers with yarn, felt, or fabric. Glue, tie, or sew.

How about clothes? Add a scarf, tie, shirt, skirt, or robe.

Get to Know Your Puppet!

Every puppet is different and will offer you insights into its personality if you take some time with your creation.

Talking—sound of voice—talks fast, slow, high, low?

Moves—happy, fast, sad, scared, sneaky, etc.

Experiment, experiment.

Always hold your puppet upright—they like good postures (arm straight up from the elbow). Make sure your puppet can see and be seen. They like looking people in the eye. Be sure your hand is bent at the wrist with fingertips pointing slightly down and toward the "audience."

Read some puppet books for more pointers!

Make Your Own Nylon Wiggler Puppet!

Use worm puppets to teach about red wigglers' behavior, illustrate their movements, learn about their anatomy or reproduction, or do skits. You'll probably come up with many other ways to use them. One group of students created their own play, *As the Worm Turns,* without teacher input!

Making and using the puppets is fun and easy. Nylon stockings work well for several reasons: color, elasticity, ease of making the "clitellum" or saddle on the worm, and general appearance. It's usually pretty easy to find a supply of reusable nylons—a few runs just add character to the puppet.

What You'll Need

- 4-5 nylon stockings
- needle and thread (optional)
- scissors
- white yarn or string
- decorations for eyes, mouth (optional)

[1] Adapted with permission from *Creative Teaching with Puppets* by Barbara Rountree, Learning Line, Inc., 1989.

How to Create Worms from Scratch

1. Cut a length of nylon stocking (from the toe end) to about as long as a knee-high stocking would be. (You could also use a knee-high type by itself.) Place 4-5 wadded up nylons in the stocking to fill it almost to the top.
2. Cut an identical length piece from the other toe of a pair (or use another knee-high stocking) and put it over the first stuffed tube, so the open end of the first tube is inside the toe of the outer stocking. You are now holding an immature (almost completed) worm puppet.
3. Next, cut two 4-inch-wide cross-sections from the leg of another (preferably lighter color) pair of stockings, making two identically sized rings.
4. Slide one ring on the worm puppet and cover it with the other ring—so they're both about two-thirds of the way to the top of the worm. This is called the clitellum, swollen band, or saddle, and is the part responsible for reproduction.
5. Tuck 3-5 small pieces of white yarn in between the two rings, which will become the newborn worms!

Put Your Nylon Wigglers to Work

Show the expanding and contracting motion of the worm by demonstrating how the puppet moves. Ask: Can you tell which end is the head and which is the tail? How? (The clitellum is near the front on a mature worm.)

Explain worm reproduction. Worms are both male and female and any two worms can produce offspring. Mature worms form an egg-case or cocoon, at the site of the clitellum, carrying 2–20 infant worms, which are tiny and white.

Have students do a short skit, interviewing other worms. ("What do you like to eat?" "Tell me about your house underground." "What happens when a bird comes to eat you?") or ask them to make up their own questions.

On a bulletin board, make a worm habitat, complete with burrows, roots, and other creatures, using cardboard, yarn, and illustrations. Attach the worms appropriately in this habitat.

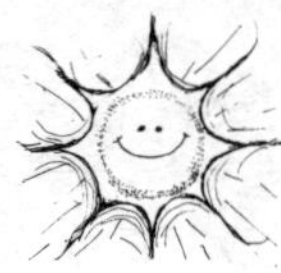

BIBLIOGRAPHY

A= GARDENING/AGRICULTURE **H** = HUNGER ISSUES
N= NUTRITION /FOOD INFO **R** = RECYCLING INFO **W** = WORM INFO / SUPPLIES

Organizations and Suppliers

Action for Healthy Kids is a public-private partnership of more than 50 national organizations and government agencies representing education, health, fitness and nutrition. AHK addresses the epidemic of overweight, sedentary, and undernourished youth by focusing on changes in schools. 4711 West Golf Road, Suite 625, Skokie, IL 60076; 800-416-5136; www.actionforhealthykids.org **N**

American Alliance of Health, Physical Education, Recreation, and Dance (AAHPERD) National organization supporting those involved in physical education, leisure, fitness, dance, health promotion, education, and all specialties related to achieving a healthy lifestyle. 1900 Association Drive, Reston, VA 20191; www.aahperd.org **N**

American Community Gardening Association ACGA a bi-national (US and Canadian) nonprofit membership organization of professionals and supporters of community greening in urban and rural communities. Offers publications, programs and conferences. ACGA c/o Franklin Park Conservatory,1777 East Broad Street, Columbus, OH 43203; 877-ASK-ACGA or 877-275-2242. **A**

American Dietetic Association ADA is the nation's largest organization of food and nutrition professionals. 120 South Riverside Plaza, Suite 2000, Chicago, IL 60606-6995; 800-877-1600 ; www.eatright.org Dietitians of Canada's website is www.dietitians.ca **N**

American Farmland Trust Works "to stop loss of productive farmland and to promote farming practices that lead to a healthy environment." Information for educators. Fun online film, *Apple as Planet Earth*, graphically depicts "It's a Small World" activity from this book. 1200 18th Street N, Suite 800, Washington, DC 20036; 202-331-7300; 800-370-4879 or 800-431-1499; www.farmland.org **A**

American Horticultural Society One of the oldest national gardening organizations in the country. Hosts the annual Children and Youth Garden Symposium and has resource lists and links on many areas of children's gardening. 7931 East Boulevard Drive, Alexandria, VA 22308-1300; 800-777-7931; 703-768-5700; www.ahs.org **A**

America the Beautiful Fund National non-profit organization, encouraging volunteer efforts to protect America's beauty. Offers free seeds to schools and other non-profit organizations periodically. Operation Green Plant, 725 15th St, NW, Suite 605, Washington, DC 20005; 800-522-3557; www.america-the-beautiful.org **A**

Banana Slug String Band. Group of zany musicians and educators who use music to teach science. We've included words to some of the songs from their tape/CD, *Dirt Made My Lunch*. ISBN 1-877737-29-1. Songs like "Dirt Made My Lunch"; "Decomposition"; "Solar Energy Rap"; and "Sun, Soil, Water, and Air" are great complements to a garden/composting curriculum. P.O. Box 2262, Santa Cruz, CA 95063; 888-32-SLUGS 5487; slugs@bananaslugstringband.com; www.bananaslugstringband.com **A N R W**

Bullfrog Films Leading U.S. publisher of independently-produced environmental videos that stress living a healthier life with concern for other inhabitants. See *A Crack in the Pavement; Recycling Is Fun!; Recycling with Worms; It's Gotten Rotten; My Father's Garden; Here's My Question: Where Does My Garbage Go?;* and *Organic Gardening.;* P.O. Box 149, Oley, PA 19547 800-543-FROG (3764) ; catalog@bullfrogfilms.com; www.bullfrogfilms.com **A R W**

Center for Ecoliteracy Dedicated to fostering a personal understanding of the environment and in living sustainably. 2522 San Pablo Avenue, Berkeley, CA 94702; www.ecoliteracy.org For a collaborative project involving schools and gardens: www.foodsystems.org **A**

Center for Science in the Public Interest Non-profit health advocacy group. Easy to understand nutrition information, *Nutrition Action Healthletter*, books, teaching aids. 1875 Connecticut Ave. NW, Suite 300, Washington, DC 20009; 202-332-9110; www.cspinet.org **N**

Center for Sustainable Agriculture at the University of Vermont State Agricultural College; mission is to bring people with a diversity of interests together to foster an understanding of agricultural issues that will lead to personal, institutional, organizational, and community decisions that encourage farming in Vermont; 63 Carrigan Drive; Burlington, VT 05405; 802-656-5459; www.uvm.edu/~susagctr **A**

Chefs Collaborative is a national network of members of the food community who promote sustainable cuisine by celebrating the joys of local, seasonal, and artisanal cooking. 262 Beacon Street, Boston, MA 02116; 617-236-5200; www.chefscollaborative.org **N A**

Community Food Security Coalition is a non-profit organization dedicated to building strong, sustainable, local / regional food systems that ensure access to affordable, nutritious, and culturally appropriate food for all people at all times, P.O. Box 209, Venice, CA 90294; 310-822-5410; www.foodsecurity.org **N H**

Division of Nutrition and Physical Activity at the Centers for Disease Control takes a public health approach to address the role of nutrition and physical activity in improving the public's health and preventing and controlling chronic diseases. Developed KidsWalk-to-School Guide, among others. 4770 Buford Highway, Atlanta, GA 30341-3717; 770-488-5820; 800-CDC-INFO; www.cdc.gov/nccdphp/dnpa **N**

Flowerfield Enterprises (Mary Appelhof) Books, worm bins, and supplies, worms, lots of information. Publishes *Worms Eat My Garbage* (small how-to guide); *Worms Eat Our Garbage* (classroom activities with Mary Frances Fenton and Barbara Loss Harris). 10332 Shaver Rd., Kalamazoo, MI 49024; 269-327-0108; www.wormwoman.com **W**

Food First/Institute for Food and Development Policy shapes how people think by analyzing the root causes of global hunger, poverty, and ecological degradation and developing solutions in partnership with movements working for social change. 398 60th Street, Oakland, CA 94618; 510-654-4400; www.foodfirst.org **H**

Food Works at Two Rivers Center was founded in 1987 to address the root causes of childhood hunger by returning students and their communities back to the land through hands-on food and gardening educational opportunities." Food Works at Two Rivers Center 64 Main Street, Montpelier, VT 05602; 802-8223-1515; www.tworiverscenter.org **A W H**

Healthy Weight Network Provides facts on weight and eating problems, offers books and materials. 402 South 14th Street, Hettinger, ND 58639; 701-567-2646; www.healthy weightnetwork.com **N**

Johnny's Selected Seeds Colorful catalog, knowledgeable staff, vegetable, flower, and herb seeds. Also a broad selection of garden supplies, books, tools. Johnny's supports school garden projects and agriculture educational programs. 955 Benton Avenue, Winslow, ME 04901; 877-johnnys (877-564-6697); www.johnnyseeds.com **A**

Just Food is a non-profit organization that works to develop a just and sustainable food system in the New York City region by fostering new marketing and food-growing opportunities. 208 East 51st Street, 4th Floor, York, NY 10022; 212-645-9880; fax 212-645-9881; www.justfood.org **N H**

Kansas Nutrition Training Resource and Information Network (KN-TRAIN) See their Pyramid Builders program. Nutrition Services, Kansas State Dept. of Education, 120 SE 10th Ave.,Topeka, KS 66612-1182 785-296-2276; www.kn-train.org **N**

Kids Can Make a Difference "The purpose of KIDS is to inspire young people to realize that it is within their power to help eliminate hunger and poverty in their communities, country, and world." Contact Jane or Larry Levine, 1 Borodell Ave.Mystic, CT 06355 (860) 245 3620; www.kidscanmake adifference.org **H**

Latino Nutrition Coalition is a consortium of industry, scientists, chefs, and Oldways Preservation Trust which promotes better Latino health through traditional foods and lifestyles. www.latinonutrition.org **N**

Leopold Center for Sustainable Agriculture Resources "explores and cultivates alternatives that secure healthier people and landscapes in Iowa and the nation" 209 Curtiss Hall, Iowa State University, Ames, IA 50011-1050; 515-294-3711; (see link to "Food, Fuel, and Freeways" for a perspective on food transportation, fuel usage and greenhouse gas emissions); www.leopold.iastate.edu/ **A**

Life Lab Science Program Inc. A private, non-profit organization dedicated to garden-based science education and stewardship of the environment. Features the science curriculum, The Growing Classroom as well as many others. 1156 High Street, Santa Cruz, CA 95064; 831-459-2001; www.lifelab.org **A**

Local Harvest An interactive internet directory of small farms, farmer's markets, CSA's, coops, and products nationwide—to attract local supporters. Encourage your local growers, market managers, etc. to add their information to the site if they aren't already listed. www.localharvest.org **A**

Medomak Valley High School Heirloom Seed Project Seed sources and historical background for hard-to-find heirloom varieties. Neil Lash, c/o Medomak Valley High School, 320 Manktown Road, Waldoboro, ME 04572; 207-832-5389; neil_lash@sad40.k12.me.us; Jon_Thurston@sad40.k12.me.us; www.msad40.org/mvhs/ **A**

MOFGA (Maine Organic Farmers and Gardeners Assoc.) Statewide advocacy and educational organization. Runs annual Common Ground Fair. MOFGA, P.O. Box 170, Unity, ME 04988; 207-568-4142; www.mofga.org **A**

National Association of Conservation Districts An association of nearly 3000 conservation districts in nearly every county—helping people to conserve land, water, forests, wildlife, and related natural resources. NACD Headquarters, 509 Capitol Court, NE, Washington, DC 20002-4946; 800-825-5547; 202-547-6223 (NACD); www.nacdnet.org **A**

National Campaign for Sustainable Agriculture, Inc. is a diverse nationwide partnership which cultivates grass roots policy toward a food and agriculture system which is healthy, environmentally sound, profitable, humane, and just. They work closely with five regional Sustainable Agriculture Working Groups (SAWGs) P.O. Box 396, Pine Bush, NY 12566; 845-361-5201; www.sustainableagriculture.net/ **A**

National Dairy Council is the nutrition marketing arm of Dairy Management Inc.™. 10255 W. Higgins Road, Suite 900, Rosemont, IL 60018. To order the "paper food models" which include a leader guide, Item #0012N, go through your state or regional affiliate. Call the National Office (847) 803-2000 to find the Dairy Council nearest you. www.national dairycouncil.org **N**

National Gardening Association (See NGA book titles.) Many excellent books, curriculum materials, lighted growing units, and science materials found in their catalog, Gardening with Kids: Tools to Help Young Minds Grow. Their newsletter, Growing Ideas: A Journal of Garden-Based Learning offers theme-based ideas for and from teachers and includes helpful resources. Apply for their "Youth Garden Grant." 1100

Dorset Street, South Burlington, VT 05403; 800-538-7476; 802-863-5251; www.kidsgardening.com and www.garden.org A W

Native Seeds/SEARCH A non-profit organization that seeks to preserve the crop seeds that connect Native American cultures to their lands. Native Seeds/SEARCH, 526 N. 4th Ave., Tucson, AZ 85705-8450; 520-622-5561; www.nativeseeds.org **A**

Natural Resources Conservation Service (NRCS) Formerly known as the Soil Conservation Service, NRCS is a federal agency under USDA that helps people conserve, improve, and sustain natural resources and the environment.; 1400 Independence Ave., SW, Room 5105-A, Washington, DC 20250; www.nrcs.usda.gov **A**

NOFA (The Northeast Organic Farming Association) is an affiliation of several state chapters which provide educational conferences, workshops, farm tours and printed materials to educate farmers, gardeners, consumers and land care professionals about local, organic agriculture. Contact NOFA c/o Bill Duesing, Box 135, Stevenson, CT 06491, 203-888-5146; www.nofa.org **A**

Oldways Preservation and Exchange Trust "Widely respected as the non-profit 'food issues think tank,' Oldways pioneered in translating the complex details of nutrition science into 'the familiar language of food.'" 266 Beacon St., Boston, MA 02116; 617-421-5500; www.oldwayspt.org N A

President's Council on Physical Fitness and Sports serves as a catalyst to encourage and motivate Americans to become physically active. 200 Independence Avenue, SW Dept W, Room 738-H, Washington, DC 20201-0004; 202-690-9000; www.fitness.gov **N**

Puppeteers of America A national, non-profit member organization dedicated to the art of puppetry. Provides information and encouragement to puppet lovers through their Puppetry Journal, newsletter, puppetry store, web site, consultants, regional guilds, festivals, and conferences; www.puppeteers.org/ **A R W**

Rodale Institute Works with people worldwide to achieve a sustainable food system that leads to environmental and human health. Their philosophy: "Healthy Soil equals Healthy Food equals Healthy People".. 611 Siegfriedale Road, Kutztown, PA 19530-9320; 610-683-1400; www.rodaleinstitute.org **A N R W H**

Rural Advancement Foundation International (RAFI-USA) "Dedicated to community, equity, and diversity in agriculture and focuses on North Carolina and the southeastern United States, but also works nationally and internationally." P.O. Box 640, Pittsboro, NC 27312; 919-542-1396; www.rafiusa.org **A**

Seed Saver's Exchange Oldest and most active non-profit group preserving heirloom seeds worldwide. 3076 N. Winn Rd., Decorah, IA 52101; 563-382-5990; www.seedsavers.com **A**

Shelburne Farms Institute is a 1,400-acre working farm, National Historic Landmark, and a non-profit environmental education center. Publisher of Project Seasons. The Shelburne Institute, Shelburne Farms, 1611 Harbor Road, Shelburne, VT 05482-7671; 802-985-8686; www.shelburnefarms.org **A N**

Slow Food USA is an international "educational organization dedicated to stewardship of the land and ecologically sound food production; to the revival of the kitchen and the table as centers of pleasure, culture, and community; to the invigoration and proliferation of regional, seasonal culinary traditions; and to living a slower and more harmonious rhythm of life." 20 Jay St., Suite 313, Brooklyn, NY 11201; 718-260-8000 ; www.slowfoodusa.org **A N**

UNIMA "Promoting International Understanding and Friendship Through the Art of Puppetry." Publishes information on and for the field of puppetry, offers support and technical assistance as well as conferences and symposia. Find a puppetry company in your area on the web site. 1404 Spring St NW, Atlanta, GA 30309-2820 404-873-3089; www.unima-usa.org

USDA: Agriculture in the Classroom Coordinated by the USDA and carried out in most states, according to state needs and interests, by individuals representing farm organizations, agribusiness, education, and government. National Program Leader USDA, 1400 Independence Avenue SW, Agriculture in the Classroom, Stop 2251, Washington, DC 20250-2251; www.agclassroom.org **A**

USDA: Agricultural Research Service Wind Erosion Unit For information and photographs about soil loss and wind erosion and its effects nationally and internationally, www.weru.ksu **A**

USDA: Cooperative State Research, Education, and Extension Service "advances knowledge for agriculture, the environment, human health and well-being, and communities through national program leadership and federal assistance. 1400 Independence Avenue SW, Stop 2201, Washington, DC 20250-2201; 202-720-7441; www.creeusda.gov **A N R W**

USDA: Sustainable Agriculture Resources See the National Agricultural Library (NAL), Alternative Farming Systems Information Center (AFSIC) at www.nal.usda.gov/afsic/ for sustainable and organic agriculture information resources, reference and referral services, online resource guides, and bibliographies. USDA, ARS, National Agricultural Library, 10301 Baltimore Ave., Room 132, Beltsville, MD 20705-2351; 301-504-6559 **A**

USDA: United States Department of Agriculture www.usda.gov See also National Agricultural Statistics Service for agricultural information by state, www.nass.usda.gov/ **N A H**

World Hunger Year WHY attacks the root causes of hunger and poverty by promoting effective and innovative community-based solutions that create self-reliance, economic justice, and food security. 505 Eighth Ave., New York, NY 10018-6582; 212-629-8850; www.worldhungeryear.org **H**

Worm Digest This non-profit organization publishes the magazine *Worm Digest*, a source of articles, suppliers, and

research on vermicomposting. (This proves that there's a publication for every topic!) 1455 East 185th St., Cleveland, OH 44145; 216-531-5374 www.wormdigest.org **W R**

Teacher's Guides

(Note: Some of the books listed in this bibliography may be out of print but are still available in libraries or through online used book sources.)

Appelhof, Mary, Mary Frances Fenton and Barbara Loss Harris. ***Worms Eat Our Garbage: Classroom Activities for a Better Environment***. Flower Press, 1993. ISBN 0-942256-05-0. An amazing range of fun lessons and activities in science, math, language arts, and art. **W R**

Barchers, Suzanne I., and Patricia C. Marden. ***Cooking up U.S. History: Recipes and Research to Share with Children.*** Teacher Ideas Press, 1991. ISBN 0-87287-782-5. Recipe-filled volume presents research, reading links, and extensive bibliographies on commonly encountered social studies units and U.S. geographic regions. **N**

Barchers, Suzanne I., Peter J. Rauen and Darcie Clark Frohardt. ***Storybook Stew: Cooking with Books Kids Love.*** Fulcrum Publishing, 1997. ISBN 1-55591-944-8. Fifty recipes, each accompanied by a summary of a featured book and a suggested activity. **N**

Bauer, Caroline Feller and Edith Bingham. ***The Poetry Break: An Annotated Anthology with Ideas for Introducing Children to Poetry***. H. W. Wilson, 1995. ISBN 0-8242-0852-8. Upbeat and down-to-earth: a useful guide offers ways to kindle children's enthusiasm for poetry. Includes suggestions for related activities and short lists of related books and poems, as well as more than 200 children's poems.

Campbell, Susan, and Todd Winant. ***Healthy School Lunch Action Guide.*** EarthSave Foundation, 1994. ISBN 0-96425-590-1. Activities to teach and motivate children to make healthy food choices and bring healthier lunches to schools. 1509 Seabright Avenue, Suite B1, Santa Cruz, CA 95062; www.earthsave.org **N**

Chewonki Foundation. ***Pathways to a Sustainable Future.*** Chewonki Foundation/Maine Waste Management Agency, 1994. Revised in 1999 by Tom Bertocci. A curriculum guide for schools exploring waste management issues. The Chewonki Foundation, 485 Chewonki Neck Road, Wiscasset, ME 04578; 207-882-7323; www.chewonki.org **R**

Dennee, Joanne, Jack Peduzzi, Julia Hand, and Carolyn Peduzzi. ***In the Three Sisters Garden: Native American Traditions, Myths, and Culture Around the Theme of the Garden.*** Common Roots Press, 1995. ISBN 0-78722-175-9. Lots of background and hands-on activities based on the traditional native garden of corn, squash, and beans. Grades 1-6. **A N**

Eames-Sheavly, Marcia. ***The Three Sisters: Exploring an Iroquois Garden*** (#142LM15) (ISBN 1-57753-269-4). Cornell Cooperative Extension. Booklet dealing with Native American gardening and preparing food from the garden is available from The Resource Center, Cornell University, 365 Roberts Hall, Ithaca, NY 14853; 607-255-2080. Mailing address for orders: PO Box 6525, Ithaca, NY 14851; http://legacy.cce.cornell.edu/store/ **A N**

______. ***Sowing the Seeds of Success.*** Cornell Cooperative Extension. Booklet dealing with Native American gardening

Evers, Connie Liakos. ***How to Teach Nutrition to Kids: An Integrated, Creative Approach to Nutrition Education for Children Ages 6-10.*** 24 Carrot Press, 2006; ISBN 0-9647970-1-1. Excellent nutrition activities for students. Companion volume: ***Leader/Activity Guide***, ISBN 0-9647970-6-2.. P.O. Box 23546, Portland, OR 97281-3546; 503-524-9318; www.nutritionforkids.com **N**

Foodplay. ***Janey Junkfood's Fresh Adventure! Activity Guidebook.*** One of several innovative resources for teachers and elementary students. Foodplay is a nutrition and health theater and video organization which creates live theater shows, video kits, curricula, media campaigns, and hands-on resources. Foodplay Productions, 221 Pine Street, Florence, MA 01062; 1-800-FOODPLAY (800-366-3752); www.foodplay.com **N**

Gonzales, Claudia and Lourdes Alcaniz. ***Gordito Doesn't Mean Healthy: What Every Latina Mother Needs to Know to Raise Fit, Happy, Healthy Kids.*** Penguin Books, 2006. ISBN 0-42520-770-6. A dietitian and a health reporter "have written a comprehensive guide for concerned parents who want to help prevent and manage their children's weight problems while still holding onto Latino culinary and cultural tradition." **N**

Goodwin, Mary, and Gerry Pollen. ***Creative Food Experiences for Children.*** Center for Science in the Public Interest, 1980. ISBN 0-89329-001-7. Excellent nutrition activities for younger elementary children. Good overview of nutrition education. Includes recipes. **N**

Hand, Julia, and Carolyn Peduzzi. ***Wonderful World of Wigglers. Food Works,*** 1995. ISBN 1-884430-00-7. Stories, guided visualizations, many hands-on activities, cute illustrations. Activities for younger children. **W**

Harmon, Alison, Rance Harmon, and Audrey Maretzki. ***The Food System: Building Youth Awareness through Involvement.*** Penn State College of Agricultural Sciences, 1999. Introduces the concept of the food system, emphasizes interactive learning, skill building, and using the community as a classroom. Grades 4-12. Contact: Alison H. Harmon, Ph.D., R.D., Alison Hiller Harmon, Assistant Professor, Food and Nutrition, Department of Health and Human Development, Montana State University, 101 MH H&PE Complex, Bozeman, Montana 59717; **A N R**

Horton, Robert L. ***4H Cycling Back to Nature Series: Soils Alive! From Tiny Rocks to Compost*** (ES #1008). National 4H Council, 1995. Hands-on guide to exploring the development of soil and soil enhancements through composting. Grades 4-12. www.4hbookstore.org or call 301-961-2934. **R**

Jaffe, Roberta, and Gary Appel. ***The Growing Classroom: Garden Based Science***. Addison Wesley, 1990. ISBN 0-201-21539-X. Curriculum on establishing a garden-based science

and nutrition program. Grades 2-6. From: LifeLab Science Program, 1156 High St., Santa Cruz, CA 95064; 831-459-2001; www.lifelab.org **A N**

Jurenka, Nancy, and Rosanne Blass. ***Beyond the Bean Seed: Gardening Activities for Grades K-6.*** Libraries Unlimited, 1996. ISBN 1-56308-346-9. Connects gardening and children's books; written for teachers, librarians, child group leaders. Companion volume by same authors: ***Cultivating a Child's Imagination through Gardening.*** Libraries Unlimited, 1996. ISBN 1-56308-452-X. Grades K-6. **A**

Kempf, Stephanie. ***Finding Solutions to Hunger: A Sourcebook for Middle and Upper Schoolteachers.*** World Hunger Year, 2005. ISBN 0-9660038-0-2. Background information and interdisciplinary activities engaging students in world hunger issues. Statistics and resources updated in 2005; www.kidscanmakeadifference.org/teac.htm **H**

Kiefer, Joseph, and Martin Kemple. ***Digging Deeper: Integrating Youth Gardens into Schools and Communities.*** Food Works, 1998. ISBN 1-884430-04-X. Excellent guide for teachers or any community member wishing to build community through gardening. **A**

Levermann, Tom. ***Dig In! Hands-On Soil Investigations.*** National Science Teacher Assoc. Press, 2001. ISBN 0-87355-189-3. Introduces soil's mysteries in an enjoyable and educational way, and designed to help students gain a greater appreciation for the value of soil. Grades K-4. www.nsta.org **A**

LiFE is an inquiry-based program that provides "science education for [urban] students in the area of biology through inquiry-based investigations in the domain of food." Designed by and based at Teachers' College, Columbia University. 525 W. 120th St.,Box 137, New York, NY 10027-6696;, 212-678-3480; www.tc.edu/centers/life/ **A N**

National Gardening Association. ***GrowLab: A Complete Guide to Gardening in the Classroom***. NGA, 1988. ISBN 0-915873-31-1. Horticultural resource for use with an indoor classroom garden, from a windowsill to a homemade or ready-to-assemble indoor GrowLab. www.garden.org **A**

_____. ***GrowLab: Activities for Growing Minds.*** NGA, 1994. ISBN 0-915873-32-X. Creative plant-based activities to stimulate science inquiry. Grades K-8. 1100 Dorset Street, South Burlington, VT 05403; 800-538-7476. www.garden.org **A**

Parrella, Deb, and Cat Smith. ***Project Seasons.*** The Shelburne Institute, 1995. ISBN 0-9642163-0-2. Interdisciplinary, hands-on activities and teaching ideas. Using the school year's seasons of fall, winter, and spring, it integrates science, agriculture and environmental themes into the curriculum and aims to show how all things are interconnected. www.shelburne-farms.org **A**

Postance, Jim. ***Introduction to Sustainable Agriculture.*** Delmar Learning, 2005. ISBN 1-4018-1091-8. Teaches concepts of sustainable agricultural production through "hands-on," safe and effective food production techniques. Examines the role individual consumers play in the global economy and ecology. **A**

Sheehan, Kathryn, and Mary Waidner. ***Earth Child 2000: Earth Science for Young Children.*** Council Oak Books, 1998. ISBN 1-57178-054-8. Thick resource for parents or teachers of young children. Activities, resources, songs in many different categories; includes a gardening chapter. A

Smith, Miranda. ***My Father's Garden.*** (VHS, 57 mins.) Miranda Productions, 1995. An engrossing and emotional documentary about two farmers, different in all details, yet united by their common goal of producing healthy food. Presents the use and misuse of technology on the American farm. Grades 7-12. Available through Bullfrog Films, P.O. Box 149, Oley, PA 19547; 800-543-FROG (3764); www.bullfrogfilms.com **A**

Steinbergh, Judith, W. ***Reading and Writing Poetry: A Guide for Teachers.*** Scholastic Publications, 1994. ISBN 0-590-49168-7. A wonderful teacher resource. K-4.

Steinbergh, Judith, and Elizabeth McKim. ***Beyond Words: Writing Poems with Children: A Guide for Parents and Teachers.*** Talking Stone Press, 1999. ISBN 0-94494-114-1.

Sweeney, Jacqueline. ***Teaching Poetry: Yes You Can!*** Scholastic Publications, 1995. ISBN 0-590-49419-8. Excellent materials for older children. Grades 4-8.

University of Wisconsin. ***Bottle Biology—Exploring the World through Soda Bottles and Other Recyclable Materials.*** Kendall Hunt Publishing Co., 2003. ISBN 0-8403-8601-X. Background information, activities, and teaching tips for creating a spider habitat, modeling a rainforest, observing the lifecycle of slime mold, or making Korean kimchee. Includes building, filling, and observing over 20 bottle constructions. Grades 2-8. Science House, 1630 Linden Drive, Madison, WI 53706; 800-462-7417; www.bottlebiology.org **R**

Watts, Linda and Steven Garrett. ***Growing with Plants: 4-H Youth Development.*** Washington State University Cooperative Extension, 1995. NAL call #QP84.W38. Emphasizes experiential learning. Goals are to improve children's self-concept; increase environmental awareness; promote life skills, and to improve nutritional practices. Excellent lesson plans based on parts of plants, good handouts, and parent outreach. Grades 1-2. www.nal.usda.gov/Kids/4hplants.htm **A N**

Zook, Douglas, (ed.). ***The Microcosmos Curriculum Guide to Exploring Microbial Space.*** Kendall Hunt, 1994. ISBN 0-84038-515-3. Child-centered curriculum filled with experiments and activities designed to look closely at our world's small things. Order from Microcosmos Program, Dr. Douglas Zook, School of EducationTwo Sherborn Street Room 315 617-353-2030 Boston MA 02215; dzook@bu.edu

Gardening/Sustainable Agriculture Sources

American Horticultural Society. ***Youth Garden Resource List.*** 7931 East Boulevard Drive, Alexandria, VA 22308; 800-777-7931; www.ahs.org/

Ausubel, Kenny. ***Seeds of Change: The Living Treasure.*** Harpercollins, 1994. ISBN 0-06-250008-2. Background information on biodiversity, discusses growing healthy food at

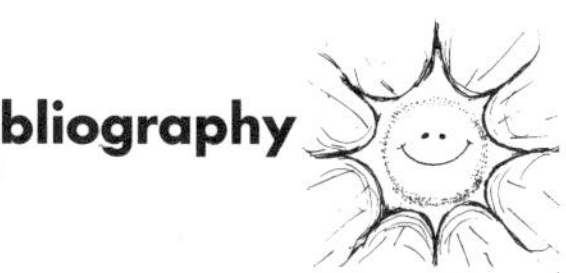

Seeds of Change farm. Includes recipes, organic growing emphasis, "The first link in saving the food chain."

Brooklyn Botanical Gardens. ***Get Ready, Get Set, Grow! A Beginner's Guide to the Joy of Gardening Based on Over 80 Years' Experience in the Children's Garden.*** Includes two booklets and a 15-minute video. 1000 Washington Avenue, Brooklyn, NY 11225-1099; 718-623-7200; http://shop.bbg.org/

Caduto, Michael, and Joseph Bruchac. ***Native American Gardening: Stories, Projects, and Recipes for Families.*** Fulcrum Pub., 1996. ISBN 1-55591-148-X. From the authors of Keepers of the Earth series. A resource book for families and teachers that explores the Native American approach to gardening.

Coleman, Eliot. Sheri Amsel, Molly Cook Field (illustrators) **The New Organic Grower: A Master's Manual of Tools and Techniques for the Home and Market Gardener.** Chelsea Green Publishing, 1995. ISBN 0-93003-175-X. Focuses on producing and marketing organic food, from planning and preparing, to planting.

Donahue, Brian, and Wes Jackson (forward). ***Reclaiming the Commons: Community Farms and Forests in a New England Town.*** Yale University Press, 2001. ISBN 0-30008-912-0. "Combines social and natural history to examine how our culture and economy favor development and consumerism at the expense of the environment."

Duesing, Bill, with Suzanne Duesing, ed. ***Living on the Earth: Eclectic Essays for a Sustainable and Joyful Future.*** Long River Books, 1993. ISBN 0-9659277-0. These were originally broadcast as public radio pieces.

Grant, Tim, and Gail Littlejohn, (editors). ***Greening School Grounds: Creating Habitats for Learning.*** New Society Publishers, 2001. ISBN 0-86571-436-3. Provides how-to instructions for composting, rooftop gardens, native plants, and creating ponds.

Green Teacher Magazine. Information- and inspiration-packed quarterly periodical from Green Teacher.PO Box 452, Niagara Falls, NY 14304-0452; (888) 804-1486; www.greenteacher.com

Gussow, Joan Dye. ***Chicken Little, Tomato Sauce, & Agriculture: Who Will Produce Tomorrow's Food?*** The Bootstrap Press, 1991. ISBN 0-942850-32-7. Explores industrial agriculture and sustainable food systems.

_____. ***This Organic Life: Confessions of a Suburban Homesteader.*** Chelsea Green Publishing, 2002. ISBN 1931498245.Explores industrial agriculture and sustainable food systems. "Blinded by the supermarket cornucopia, most of us need to be reminded that food is the generous result of a collaboration between our species and the rest of nature, not simply another product of industrial civilization."

Guy, Linda A., Cathy Cromell, and Lucy K. Bradley. ***Success with School Gardens: How to Create a Learning Oasis in the Desert.*** Arizona Master Gardener Press, 1996. ISBN 09651987-0-7. 4341 E. Broadway Road, Box 192, Phoenix, AZ 85040-8807; 602-470-8086. A great gardening resource, especially for areas in the Southwest. http://.cals.arizona.edu/maricopa/garden/

Hart, Avery, Paul Mantell; Loretta Braren, Jennie Chien (illustrators). ***Kids Garden: The Anytime, Anyplace Guide to Sowing and Growing Fun.*** Williamson Publishing,1996. ISBN 0-91358-990-X. A fun resource book of indoor/outdoor gardening activities.

Harvest of History. An interactive and interdisciplinary website dedicated to agriculture and rural life, featuring video clips of farming, both past and present, a database of primary sources, museum objects and documents, as well as a fourth-grade curriculum. Farmer's Museum (Cooperstown, NY) and National Gardening Association. www.harvestofhistory.org

Herd, Meg, and Andrew Elton. ***Learn and Play in the Garden: Games, Crafts, and Activities for Children.*** Barrons Juveniles, 1997. ISBN 0-8120-9780-7. Geared toward younger children and early elementary students; an introduction to natural science and horticulture includes instructions for planting vegetables, an herb garden, making a scarecrow, and more.

Hogue, Jane. ***Gardens That Children Will Dig*** (theme gardens). This booklet is available from Prairie Pedlar, 1609 270th St., Odebolt, IA 51458; http://showcase.netins.net/web/ppgarden/

Jackson, Dana L., and Laura L. Jackson, eds. ***The Farm as Natural Habitat: Reconnecting Food Systems with Ecosystems.*** Island Press, 2002. ISBN 1-55963-847-8. Various contributors speak of an alternative agriculture that can not only produce healthy food, but also protect populations of native species and their functioning ecosystems.

Jackson, Irene. ***Hot Biscuits and Shanty Boys***. Maine Folklife Center, 1998. # ED480702 from the Educational Resources Information Center. "This curriculum guidepresents an introduction of 4 units: conducting oral histories; games; the lumbering life; and romance and reality."

Jeavons, John. ***How to Grow More Vegetables Than You Ever Thought Possible in Less Space Than You Can Imagine.*** Ten Speed Press, 1995 5th ed, 2002. ISBN 1-58008-233-5. www.tenspeedpress.com

Jeavons, John and Carol Cox. ***The Sustainable Vegetable Garden: A Backyard Guide to Healthy Soil and Higher Yields.*** Ten Speed Press, 2002. ISBN 1-58008-016-2. Introduction to bio-intensive gardening describes how to grow "astonishing crops of healthful organic vegetable and fruits while conserving resources and helping the soil." www.tenspeedpress.com.

Kids in Bloom Seed Company Works with school children to help save heirloom seeds—"Seed Guardians." P.O. Box 344, Zionsville, IN 46077; 317 636-3977; www.kidsgardening.com/resources/browse.taf? Type=detail&ID=8

Kimbrell, Andrew, ed. ***Fatal Harvest: The Tragedy of Industrial Agriculture.*** Island Press, 2002. ISBN 1-55963-941-5. Thoughtful essays by leading agricultural figures "provide a wealth of clarifying information and illuminating interpretations on the failures and hazards of current American agriculture"—as well as the solutions.

Klinkenborg, Verlyn. "A Farming Revolution: Sustainable Agriculture." ***National Geographic***, pp. 60-89, December 1995. Comprehensive article on sustainable agriculture, including helpful illustration. Good for upper grades.

Lopez, Ruth Kantor. ***Gardens for Growing People—A Guide for Gardening with Children.*** 1990 ISBN 0-9627463-3-9. Highlights all of the basics: from first inviting children to the harvesting stage. Information is given in a compact but complete format, short and sweet. Topics include planning and designing the garden, tools needed, types of things to grow, cold season/warm season growing, and container gardening.

Masumoto, David. ***Epitaph for a Peach: Four Seasons on My Family Farm.*** Harper, 1996. ISBN 0-06-251025-8. Farmer describes his attempt to grow Suncrest peaches—poignant firsthand account of one farmer's struggles.

_____. ***Four Seasons in Five Senses: Things Worth Savoring.*** W. W. Norton & Co., 2003. ISBN 0-39301-960-8. Appreciating the fruits of one's labors requires all the senses. "Follow your nose" with the nation's favorite literary farmer while witnessing the cycle of the harvest and taking time to "smell the roses."

_____. ***Harvest Son: Planting Roots in American Soil.*** W. W. Norton & Co., 1999 ISBN 0-3933-1974-1. A Japanese-American farmer recounts the challenges of taking over and renewing his family's farm in Del Ray, California, describing the pains and pleasures of farm work and the perseverance of his grandfather.

Morash, Marian. ***Victory Garden Cookbook.*** Alfred A. Knopf, 1982. ISBN 0-394-70780-X. A good cookbook (though tends to use higher-fat ingredients) with more: basic gardening, harvesting, and preparation techniques for most vegetables—as well as shopping tips for non-gardeners.

Ocene, Lynn, and Eve Pranis. ***National Gardening Association's Guide to Kids Gardening.*** John Wiley and Sons, Inc., 1990. ISBN 0-471-52092-6. Lots of helpful organizational and planning details such as funding, basic equipment checklist, site development, and design.

Potter-Springer, Wendy. ***Grow a Butterfly Garden***.Storey Country Wisdom Bulletin #A-114. Storey Publishing, 1990. 0-88266-600-2 32 pages of ideas for designing, planting, and maintaining a butterfly garden. Includes a detailed list of herbs and flowers suitable as butterfly habitat (available through Johnny's Selected Seeds).

Reilly, Ann. ***Starting Seeds Indoors*** Storey Country Wisdom Bulletin #A-104. Storey Publishing, 1989. ISBN 0-88266-519-7. Practical, hands-on instructions and earth-friendly information to help you master dozens of country living skills. See also Seed Sowing and Saving by Carole B. Turner. ISBN 1-58017-001-3; www.storeybooks.com

Tilgner, Linda. ***Tips for the Lazy Gardener***. Storey Publishing, 1998. ISBN 1-58017-026-9. Time- and labor-saving tips for the home gardener.

Vaughn, J. G. and Catherine Geissler, and B. E. Nicholson, Elizabeth Dowle, Elizabeth Rice (Illustrators) ***The New Oxford Book of Food Plants: A Guide to the Fruits, Vegetables, Herbs, and Spices of the World.*** Oxford University Press, 1999. ISBN 0-19-850567-1. A guide to edible plants describes each variety's edible parts, historical and current uses, method of preparation, and nutritional value.

Nutrition, Health, and Food-Related Sources

Barchers, Suzanne I. and Peter J. Rauen, Darcie Clark Frohardt (Illustrator). ***Holiday Storybook Stew: Cooking through the Year with Books Kids Love.*** Fulcrum Pub., 1998. ISBN 1-55591-972-3. Celebrate diverse cultural traditions by combining activities, reading, and cooking. Organized by month with 30 recipes.

Braunstein, Mark Matthew. ***The Sprout Garden.*** Book Publishers Co., 1999. ISBN 1-57067-073-0. From seed selection to meal preparation, this book is a definitive guide to growing and enjoying over 40 varieties of sprouts.

Brody, Jane. ***Jane Brody's Nutrition Book.*** Bantam Doubleday Dell, 1989. ISBN 0-553-34721-7. One of several Jane Brody favorites for a wealth of nutrition information, menu ideas, shopping tips, and plenty of tasty, healthy recipes.

Burns, Marilyn. ***Good for Me! All about Food in 32 Bites.*** Econo-Clad Books, 1999. ISBN 0-808-50599-8. New edition of an old favorite. Wonderful resource when teaching about nutrition and the human body.

Center for Science in the Public Interest. (CSPI) ***Nutrition Action Healthletter and Healthy Eating Pyramid.*** Excellent all-round nutrition educational publication for adults, but contains "Kids Against Junk Food" section. Also Food Additive Dictionary. www.cspinet.org

Collins, Tracy Brown, (ed). ***Fast Food.*** Greenhaven Press, 2005. A collection of 10 essays exploring varied opinions about different aspects of the fast food debate.

Farb, Peter, and George Armelagos. ***Consuming Passion: The Anthropology of Eating.*** Pocket Books, 1983. ISBN 0-671-43420-9. Explores the anthropological connections between various eating habits and human behavior.

FOODPLAY Productions Emmy Award-winning nutrition and health theater and video company. The purpose of their school theater shows, video kits, and educational resources is to improve the health of children. 221 Pine Street, Florence, MA 01062; 1-800-FOODPLAY (800-366-3752). Contact Barbara Storper. www.foodplay.com/

Gabaccia, Donna. ***We Are What We Eat: Ethnic Food and the Making of Americans***. Harvard University Press, 1998. ISBN 0-674-94860-2. Explores how ethnicity has influenced American's eating habits; looks at food as a social and political symbol in our history.

Guhin, Paula. ***Can We Eat the Art? Incredible Edibles and Art You Can't Eat***. Incentive Publications Inc., 2001. ISBN 0-86530-471-8. Edible art for older children. Hands-on art experiences designed for teachers, parents, scout leaders, etc. Includes recipes for art materials.

Ichord, Loretta Frances. ***Hasty Pudding, Johnny Cakes, and Other Good Stuff: Cooking in Colonial America.*** Millbrook Press, 1998. ISBN 0-7613-1297-8. Presents colonial

food preparation with a look at the influences of available ingredients, cooking methods, and equipment. Includes recipes and appendix of classroom cooking directions.

Jacob, H. E. ***Six Thousand Years of Bread: Its Holy and Unholy History*** (The Cooks Classic Library). The Lyons Press, 1997. ISBN 1-55821-575-1. Bread "has caused wars, festivals, visions, and plagues." A historical and philosophical look at bread, starting with its early beginnings in Egypt, through the Middle Ages, and on to the author's own experiences—bread made of sawdust in a Nazi concentration camp.

Jacobson, Michael, and Bruce Maxwell. ***What Are We Feeding Our Kids?*** Workman Publishing Co., 1994. ISBN 1-56305-101-X. Guide explains connection between childhood diet and disease, good and bad influences on your child's food preferences, strategies for eating out of the home, TV's influence, etc.

Katzen, Mollie. ***Honest Pretzels.*** Tricycle Press, 1999. ISBN 1-883672-88-0.

_____. ***Pretend Soup.*** Tricycle Press, 1993. ISBN 1-883672-06-6. Children's cookbooks by well-known whole foods chef;

Lappé, Frances Moore, and Anna Lappé. ***Hope's Edge: The Next Diet for a Small Planet.*** J. P. Tarcher, 2002. ISBN 1-58542-149-9. The author of the classic *Diet for a Small Planet* and her daughter travel the world, discovering practical visionaries who are making a difference in world hunger, sometimes one village at a time. Discusses the urgent food issues of our time and how "what's best for our bodies is best for our communities and for the earth itself." www.annalappe.org

Larrimore, Bertha. ***Sprouting for All Seasons: How and What to Sprout, Including Delicious, Easy-to-Prepare Recipes***. Horizon, 1993. ISBN 0-88290-055-2.

Nabhan, Gary. ***Coming Home to Eat: The Pleasures and Politics of Local Foods.*** Norton, 2002. ISBN 0-393-32374-9. A celebration of food and culture with a social conscience, in the tradition of M. F. K. Fisher and Frances Moore Lappé. Presents a compelling case for eating from our local "foodshed."

Pennington, Jean A. T., Ph.D., R.D., and Judith A. Douglass. ***Bowes & Church's Food Values of Portions Commonly Used.*** 18th ed., Lippincott, Williams & Wilkins Publishers, 2004. ISBN 0-397-55435-4. Nutrient reference manual and nutrition almanac.

Ripley, Catherine, ed. ***Kitchen Fun.*** Little, Brown and Co., 1988. ISBN 0-920775-33-0. "Tasty treats, magic tricks, super crafts, puzzles, and games." Grades PreK-2.

Rodale Institute. ***Empty Breadbasket? The Coming Challenge to America's Food Supply and What We Can Do about It.*** St. Martin's Press, 1982. ASIN 0878574026. The Cornucopia Project of the Rodale Institute documents the vulnerabilities in the U.S. food system and suggests ways to develop a secure and affordable food supply that is also ecologically sustainable.

Schlosser, Eric. ***Fast Food Nation: The Dark Side of the All-American Meal.*** Harper Perennial 2005. ISBN 0-395-97789-4. Well-researched and fascinating investigative narrative into the nation's food system, looking primarily at the effect of large fast-food purveyors on industry, agriculture, employment, and our health.

______.Chew on This: Everything You Don't Want To Know About Fast Food. Houghton Mifflin Co., 2006. ISBN 0618710310.

Shephard, Sue. ***Pickled, Potted, and Canned: How the Art of Food Preserving Changed the World.*** Simon and Schuster, 2001. ISBN 0-7432-1633-4. Sixteen chapters on the history of preserving foods—from Attila the Hun to the space-bound NASA astronauts.

Surgeon General's Call to Action to Prevent and Decrease Overweight and Obesity. "Public health approaches in schools should extend beyond health and physical education to include school policy, the school physical and social environment, and links between schools and families and communities." www.surgeongeneral.gov/topics/obesity/calltoaction/toc.htm

Teitel, Martin. ***Rain Forest in Your Kitchen: The Hidden Connection between Extinction and Your Supermarket.*** Island Press, 1992. ISBN 1-55963-153-8. Proposes restoring biodiversity on the earth by restructuring agricultural practices and eating habits of Americans.

Visser, Margaret. ***Much Depends on Dinner: The Extraordinary History and Mythology, Allure and Obsessions, Perils and Taboos, of an Ordinary Meal.*** Grove Press, 1999. ISBN 0-8021-3651-6. Each chapter is a meal unto itself—well-researched and amusingly presented. Explores how a typical American meal can teach us about our history and culture.

Wilkins, Jennifer, and Jennifer Bokaer-Smith. ***Northeast Regional Food Guide Pyramid*** poster and educational handouts promoting local seasonal eating. Cornell University Resource Center, 7 Business & Technical Park, Ithaca, NY 14850; 607-255-2080; (Poster #399NRFGP, Fact sheets #399NRFGFS); www.nutrition.cornell.edu/FoodGuide/archive

Zeller, Paula A. ***Eat, Think, and Be Healthy: Creative Nutrition Activities for Children.*** Center for Science in the Public Interest, 1987. ISBN 0-89329-016-5. CSPI nutrition activities for the older child.

Worms, Composting, and Environmental Education Sources

Appelhof, Mary, Mary Frances Fenton and Barbara Loss Harris. ***Worms Eat My Garbage.*** Flower Press, 1997. ISBN 0-942256-10-7. How-to guide with extensive information on worms and worm composting. A must-read! See also Teacher's Guides.

_____. ***Wormania!*** (26 min. video). Flower Press, 1999. ISBN 0-942256-09-3. Worm woman visits the Brennan kids and teaches them about soil ecology, worms, and composting. Lively songs written for the video. Grades 2 and up

Caduto, Michael, and Joseph Bruchac, and Ka-Hon-Hes, Carol Wood (illustrators). ***Keepers of the Earth: Native American Stories and Environmental Activities for***

Children. Fulcrum Publishers, 1997. reisssue 2001. ISBN 1-5559-102-7. Ways to present Native American stories. Provides background to activities, and encourages earth stewardship and environmental awareness.

Campbell, Stu. ***Let It Rot! The Gardener's Guide to Composting.*** Storey Books, 3rd ed, 2002. ISBN 1-58017-023-4. Home gardener's guide to composting.

Ernst, David. ***The Farmer's Earthworm Handbook: Managing Your Underground Money-Makers.*** Lessiter Publications, 1995. ISBN 0-94407-903-2. A more technical resource for farmers, educators, etc. Everything you may want to know about worms (or not!) and composting with them.

Fewell, Roy, and Dianne Fewell, Teresa E. Adkins (Illustrator). ***As the Worm Turns: New & Easy Methods for Raising Earthworms.*** Shields Publications, 1998. ISBN 0-914116-34-7. Based on their own experience, the authors present helpful information and good guidelines for successfully raising earthworms.

Hopp, Henry. ***What Every Gardener Should Know about Earthworms.*** Storey Publishing Bulletin# 66195. 32 pages of facts on earthworms, what they do for the soil, and their effect on soil moisture, aeration, and nutrients. It addresses questions about whether it's necessary to "plant" earthworms and how to build up populations www.storey.com

In-Touch Science: Plants & Engineering, Foods & Fabrics, Chemistry & Environment, Fiber & Animals. ISBN 1-57753-263-5. Four individual units can also be purchased as a set. The Resource Center, Cornell Cooperative Extension, 365 Roberts Hall, Ithaca, NY 14853 607 255-2080. Mailing address for orders: PO Box 6525, Ithaca, NY 14851.

Larson, Gary. ***There's a Hair in My Dirt: A Worm's Story.*** HarperCollins, 1998. ISBN 0-06-019104-X. Comedic story of a young worm and his world. For older students and adults (some editing required). Hilarious cartoons.

Leslie, Clare Walker, and Charles Edmund Roth. ***Nature Journaling: Learning to Observe and Connect with the World around You.*** Storey Books, 1998. ISBN 1-58017-088-9. Adapted from Keeping a Nature Journal. Use the simple techniques described to create your own work of art while learning a new way to see your surroundings.

Nancarrow, Loren, and Janet Hogan Taylor. ***The Worm Book: The Complete Guide to Worms in Your Garden.*** Ten Speed Press, 1998. ISBN 0-878-15994-6. Humorous resource with helpful tips on vermiculture. Good book for gardeners interested in environmentally friendly gardening.

Nelson, Joshua. ***Worm Composting.*** A Storey Country Wisdom Bulletin, A-188, Storey Books, 1998. ISBN 1-58017-140-0. Practical, hands-on instructions and earth-friendly information. www.storeybooks.com

Oliver, Bill. ***Have to Have a Habitat*** (album and song). An original song that's become standard in classrooms and nature centers all over the country. As a result, he's now known as "Mr. Habitat." See his other albums of eco-music. www.mrhabitat.net

Payne, Binet. ***The Worm Cafe—Mid-Scale Vermicomposting of Lunchroom Wastes.*** Flower Press, 1999. ISBN 0-942256-11-5. A teacher and her students developed a manual for schools, community groups, and small businesses—and saved their own school some money in the process. To order: www.wormwoman.com

Rathje, William, and Murphy Cullen. ***Rubbish! The Archeology of Garbage.*** University of Arizona Press, 2001. ISBN 0-81652-143-3. A scientific approach to rubbish! Delves into the history, habits, problems of, and solutions for what we throw "away."

Ryan, John C., and Alan Thein Durning. ***Stuff: The Secret Lives of Everyday Things.*** Sightline Institute (formerly Northwest Environmental Watch), 1997. ISBN 1-88609-304-0. " If you don't know your stuff, you don't know your world." Life-cycle analyses (where stuff comes from and where it goes) for common, everyday items. www.sightline.org/

Puppetry

Bauer, Caroline Feller. ***Leading Kids to Books through Puppets.*** American Library Association Editions, 1997. ISBN 0-8389-0706-7. Promotes books and reading to children through simple puppetry. Comes with theme-based programs to act out, poems, and lists of related books.

Buetter, Barbara Macdonald, and Nancy Buetter. ***Simple Puppets from Everyday Materials.*** Sterling Publishing Company, 1998. ISBN 1-895569-35-4. Easy-to-follow ideas (often using recycled materials) for constructing puppets. Encourages the use of imagination and looking at ways to alter the designs for one's own purposes. Good classroom reference. Grades K-3.

Flower, Cedric, and Alan Fortney. ***Puppets—Methods and Materials.*** Sterling Publishers, 1983. ISBN 0-87192-142-1. A great overview of the diversity within the field of puppetry. Includes some history as well as practical tips for constructing a variety of puppets.

Frazier, Nancy, and Nancy Renfro, Lori D. Sears. ***Imagination: At Play with Puppets and Creative Drama.*** Nancy Renfro Studios, 1987. ISBN 0-931044-16-2. Activities combining creative drama and puppetry using simple materials. Full of neat ideas to help children use their imaginations.

Fujita, Hiroko, and Fran Stallings, eds. ***Stories to Play with: Kids' Tales Told with Puppets, Paper, Toys, and Imagination.*** August House, 1999. ISBN 0-87483-553-4. A selection of simple stories and easy-to-make puppet/props to help tell a tale with a flourish

Henson, Cheryl, and the Muppet Workshop. ***The Muppets Make Puppets.*** Workman Publishing Company, Inc., 1994. ISBN 1-56305-708-5. A fun "how-to" book with lots of great ideas for making puppets with ordinary materials. Includes a few materials for making your own puppet.

MacLennon, Jennifer. ***Simple Puppets You Can Make.*** Sterling Publications, 1988. ASIN 0806968168. Whether making simple fabric finger puppets or elaborate fabric hand puppets, the designs are all within the skills of the average seamstress. Patterns included.

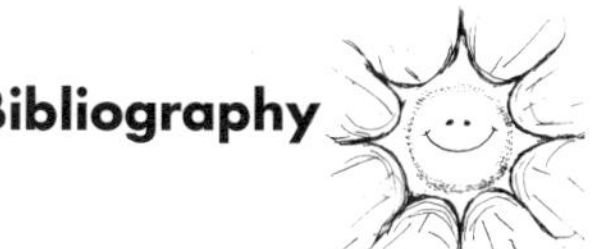

Robson, Denny, and Vanessa Bailey. ***Puppets—Games and Projects (Rainy Days).*** Gloucester Press, 1991. ISBN 0531172694. How to make a variety of puppets—glove and sock puppets to stick puppets and marionettes.

Rountree, Barbara S., Melissa B. Shuptrine, Jean F. Gordon, and Nancy Y. Taylor. ***Creative Teaching with Puppets: Resources for Six Integrated Units.*** The Learning Line, Inc. 1989. ISBN 0-940678-00-4. "We feel there is no better or more exciting technique of teaching than through the use of puppets to make your . . . classroom come alive." Along with units and projects very suitable to young children, these women make the case and provide the examples of why and how to use puppets to enhance your curriculum.

Rump, Nan. ***Puppets and Masks: Stagecraft and Storytelling.*** Sterling Publications, Inc., 1995. ISBN 0-87192-298-3. Masks, storytelling, puppets of all sizes and types, as well as skit ideas, scenery, and sound effects suggestions. A fun book for teachers and kids.

Literature Links: Books for Children

Albyn, Carole, and , Lois Sinaiko Webb. ***The Multicultural Cookbook for Students.*** Oryx Press, 1993. ISBN 0-89774-735-6. The book is filled with recipes (one from each of 122 countries), including descriptions of multicultural feasts, and lots of activities. 4-8.

Aliki. ***Corn is Maize: The Gift of the Indians.*** HarperTrophy, 1986. ISBN 0-06-4450260. This award-winning author-illustrator tells the story of corn, from its cultivation by Native Americans thousands of years ago to how it's used today. K-3.

Altman, Linda Jacobs, Enrique O. Sanchez (illustrator). ***Amelia's Road.*** Lee & Low Books, 1995. ISBN 1-880000-27-X. The daughter of migrant farm workers dreams of a stable home.

Amos, Janine. ***Feeding the World.*** Raintree Steck-Vaughn, 1994. ISBN 0-8114-3407-9. An explanation of the issue of world hunger and some suggestions on ways kids can help.PreK-3.

Ancona, George, and Joan Anderson. ***The American Family Farm: A Photo Essay.*** Harcourt, 1997. ISBN 0-606-11038-0. A tribute to the American farm life. Reflections on the adversities of farm life and its benefits. 4-6.

_____. ***Harvest***. Marshall Cavendish, 2001. ISBN 0-7614-5086-6. A spotlight on the Mexican migrant workers and their families who harvest produce in the United States. Also looks at the work of Cesar Chavez, the use of pesticides and the cultural life of the families. 4-6.

Artley, Bob. ***Once Upon a Farm.*** Pelican Publishing, 2000. ISBN 1-56554-753-5. Describes each season of farm life experienced by the author on his farm during the 1920s and '30s and illustrates seasonal farm work from spring plowing to fall harvesting.

Ayers, Patricia. ***A Kid's Guide to (series): How Flowers Grow*** (ISBN 0-8239-5462-5); ***How Fruits Grow*** (ISBN 0-8239-5466-8); ***How Herbs Grow*** (ISBN 0-8239-5464-1); ***How Plants Grow*** (ISBN 0-8239-5465-X); ***How Trees Grow*** (ISBN 0-8239-5463-3); ***How Vegetables Grow*** (ISBN 0-8239-5461-7). PowerKids Press, 2000. PreK-3.

Azarian, Mary. ***A Farmer's Alphabet.*** David R. Godine Pub., 2004. ISBN 0-87923-397-4. Beautiful block print-illustrated alphabet pages of farm life in the past. PreK-2.

Beinicke, Steve and Candace Savage. ***Trash Attack: Garbage, and What We Can Do about It.*** Firefly Books, 1991. ISBN 0-92066-873-9. Explains the background of the garbage crisis, discusses landfills, incinerators, and toxic waste, and tells what people can do to reduce trash.

Berenstain, Stan and Jan. ***The Berenstain Bears and Too Much Junk Food.*** Random House, 1985. ISBN 0-394-87217-7. When Mama decides they have to eat healthy snacks, everyone, including Papa, protests.

Berggren, Don, and Dorothy Weeks. ***The Jar Garden—Making Delicious Sprouts: A How-To Book for Boys and Girls.*** Woodbridge Press, 1997. ISBN 0-88007-211-3. A rhyming guide to sprouting seeds in a jar to use for healthful salads and sandwiches.

Beskow, Elsa. ***Christopher's Harvest Time.*** Floris Books, 1999. ISBN 0-86315-151-5. As Christopher searches for a lost ball, he encounters fairies and magical creatures in his garden. Includes song lyrics. Written in Swedish in early 1900s; has unusual illustrations.

Bial, Raymond, ***The Farms (Settling America Series).*** Marshall Cavendish, 2001. ISBN 0-76141-332-4. One in a series of books on early America. Clearly written, including some primary sources, photos, period paintings, etc. 4 -6.

_____. ***Portrait of a Farm Family.*** Houghton Mifflin Co., 1995. ISBN 0-395-69936-3. Although it's becoming increasingly difficult for a family farm to survive, the Steidinger family is approaching its fourth generation on the farm. Portrait of a way of life. 3-7.

_____. ***A Handful of Dirt.*** Walker & Co., 2000. ISBN 0-8027-8699-5. Discusses the nature and importance of soil and the many forms of life it supports. 2-6.

Bjork, Christina, Lena Anderson (Illustrator), Joan Sandin (Translator). ***Elliot's Extraordinary Cookbook.*** Sweden: Farrar, Straus & Giroux, 1991. ISBN 91-29-59658-0. Filled with easy, delicious recipes and brimming with Elliot's infectious enthusiasm. He investigates what's healthy and finds out about nutrients and the digestive system. 3-6.

_____, Lena Anderson (Illustrator), Joan Sandin (Translator) ***Linnea's Windowsill Garden***. Sweden: R & S Books, 1988. ISBN 91-29-59064-7. This sprightly young girl who grows plants everywhere—in pots, crates, and glass jars—takes the reader on a tour of her green menagerie and teaches kids how to start their own gardens. Great resource for indoor gardening. 1-5.

Blood, Peter, and Annie Patterson, eds. ***Rise up Singing—A Group Singing Book.*** Sing Out Publications, 1992. ISBN: 0-9626704-7-2. Words to hundreds of folk tunes.

Bramwell, Martyn and Catriona Lennox. ***Food Watch: Protecting Our Planet***. DK Publishing, 2001. ISBN 0-7894-7765-3. Explores issues of food—from problems of world hunger to the effects of pest controls. Offers solutions for protecting our future.

Branzei, Sylvia. ***Grossology and You: Really Gross Things about Your Body.*** Sagebrush, 2003. ISBN 0-8431-7736-5. Presents scientifically accurate information in a manner that is kid-friendly yet informative.

_____. ***Grossology: The Science of Really Gross Things (Grossology Series).*** Price Stern Sloan Pub., 2002. ISBN 0-8431-4914-0. "An outrageous alternative to a really boring health class." Introduces real science about the most disgusting features of the human body—snot, vomit, scabs, and ear wax—in ways that kids just can't resist.

Brown, Craig. ***Tractor***. Greenwillow, 1995. ISBN 0-688-10499-1. Simple text introduces machinery used on a farm and illustrations depict the richness of farm life and the process of growth. Illustrated farm machinery glossary included. K-3.

Brown, Marcia (Illustrator). ***Stone Soup: An Old Tale.*** Aladdin, 1997. ISBN 0-689-71103-4. Three soldiers get a village to share their food when they get donations for their stone soup.

Brown, Mark Tolon. ***Arthur's TV Trouble.*** Little, Brown & Co., 1995. ISBN 0-316-10919-3. This amusing picture book will give parents a good lead into discussions of "truth in advertising." Arthur's fans will enjoy the humor of his predicament and the edgy interplay between Arthur and his sister.

Bruchac, Joseph, and Jonathan London, Thomas Locker (Illustrator). ***Thirteen Moons on Turtle's Back: A Native American Year of Moons.*** The Trumpet Club, 1992. ISBN 0-440-83438-4. Each page beautifully displays and explains each of the year's moons (months) through the eyes and beliefs of different North American Indian tribes.

Burke-Weiner, Kimberly. ***The Maybe Garden.*** Beyond Words Pub. Co., 1992. ISBN 0-941831-56-6. A little girl envisions a garden of her dreams which is nothing like the immaculate garden her mother enjoys. Gentle treatment of important themes—individual identity and the creative aspect of planning a garden. Read aloud and then invite students to create fantastic visions for gardens they might like to grow. K-2.

Burton, Jane, Kim Taylor. ***The Nature and Science of Waste (Exploring the Science of Nature).*** Gareth Stevens, 1999. ISBN 0-8368-2186-6. Describes different kinds of waste—including leaf litter, food, and liquid waste—and how they can be disposed of. 3-6.

Byles, Monica. ***Experiment with Senses.*** Lerner Publishing Group, 1993. ISBN 0-822-52455-4. Simple science experiments help explain the senses: sight, smell, taste, touch, and hearing. 4-6.

Carle, Eric (illustrator). ***The Tiny Seed.*** Aladdin, 2001. ISBN 0-689-84244-9. The simple life cycle of a plant is turned into an exciting story and nature lesson as we also learn about the importance of perseverance. PreK-3.

Carlson, Laurie. ***Ecoart! Earth-Friendly Art & Craft Experiences for 3- to 9-Year-Olds.*** Williamson Publishing Co., 1993. ISBN 0-913589-68-3. Learn how to make non-toxic art materials, utilize natural materials, transform trash into useful and artistic treasures, and safely recycle or compost dozens of common household materials. PreK-4.

Casely, Judith. ***Grandpa's Garden Lunch.*** Greenwillow Books, 1990. ISBN 0-688-08816-3. Sarah and her grandfather plant a garden and care for it. One day grandpa announces they are "having the garden for lunch," and they sit down to a garden-grown feast. K-3.

Cobb, Vicki, Cynthia C. Lewis (illustrator). ***Feeling Your Way: Discover Your Sense of Touch (Five Senses Series).*** ISBN 0-7613-1657-4. ***Follow Your Nose:*** ISBN 0-7613-1521-7. Millbrook Press, 2001. Provides basic facts related to each sense and utilizes interactive, experimental approaches to allow the reader to learn how each sense transmits its information—humorous tone. K-3.

Cole, Henry. ***Jack's Garden.*** Greenwillow Books, 1995. ISBN 0-688-13501-3. Cumulative text and illustrations depict what happens in Jack's garden after he plants his seeds. Done in the tradition of "This is the House That Jack Built." Beautiful artwork with seeds, flowers, and insects. K-2.

Cole, Joanna, and Bruce Degen (illustrator). ***The Magic School Bus Activity Guide: Inside the Human Body.*** Scholastic, 1990. ISBN 0-590-41426-7. A special field trip on the magic school bus allows Ms. Frizzle's class to get a firsthand look at major parts of the body and how they work. K-3.

_____. ***The Magic School Bus Activity Guide: Plants and Seeds/A Book about How Living Things Grow.*** Scholastic, 1995. ISBN 0-590-22296-1. Accompany the bus on a nature adventure following seeds. K-3.

_____. ***The Magic School Bus Explores the Senses.*** Scholastic, 2001. ISBN 0-590-44698-3. Ms. Frizzle and her class explore the senses by traveling on the magic school bus in and out of an eye, ear, mouth, nose, and other parts of both human and animal bodies. K-3. poos

Cole, Joanna, and Carolyn Bracken (illustrator). ***The Magic School Bus Meets the Rot Squad: A Book about Decomposition.*** Scholastic, 1999. ISBN 0-590-40023-1. Ms. Frizzle's class learns about decomposition in a rotting log and how it makes rich soil. www.scholastic.com/magicschoolbus/home.htm K-3.

Cook, Deanna F. and Michael P. Kline (illustrator). ***The Kids's Multicultural Cookbook: Food and Fun around the World,*** Vol. 10. Williamson Publishing, 1995. ISBN 0-913589-91-8. Want to prepare some delicious meals for your family?

Coronado, Rosa. ***Cooking the Mexican Way (Easy Menu Ethnic Cookbooks).*** Lerner Publishing Group, 2001. ISBN 0-8225-4117-3. This is just one in a series of 40 cookbooks (different authors), devoted to a specific ethnic cuisine. Also includes each country's food-related customs as well as festivals. Revised and expanded to include new low-fat and vegetarian recipes. 5-10.

Creasy, Rosalind and Ruth Heller (Illustrator). ***Blue Potatoes, Orange Tomatoes: How to Grow a Rainbow Garden.*** Sierra Club Books for Children, 1994. ISBN 0-87156-576-5. Wonderful illustrations detail how to grow colorful fruits and vegetables. Includes instructions, tips, and recipes. 1-5.

_____. ***The Edible Italian Garden (Edible Garden Series).*** Periplus SGP, 1999. ISBN 962-593-295-X. One of three books—(including The Edible Asian Garden and The Edible Mexican Garden) that encourage children to sow a special theme garden based on a specific ethnic cuisine. Recipes included.

Cutler, Jane, and Philip Caswell. ***Family Dinner***. Farrar, Straus, Giroux, 1992. ISBN 0-374-32267-8. Great-uncle Benson is appalled that Rachel's family doesn't gather for dinner. He takes matters into his own hands and prepares exotic dishes in order to lure Rachel's family to a communal meal. 4-6.

Cyrus, Kurt. ***Oddhopper Opera: A Bug's Garden of Verses.*** Harcourt, 2001. ISBN 0-15-202205-8. An "odd" book about creepy-crawlies that children and adults will love. Cyrus does a wonderful job of blending poetry and beautiful illustrations that spread across two pages at a time to give the reader a bug's-eye view of life. K-4.

D'Amico, Joan, and Karen Erich Drummond. ***The Healthy Body Cookbook: Over 50 Fun Activities and Delicious Recipes for Kids.*** John Wiley, 1999. ISBN 0-471-18888-3. This book has three special ingredients. Each chapter 1) examines a body part or a topic of importance for maintaining good health; 2) includes science activities that explore those topics or body parts, and 3) provides several nutritional recipes meant to boost the function of the body part covered.

Day, Nancy. ***Advertising: Information or Manipulation? (Issues in Focus).*** Enslow Publishers, Inc., 1999. ISBN 0-7660-1106-2. Examines the impact of advertising and looks at its effects on children.

de Paola, Tommie. ***Strega Nona.*** Prentice-Hall Inc., 1975. ISBN 0-13-851600-6. When Strega Nona leaves him alone with her magic pasta pot, Big Anthony is determined to show the townspeople how it works.

_____. ***The Popcorn Book.*** Holiday House, 1984. ISBN 0-82340-533-8. Some interesting popcorn stories and legends as well as two original recipes accompany explanations of popcorn's origins and mancture.

Degen, Bruce. ***Jamberry***. Harperfestival, 1995. ISBN 0694006513. Every character seems giddy with well-fed joy in this veritable jamboree of flavorful fun. PreK.

de Regniers, Beatrice Schenk, ed., M. White, Ed Moore, and Nine Caldecott (Illustrator). ***Sing a Song of Popcorn: Every Child's Book of Poems.*** Scholastic Trade, 1988. ISBN 0-590-43974-X. A collection of modern and old-fashioned poems by a variety of famous authors and nine Caldecott Medalist illustrators—includes sections on weather, animals, silly topics, etc.

Diepenbrock, Katie B. ***Annelida the Wonder Worm.*** Sagittarian Press, 1991. Annelida tells a human boy just how important earthworms really are. Order from Worm Digest at www.wormdigest.org

DiSalvo-Ryan, DyAnne. ***Uncle Willie and the Soup Kitchen.*** HarperCollins, 1997. ISBN 0-688-15285-6. When Uncle Willie invites his nephew to help out in the soup kitchen, the boy is hesitant at first but soon sees that to Uncle Willie, the soup kitchen visitors aren't strangers, they are guests.

_____. ***City Green.*** William Morrow and Company, 1994. ISBN 0-688-12786-X. Marcy and Miss Rosa start a campaign to clean up an empty lot and turn it into a community garden—improving community spirit on their way. K-3

Dooley, Norah and Peter J. Thornton (illustrator). ***Everybody Brings Noodles!*** Carolrhoda Books, Inc., 2002. ISBN 0-87614-455-5. Everyone brings different and delicious noodle dishes to the block party. Recipes from many countries.

_____ and Peter J. Thornton (illustrator). ***Everybody Cooks Rice.*** Carolrhoda Books, 1991. ISBN 0-87614-412-1. Carrie visits her neighbors who were originally from various countries while looking for her brother. At each house she samples their rice dishes, finally coming home to her mother's rice dish from Italy. Recipes included. 1-5.

Egan, Robert. ***From Wheat to Pasta.*** Children's Press, 1997. ISBN 0-51-626069-3. Lively narrative and detailed photographs clearly present each step in making pasta.

Ehlert, Lois. ***Eating the Alphabet: Fruits and Vegetables from A to Z.*** Red Wagon, 1996. ISBN 0-15-201036-X. Colorful depiction of usual and unusual fruits & vegetables from A to Z. K-3.

_____. ***Growing Vegetable Soup.*** Harcourt Brace Jovanovitch, 1990. ISBN 0-15-232575-1. Bold print combines with colorful illustrations to show a father and child growing vegetables and then making them into a soup. PreK-2.

_____. ***Planting a Rainbow.*** Voyager, 1992. ISBN 0-15-262610-7. Mother and child plant bulbs, seeds, and seedlings, which result in a rainbow of flowers. K-2.

Elffers, Joost, and Saxton Freymann. ***How are You Peeling? Foods with Moods.*** Scholastic Paperbacks, 1999. ISBN 0-439-10431-9. (See description below.)

_____. ***Play with Your Food.*** Stewart, Tabori & Chang, Inc., 1997. ISBN 1-55670-630-8. Both of the books in this series use leading questions and evocative expressions on whimsical food sculptures and carvings which introduce the language of emotions in an "a-peeling" and non-threatening way.

Featherstone, Jane. ***Farming (Ecology Alert).*** Raintree Steck-Vaughn, 2000. ISBN 0-817-25371-8. Different methods of farming and soil preservation are discussed. 3-7.

Finch, Mary. ***The Little Red Hen and the Ear of Wheat.*** Barefoot Books, 1999. ISBN 1-902283-47-3. An adaptation of the old folktale. The Little Red Hen asks but receives no help each step of the way (from planting wheat to baking the bread) until she is ready to eat it. Her friends are not invited to eat the bread and they change their ways. Whole wheat bread recipe included.

Fleischman, Paul and Judy Pedersen (Illustrator). ***Seedfolks.*** HarperTrophy, 2004. ISBN 0-06-447207-8. One by one, thirteen people of varying ages and ethnic backgrounds transform a trash-filled inner-city lot into a productive and beautiful garden. In doing so, the gardeners are themselves transformed. K-6.

Foster, Joanna. ***Cartons, Cans, and Orange Peels: Where Does***

Your Garbage Go? Houghton Mifflin Co., 1993. ISBN 0-39566-504-3. Outlines the composition of garbage and trash and discusses the various methods of disposing it.

French, Vivian and Alison Bartlett (Illustrator). ***Oliver's Vegetables.*** Orchard Books, 1995. ISBN 0-531-09462-6. When Oliver, who eats only french fries, visits his grandparents, he is interested in their garden—only for the potatoes. His grandfather finds a way for Oliver to sample other vegetables on his search. K-3.

Freymann, Saxton and Joose Elffers. ***Fast Food.*** Arthur A. Levine Books, 2006; ISBN 0-43911-019-X. *Booklist* says: "This handsome book is both a uniquely entertaining addition to preschool and primary-grade units on transportation and an irresistible invitation for children to play creatively with their food. PreK-3.

Friedman, Ina and Allen Say (Illustrator). ***How My Parents Learned to Eat.*** C Mifflin, 1984. ISBN 0-395-35379-3. An American sailor C a Japanese girl and each tries, in secret, to learn the other's way of eating. PreK-3.

Friedrich, Elizabeth, and Michael Garland (illustrator). ***Leah's Pony.*** Boyds Mills Press, 1996. ISBN 1563971895. A young girl sells her horse and raises enough money to buy back her father's tractor, which is up for auction, in this story of a Depression-era farm.

Frost, Helen. ***The Digestive System.*** Pebble Books, 2000. ISBN 0-7368-0649-0. Basic facts, in simple language accompanied by color photos. K-3.

Gay, Kathlyn. ***Keep the Buttered Side Up: Food Superstitions from around the World.*** Walker & Co., 1995. ISBN 0-8027-8228-0. Relates beliefs and superstitions attributed to different categories of foods, the origins of these superstitions, and carryover practices found today. PreK-3.

Gerson, Mary Joan and Carla Golembe (Illustrator). ***Why the Sky is Far Away: A Nigerian Folktale.*** Joy Street, 1992. ISBN 0-316-30852-8. People could just reach up into the sky to get their food until they became too wasteful. Ever since then, they've had to grow their own. K-3.

Gibbons, Gail. ***From Seed to Plant.*** Holiday House, 1991. ISBN 0-8234-0872-8. With colorful illustrations and simple text, the author explains how seeds grow into plants. Includes plant reproduction, seed dispersal, seed germination, and pollen transfer. K-3.

_____. ***Recycle! A Handbook for Kids.*** Little, Brown and Co., 1996. ISBN 0-316-30943-5. Children collect and separate recyclables. Captions and text stress the need to reduce waste and save natural resources. Printed on recycled paper.

_____. ***The Pumpkin Book.*** Holiday House, 1999. ISBN 0-8234-1465-5. Account of the life cycle of the pumpkin. Explains role of the pumpkin in traditional American fall holidays and includes information for home and classroom projects. K-3.

_____. ***The Seasons of Arnold's Apple Tree.*** Harcourt Brace Jovanovitch, 1984. ISBN 0-15-271246-1. As the seasons pass, Arnold enjoys a variety of activities as a result of his apple tree. Includes a recipe for apple pie and a description of how an apple cider press works. K-3.

Glaser, Linda. ***Compost! Growing Gardens from Your Garbage.*** Millbrook Press, 1996. ISBN 0-7613-0030-9. Rhythmic text in the voice of a child explains how her family turns garbage and garden waste into soil using the compost bin. PreK-3.

Glaser, Linda, and Loretta Krupinski. ***Wonderful Worms.*** Millbrook Press, 1994. ISBN 1-56294-730-3. Describes physical characteristics, behavior, and life cycle of the common earthworm. Nice illustrations of worms underground. PreK-3.

Goodman, Susan. ***Seeds, Stems, and Stamens: The Way Plants Fit into their World.*** Millbrook Press, 2001. ISBN 0-7613-1874-7. In a creative and inviting manner, looks at the ways plants survive in their various habitats. Short chapters discuss fitting into the environment; getting sun, water, and food; inherent defenses; and propagating. 3-8.

Gourley, Catherine. ***Media Wizards: A Behind-the-Scenes Look at Media Manipulations.*** Twenty-First Century, 1999. ISBN 0-7613-0967-5. Examines how TV producers, advertisers, and others in the media can influence the public. Black-and-white photographs with the text present examples from the present and past. 5-11.

Greenfield, Eloise and Leo and Diane Dillon (Illustrators). ***Honey, I Love and Other Love Poems.*** HarperTrophy, 1986. ISBN 0-690-01334-5. Fifteen poems for children that express the feelings of one little girl; could be used to think about what your students love about themselves, gardening, food, etc. 1-3.

Greenstein, Elaine. ***Mrs. Rose's Garden.*** Simon & Schuster, 1996. ISBN 0-689-80215-3. Mrs. Rose's unusual mix of fertilizers produces a whole garden full of prizewinning vegetables, and some additional surprises. K-3.

Haduch, Bill. ***Food Rules! What You Munch, Its Punch, Its Crunch, and Why Sometimes You Lose Your Lunch.*** Penguin Putnam Books for Young Readers, 2001. ISBN 0-525-46419-0. Cool enough for kids to savor, scientific enough to be an invaluable resource. Stories, jokes, recipes, rumors, and fact. 3-6.

Hall, Eleanor. ***Garbage.*** Greenhaven Press, 1997. ISBN 1-560-06188-X. Discusses our waste problem and how we can manage what we produce—including recycling and reducing waste production. 3-8.

Handelsman, Judith. ***Gardens from Garbage: How to Grow Indoor Plants from Recycled Kitchen Scraps.*** Econo-Clad Books, 1999. ISBN 1-56294-843-1. Provides instructions for growing houseplants from pieces of potatoes, corn, watermelons, and other kitchen scraps including a bit of plant folklore. 4-6.

Harbison, Elizabeth M. ***Loaves of Fun: A History of Bread with Activities and Recipes from around the World.*** Chicago Review Press, 1997. ISBN 1-55652-311-4. A collection of recipes for various kinds of breads arranged in a timeline format that charts the history of this staple food from the earliest civilization to the present day. Includes instructions for related activities. 1-6.

Hatch, Warren A. ***Worm Bin Creatures Alive through a***

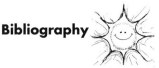

Microscope. (Video, 31 minutes). ASIN 1-884195-36-9. Captivating video shows tiny organisms often seen but rarely identified in a worm bin. Springtails and pseudo-scorpions amuse and entertain as they search for food or shelter. Available from www.wormwoman.com

Heddle, Rebecca. ***Science in the Kitchen.*** EDC Publishing, 1992. ISBN 0-7460-0974-7. Safe and easy science experiments from blowing bubbles to making soft drinks. Clear and simple so children can use the book by themselves. K-4. Find book through publisher, Educational Development Corporation. www.edcpub.com

Heller, Ruth. ***The Reason for a Flower (World of Nature Series).*** Penguin Putnam Young Reader; reissue edition, 1999. ISBN 0-698-11559-7. In her trademark style, Heller uses brief text and colorful illustrations to explain plant reproduction and the purpose of a flower to young readers. 1-4.

Henwood, Chris. ***Keeping Minibeasts: Earthworms.*** Franklin Watts, Inc., 1988. ISBN 0-531-10620-9. Part of a series exploring how to care for small creatures. Simple text, close-up color photos, shows how to find, house, feed, care for, and observe earthworms.

Hess, Lilo. The Amazing Earthworm. Atheneum, 1979. ISBN 0-68416-079-X. Describes the characteristics and habits of earthworms. Preschool.

Hines, Anna Grossnickle. ***Daddy Makes the Best Spaghetti.*** Sagebrush, 1999. ISBN 0-8335-2786-X. Not only does Corey's Dad make the best spaghetti, he also does shopping, plays Batman, and carries Teddy to bed.

Hubbard, Vicki, and Nancy Killion. ***Kinder Spirits: Children Helping Children in the Fight Against Hunger.*** Universe.com Inc., 2000. ISBN 0-595-13542-0. Poetry written by children in appreciation of the riches in life—and expressing that children of all ages can understand that hunger exists and that they can help in their own way. Proceeds benefit charities that serve hungry people. 3-7.

Hughes, Meredith Sayles. ***Green Power: Leaf and Flower Vegetables (Plants We Eat Series).*** Lerner Publishing Group, 2001. ISBN 0-8225-2839-8. Describes the history, growing requirements, uses, and food value of various leafy green vegetables and vegetable flowers, including cabbage, broccoli, artichokes, spinach, Belgian endive, and lettuce. Includes recipes. 3-6

Inglis, Jane. ***Fiber (Food Facts).*** Carolrhoda, 1993. ISBN 0-87614-793-7. Easy-to-read chapters accompanied by cartoon-like drawings and photographs providing general information about fiber in our diet. 3-6.

Jackson, Ellen. ***The Autumn Equinox: Celebrating the Harvest.*** Millbrook Press, 2000. ISBN 0-7613-1442-3. Explains the relevance of the autumn equinox and the importance of the harvest as well as a variety of cultural celebrations. Projects and recipes included. Pre-K-3.

Jimenez, Francisco, Simon Silva (illustrator). ***La Mariposa.*** Houghton Mifflin, 2000. ISBN 0-618-07317-5. Son of a Mexican migrant worker trying to befriend his English-speaking classmates. His fascination with a caterpillar helps him fit in. PreK-3.

Johnson, Paul Brett. ***Farmers' Market.*** Orchard Books, 1997. ISBN 0-531-30014-5. Laura goes with her family on Saturdays in the summer to help sell their produce at the farmer's market. K-3.

Johnson, Siz A. ***Wheat (Natural Science Series).*** Lerner Publishing Group, 1990. ISBN 0-8225-1490-7. Describes the life cycle of different kinds of wheat; plant parts shown in microscopic detail in color photos. 4-6.

Jordan, Helene. ***How a Seed Grows.*** HarperCollins, 1992. ISBN 0-06-020104-5. Tells how a seed becomes a flower or vegetable with the right mix of things. K-3.

Kalbacken, Joan. ***Food Pyramid (True Books, Food & Nutrition).*** Children's Press, 1998. ISBN 0-516-26376-5. A simple guide for younger children to learn the values of good nutrition. K-3.

Kalman, Bobbie. ***Early Stores and Markets (Early Settler Life Series).*** Crabtree Publishers, 1981. ISBN 0-86505-994-X. A glimpse into eighteenth and nineteenth century markets, storefronts, and the items that were sold. 3-6.

Kalman, Bobbie, and Janine Schaub. ***Squirmy Wormy Composters.*** Crabtree Publishers, 1992. ISBN 0-86505-555-6. Clear illustrations and language about worm composting, worm anatomy and reproduction on a child's level. 1-6.

Keen, Martin, Harris Petie (illustrator). ***The World Beneath Our Feet: The Story of Soil.*** Julian Messner, 1974. ISBN 0-67132-673-2. Introduction to soil's formation, importance and conservation, as well as the life found in it.

Kindersley, Barnabas, and Anabel Kindersley. ***Children Just Like Me: Celebrations! Festivals, Carnivals, and Feast Days Around the World***. DK Publishers, 1997. ISBN 0-7894-2027-9. A calendar of celebrations, describing holidays and festivals from all major religions and cultures around the world. 3-6.

Kite, Patricia. ***Gardening Wizardry for Kids.*** Barrons Juveniles, 1995. ISBN 0-8120-1317-4. Three hundred indoor gardening projects, crafts, and folklore tales. PreK-6.

Kohl, Mary Ann. ***Good Earth Art: Environmental Art for Kids,*** Vol. 1. Bright Ring Publishing, 1991. ISBN 093560. Kids collect "discards" from inside and out—fallen leaves, pinecones, newspaper, envelopes to use in 150 open-ended projects.

Kohl, Mary Ann F., and Jean Potter. ***Cooking Art: Easy Edible Art for Young Children.*** Gryphon House, 1997. ISBN 0-87659-184-5. Kid-friendly instructions for 150 edible and healthy "masterpieces." Organized by themes including: shapes and forms, numbers and letters, animals and creatures. PreK-2.

Krauss, Ruth. and Crockett Johnson (Illustrator). ***The Carrot Seed.*** Scholastic Paperbacks, 1990. ISBN 0-590-73301-X. Despite everyone's dire predictions, a little boy has faith in the carrot seed he plants. Delightful book for young children. K-1.

Krull, Kathleen and Melanie Hope Greenberg (Illustrator).

Supermarket. Holiday House, 2001. ISBN 0-8234-1546-5. Interesting tidbits, behind the scenes looks, the story of how food gets from farm to table, and artwork filled to the brim with products, peoples, signs, and advertisements. PreK-3.

Kuhn, Dwight. ***More Than Just a Vegetable Garden.*** Silver Burdett Press, 1990. ISBN 0-67169-643-2. Text and photos present life among the animals and plants in a vegetable garden, and gives instructions for starting your own vegetable garden indoors. 3-6.

Lade, Roger. ***The Most Excellent Book of How to Be a Puppeteer.*** Copper Beech Books, 1996. ISBN 0-7613-0505-X. Advice for the young, practicing puppeteer. Includes tips for hand and finger manipulation, dialogue, and how to make puppets "come alive." 4-7.

Lambourne, Mike. ***Down the Hatch: Find Out about Your Food.*** Millbrook Press, 1992. ISBN 1-56294-150-X. A colorful "mess" of caricatures—appealing to kids more than adults—points to the benefits of eating a balanced diet. Pre K-3.

Landau, Elaine. ***Sugar.*** Children's Press, 2000. ISBN 0-51626-772-8. Examines the history, sources, refinement, and uses of sugar. PreK-3

Lasky, Kathryn and Christopher G. Knight (Illustrator). ***Sugaring Time.*** Aladdin Paperbacks, 1986. ISBN 0-6897-1081-X. Shows how a family taps the sap from maple trees and processes it into maple sugar. 4-6

Lauber, Patricia. ***Seeds: Pop, Stick, Glide.*** Knopf Books for Young Readers (1988). ISBN 0-517-54165-3. Text and black-and-white photographs describe the many different ways that seeds travel and disperse. 2-5

Lavies, Bianca. ***Compost Critters.*** Dutton Children's Books, 1993. ISBN 0-525-44763-6. Describes what happens in a compost pile and how creatures, from bacteria and mites to millipedes and earthworms, aid in the process of turning compost into humus. Up-close, enlarged color photographs follow the compost pile through an entire year. K-4

Lerner, Carol. ***My Indoor Garden.*** William Morrow, 1999. ISBN 0-688-14753-4. An indoor grower's well-organized introduction to growing, propagating and caring for "houseplants." Combines savvy and systematic advice with pleasant, muted watercolors. PreK-.

Levenson, George. ***Pumpkin Circle: The Story of a Garden.*** Tricycle Press, 2002. ISBN 1-58246-078-7. Captures each phase of the pumpkin's life with time-lapse photography: seeds sprouting, flowers blooming, bees buzzing, pumpkins growing, and finally the pumpkin returning to earth. Pre K-3.

Lewin, Ted. ***Market!*** Lothrop, Lee & Shepard, 1996. ISBN 0-688-12161-6. Markets around the world are featured in this informative and brightly illustrated book. PreK-3

Lewis, Patrick J. and Lisa Desimini (Illustrator). ***Doodle Dandies: Poems That Take Shape.*** Atheneum/Schwartz, 1998. ISBN 0-689-81075-X. Mixed-media collages provide the form in which these poems take their shape. (Poems within in the shapes of their subjects.) K-3.

Lin, Grace. ***The Ugly Vegetables.*** Charlesbridge Publishing, 1999. ISBN 0-88106-336-3. A young girl is disappointed with her family's Chinese vegetable garden compared to the neighbors' "rainbow of flowers" until she discovers how her mother's aromatic vegetable soup attracts the whole neighborhood for a taste of their garden. PreK.

Little, Lessie Jones and Jan Spivey Gilchrist (Illustrator). ***Children of Long Ago Poems.*** Lee & Low Books, 2000. ISBN 1-58430-009-4. Poems about life before modern conveniences; focuses on families and children.

Livingston, Myra Cohn. ***Poem-Making: Ways to Begin Writing Poetry.*** HarperCollins, 1991. ISBN 0-06-024019-9. The mechanics of poetry are provided in an understandable and organized fashion by this poet/anthropologist/teacher. 4-6.

Livo, Norma J. ***Moon Cakes to Maize: Delicious World Folktales.*** Fulcrum Publishing, 1999. ISBN 1-55591-973-1. This collection of more than 50 world folktales, riddles, and fables features food, and provides a delectable feast for parents, teachers, storytellers, and children. 3-8.

Llewellyn, Claire and Barrie Watts ***Earthworms (Minibeasts).*** Franklin Watts, 2002. 0531148254. Full color photos show how earthworms grow, where they live, what they eat and who eats them. PreK-3.

Lovejoy, Sharon. ***Roots, Shoots, Buckets, and Boots: Gardening Together with Children.*** Workman Publishing Co., 1999. ISBN 0-7611-1056-9. A unique guide to gardening for the entire family offers fun, action-packed advice on how to plant a pumpkin seed, create theme gardens, and plant a "pizza patch" complete with tomatoes, zucchini, oregano, and basil. All ages.

Lovejoy, Sharon and Robert Shetterly (Illustrator). ***Sunflower Houses.*** Interweave Press, 1991. ISBN 0-934026-70-X. Garden discoveries for children of all ages: stories, poems, nostalgic garden projects. 1-6

Maass, Robert. ***Garbage.*** Henry Holt & Co., 2000. ISBN 0-8050-5951-2. This photo essay offers young readers an in-depth look at the steps involved in the processing of garbage as it is carried from the home to the landfill. PreK-3

McLaughlin, Molly. ***Earthworms, Dirt, and Rotten Leaves.*** HarperCollins, 1990. ISBN 0-380-71074-9. Introduces young ecologists to the fascinating world of earthworms, describing the creature's structure, behavior, habits, habitat, and role in soil ecology. 4-7

McNulty, Faith, and Bob Marstall. ***The Lady and the Spider.*** Harper and Row Pub., 1986. ISBN 0-06-024191-8. A spider who lives in a head of lettuce is saved when she is put back in the garden by the lady who finds her. K-3

Mitgutsch, Ali. ***From Seed to Pear.*** Carolrhoda Books, 1981. ISBN 0876141637. This simple book shows a gardener planting pear seeds and tending the tree until it grows large enough to produce fruit. Contains enough information for young readers to understand the growth process. PreK-3

Moore, Eva. ***The Story of George Washington Carver.*** Scholastic, 1990. ISBN 0-590-42660-5. Biography of famous scientist who was born a slave. Discovered how to improve soil conditions in the South, and invented hundreds of ways

to use peanuts and sweet potatoes. 4-6

Moore, Lillian, and Sharon Wooding (illustrator). ***I'll Meet You at the Cucumbers.*** Atheneum, 1988. ISBN 0-689-31243-1. Adam and Junius, two country mice, go for a visit to the city, where Adam despairs when his dear friend admits he might like to stay. PreK-3

Muller, Gerda. ***The Garden in the City.*** Dutton, 1992. ISBN 0-525-44697-4. Ben and Caroline grow a garden and learn how to care for many kinds of plants. Complete with helpful hints and ideas for projects. PreK-3.

Needham, Bobbe. ***Ecology Crafts for Kids: 50 Great Ways to Make Friends with Planet Earth.*** Sterling Publishing, 1999. ISBN 0-8069-2024-6. Create "nifty" stuff with recycled objects: newspaper, bottles, cans, wrapping paper—and learn about garbage issues.PreK-3

Nottridge, Rhoda. ***Sugars.*** Carolrhoda Books, 1993. ISBN 0-87614-796-1. A look at how sugar is processed, its use in foods, and how it affects health. PreK-3.

Overbeck, Cynthia. ***The Magic School Bus Activity Guide: How Seeds Travel.*** Lerner Publishing Group, 1990. ISBN 0-8225-9569-9. Color photographs trace the seeds back to their source. Seeds and fruit are explained as well as plant reproduction. 2-5.

Paladino, Catherine. ***One Good Apple: Growing Our Food for the Sake of the Earth.*** Houghton Mifflin Co., 1999. ISBN 0-395-85009-6. Discusses the problems created by the use of pesticides and chemical fertilizers to grow food crops and the benefits of sustainable and organic farming. 4-8. .

Parker, Steve. ***Eating a Meal: How You Eat, Drink, and Digest.*** Franklin Watts, Inc., 1991. ISBN 0-5311-4086-5. 2-5. See also The Body Atlas. Dorling, 1993. ISBN 1-56458-224-8. 5-10; and ***How the Body Works*** by Carol Vorderman. Reader's, l994. ISBN 0-89577-575-1. How organs and body systems work 4-6

_____. ***Food and Digestion.*** Franklin Watts, 1990. ISBN 0-5311-4027-X. An introduction to the digestive system, discussing each stage of digestion, the organs which aid in the process, and the assimilation of nutrients into the body. 3-6.

Pascoe, Elaine. ***Earthworms (Nature Close Up Series).*** Blackbirch Press, 1997. ISBN 1-56711-177-7. Describes the digging habits, physical characteristics, reproductive process, and habitat of the earthworm and provides instructions for related hands-on science projects. Amazing earthworm facts and photos! PreK-6.

Patraker, Deborah. ***What is a Farmer's Market?*** Books for Children, 1997. ISBN 0965843106. A coloring book about farmers who grow and sell food at the market. Underlying themes of fun and nutrition.

Paulsen, Gary. ***The Tortilla Factory.*** Harcourt Brace & Company, 1995. ISBN 0-15-292876-6. "In simple and eloquent language . . . pays tribute to a cycle of life—from seed to plant to tortilla." K-2.

Pelham, David. ***Worms Wiggle.*** Little Simon, 1989. ISBN 0-671-67218-5. A cleverly engineered and rhyming pop-up book focuses on how creatures get around. PreK-3.

Pennington, Daniel. ***Itse Selu: Cherokee Harvest Festival.*** Charlesbridge Publishers, 1994. ISBN 0-88106-850-0. Many Cherokee traditions are incorporated into the story as the tribe celebrates at the Green Corn Festival. PreK-3.

Perez, L. King and Robert Casilla (Illustrator). ***First Day in Grapes.*** Lee & Low Books, 2002. ISBN 1-584-30045-0. The life of Chicos—from a migrant worker family— and how he copes in school. 1-3

Perl, Lila. ***Junk Food, Fast Food, Health Food: What America Eats and Why.*** Houghton Mifflin Co., 1980. ISBN: 0-39529-108-9. Explores 20th-century American eating patterns and includes a selection of recipes reflecting contemporary tastes.

Peet, Bill. ***The Wump World.*** Houghton Mifflin, 1970. ISBN 0-395-19841-0. A clever parable built on the subject of pollution and the waste of natural resources. PreK-4.

Peterson, Cris and Alvis Upitis (Photographer). ***Century Farm: One Hundred Years on a Family Farm.*** Boyds Mills Press, 1999. ISBN 1-56397-710-9. The story of a family farm in Wisconsin and the three generations of Petersons who farmed the land. PreK-5.

_____. ***Harvest Year.*** Boyds Mills Press, 1996. ISBN 1-56397-571-8. Wonderful farm, family, and food photos. A month-by-month sampling of what's grown throughout the U.S. K-5.

Plater, Inge. ***Earthworms and Their Food*** (0-7802-2707-7), ***How Earthworms Live*** (0-7802-2709-3), and ***How Earthworms Grow*** (0-7802-2705-0). The Wright Group, 1995. Picture book series with great photographs and illustrations for young children.

Pluckrose, Henry. ***In the Supermarket (Machines at Work Series).*** Scholastic, 1999. ISBN 0-5311-5357-6. PreK-2.

Poortlviet, Rien. ***The Farm Book.*** Harry N Abrams, 1994. ISBN 0810908174. Life on an old-fashioned Dutch farm. Depictions of real farm life, tools, and animals. Humorous text.

Portman, Michelle Eva. ***Compost, By Gosh!*** Flower Press, 2002. ISBN 0-942256-16-6. Poetic, rhyming couplets explain the process of vermicomposting that young readers/listeners will enjoy. PreK-3

Powell, Jillian. ***Everyone Eats Pasta.*** Raintree Steck-Vaughn, 1997. ISBN 0-8172-4760-2. Presents basic facts and history of pasta as well as methods of production and preparation, uses around the world, and a few easy recipes. PreK-4

_____. ***Food and Your Health (Health Matters Series).*** Raintree Steck-Vaughn, 1998. ISBN 0-8172-4925-7. Introduction to basic nutrition and the relationship between food and health. 2-5.

Pratt, Dianne, Sherri Eldridge (Editor) and Janet Winter (Illustrator). ***Hey Kids! You're Cookin' Now! A Global Awareness Cooking Adventure.*** Harvest Hill Press, 1998. ISBN 1-886862-07-9. Recipes for children who are interested in making breakfasts, breads, lunches, snacks, dinners, desserts, beverages, and "marvelous mixes." Also includes facts about diet, nature, and ecology. 3-6

Prelutsky, Jack and James Stevenson (Illustrator). ***Something Big Has Been Here.*** HarperCollins, 1990. ISBN 0-688-06434-5. Humorous poems about characters like ancient tortoises, a solid meatloaf, and five flying hotdogs. K-3.

Prelutsky, Jack, ed. and Marc Brown (Illustrator). ***Read-Aloud Rhymes for the Very Young.*** Alfred A. Knopf, 1986. ISBN 0-394-87218-5. A richly illustrated collection of over 200 verses, silly rhymes, and poems relating to all sorts of subjects. PreK–K.

Priceman, Marjorie. ***How to Make an Apple Pie and See the World.*** Dragonfly, 1996. ISBN 0679880836 . A girl makes a trip around the world in search of the ingredients to make an apple pie.

Pringle, Laurence. ***Explore Your Senses Series: Hearing*** (ISBN 9-7614-0735-9); Sight (ISBN 9-7614-0734-0); ***Smell*** (ISBN 9-7614-0737-5); ***Taste*** (ISBN 9-7614-0736-7); ***Touch*** (ISBN 9-7614-0738-3). Marshall Cavendish, 2000.

Quinn, Greg Henry and Lena Shiffman (Illustrator). ***The Garden in Our Yard.*** Scholastic, 1995. ISBN 0-590-48536-9. Follow family from planting through harvest. PreK-3.

Ray, Mary Lynn and Barry Root (Illustrator). ***Pumpkins: A Story for a Field.*** Turtleback, 1996. ISBN 0-606-11-770-9. A man harvests and sells a bountiful crop of pumpkins so that he will be able to preserve the field from developers. K-3.

Regguinti, Gordon. ***The Sacred Harvest: The Ojibway Wild Rice Gathering.*** Lerner Publishing Group, 1992. ISBN 0-8225-9620-2. An eleven-year-old Ojibway boy goes with his father to harvest wild rice, the sacred food of his people. Part of the ***We Are Still Here Series*** by Native American authors. 3-6.

Rhatigan, Joe and Heather Smith. ***Earth-Friendly Crafts for Kids: 50 Awesome Things to Make with Recycled Stuff.*** Sterling Publishing, 2002. ISBN 1579903401. Create a wealth of easy toys and even gifts from plastic, metal, paper, fabric, glass, and miscellaneous. Sidebars show things people worldwide do with their trash.

Ring, Elizabeth. ***What Rot! Nature's Mighty Recycler.*** Millbrook Press, 1996. ISBN 1-56294-671-4. Text and photos show how rot works and how all the tiny organisms that cause it maintain the cycle of life. 1-4.

Robinson, Fay. ***Too Much Trash.*** Children's Press, 1995. ISBN 0-51606-042-2. Follows garbage from cafeteria to landfill and describes methods to deal with trash. PreK-3

Robinson, Fay, and Allan Fowler. ***Recycle That!*** Children's Press, 1995. ISBN 0-516-46033-1. Explains what recycling means, tells why it's important not to be wasteful, and shows how old cans, bottles, and paper can be made into new products. Pre-K-2.

Rockwell, Lizzy. ***Good Enough to Eat: A Kid's Guide to Food & Nutrition.*** HarperCollins, 2000. ISBN 0-06-445174-7. Clear, detailed presentation of facts about nutrients we need and foods they are in. Enough information for older kids and adults. K-3.

Rohmer, Harriet, Gomez Cruz and Enrique Chagoya. ***Mr. Sugar Came to Town/La visita del Sr. Azucar.*** Children's Book Press, 1989. ISBN 0-89239-045-X. Mr. Sugar tries to lure children away from Grandma's tasty tamales, using his truck of sweets. PreK-3.

Rosen, Michael J., ed. ***Down to Earth: Garden Secrets! Garden Stories! Garden Projects You Can Do!*** Harcourt Children's Books, 1998. ISBN 0-15-201341-5. A collection of stories, recipes, garden projects, and works of art fill this beautiful book. Thanks to the artistic contributions of 41 children's authors and illustrators, sales of this book will benefit an anti-hunger organization. 4-6.

_____, ed. ***Food Fight: Poets Join the Fight Against Hunger with Poems to Favorite Foods.*** Diane Publishing Company, 2000. ISBN 0-78819-112-8. The work of 33 favorite children's poets fills this anthology with poems devoted to favorite foods and the fight against hunger. 4-6. Proceeds to benefit Share Our Strength (SOS), an anti-hunger organization that mobilizes industry and individuals (chefs, poets, artists) to contribute their talents to fight hunger. 4-7

Ross, Bill. ***Straight from the Bear's Mouth: The Story of Photosynthesis.*** Atheneum, 1995. ISBN 0-689-31726-3. Trying to perform an experiment with aspen trees, Dina and Jake seek the advice of eccentric science teacher Dr. Mildew and are astounded when the doctor's pet bear breathes on the trees, an act that has surprising results. 5-9.

Ross, Kathy, ed. and Hank Schneider (Photographer) ***Recycle Art: Look What You Can Make with Plastic Bottles and Tubs.*** Boyds Mills Press, 2002. ISBN 1-56397-567-X. Dozens of ideas and over 80 photographed crafts. PreK-3.

Ross, Michael Elsohn and Brian Grogan (Photographer), Darren Erickson (Illustrator). ***Wormology.*** Lerner Publishing Group, 1996. ISBN 0-87614-937-9. Presents rigorous scientific observational skills as attainable by children patient enough to take the time to carefully study worms.

Rotner, Shelley, and Julia Permberton Hellums. ***Hold the Anchovies! A Book about Pizza.*** Orchard Books, 1996. ISBN 0-531-09507-X. Describes the ingredients that are used to make a pizza, where each comes from, and how they are used to prepare the final product. Includes recipe. PreK-3

Savage, Candace and Gary Clements (Illustrator). ***Eat Up! Healthy Food for a Healthy Earth.*** Firefly Books, 1993. ISBN 1-89556-513-8. Environmentally oriented book for older students; discusses the advantages of natural versus processed foods, describes the environmental impact of the foods we buy, and tells how to shop wisely. (Available through Green Brick Roads, see Organizations. 4-7

Schmid, Eleonore. ***Living Earth: Soil.*** North South Books, 2000. ISBN 0-61326-040-6.Presents the delicate balance between natural processes and the human-induced modifications on soils.PreK-3

Schomp, Virginia. ***If You Were a Farmer***. Benchmark Books, 2001. ISBN 0-7614-1001-5. Gives very young readers a look inside the life and work of a farmer. PreK-3.

Sekido, Isamu. ***Fruits, Roots, and Fungi: Plants We Eat (Science All Around You Series).*** Lerner Publishing Group, 1993. ISBN 0-8225-29025. Nine common foods, seen in close-up, color photographs, are presented for study as a guessing game; which is a fruit and which a vegetable? K-3.

Sendak, Maurice. ***Chicken Soup with Rice.*** HarperCollins Children's Books, 1969. ISBN 0-06-025535-8. Each month is gay, each season is nice, when eating chicken soup with rice. It's nice in January, April, June, and December—here's the every-month dish for everyone to remember. PreK-3

Sharmat, Michael and Ariane Dewey, Jose Aruego (Illustrators). ***Gregory, the Terrible Eater.*** Scholastic, 1980. ISBN 0-590-43350-4. Mother Goat is alarmed by Gregory's bizarre dietary preferences—he prefers toast and scrambled eggs to shoe boxes and tin cans. PreK-2.

Showers, Paul and Edward Miller (Illustrator). ***What Happens to a Hamburger.*** HarperCollins, 2001. ISBN 0-06-445013-9. Explains the process by which a hamburger and other foods are used to make energy, strong bones, and solid muscles as they pass through the digestive system. PreK-3

_____and Randy Chewning (Illustrator). ***Where Does the Garbage Go? (Let's-Read-and-Find-Out Science Book).*** HarperCollins Juvenile, 1994. ISBN 0-06-445114-3. Explains how people create too much waste and how waste is recycled and landfilled. PreK-3

Silverstein, Alvin, Virginia Silverstein, and Laura Silverstein Nunn. ***Tooth Decay and Cavities.*** Franklin Watts, Inc, 1999. ISBN 0-531-11580-1. Explains the process of tooth decay and how science has evolved to intervene. Full-color photographs and "Did You Know" sidebars provide additional information. 4-6.

Silverstein, Alvin, Virginia Silverstein and Robert Silverstein. ***Fats (Food Power! Series).*** Millbrook Press, 1992. ISBN 1-56294-208-5. Fats are described in an easy-to-read style. Discussion includes what is necessary for the human body. Helpful charts and sidebars of little known facts enhance the book's use. 4-7.

Smith, Alastair. ***What Happens to Your Food?*** Usborne Flip Flaps, 1997. ISBN 0-7460-2504-1. An interactive book with flaps (to see what happens inside when you eat) accompanied by simple explanations. PreK-3

Solheim, James and Eric Brace (Illustrator). ***It's Disgusting and We Ate It! True Food Facts from around the World and throughout History.*** Simon and Schuster, 1998. ISBN 0-689-80675-2. A book of zany illustrations accompanying a "menu" of food trivia—and what people eat—from seaweed to worm soup! K-4.

Stevens, Jan Romero. ***Carlos and the Cornfield (Carlos y la milpa de maiz).*** Northland Publishers, 1999. ISBN 0-87358-735-9. When he sees the results of not following his father's instructions on the proper way to plant corn, a young boy tries to make things right. Includes recipe for blue corn pancakes. PreK-3

Stevens, Janet. ***Tops and Bottoms.*** Harcourt Brace & Company,1995. ISBN 0-15-201034-3. Hare makes a clever deal with bear—a 50:50 split on the vegetable harvest based on the part of the plants. Bear always seems to end up getting the wrong part. K-3.

Stewart, Sarah and David Small (Illustrator). ***The Gardener***. Farrar, Straus, Giroux, 1997. ISBN 0-374-32517-0. Lydia Grace goes to live with her Uncle Jim in the city but takes her love for gardening with her. K-5.

Stuve-Bodeen, Stephanie. ***Elizabeti's Doll.*** Lee & Low Books, 2002. ISBN 1-880000-70-9. Details of life in contemporary Tanzania are included in the story of Elizabeti who uses her imagination and what is available to her to solve a problem. PreK-3.

Suzuki, David and Barbara Hehner (illustrator). ***Looking at Plants.*** John Wiley & Sons, 1999. ISBN 0-471-54049-8. Explains the importance of plants—all the various and incredible ways they've had to develop in order to protect themselves, etc. 4-6.

Takaki, Ronald and Rebecca Stefoff. ***Raising Cane: The World of Plantation Hawaii (Asian American Experience Series).*** Chelsea, 1994. ISBN 0-7910-2178-5. Explores the lives and includes personal recollections of the Chinese, Korean, Japanese, and Filipino immigrants who came to the United States by way of Hawaii and worked on the island's sugar plantations. 5-11.

Talmage, Ellen and Bruce Curtis (Illustrator). ***Container Gardening for Kids.*** Sterling Publications, 1997. ISBN 0-80691-378-9. Clear and concise instructions for 25 container projects. Great introduction to gardening with lots of photographs. 3-6.

Thomson, Bob, and Jerry Pallotta and Edgar Stewart (Illustrator). ***The Victory Garden Vegetable Alphabet Book.*** Monarch Books 2002. ISBN 0-88106-469-6. A range of vegetables (from A to Z) that can grow in a garden are illustrated and described. K-3.

Titherington, Jeanne. ***Pumpkin, Pumpkin.*** Morrow Avon, 1990. ISBN 0-688-09930-0. Jamie plants a pumpkin seed and, after watching it grow, carves it, and saves some seeds to plant in the spring. K-3.

Vezza, Diane Simone and Susan Greenstein (Illustrator). ***Passport on a Plate: A Round-the-World Cookbook for Children.*** Simon & Schuster, 1997. ISBN 0-689-80155-6. Describes the culinary styles of twelve regions around the world and provides recipes for each. 4-7

Wake, Susan and John Yates (Illustrator). ***Vegetables.*** Carolrhoda Books, 1990. ISBN 0-87614-390-7. Looking at different types of vegetables through their history, their role in our diet, and how they are grown. Includes recipes. PreK-3

Waters, Alice. ***Fanny at Chez Panisse.*** Scott Foresman, 1997. ISBN 0-06-092868-9. Opening up the magic world of cooking to children, Alice Waters describes, in the words of seven-year-old Fanny, the path food travels from the garden to the kitchen to the table. 3-7.

Watts, Barrie. ***Potato.*** Silver Burdett Press, 1990. ISBN 0-38224-018-9. Describes how a potato develops from a shoot to a plant. PreK-2.

Weitzman, David. ***My Backyard History Book.*** Little, Brown and Company, 1975. ISBN 0-316-92901-8. Activities and projects, such as making time capsules and rubbings and tracing genealogy, demonstrate that learning about the past begins at home. 4-7

Welch, Catherine A and Laurie K. Johnson (illustrator). ***Clouds of Terror.*** Carolrhoda Books, Inc., 1994. ISBN 0-87614-771-6. Living on a farm in southwestern Minnesota in the 1870s, a brother and sister try to help their family cope with plagues of locusts. 2-4.

Wheeler, Jill. ***The Throwaway Generation.*** Abdo Pub. Co., 1991. ISBN 1-56239-030-9. Discusses the trash problem in this country, caused by both people and technology, and suggests ways to cut down on what we throw away.

Wigginton, Eliot. ***Sometimes a Shining Moment.*** Anchor,1986. ISBN 0385133596. is the story of a teacher's struggles with his class as they put together a literary magazine that becomes famous: *The Foxfire Books.*

Wilkes, Angela. ***A Farm through Time: The History of a Farm from Medieval Times to the Present Day.*** DK Publishing, 2003. ISBN 0-7894-7902-8. Farming chores from medieval times to the present, showing the changes over centuries. 3-7.

Wilder, Laura Ingalls and Garth Williams (Illustrator). ***Farmer Boy.*** HarperTrophy, 1973. ISBN 0-06-440003-4. While Laura Ingalls grows up in a little house on the western prairie, her husband-to-be Almanzo Wilder is living on a big farm in New York State. Almanzo and his brother and sisters work at their chores from dawn to supper most days—no matter what the weather. Wonderful descriptions of farm food. See other books in the series for more descriptions and tales of life on the prairies in the 1800s. 3-6.

Williams, Karen L. and Catherine Stock (Illustrator).***Galimoto.*** Turtleback, 1991. ISBN 0-606-00456-4. A determined African boy searches for materials to make a galimoto—a toy vehicle made of wire. PreK-3.

Winckler, Suzanne, and Mary M. Rodgers. ***Our Endangered Planet: SOIL.*** Lerner Publishing Group, 1993. ISBN 0-8225-2508-9. Global in its perspective, this effective introduction to soil science provides everything from nature's recipes for making soils to an examination of the human mismanagement of this valuable natural resource. 3-7

Wittstock, Laura. ***Ininatig's Gift of Sugar: Traditional Native Sugarmaking.*** Lerner Publishing Group, 1993. ISBN 0-8225-9642-3. Beginning with the legend of Ininatig, who gave the people maple sugar, the book explores how an Ojibway man makes maple sugar today. 3-7

Wyler, Rose and Pat Ronson Stewart (Illustrator). ***Science Fun with Mud and Dirt.*** Julian Messner, 1987. ISBN 0-671-55569-3. Instructions for performing a variety of experiments, indoors and out, with soil and rocks. PreK-3.

Zamorano, Ana and Julie Vivas (Illustrator). ***Let's Eat.*** Scholastic, 1997. ISBN 0-590-13444-2. Each day Antonio's Mama tries to get everyone to sit down together to eat, but someone is always busy elsewhere, until the family celebrates a new arrival. Spanish dishes and words sprinkled in with a brief Spanish translation glossary in the back. K-3.

Zemach, Margot. ***The Little Red Hen: An Old Story.*** Farrar, Straus and Giroux, 1993. ISBN 0-374-44511-7. A hardworking little red hen decides to plant some wheat and eventually make bread. But every time she asks for help, her friends refuse. After doing every step alone, she declares that she also would eat it alone. And she does. K-3.

Web Sites

(See also additional web addresses and descriptions under specific organization listing.) If a web address doesn't send you to the site at first, try a few alternatives.

1. Go to the home page of the site and "surf" (i.e., erase everything after the .org, .edu, .net, .com, etc. and try again).
2. Do a search using the words in the web address or the titles.

Agricultural Museums Locator: www.alhfam.org/alhfam.links.html or www.museumstuff.com

Center for Science in the Public Interest www.cspinet.org

Children's Health and Nutrition: This site is designed for kids. Bright graphics and good information on many subjects relating to their own health. www.kidshealth.org/kid/

City Farmer's Urban Agriculture Notes: Information on gardening—school, community, rooftop, condo farming. www.cityfarmer.org/schgard15.html

Community Alliance with Family Farmers: rural and urban people interested in supporting family-size farms will find many helpful resources when they visit this California-based site: www.CAFF.org

Community Gardening Association www.communitygarden.org

Cooperative Extension: Find your state and county offices. http://www.esrees.usda.gov/Extension/index.html

Cultural and Ethnic Food and Nutrition Education Materials a resource list for educators at www.nal.usda.gov/fnic/pubs/bibs/gen/ethnic.html

Education Resources Information Center (ERIC) produces the world's premier database of journal and non-journaleducation literaature, providig access to a million citations and 110,000 full-text materials at no charge. http://eric.ed.gov/

EPA Kids' Activities (Environmental Explorer's Club): www.epa.gov/kids and EPA teacher's lessons www.epa.gov/teachers

Ethnic Groups Nutrition Issues (USDA): www.nal.usda.gov/fnic/ Click on ethnic and cultural food guide pyramids.

Farmer's Market Locator: www.ams.usda.gov/farmersmarkets/

Flowerfield Enterprises: www.wormwoman.com (founded by the late Mary Appelhof, author and vermicomposting expert)

Food and Nutrition Information Center (USDA): http://riley.nal.usda.gov/nal_display/index.php?info–center=4&tax_level=1&tax_subject=242 or www.nal.usda.gov/fnic/

Food Cooperative Locator: www.coopdirectory.org

Food Guide Pyramid Information: www.usda.gov/news/usdakids/index.html

Food Origins: From tea to potato chips! This site links visitors to information about origins of many of the most popular foods we eat. www.asiarecipe.com/foodline.html

Food Pyramids across Cultures: This site illustrates healthy eating patterns for the Mediterranean, Asian, and Latin cuisines. www.oldwayspt.org

Food Resource and Action Center Gateway to federal nutrition and hunger-related information: www.frac.org

Food Systems www.foodsecurity.org/links.html has a large variety of resources dedicated to food systems, food security, gardening, nutrition, and sustainable agriculture.

Food Timeline: A collection of related web sites for parents and teachers on food history and traditions across cultures. This site links to multiple lesson plans. www.foodtimeline.org

"Green" Schools: This site helps interested teachers learn how to start and sustain a "green" school. www.greenschools.net

Hunger Donations: www.thehungersite.com

Hunger: the Community Food Security Coalition: Dedicated to building strong sustainable, local and regional food systems that ensure access to affordable, nutritious, and culturally appropriate food for all people at all times. www.foodsecurity.org

Indicators of Children's Well-Being: www.childstats.gov/

Invertebrates of the Compost Pile: http://compost.css.cornell.edu/invertebrates.html

Kids Can Make a Difference: www.kidscanmakeadifference.org

Kinder Garden: http.aggie-horticulture.tamu.edu/kinder/garden/kinder.htm

Local Food Solutions: The Wisconsin Foodshed Research Project. This well-designed site aims to provide tools and resources for eaters and educators who want to change the way we grow, process, market, and eat food. www.cias wisc.edu/foodshed/

Local Harvest: Nationwide directory of local sources of sustainably grown food. www.localharvest.org/

Maine Organic Farmers and Gardeners Association: www.mofga.org

Museum Locator: www.musee-online.org or www.museumstuff.com

National Cancer Institute's Eat 5-to-9-a-Day Program: www.5aday.gov

National Digestive Diseases Information Clearninghouse: Your Digestive System and How It Works http://digestive.niddk.nih.gov/ddiseases/pubs/yrdd/index.htm

National Science Teachers Association Store: www.nsta.org/scistore

Nutrition and School Gardens: Texas A&M's web site has lesson plans and slide shows to illustrate how and why gardening and composting projects in schools are valuable. http://aggie-horticulture.tamu.edu/kindergarden/index.html

Nutrition for Kids/Connie Evers: www.nutritionforkids.com

Nutrition Information: Tufts University developed the "Nutrition Navigator" to help consumers evaluate the information overload on food, nutrition, and health. www.navigator.tufts.edu

Nutrition Label Reading Information www.cfsan.fda.gov/label.html or www.nal.usda.gov/fnic/foodcomp/Data/SR14/wtrank/wt rank.html

School Gardening Listserve majordomo@ag.arizona.edu (Put "subscribe school garden digest" in message.)

School Gardens: City Farmer has many requests about school-based garden projects. A portion of their site provides opportunities for students to explore such gardens on their own. www.cityfarmer.org.schgard.15html

School Gardens: A step-by-step guide to starting one. http.aggie-horticulture.tamu.edu/kindergarden/child/school/step.htm

Schoolyard Wildlife Habitats: National Wildlife Federation: www.nwf.org/backyard/

SlowFood—Antidote to Fast Food: www.slowfood.com

Snack Handout—Reproducible: www.fns.usda.gov/tn/Educators/yrslf07.pdf

Soil—Microorganisms: http://school.discovery.com/school adventures/soil/

Square-Foot Gardening: (The official site of originator and author Mel Bartholomew.) www.squarefootgardening.com

Sugar Facts: Learn about the effects of sugar on health and the sources of sugar in our diet. www.cspinet.org/new/sugar.htm

Sustainable Agriculture: Sustainable agriculture and "no-till" farming are practiced at Cedar Meadow Farm in Pennsylvania. This farm was one of the five in the world featured on a PBS documentary about sustainable agriculture. www.cedarmeadowfarm.com

Sustainable Agriculture: Research Program of North Carolina State; good links to national sustainable agriculture sites. www.sustainable-ag.ncsu.edu/

Sustainable Agriculture: Leopold Center for Sustainable Agriculture, Ames, Iowa. This site offers information and graphics which illustrate food issues, including the distance produce travels to reach the market. www.leopold.iastate.edu/pub/staff/ppp/index.htm

Sustainable Agriculture Resource for Teachers: www.nal.usda.gov/afsic/AFSIC pubs/k-12.htm

TV-Free America: www.tvfa.org

TV Turnoff Network: www.turnoff.org

USDA for Kids: (Food Guide Pyramid information and other great resources) www.usda.gov/news/usdakids/index.html

Vermicomposting: Frequently Asked Questions—click on Earthworm FAQ www.oldgrowth.org/compost/wormfaq.html

Waste Awareness Quiz: www.ciwmb.ca.gov/PublicEd/Quiz/default.asp See also "The Adventures of Vermi the Worm" game www.ciwmb.ca.gov/vermi/Game/default.html

Worm Digest: www.wormdigest.org/

Youth and Kids' Pages in Agriculture:www.nal.usda.gov/outreach/youthkids.htm

Yuckiest Site on the Internet! www.nj.com/yucky. Go directly to "worm world" and "gross and cool body." yucky.kids.discovery.com/

INDEX

Y

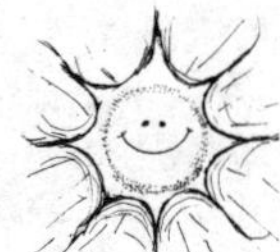

The Salad Garden Café and a Salsa Fiesta!

Inspiration from Two Teachers to Get You Going!

Walter Lunt, an inventive teacher from the Soule Program at the Mast Landing School in Freeport, Maine, demonstrated the entire cycle of the ***Healthy Foods from Healthy Soils*** program with his upper-elementary students. They planted and harvested a spring garden of early crops just outside their classroom windows, tasted the various leafy green varieties, and then prepared and served simple salads at an outdoor school-side "Salad Garden Café." It was the culinary feature of an end-of-school-year curriculum fair, so lots of families attended.

Certain early greens such as lettuce, spinach, radish, arugula (also called "rocket"!), mesclun, cress, peas, some beans, and chives are nutritious and—being quick-growing—ensured a crop before school ended. Edible flowers lent color and spirit.

Weeks of fun planning, gardening, vermicomposting, and learning about the salad garden preceded the "Café Night."The students also created small colorful posters with illustrations of garden greens, food trivia, and nutrient explanations of the garden plants that they'd researched. These were laminated and became the menus/placemats for the café.

In the one-evening café, "patrons" (invited parents, school staff, other students) arrived, received a handmade menu, chose garden produce *à la carte* with the help of student waiters, who then picked it, rinsed it clean, spun it (in donated salad spinners), and served the salads. Patrons selected from a variety of homemade and store-bought salad dressings, some purchased with the help of volunteer parents.

Delicious!

A variation on the Salad Garden Café was a "Salsa Fiesta" which Judy Higbea (a dedicated teacher-principal at the same school) and her class held in the fall.

"I gave the kids a generic salsa recipe and had the different ingredients available: lemons and limes, salt and pepper, olive oil (I supervised its use), cilantro and parsley, some sweet and hot peppers—both of which we grew in the garden—garlic, chives, and onions, and, of course, the tomatoes.

"I talked with each group and encouraged the students to try a little of the different things such as garlic, hot peppers, lemon or lime, and salt and pepper. They did a great job experimenting and taste-testing.

"We ended up with five very different salsas: including one that was very tart, one that was almost sweet, another that was very, very spicy, a fourth that was fairly bland, and the fifth that was a wonderful combination—the one that by my standards was just right!

"The groups were delighted with their results—each group, of course, felt that its salsa was the best. They worked very cooperatively and quite industriously. It was quite wonderful!"

Award-Winning Environmental Education Titles from Tilbury House

See our website at www.tilburyhouse.com for more information and for sample activities, literature links, and further resources for each book.
If you would like a free catalog of our books, please call 800–582–1899.

Life Under Ice—by Mary M. Cerullo; photographs by Bill Curtsinger
Hardcover, $16.95; ISBN 0-88448-237-5; paperback, $7.95; ISBN 0-88448-247-2; 9 x 10; 40 pages; color photographs; Grades 3–6
- "Editor's Choice" —*Audubon Magazine*
- "...there's enough weirdness and beauty combined to draw reluctant readers as well as animal lovers and junior ecologists." —*Bulletin of the Center for Children's Books*

Saving Birds: Heroes Around the World—An Audubon Book by Pete Salmansohn and Stephen W. Kress
Hardcover, $16.95; ISBN 0-88448-237-5; 9 x 10; 40 pages; color photographs; Grades 3–6
- "At last a book that says, 'Yes, it can be done!'...This is the happiest book I have read in a long, long time." —Jean Craighead George

Project Puffin: How We Brought Puffins Back to Egg Rock —An Audubon Book by Stephen W. Kress and Pete Salmansohn
Paperback, $7.95; ISBN 0-88448-171-9; 9 x 10; 40 pages; color photographs; Grades 3–6
- "Notable Books for Children" —*Smithsonian*
- "Outstanding Science Trade Books for Children, 1998" —CBC/NSTA

Giving Back to the Earth: A Teacher's Guide to Project Puffin and Other Seabird Studies
An Audubon Book by Pete Salmansohn and Stephen W. Kress
Paperback, $9.95; ISBN 0-88448-172-7; 8.5 x 11; 80 pages; illustrated; Grades 3–6. Can also be used with *Saving Birds!*
- "Educationally sound, it offers a wide variety of experiences to enhance and enrich the student's understanding of puffins, seabirds, and the oceans....This is a marvelous and fun resource." —*Appraisal*

Muskrat Will Be Swimming—by Cheryl Savageau; illustrated by Robert Hynes
Paperback, $7.95; ISBN 0-88448-280-4; 9 x 10; 32 pages; illustrated; Grades 3–6
- "Notable Books for Children" —*Smithsonian*
- Skipping Stones Book Award for Exceptional Multicultural and Nature/Ecology Books
- "No children's writer I know has done a better job of putting our traditions into the context of modern times while also dealing with the issue of mixed-blood ancestry in a way that is both honest and heart-lifting." —Joseph Bruchac

Just for Elephants—by Carol Buckley
Hardcover, $16.95; ISBN 0-88448-283-9; 9 x 10; 32 pages; color photographs; Grades 3–6
Outstanding free teacher's guides can be downloaded from the Elephant Sanctuary's web site: www.elephants.com
- "This amazing book reveals the complexity and intelligence of elephants. Jenny and Shirley's story shows us the strength of the bonds between individual elephants, their amazing memories, and their ability to feel and express intense emotions...." —Cynthia Moss, Amboseli Trust for Elephants, Langata, Nairobi

Travels with Tarra—by Carol Buckley
Hardcover, $16.95; ISBN 0-88448-241-3; 9 x 10; 40 pages; black and silver photographs; Grades 3–6
Outstanding free teacher's guides can be downloaded from the Elephant Sanctuary's web site: www.elephants.com
- "Notable Books for Children" —*Smithsonian*
- "...a wondrous story." —NSTA *Science Scope*

Shelterwood—by Susan Hand Shetterly; illustrated by Rebecca Haley McCall
Paperback, $7.95; ISBN 0-88448-256-1; 9 x 10; 40 pages; illustrated; Grades 3–6
- "Outstanding Science Trade Books for Children" —CBC/NSTA
- "Best Books for Children" —*Science Books & Films*

Shelterwood Teacher's Guide: Discovering the Forest—by Judy Markowsky; illustrated by Rosemary Giebfried

Paperback, $9.95; ISBN 0-88448-211-1; 8.5 x 11; 80 pages; illustrated; Grades 3–6

- "...a loving tribute to the working forest...bursting with well-thought-out forest-related activities...a sure-fire, hands-on way to introduce children to the delights of the woods around us." —*Habitat Magazine*

Sea Soup: Phytoplankton & Sea Soup: Zooplankton—by Mary Cerullo; photography by Bill Curtsinger

Hardcover, $16.95; ISBN 0-88448-208-1 (Phytoplankton) and ISBN-0-88448-219-7 (Zooplankton); 9 x 10; 40 pages; color photographs; Grades 3–7

- "Notable Books for Children," —*Smithsonian*
- "Outstanding 1999 Books" —*Appraisal*
- "Outstanding Science Trade Books for Children" —CBC/NSTA
- "Best Books for Children" —*Science Books & Film*

Sea Soup Teacher's Guide: Discovering the Watery World of Phytoplankton and Zooplankton by Betsy T. Stevens; illustrated by Rosemary Giebfried

Paperback, $9.95; ISBN 0-88448-209-X; 8.5 x 11; 96 pages; illustrated; Grades 3–7

- "...a valuable resource for understanding ocean food chains and the ecology of oceans." —*Booklinks*

Everybody's Somebody's Lunch—by Cherie Mason; illustrated by Gustav Moore

Hardcover, $16.95; ISBN 0-88448-198-0; Paperback, $7.95; ISBN 0-88448-200-6; 9 x 10; 40 pages; illus.; Grades 3–6

- "This is one of the best books I have seen on predators and prey." —*Portals*

Everybody's Somebody's Lunch Teacher's Guide: The Role of Predator and Prey in Nature by Cherie Mason and Judy Kellogg Markowsky; illustrated by Rosemary Giebfried

Paperback, $9.95; ISBN 0-88448-199-9; 8.5 x 11; 70 pages; illustrated; Grades 3–6

- "...provides a wealth of material for studying the roles of predator and prey in nature." —*Science Books & Films*

Stone Wall Secrets—by Kristine and Robert Thorson; illustrated by Gustav Moore

Hardcover, $16.95; ISBN 0-88448-195-6; Paperback, $7.95; ISBN 0-88448-229-4; 9 x 10; 40 pages; illus.; Grades 3–7

- "Notable Books for Children" —*Smithsonian*
- "...chock-full of real geology." —*Appraisal*

Stone Wall Secrets Teacher's Guide: Exploring Geology in the Classroom by Ruth Deike

Paperback, $9.95; ISBN 0-88448-196-4; 8.5 x 11; 90 pages; illustrated; Grades 3–7

- "an extensive supplement of facts, lesson ideas, and experiments for learning about the universe and the rock cycle...together, the two books offer an innovative way to teach about rocks and minerals and encourage reading at the same time," —*Green Teacher*